Robert K. DeArment

Bat
Masterson
The Man and the Legend

The University of Oklahoma Press : Norman

DeArment, Robert K   1925—
    Bat Masterson, the man and the legend.

    Bibliography: p. 417
    Includes index.
    1.   Masterson, William Barclay, 1853–1921.
2.   Frontier and pioneer life—The West.   3.   The West—
History—1848–1950.   4.   Pioneers—The West—Biography.
I.   Title.
F594.M33D4   978'.02'0924 [B]   78-21383

To

MAR

Who helped follow the old trails

ACKNOWLEDGMENTS

The following people were most helpful to me during the years I spent gathering material for his book, and to them I should like to express my sincere appreciation:

Nyle H. Miller and Joseph W. Snell of the Kansas State Historical Society, Topeka, Kansas,

Mrs. Opal Harber and her fine staff at the Western History Department of the Denver Public Library, Denver, Colorado,

Mrs. Cassandra Tiberio of the University of Colorado, Boulder, Colorado,

Waldo E. Koop of Wichita, Kansas,

Colonel Bailey C. Hanes of Guthrie, Oklahoma,

James P. Reinhold of the Atchison, Topeka & Santa Fe Railway,

The late Nat Fleischer, editor of *Ring Magazine* and for forty years the foremost authority on boxing in America,

Zoe A. Tilghman, author, the widow of Bill Tilghman,

Joseph G. Rosa, Middlesex, England,

Chris Penn, Norfolk, England,

Ruth Henritze, State Historical Society of Colorado, Trinidad, Colorado,

Marjorie A. Morey, Curator of Photographic Collections, Amon Carter Museum of Western Art, Forth Worth, Texas,

Andrie Raymond of the Office of the Prothonotary, St. Jean, Quebec, Canada,

and

Madeleine Y. DeArment, who said it could be done and helped do it.

ROBERT K. DEARMENT

vii

CONTENTS

ILLUSTRATIONS

MAP

BAT MASTERSON

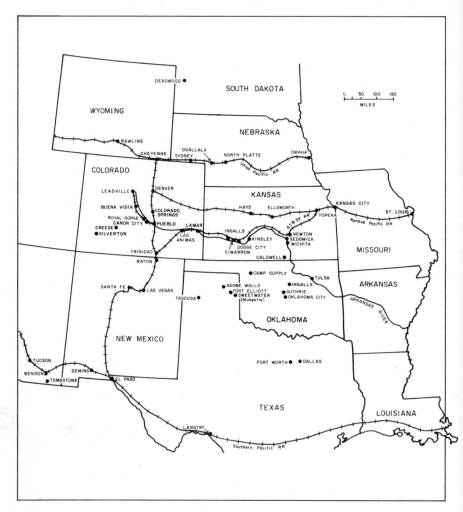

Bat Masterson Country

CHAPTER ONE

THE SEED OF LEGEND

The time was August, 1881, the place the Tabor House in Gunnison, Colorado. The correspondent for the *New York Sun*, in town to cover the excitement in this latest of a long line of boom camps, needed a story. Knowing that nothing titillated eastern readers like tales of the great gunfighters of the Wild West, but having seen no six-shooter antics during his stay, the newsman inquired of his western acquaintances, Dr. W. S. Cockrell and U.S. Army Lieutenants Febringer, Wagner, and Wetherill, whether reports of killings had not been greatly exaggerated.

Dr. Cockrell nodded his head and agreed that many such tales were fabrications, mere fiction concocted to bemuse the gullible. The officers expressed agreement, and the correspondent's heart sank. However, the doctor continued, there were instances in which the truth had never been told. As he scanned the crowded lobby of the hotel, the doctor saw a well-dressed young man standing at the doorway to the billiards room. "There is a man," he said, "who has killed twenty-six men, and he is only twenty-seven years of age."

The newsman's interest quickened and he leaned forward, pad in hand and pencil poised. The doctor continued:

He is W. B. Masterson, of Dodge City, Kansas. He killed his men in the interest of law and order. Once he shot seven men dead within a few minutes. While in a frontier town, news was brought to him that his brother had been killed by a squad of ruffians just across the street. Taking a revolver in each hand, for he shoots readily with both, in this manner [Dr. Cockrell demonstrated by crossing his wrists to form an X], he ran over to avenge his brother. The murderers became terror-stricken when they saw him coming, and hastily locked the door. Masterson jumped square against the door with both feet, bursting it open at the first attempt. Then he sprang inside, firing immediately right and left. Four dropped dead in a shorter time than it requires to tell it. The remaining

3

three men ran for their horses in a vain attempt to escape from the town. He followed them up so closely that before they reached the outskirts all three had bitten the dust.

The pencil was fairly flying over the pad now. Doctor Cockrell, warming to his yarn, told how Masterson had tracked two desperadoes, with bounties on their heads, to their hideout in the mountains and had dispatched them with well-placed rifle shots.

He paused to allow the newspaperman to catch up on his notes before adding a last sensational fillip to this tale.

Cutting off their heads, Masterson placed them in his sack, and started to exhibit his trophies in order to obtain the promised reward. A two days' ride under a hot sun swelled and disfigured the heads so that they were unrecognizable, taking advantage of which the authorities refused to pay the reward.

It was a fine story the doctor had spun, and in due time it appeared in the *Sun* under the head: "A Mild-Eyed Man Who Has Killed Twenty-six Persons." The story might have ended there, having provided a bit of vicarious Wild West thrill for effete New Yorkers, but for the fact that it was picked up and reprinted by several Western newspapers, including the Ford County *Globe*, published in Dodge City, Kansas.[1] The story created something of a stir in the border towns, and when a reporter for the Kansas City (Missouri) *Journal* heard that Masterson the mankiller was at that moment in town, he arranged for an interview.

Under the headline, "BAT'S BULLETS," the writer pointed out that "the gentleman who has 'killed his man' is by no means a *rara avis* in Kansas City. He is . . . a ubiquitous individual in this city, and may be met at every corner. . . . but when you see a man who has entered upon his third dozen, it is about time to be civil . . . ."

The previous evening, said the reporter, he had met "the famous H. B. Masterson, of Dodge City — known, by those whom he has not shot, as 'Bat' Masterson," whom he described as "a medium sized man, weighing perhaps 150 pounds, and reaching five feet, nine inches in height. His hair is brown, his rather small mustache of the same tint, and his smooth shaven cheeks plump and rosy. His eyes are blue and gentle in expression, his attire modest but neat, and withal he is about as far removed in appearance from the Bowery frontiersman as one could well imagine."

When asked pointedly about his reported string of killings, Masterson replied that he had not killed as many men as was popularly supposed but that he had "had a great many difficulties." He was quoted as saying he had been tried four times for first-degree murder and had been acquitted each time.

How about shooting some Mexicans, cutting off their heads, and carrying the gory trophies back in a sack? he was asked. "Oh, that story is straight, except that I did not cut off their heads," he said.

Regarding the gunfight in which one of his brothers was killed and Bat was reported to have killed seven men, the Kansas City reporter furnished details. While arresting a man named Walker, Ed Masterson was attacked by a gang of toughs led by a desperado named Wagner. Walker pulled a pistol and killed Ed. Just then, Bat arrived and opened fire. "His first bullet laid Walker low," wrote the reporter, "his second struck Wagner in the breast and glanced around, inflicting a dangerous but not fatal wound. His third and fourth laid low two more of the mob, and three more were forever forbidden to come to Dodge City by Masterson. They walked out of town and never returned."

Another Masterson was killed at Dodge City in April, 1881, continued the reporter. The killers, named Peacock and Updegraff, snorted, "The Mastersons were born to run." Eleven hundred miles away in Tombstone, Arizona, Bat was telegraphed the news; the remark "infuriated him more even than the death of his brother." Bat headed for Dodge City, where he "shot Peacock and Updegraff dead, disproving, at least, the assumption that 'the Mastersons were born to run.' "

Asked about a reported run-in with soldiers in Texas, "Mr. Masterson was quite reticent. In answer to a direct question he said, 'I had a little difficulty with some soldiers down there, but never mind, I dislike to talk about it.' It is popularly supposed that he annihilated a whole regiment, and this belief is strengthened by the fact that there was an urgent call for recruits about that time. Only West Point graduates escaped, and being officers they sought places of safety early in the engagement."

The *Journal* reporter concluded his article:

Whether he has killed twenty-six men as is popularly asserted, cannot be positively ascertained without careful and extensive research, for he is himself quite reticent on the subject. But that many men have fallen by his deadly revolver and rifle is an established fact, and he furnishes a rare illustration of the fact that the thrilling stories of life on the frontier are not always overdrawn.[2]

Thus was a legend born. By word of mouth and by pen, tales about Bat Masterson, man killer, spread throughout the West, the nation, and the world, becoming an integral part of the fabric of history, half-truths, and tall tales that make up the story of the Wild West.

The number of dead men credited to Masterson's smoking guns fluctuated after 1881. Writing about Masterson in 1887, a news-paperman in Leoti, Kansas, said Bat had been accused of killing a man on every birthday since he was a lad. Called before the Kansas Supreme Court in an election fraud case, Masterson was asked if he had killed thirty-eight men. He had not, Bat is supposed to have answered, unless Indians were counted; he admitted killing a good many of them.[3]

Cy Warman, who had known Bat Masterson personally in Creede, Colorado, and other towns, wrote in his book *The Story of the Railroad*, published in 1898, of "a string of slaughterers headed by 'Bat' Masterson, whose hands were red with the blood of no less than a score of his fellow men."[4] And Fred E. Sutton, who as a youngster in Dodge City had known and hunted with Masterson, set it down in 1926 that "Bat Masterson, as peace officer of Dodge City when it was the most lawless and disorderly town in America, added thirty-seven to the graves on Boot Hill."[5]

Making up the legend of Bat Masterson were the same factors that go into all legends: a skeleton of truth, fleshed with prejudice, clothed with awe. This book is an attempt to dissect the legend, to extricate the framework of truth from the body of myth and rags of rumor that have grown around it. The story of Bat Masterson requires no sensational embellishments. His was an exciting life, spanning the latter half of the nineteenth century and the first quarter of the twentieth, when the nation was maturing. As buffalo hunter, army scout, frontier peace officer, professional gambler,

Bat Masterson (standing) and Wyatt Earp, Dodge City lawmen, 1876. Bat's hand rests on the butt of his sixgun, holstered for the cross-draw. Courtesy Jack DeMattos Collection.

sportsman, promoter, and newspaperman, Masterson had a stormy and colorful career. But wherever he went and whatever he did after 1881, his legend went with him. This is ironic, for after a long career during violent times, in violent places and in associations with violent men, *there is no hard evidence that Bat Masterson ever killed anyone.*

"His baptismal name was William Barclay." These were the first words in Chapter 1 of a book published in 1905 by Alfred Henry Lewis. Entitled *The Sunset Trail*, it purported to be an account of the frontier adventures of the widely known westerner. "To William Barclay Masterson This Volume is Inscribed By His Friend The Author" proclaimed the dedication. "I have seized on a real man, and in its tragedy at least, told what really happened," Lewis wrote in his introduction. "Speaking in its broader lines, this book is true, and there be scores who will recognise its incidents."

On the opening page of Chapter 1, Lewis explained the derivation of *Bat*:

Before the corn-coloured penciling on his upper lip had foretold the coming of a moustache, he was known throughout that wide-flung region lying between the Platte and the Rio Grande, the Missouri and the Mountains, as Bat. This honour fell to the boyish share of Mr. Masterson because his quick eye, steady hand, and stealthy foot rendered him invincible against bears and buffaloes and other animals, *ferae naturae*, and gray oldsters of the plains were thereby reminded of a Baptiste Brown who had been celebrated as a hunter in the faraway heroic days of Chouteau, Sublette, Bridger, and St. Vrain.[6]

Two years later, in an article in the magazine *Human Life*, which he edited, Lewis repeated his version of the nickname's origin and further informed his readers that "William Barclay Masterson was born in Iroquois County, Illinois, about fifty-three years ago. His father was a farmer and came originally from St. Lawrence County, New York."[7]

In the late 1930's, George G. Thompson researched Masterson's Kansas career and in 1943 published the results under the title *Bat Masterson: The Dodge City Years*. Basing his statements concerning Masterson's early life on a November 4, 1937, interview with one of Bat's brothers, Thomas Masterson, Jr.,

Thompson wrote: "On a farm near Fairfield, Illinois, November 24, 1853, a boy was born. . . . This infant was christened William Barclay Masterson." Without explaining why, he added: "The stately title of William Barclay would one day be discarded for the short and unusually descriptive title, 'Bat.' "[8]

In his book *Dodge City, Queen of Cowtowns*, published in 1952, Stanley Vestal suggested that the nickname was attached to Masterson in 1876 when he served as a Dodge City police officer and, still limping from a gunshot wound, used a walking stick to bat down troublemakers.[9] Other writers have picked up the idea, including Richard O'Connor. His *Bat Masterson* (1957) was the first attempt at a full-length factual biography, and a television series of the same title was very loosely based on it. Without supplying a date, O'Connor affirmed that Bat was born on a farm in Iroquois County, Illinois. "The elder Mastersons," O'Connor wrote, "met and married in upstate New York, began raising a family in Illinois, moved to Missouri . . . and settled on a homestead . . . north of Wichita."[10]

In 1921, Skater Reynolds, who claimed to be a longtime friend of the Masterson family, pinpointed the site of Bat's birth as "the south bank of the Iroquois River, just over the Indiana state line, near Momence, Illinois."[11] However, recent research shows that Bat was not born in Illinois, was not christened William Barclay, and was not given his nickname because of his shooting or cane-wielding prowess. He was born on November 26, 1853, in the parish of St. George, Henryville, county of Iberville, province of Quebec, Canada. His baptismal name was Bartholomew, which the family shortened to Bart or Bat.

Thomas Masterson, Bat's father, was born in Canada in 1827. In 1852, he married Catherine McGurk of St. Johns. On September 23, 1852, the first of seven children in this marriage was born and was christened Edward John the following day. When a second son was born fourteen months later, the parents named him Bartholomew. The baptismal record, in French, with the name spelled Bertholomiew, is still on file in the Register of the Parish of St. George:

November 27th, 1853, we undersigned Priest, have baptised Bertholomiew born yesterday of Thomas Masterson and Catherine McGurk

of this parish. Godfather Charles McGurk and godmother Mary Anne
Oshea who except the godfather have signed.

[*Signed*] Tho. Masterson
Mary Anne Oshea
Ft. St. Aubin, priest[12]

Other children followed: James in 1855; Nellie in 1857;
Thomas, Jr., in 1858; George Henry in 1860; and Emma (or
Minnie, as the family called her) in 1862. All of these births are
recorded in the files of the parish of St. George with the exception
of the last. It is believed that sometime in 1861, Thomas Masterson
determined to leave Canada and enter the United States. He did not
have far to go. Henryville, thirty miles southeast of Montreal near
the northern reaches of Lake Champlain, is about eight miles from
the U.S. border.

It was the virgin farmland of the American frontier that Masterson sought, and he and the family began a westward trek of ten
years' duration. It seems likely that the various localities mentioned as early homes of the Mastersons — upstate New York;
Iroquois County, Illinois; Fairfield, Illinois (which is in Wayne
County); and a farm "in the vicinity of St. Louis" — actually were
temporary stopping points for Thomas Masterson and his family in
their slow advance westward.

Thomas Masterson, Sr., was no drifter, however; when at last
he found the land he sought, he put his roots down deep. On June 6,
1871, he settled on an eighty-acre tract in Grant Township,
Sedgwick County, Kansas, some fourteen miles northeast of
Wichita, which was emerging as one of the storied Kansas cattle
towns. Four years later, he paid five hundred dollars for an additional 160 acres in nearby Garden Plain Township and worked two
farms. He remained a resident of Sedgwick County for fifty
years — until his death in 1921 at the age of ninety-six.

Thomas Masterson's second son apparently did not like the
name he was given. As a young man, he adopted another one,
William Barclay, and people close to him, such as his brother Tom
and Alfred Henry Lewis, either did not know his real name or
respected his wishes and never referred to it. Bat signed as either
W. B. Masterson or Bat Masterson. In the only known instance
where his full signature appears in his own handwriting (his will,

Bat's parents, Thomas Masterson, Sr., and Catherine McGurk Masterson. Note the father's pale eyes and heavy, dark eyebrows—distinguishing features inherited by Bat. Courtesy Denver Public Library.

Mr. and Mrs. Thomas Masterson, Sr., in front of their home near Sedgwick, Kansas. Courtesy Denver Public Library.

Ed Masterson, the first born and the first to die. Easygoing Ed wore the star in Dodge and on two occasions went down in the roar of gunfire. The second time, he did not come back. Courtesy Denver Public Library.

Jim Masterson survived Dodge and other frontier hellholes only to be cut down by galloping consumption. Jim was a law officer in Kansas, Colorado, New Mexico, and Oklahoma, but it was his lot to be remembered only as "a brother of Bat Masterson." Courtesy Denver Public Library.

dated August 3, 1907), the name is William Barclay Masterson.

In addition to the Canadian baptismal record, there are two known published references to Bartholomew Masterson. A. T. Andreas' *History of the State of Kansas*, published in 1883, contained a short sketch on Sedgwick County pioneer Thomas Masterson with a reference to a son "Bartholomew . . . Marshal of Trinidad, Colorado."[13] And the *Kansas City Star* of December

Thomas Masterson, Jr. Courtesy Denver Public Library.

George Masterson. Courtesy Denver Public Library.

Nellie Masterson. Sister to three cow-town lawmen, she married another, James Cairnes. Courtesy Denver Public Library.

Emma Masterson, called Minnie by the family. Courtesy Denver Public Library.

10, 1897, contained a story recounted by one Joe Forsythe, a hotelkeeper from Reno, Nevada. He told of an 1886 visit by Masterson, who signed the hotel register thus: Bartholomew Masterson, Leadville, Col.

Little is known of Bat Masterson's early life. His formal education undoubtedly was minimal, but he was an apt pupil in the school of life, as is attested by his later accomplishments. He was introduced to the three R's in one-room country schoolhouses, but most of his education was self-acquired. He was an avid reader, and although the greater portion of his acquired knowledge undoubtedly was weighted heavily on the side of sports, politics, and similar competitive games, he was not entirely ignorant of the arts, science, and other fields of knowledge. As a successful professional gambler, he necessarily became learned in the mathematical laws of probability; he developed enough skill in the use of the written word to make his living for almost twenty years as a newspaper columnist; and he somehow acquired sufficient knowledge of the intricacies of the law to use it to his advantage, both as a peace officer and when he was operating with no legal authority whatsoever.

When he moved to Sedgwick County, Kansas, in June, 1871, Thomas Masterson took his family to the edge of the advancing frontier. Here young Bat got his first glimpse of life in the wild and woolly West. Sedgwick lay directly between two rip-roaring new cow towns, Newton to the north and Wichita to the south, and, as Bat reminisced a half-century later, "it was only a few miles west of the Arkansas River to the buffalo range. Griffin's ranch on the Medicine Lodge was, as a matter of fact, right in the center of the buffalo range. It was also right in the center of the Indian range."[14]

The older Masterson boys, Ed and Bat, stayed with their father that first summer in Kansas, helping him to construct a sod house and turn the virgin grassland for crops. The spirit of adventure was strong within them, however, and after they had helped with the harvest, they announced they were heading for the buffalo ranges to seek fame and fortune.

CHAPTER TWO

"A CHUNK OF STEEL"

In 1870, General George Crook estimated for the government that there were fifty million buffalo on the plains, ten million of them grazing between Fort Dodge and Camp Supply. During the 1860's, buffalo had been slain by white men for sport, for warm winter robes, and for meat to feed the railroad gangs who pushed the steel of the Kansas Pacific and Santa Fe railroads across Kansas. Hide hunters had taken their harvest only during the winter, when the bulls acquired their heavy coats. In 1871, however, about the time the Masterson brothers set out for the buffalo ranges, word reached Kansas of an unlimited market for hides. Although unsuitable for shoe leather, buffalo hide could be worked into an excellent buff, tannery operators reported. Machine designers found that buffalo leather was quite serviceable as power belting. With the new demand for hides, hunting could continue the year round, and cows and calves, as well as the superbly robed bulls, would become prey of the hunters. The Great Slaughter was on, and the days of the "crooked back oxen," which had ruled the plains for centuries, were numbered.

Nineteen-year-old Ed Masterson and Bat, not yet eighteen, headed south from their father's farm to Stone's Store, where the hide hunters provisioned. Here, where the free-wheeling town of Caldwell would stand a few years hence, they learned how buffalo were hunted on a grand scale. The hide hunter, they found, was a businessman with employees, much valuable equipment, and much skill in his craft. A typical hunter owned five four-horse wagons. His retinue included a driver, a stock tender, a watchman, and a cook; these men doubled as skinners when the hunter set up shop far out on the prairie. The armament of the hide man was prodigious. He wore a brace of six-guns for his personal defense. To vary the monotony of buffalo meat at camp meals, he kept a shotgun for small game. But his business tools were Sharps buffalo guns, of which he usually had several. The .50-caliber Sharps had gradually evolved from a seven-pound cavalry carbine to what became known as the Big Fifty: sixteen pounds unloaded. The hunter himself picked the ammunition for this huge single-shot. Cartridges about three inches long were loaded with up to one hundred twenty grains of black powder and a smooth leaden bullet weighing eleven to the pound. The cartridges were loaded for short, medium, and long ranges.

Bat and Ed found jobs as skinners and stock tenders and moved west toward the Medicine Lodge River with a hunting party. Already deep in buffalo country, they saw thousands of the lumbering beasts and heard the banging of buffalo guns from other camps. However, the man who was bossing the Mastersons' outfit pushed on toward hunting grounds he had picked out the previous spring. They crossed the Medicine Lodge and continued on until they reached the Nescatunga, a tributary of the Salt Fork of the Arkansas. They picked a campsite near the creek and began to construct a dugout.

The buffalo herds, moving slowly southward for the winter, were near by. The following morning, the boys had an opportunity to watch a professional hide hunter in action. Riding a short distance from camp, the hunter dismounted several hundred yards from a herd and continued forward on foot. He carried with him his Sharps, a pair of rest sticks for the barrel, a supply of ammunition, a canteen of water, and a rag. About a hundred yards from the herd, which had taken no notice of his approach, the hunter eased to the ground, propped the rifle barrel on his rest sticks, and commenced shooting. He dropped the leaders of the herd with shots directly through the lungs. The stricken animals pawed the earth, threw blood from their nostrils, then slowly sank to the ground and died. The other brutes watched them stupidly, seemingly oblivious to the roar of the Big Fifty and their own danger. When one would start to move off and others follow, the hunter would quickly drop the lead animal in its tracks to keep the remainder in place. Occasionally, he swabbed the hot barrel of his rifle with the wetted cloth to cool it. The spectacle was brutal, bloody, and fascinating.

There was little time to stand idle and watch. Soon, thirty or forty dead buffalo lay scattered in the area, and the hunter stood up and waved his wagons forward. Bat, Ed, and the others drove to the carcasses and began the hard, bloody, dirty work of removing the hides.

With razor-sharp skinning knives, they ripped a carcass down the belly and the inside of each leg. A cut was made around the neck and the hide loosened along the incisions. A rope was tied to the skin at the neck, a hitch taken on a saddle horn, and the skin peeled straight back from head to tail. The heavy hides were loaded into the wagons to be taken back to camp and staked out for drying. While his men were busy skinning his first kill, the hunter stalked another herd for a second stand. No sooner had the skinners finished stripping the hides from the first batch than it was time to move on to the next stinking, fly-covered pile of dead buffalo. The stripped carcasses were left to rot where they lay, only the tongues being taken for food.

The work continued seven days a week, week after week. The nights grew cold, then the days, as autumn passed into winter. Still, from atop a rise in the prairie, Bat could see thousands of buffalo stretching into the distance. The flies were gone now, but the skinning knives slipped from numbed fingers, and buffalo carcasses froze quickly in the zero temperature.

There were many other outfits working the Salt Fork that winter, some of them quite near. Sometimes in the evening the men would pay a visit to a neighboring camp, there to renew old friendships and make new ones. On these short trips, Bat first met many of the men who later were to play a prominent role in his life. He formed acquaintanceships with Billy Dixon, Jim Hanrahan, Old Man Keeler, Billy Ogg, Mike Welsh, Andy Johnson, Billy Tyler, and Bermuda Carlisle, all of whom would fight shoulder to shoulder with him in a historic Indian battle several years later. Here, too, he first met many of the men who in years to come would serve as lawmen with him: Charlie Trask, Tom Nixon, Dave Morrow, Neal Brown, Fred Singer, and the man who perhaps had a greater effect upon the course of Bat's life than any other, Wyatt Earp.

On the surface, the friendship that developed between Bat Masterson and Wyatt Earp early in 1872, and which was to last throughout their lives, would seem rather surprising. At twenty-four, Earp was already a veteran frontiersman, having been to California and back by covered wagon. Bat, although he was learning fast, was still a greenhorn. He was so youthful in appearance that Wyatt mistakenly told his (Earp's) biographer that Bat was sixteen at the time of their meeting. Actually, Masterson was several months past his eighteenth birthday. The two were strikingly dissimilar in physical appearance. Earp was more than six feet tall and slender, weighing about one hundred fifty pounds. His erect posture and lean frame made him appear taller than he actually was. His long hair and flowing moustache were blond. His expression was habitually tight lipped and serious, and people who did not know him well regarded him as cold and calculating, utterly devoid of humor. His reputation as a fighter, a dangerous man with whom to have trouble, was being established, and he looked every inch the part.

Bat seemed short and thick set beside Wyatt. He stood about five feet nine and was compactly constructed, with broad shoulders, a deep chest, and muscular arms. His hair was dark, and his distinctive heavy black eyebrows were more inclined to arch upward in laughter than to knit in anger.

In the eyes alone were the two alike. Both had pale gray-blue eyes, keen, intelligent, perceptive. In Bat's eyes Wyatt saw the qualities he himself possessed and which, as later events were to prove, were not lacking in Bat: courage, loyalty, resourcefulness.

It was in the buffalo camps that winter of 1871–72 that Bat began his apprenticeship in the two favorite sports of the West: drinking and gambling. Whiskey peddlers toured the camps, selling rotgut out of a barrel from a wagon tailboard. The hunters would line up behind one of these rolling saloons, tin cups in hand, lips smacking in anticipation of the tang of whatever evil concoction the particular camp follower was vending. Raw alcohol often was sold to the undiscriminating drinkers. The hardy hide hunters judged a beverage by its potency, seemingly were endowed with cast-iron gullets, and demanded firewater of high thermal rating. The whiskey venders obliged by spiking their wares with everything from red pepper to — in one case, at least — rattlesnake heads. This was the drinking fraternity from which Bat learned the art of the bent elbow. Having survived the apprenticeship, he was to be affected little by the huge quantity of alcohol he consumed during the remainder of his life.

Gambling, the second great avocation of the West, was not neglected in the camps. When two or more men could sit down together for a few minutes' rest, a greasy deck of cards appeared and a poker or monte game got under way. Bat learned that there was much more to a gambling game than keeping track of the cards and figuring percentages. A successful gambler had to be a canny judge of men. He had to know who would try to run a bluff and how often. He had to know whom he could bluff. The allied skill of card playing was card or money manipulation, baldly called cheating. Bat had to learn the many and devious forms of this skill and the countermeasures required. That he was well schooled is attested by his later life, when for many years he was a successful professional gambler, matching luck, skill, and wits with some of the shrewdest operators in the western gambling circuit.

In the spring and early summer of 1872, the Atchison, Topeka & Santa Fe was frantically pushing steel across the buffalo ranges of western Kansas. The government land grant giving the railroad a right-of-way through the state stipulated that the line had to be completed to Colorado by 1873. Delay after delay had held up construction until now only a prodigious effort would make it possible to meet the deadline. The company needed help badly and was willing to pay well to get it.

The Masterson boys met a man named Raymond Ritter, a subcontractor for the Topeka firm of Wiley & Cutter, which held the grading contract for the railroad. Ritter offered high wages to the brothers for help in grading a five-mile section between Fort Dodge and Buffalo City, a small settlement on the Arkansas River. With a Sedgwick homesteader named Theodore Raymond, who contributed an old wagon and a team, the Masterson boys headed for Fort Dodge. Raymond was an Illinois native who had become friendly with Thomas Masterson in Missouri and had followed his example by staking out a claim in Kansas.

Fort Dodge was established in 1864 to provide protection from Indian attack for wagon trains moving west over the Santa Fe Trail. In 1871, H. L. Stitler, a teamster, constructed a sod house five miles upstream from the post; later that year, several tent saloons

Theodore Raymond helped Bat and Ed Masterson grade the railroad right-of-way through Dodge City and hunted buffalo with them. Courtesty Kansas State Historical Society.

Henry Raymond. His diary affords a close look at the life of the buffalo hunter on the plains of western Kansas in the early 1870's. Courtesy Kansas State Historical Society.

sprang up near the Stitler place. Liquor could not be sold legally within five miles of a military installation, so the location was perfect for the saloonkeepers, who catered to soldiers from the fort and buffalo hunters who happened to be in the area.

Ed and Bat Masterson and their friend Theo Raymond toiled hard and long that spring and summer. By July, they had reached Buffalo City, as the new tent town was called. They were present that month when A. A. Robinson, chief engineer for the Santa Fe, laid out streets for the new town, the name of which was changed to Dodge City and soon shortened to Dodge by the laconic plainsmen. Steel rails followed the grading crews closely, and in September the first work train rolled into town.

Ritter gave Ed and Bat a small amount of money, a partial payment, when they finished their work. He then departed for points east, saying he had to get the balance, some three hundred dollars, from Wiley & Cutter. He promised to return immediately, but days passed into weeks with no sign of Ritter. Gradually, it dawned on the Masterson boys and Raymond that they had been cheated. Broke and bitterly discouraged, they returned to the buffalo ranges, taking Raymond's wagon and heading for the camp of Tom Nixon and Jim White on Kiowa Creek.

Nixon, a leading citizen who built one of Dodge's first permanent homes, had many business interests. He kept a sod feed store, a saloon, and a blacksmith shop in town and freighted commercially. He also was a buffalo hunter, one of the most successful in the West. His freighting outfit gave him the capacity to handle a huge number of hides, and when he set up a stand, he kept the muzzle of his Big Fifty red hot. On one occasion, he kept it too hot; from a single stand, he shot 120 buffalo in forty minutes, burning out the barrel of his Sharps in the process. In a little over a month one year, he killed 2,173 buffalo. During another hunt on Rattlesnake Creek, only thirty-five miles from Dodge, he slew 3,200 in thirty-five days.

White, Nixon's buffalo-hunting partner, was a tall, angular Illinoisan with a hawklike visage. In the 1850's, he was a bullwhacker and wagonmaster on the Santa Fe Trail, where he was known by his real name, Jim Wilson. He later freighted to the army forts along the trail and was involved in many skirmishes with the Indians. He was one of thirty-two soldiers and civilians who successfully withstood an attack by 1,500 Sioux and Cheyennes under Chief Red Cloud near Fort Phil Kearny in 1867. A year later, he got into a fight with Mexicans near Fort Union and killed two. He and a friend saddled up and rode east. They were overtaken by a Mexican posse near Las Vegas, but they killed two possemen and wounded another, routing their pursuers. It was after this narrow escape that Jim Wilson became Jim White.

During 1869 and 1870, White hunted buffalo on the Platte. He teamed up with Nixon in 1871 to hunt along the tributaries of the Arkansas in western Kansas. The partners established a large camp on Kiowa Creek the following year, and from this base several other hunting parties operated.

It has been estimated that more than 10,000 buffalo hunters were on the plains at this time, and many of the more well-known hide men were working the range near Dodge. Orlando A. ("Brick") Bond, who once killed 300 buffalo in a single day, was there, as was Josiah Wright Mooar, who accounted for 20,500 hides in a nine-year hunting span. Bob and Jim Cater were there; Jim estimated that he killed 16,000 buffalo during the peak years of the Great Slaughter, 1872–75. Emanuel Dubbs, Vic Smith, Rufe Tarbox, John Goff, Frank Mayer, Bob McRae, Alex Vimy, John R. Cook, Dave Dudley, Levi Richardson, Mack Hart, Joe McCombs, Zack Light, Hugh Henry, George W. ("Hoodoo") Brown, and Kirk Jordan were all harvesting hides near Dodge.

The 1872–73 season was the zenith of buffalo hunting in Kansas. Billy Dixon estimated that 75,000 were killed within sixty to seventy-five miles of Dodge that winter. A line of camps extended all the way from Dodge to Granada, Colorado. "The noise of the guns of hunters could be heard on all sides, rumbling and booming hour after hour, as if a heavy battle were being fought," Dixon said.[1]

At twenty-two, long-haired Billy already had achieved fame on the frontier as a hunter, Indian fighter, and crack shot. He and Bat Masterson became close friends. Bat wrote many years later:

I first became acquainted with Billy Dixon on the buffalo range in the fall of 1872 and continued to know him well and intimately for several year thereafter . . . Billy Dixon was a typical frontiersman of the highest order. The perils and hardships of border life were exactly suited to his stoical and imperturbable nature. This does not mean that Billy was not a kind-hearted, generous and hospitable man, for he possessed all these admirable qualities to a high degree, but he was cool, calculating and uncommunicative at all times.[2]

Evidence that Masterson's respect and admiration for Dixon were reciprocated is found in the latter's colorful and oft-quoted description of young Bat: "He was a chunk of steel and anything that struck him in those days always drew fire."[3]

Bat and Ed Masterson and their pal Theo Raymond were joined in the fall by several other men from Sedgwick County. Abe

Mahew and his son Steve, neighbors of the Mastersons, showed up in Dodge with Jim Masterson, now seventeen and eager for adventure with his older brothers. In November, Theo's younger brother Henry left the Raymond home in Carlinville, Illinois, to join Theo in western Kansas. Henry kept a diary of his experiences as a buffalo hunter, and the brief notes he jotted down, often by the flickering light of a campfire and sometimes written in gunpowder mixed with water when the inkwell ran dry, provide us with a unique look at the day-to-day experiences of the Masterson brothers and their friends in and around Dodge in 1872–73.

Henry Raymond arrived by train in Dodge City at 6:55 on the morning of November 16, 1872. He recalled in a letter written many years later:

It was just showing signs of the arrival of a new day, and, seeing a light across the street . . . I wended my way to this light. In entering there appeared a cardtable with men around it; and on the table were stacks of poker chips and piles of money indicating that the game had perhaps been going on all night. The man with his back to me as I entered wore a blouse and protruding below it were the barrels of two large revolvers. I learned later this was Bill Brooks. Quite an unusual sight for a tenderfoot!

Raymond walked west a quarter of a mile to Tom Nixon's house, where he was welcomed by Nixon's wife:

Mrs. Nixon, on learning my identity, kindly suggested that, since I was just from "The States" the town would be a rather rough place for me; and if I wished, might remain there until my brother came in, as he was camped with her husband, hunting buffalo.[4]

Two days later, Theo came in with a load of hides, and on November 21, the Raymond brothers left for the Kiowa Creek camp.

In the days that followed, Henry began his education in the arduous profession of hide hunting under the tutelage of his brother Theo, the Mayhews, and Ed, Bat, and Jim Masterson. Ed and Bat did most of the shooting, and the Raymonds and the Mayhews skinned and butchered meat. Jim, the youngest, usually was assigned the job of pegging the hides to the ground to dry. It is clear that the boys were hauling buffalo meat to Dodge, probably to feed the Santa Fe's construction crews, who were still hard at work

Tom Nixon, well known in the
camps of the buffalo hunters,
came to an untimely end as a
Dodge City law officer.
Courtesy Kansas State
Historical Society.

laying track to Colorado. The young hunters were bringing down
ten to twenty-five animals a day, so Theo's ox team was given little
rest.

On December 4, Henry saw his first wild Indians: three
Arapahoes who wandered into camp. Several days later, he, Ed,
and Jim went to the Arapahoe village, which was near by, and
watched the women tan robes. He made another trip to the village
with Bat, Jim, and Ed Masterson, Abe Mayhew, and Jim Rignyer,
another hunter from Nixon's outfit, to do some trading. His diary
contains the simple line "Saw Indians eating lice."[5] He later
elaborated on that sight:

Sitting on the ground was a "Brave," his back against a log on which
sat another while at his back still another was standing; the two latter
carefully searching their companion's heads for what we sometimes hear

called "Jerusalem Creepers" and judging from the frequency of the hand to the mouth, they must have found a rich harvest. I don't know whether they eat them for the nourishment they furnish or whether it is just simply to rid themselves of the pests.[6]

Christmas Day was celebrated in the morning by a shooting contest among the boys. "Shot at mark to see whos treat. Ed and me best," reads the proud entry in Raymond's diary. At the invitation of Tom Nixon, they headed for his camp in the afternoon. "They were to have pie and cake like they do 'back in the states' and a dance at night," Raymond wrote later. "Of course, there were no girls there, so half of the men had to take the role of the gentler sex in the quadrille."[7] Henry, who was packing a violin he had purchased in St. Louis en route to Kansas, was enlisted to provide the music. "Played fiddle for stag dance in dug out," he noted in his diary that night. "terrible windy and cold. Stayed all night. I slept with boss Jim White."

With the onset of the frigid weather, the buffalo suddenly became scarce along the creeks, and there was talk of breaking camp. Tom Nixon was the man they all looked up to, and when he pulled out on the last day of the year, the others started packing.

Bat and Theo Raymond had already returned to Dodge. On January 1, 1873, the other members of the party put thirty buffalo hams and tongues in the wagon and headed for town. As recorded in Henry's diary, it was a harrowing trip in a snowstorm:

[January 1] got lost on prairie, made bed down in the snow. no fire nor supper. Snowed and sleeted all day and part of night.

[January 2] got up this morning found ourselves snowed under, and surrounded by wolves. I shot at them. very cold day. . . .

[January 3] crossed river got to Dodge City. couldnt sell meat. . . .

Theo had already departed for Sedgwick, and Henry and Ed and Jim Masterson, having had their fill of winter on the plains, decided to follow his lead. On January 5, they sold their hams and tongues, totaling 990 pounds, for a penny a pound and set out the next day for Sedgwick in Theo's wagon. Bat told them good-bye; he had chosen to remain in Dodge.

CHAPTER THREE

THE DAUGHTER OF THE HIDE HUNTERS

The little town had mushroomed since the coming of the railroad. Nearly one thousand buffalo hunters and the entrepreneurs who serviced them were in and around town that winter.

The general-merchandise store operated by veteran plainsmen Bob Wright and Charlie Rath was the focal point of business by day. Most of the hunters outfitted and sold their hides there. Since there was no bank, the storekeepers acted as bankers for the hunters. Wright was a sutler at Fort Dodge before the town was founded. He became Dodge's most successful businessman and a power in the politics of western Kansas. His book *Dodge City, the Cowboy Capital, and the Great Southwest*, published in 1913, is a prime source of information on the well-known frontier town. He wrote of these early days:

> What a tremendous business was done in Dodge City! For months and months there was no time when one could get through the place on account of the blocking of the street by hundreds of wagons — freighters, hunters and government teams. Almost any time during the day, there were about a hundred wagons on the streets, and dozens and dozens of camps all around the town, in every direction.[1]

Those who did not sell their hides to Rath and Wright usually dealt with Eugene LeCompt, buyer for Lobenstein, the large Leavenworth hide concern. LeCompt operated without an office, standing on Front Street, his pockets bulging with banknotes, buying up wagonloads of hides as they rolled in.

By night, the centers of activity were the Alhambra Saloon, Gambling-Hall and Restaurant, run by James H. Kelley and Peter L. Beatty, and Tom Sherman's dance hall. Kelley, an Irish immigrant, served the Confederacy during the Civil War and fought Indians under Custer. He and Beatty put up one of the first frame buildings in Dodge, freighting it in sections from Hays City to the new town in August, 1872, and erecting it on the corner of Front Street and First Avenue as the Alhambra. In later years, he became well known throughout the West for his pack of racing greyhounds (hence he was commonly referred to as Dog Kelley) and was mayor of Dodge during its heyday.

The dance hall kept by fat Tom Sherman was the other favored resort of the hunters. Here, Nell St. Clair, Lil Thompson, Nell Pool, and other frontier fancies disported with the bewhiskered hunters who came to Dodge, horny of hand and mind. Sherman was a vicious killer who contributed to the reputation for bloodletting that Dodge City soon acquired.

Bob Wright recorded that during the first year at Dodge, twenty-five men were killed and twice that number wounded. Although this figure may be exaggerated, there undoubtedly were many killings when the town was known as the Daughter of the Hide Hunters. Recalled Wright: ''We were entirely without law or order, and our nearest point of justice was Hays City, 95 miles northeast of Dodge City. Here we had to come to settle our differences, but, take it from me, most of those differences were settled by rifle or sixshooter on the spot.''[2]

The town was full of violent men, the most notorious of whom was probably Bill (''Bully'') Brooks, the card player with the pair of long-barreled six-guns, who was the first man greenhorn Henry Raymond saw when he arrived in Dodge. A former stage driver and sometime police officer, Brooks had been involved in several gun scrapes elsewhere. Only the previous June, while acting as marshal at Newton, he had been shot three times in a fracas with Texas cattlemen. He had seen action as a lawman in wild and woolly Ellsworth before transferring to Dodge in late 1872. The saloonkeepers and gamblers kittied up the cash to hire Brooks as marshal. His job was to keep inebriated and cantankerous hunters from taking the resorts apart. After a few months with Bully Brooks riding high, they may have regretted their action.

Emanuel Dubbs has said that in his first month at Dodge Brooks killed or wounded fifteen men. Four of them fell in the space of a few seconds during a gunfight Dubbs said he witnessed.[3]

On March 4, 1873, tough old buffalo hunter Kirk Jordan determined to put out Bill Brooks's lights. The reported motive, as might be expected, was revenge for Brooks's murder of one of Jordan's friends. His long needle gun steadied on a door frame, Jordan drew a bead on Brooks as the latter approached on Front Street. Just before Jordan squeezed trigger, someone stepped from a doorway in front of Brooks, and Jordan raised his rifle. Brooks saw the movement and leaped behind a pair of the water barrels that were strategically placed along Front Street for firefighting. Jordan took aim and drove a ball through both barrels. The bullet lodged in the iron hoop next to the crouching Brooks, who turned and ran before the buffalo hunter could reload. The next day, friends of the two men arranged a meeting and they shook hands, but Bill Brooks was finished in Dodge and he knew it. He quietly left town. On July 29, 1874, vigilantes in Sumner County, Kansas, hanged him as a common horse thief.

Many of the men with whom Bat Masterson was acquainted during this period were destined to die violently within a few years. Dave Dudley, who often hunted with the Masterson brothers in 1873, was killed by Indians on the Canadian River in June, 1874. That same month, Billy Tyler and Dodge City restaurateur William Olds died in a well-known Indian battle in which Bat participated. Levi Richardson was killed in a gunfight at a Dodge saloon in 1879. In 1881, Bat heard that plains-wise Jim White had been killed by the Sioux while hunting the last of the buffalo on Montana's Milk River, and in 1884, he testified at the inquest into the death of Tom Nixon, gunned down in Dodge City by Mysterious Dave Mather.

Ed Masterson, who also died violently in Dodge City, returned to the town in February, 1873, accompanied by Henry Raymond. Jim Masterson did not leave for Dodge at this time, but he did rejoin his brothers in a few months. Raymond later wrote that he had tried to find work in Sedgwick County "but found it slow business. I soon made known my decision to return to Dodge where money was plenty. Ed said if I went back he was going too at which his mother began to cry."[4]

Thomas Masterson took Ed and Henry by wagon as far as the town of Sedgwick, from which they walked ten miles to the railroad at Newton. There, Henry's diary tells us, they purchased thirty-five cents' worth of crackers and two pounds of bologna for fifty cents, boarded car 5167 behind Santa Fe engine 32, *The Kansas*, and "beat our way to Dodge City," arriving on February 19.

During January and February, Bat hunted with Tom Nixon and Jim White when the weather permitted, and he was at their camp when Ed and Henry arrived. On the twenty-fourth, Nixon's outfit came into town and the boys had a big night at Tom Sherman's dance hall. Henry, who spoke German, occasionally used that language for diary entries of a somewhat delicate nature, items he felt everyone should not be able to understand. He noted on February 27: "Bat and Ed *geschlaft mit freunden litzten nacht* [slept with friends last night]." It's a good bet that the "friends" were a pair of Tom Sherman's girls.

Ed took a job in Jim Kelley's Alhambra, while Bat and Raymond in the following weeks divided their time between the buffalo camps and Dodge City.

Raymond's diary contains frequent references to the violence in Dodge, which seemed to increase with the warming weather. Henry and Bat were in town on March 4 when Kirk Jordan threw down on Bill Brooks. Henry wrote in his diary that night: "beautiful day. down in town. Bill Brooks got shot at with needle gun the ball passing through two barrels of watter lodging in outside iron hoop. Jordan shot at him. . . . Pat [Baker] and Bat went to hunt the horses. Soldier got beat over the head with boot and $5 taken from him in town."

As the lawlessness increased, a vigilance committee was organized, but, as often happened with mob action of this kind, some of the worst elements in town soon gained control and used it for their own nefarious ends. "Last night the vigilante committee shot McGill, a buffalo hunter, for firing pistol in dance hall. I went down town saw him," Raymond noted on March 12. Although McGill was reputed to be a desperate character who, among other depredations, had murdered a sixteen-year-old boy the previous New Year's Day, Raymond and others were repelled by the callousness of his killing.

The very next night there was another wanton and cold-blooded murder. Tom Sherman, "a big lubberly fellow, who ran with a limp," chased a man named Burns out of the dance hall and dropped him in the street with a shot. Henry Raymond was there and later recalled seeing Sherman standing over the writhing Burns. "I'd better shoot him again, hadn't I, boys?" Sherman asked, and without waiting for an answer, he aimed his revolver at Burns's head and fired. "The bullet went a little high and scattered his brains in his hair."[5]

The violence in Dodge continued unabated until a crisis was reached in June with the murder of William Taylor, who operated a restaurant. John Scott and William Hicks, Taylor's slayers, were members of the vigilance committee and thought their deed would go unchallenged. Taylor, however, a quiet, hard-working Negro, had been the private cook of Major Richard I. Dodge, the commanding officer at Fort Dodge, before he opened his restaurant. When the major heard of the murder, he wired Kansas Governor Thomas Osborn:

> A most foul and cold-blooded murder committed last night by ruffians in Dodge City. County organized but no election yet. Had nobody with power to act. Please authorize the arrest of the murderers.[6]

Osborn replied immediately:

> Until Ford County is fully organized you are authorized to hold, subject to orders of the civil authorities of the proper judicial districts, all persons notoriously guilty of a violation of the criminal laws of this state. I desire that you should exercise authority with great care and only in extreme cases.[7]

Major Dodge acted. "This morning the town surrounded by soldiers trying to arrest the murderer of Taylor who was killed last night," Henry Raymond wrote in his diary on June 4. Hicks was arrested, but Scott hid in the icebox at Peacock's Saloon and managed to escape. He was still a fugitive with a price on his head six years later when Bat Masterson became sheriff of Ford County.

The next day, Major Dodge's troops were back in town. "Soldiers again surrounded the town, put five men in jail. viz. Sherman, Gilkerson, Cook and the two Micks," noted Raymond.

In a letter to Governor Osborn, Major Dodge described the problems of suppressing lawlessness in a frontier community like Dodge City.

Everyone who has had experience of life in railroad and mining towns in unorganized counties or territories beyond the reach of civil law is perfectly aware of the necessity of "vigilance committees," so-called organizations which take upon themselves the right and duty of punishing crime when otherwise it would go unpunished and unpunishable.

So long as these organizations confine themselves to the legitimate object of punishing crime they are not only laudable but absolutely necessary. It is not often that the property-owning and valuable class of citizens is strong enough to do this work alone. They are obliged to receive into their organizations some of the roughs. These in turn take in others worse than themselves, until, as I have often seen, a vigilance committee organized by good men in good faith has become simply an organized band of robbers and cutthroats. . . . The town of Dodge City is under the control of such a band of vigilantes — some good men, some bad. The murder of Taylor was committed by these vigilantes, who . . . aided, abetted and became "particeps criminis" in the most cowardly and cold-blooded murder I have ever known in an experience of frontier life dating back to 1848.

Of course the vigilantes are only a small portion of the population of Dodge City. It is probable they do not number over thirty or forty men; but, being organized and unscrupulous, they are able to exercise a complete tyranny of terror over the really good citizens who lack organization. . . . The government is supposed to give protection. It protects these citizens from the Indians at great expense, yet leaves them to the tender mercies of a foe a thousand times more bloody and brutal than the Indians and infinitely more dangerous because he is in our very midst.[8]

On June 5, 1873, the same day Major Dodge arrested the five men whom he considered the most vicious of the vigilantes, a special election was held in Dodge City by order of the governor. Charles E. Bassett was elected Ford County's first sheriff. He was returned to office at two regularly scheduled elections and served four and a half years before he was succeeded by young Bat Masterson. The murder of William Taylor had turned the tide against lawlessness in Dodge City. Although there were many bloody episodes to come, the rule of law prevailed, for the most part, and the vicious element, so much a part of every frontier community, remained on the defensive.

There is no evidence that the Masterson brothers were involved in Dodge vigilante activities. It can be safely conjectured, however, that the murderous excesses of the vigilance committee had a

profound influence on young Bat. He definitely acquired an intense feeling of repugnance for mob rule and on many occasions
throughout his career acted in defiance of angry mobs, often at
extreme risk to his life.

Although Henry Raymond's diary contains brief mentions of
these dramatic events in Dodge, most of the entries are concerned
with daily routine. He and his friends journeyed to the creeks after
buffalo or worked at various jobs in Dodge. In March, Raymond
was working for Charlie Rath and Eugene LeCompt, stacking and
loading freight cars with buffalo hides and salting meat and
tongues preparatory to shipment. Ed was still employed by Jim
Kelley, and Bat was in and out of town with wagonloads of hides.
Then, on Tuesday, April 15, Raymond wrote in his diary: "Bat
took Ritter prisoner. I went on train got his valice."

Josiah Wright Mooar furnishes the details of this enigmatic
entry.[9] One of Bat's friends had been to end of track at Granada,
Colorado. When he returned to Dodge, he told Bat he had seen
Raymond Ritter, the man who had decamped eight months before
without paying the Mastersons and Theo Raymond for their grading work. What was even more interesting to Bat was the information that Ritter was flush, with a roll of two or three thousand
dollars in his pocket, and that he would be coming east on the next
train.

The news quickly spread in Dodge, and when Bat went to meet
the train, a crowd, including Mooar and Henry Raymond, followed him, curious to see what the young man would do. As the
train ground to a halt, Bat entered the cars alone. A few minutes
later, he marched Ritter onto the rear platform at gunpoint and
demanded the three hundred dollars Ritter had neglected to pay. If
the contractor did not fork over, Bat warned, he was not going back
into the car alive. Ritter began to protest that he was being robbed,
but after another look at the young man's determined jaw, chilly
blue eyes and cocked six-gun, he shrugged and mumbled that his
money was in a valise in the car. Bat motioned for Henry Raymond
to get the bag, never taking his eyes off Ritter. When Raymond
returned, Bat had Ritter open the case and count out the correct
amount. Taking the money, he waved Ritter back into the car and
then led the way to Kelley's to set up drinks for the cheering,

Bob Wright, Dodge City pioneer, businessman, and politician, devoted friend and admirer of Bat Masterson. Courtesy Kansas State Historical Society.

Richard I. Dodge. As a major, he commanded the garrison at Fort Dodge and had problems with civilians in the raw town that sprang up five miles away. Courtesy Denver Public Library.

back-slapping crowd. Mooar said Bat had not been noticed much before this incident but thereafter was considered a man to be reckoned with. Those who saw Bat's pale eyes harden and noticed the steadiness of his gun hand were convinced that had Ritter not paid his debt, he would never, as Bat promised, have reboarded the train.

With the arrival of spring, buffalo hunting was resumed in earnest. In May, Bat teamed up with a man named George Mitchell and left Dodge on a long hunt. Sometime later, Henry Raymond went into partnership with Dave Dudley. On July 7 there is a reference in Raymond's diary to the Alexander Jester affair, which was the cause of some excitement in the buffalo camps that month: "crossed rivr. camped at Jones. . . . drove to big hollow between Mulberry and Kiowa and camped. stoped at [Emanuel] Dubbs. . . . Saw remains of Jester."

Like the Mastersons and Raymonds, Jester was from Sedgwick County. He had been tried and convicted of killing a man but had escaped to southwest Kansas. There he reportedly tried to kill a man in order to steal his team. The man escaped and sought help at the camp of Mike O'Brien near the mouth of Bluff Creek. O'Brien led a gang of hunters who ran down a man believed to be Jester near Big Hollow and lynched him.

Twenty-six years later when Henry Raymond wrote Bat Masterson to ask whether Bat remembered the incident, Masterson answered:

> Since you spoke about the case I recall the killing of a man near big hollow who had attempted to kill some one for his team. I can not now recall the names of any one connected with the tragedy excepting Mike O'Brien who I believe killed the man in the vicinity of big hollow. I remember the killing more from the fact that the Coyotes had dug up the body which remained exposed for some days and was finally reburied by some buffalo hunters.[10]

Several years later, Alexander Jester showed up in Wichita, and apparently it has never been determined who the victim of the O'Brien "posse" was.

The 1873 migration did not measure up to that of 1872, and by the spring of 1874 the buffalo had virtually disappeared from Kansas. As far as the hunters were concerned, the seemingly limitless Arkansas herd had been exterminated. A few scattered herds still crossed the Kansas plains, but the hide men were not yet ready to chase down these pitiful remnants. They had turned their eyes southward, across the Cimarron, to the Texas Panhandle. A few bold hunters had ventured into that country, forbidden to white hunters by the Medicine Lodge Treaty of 1867, and had returned with tales of vast black columns of buffalo, the great Texas herd, practically untouched by the sting of the Big Fifty.

The white hunters had no compunction about violating the terms of the treaty and encroaching on the private game preserves of the red men, for the Indians had been violating the treaty with impunity for years. Bat summed up the hunters' view:

> From 1870 until 1875 the Cheyenne and Arapahoe tribes made the Medicine Lodge Valley their private hunting grounds although it was strictly against their treaty agreement to leave their reservation and cross into Kansas for the purpose of killing buffalo. But as there was no one there in authority to prevent their invasion of Kansas for hunting purposes, the Indians did pretty much as they pleased, just as the white hunters did. It was simply a case of the survival of the fittest.[11]

As he set down these remarks in his New York newspaper office almost fifty years later, Bat may well have recalled a harrowing experience that befell him during the winter of 1873, an adventure he related to Alfred Henry Lewis, who retold it in his 1907 article "The King of the Gun-Players."

Bat, alone, was surprised one day by five Cheyennes, members of Chief Bear Shield's band, which was camped on the Medicine Lodge. He was skinning a buffalo he had shot when the warriors suddenly appeared. One of them picked up Bat's Sharps rifle, which was lying several feet away. Another darted up behind him and snatched his revolver from its scabbard. As Bat whirled, he was felled by a blow on the head; he had been struck by the heavy octagonal barrel of his rifle. Blood streamed down his face from an ugly gash.

With impatient gestures and guttural commands, the Indians made it clear they wanted Bat to vacate the area. With his head throbbing and the muzzles of his own weapons directed at him, he made haste to do just that. He ran a half-mile to his camp and conferred with his partners. Bat was for returning to fight for his property, but the other hunters outvoted him; the decision was made to pull out for Dodge immediately.

To this point, the tale has the ring of truth, but Lewis goes on to tell how Bat, in retaliation, raided Bear Shield's encampment on Christmas night and ran off forty ponies, which he somehow drove to Dodge, where they fetched twelve hundred dollars. Now this sounds suspiciously fictional, inserted to restore the hero's image, diminished somewhat by Bat's being victimized by the Cheyennes.

In March, 1876, a group of hunters met in Dodge City to discuss the possibility of a large-scale expedition to the heart of the Texas buffalo country. The hide hunters, many of them veterans of Indian scrapes similar to Bat's experience, recognized the danger of the proposed undertaking. They were considering a venture into the home grounds of the Kiowa, Cheyenne, and Comanche tribes, bold, fierce warriors who were certain to resent white intrusion into their private hunting domain. The hide men would be more than one hundred miles from Dodge, the nearest source of assistance in the event of trouble.

The danger was great, but the prospective rewards were greater. Many of the men were anxious to take the risk, but they faced a major problem: they needed a source of supplies and a market for hides. No site for a camp had been agreed upon, other than a location somewhere on the Canadian River, but it was obvious that there would be no hide buyer nearer than Dodge and it would be too long a haul to that town.

A. C. Myers, who kept a general store in Dodge and had been a buffalo hunter himself, resolved the difficulty by agreeing to accompany the expedition and set up a store at the base camp. He would make supplies available there at Dodge City prices. If the hunters were happy about this offer, they were overjoyed when Jim Hanrahan, a big, hearty Irish frontiersman, said he would establish a saloon at the camp. Charlie Rath and Bob Wright hopped on the bandwagon, saying they would build a store to buy the hides after the hunters found a location.

Always the most adventuresome of the Mastersons, Bat was eager to take part in the venture, but Ed and Jim demurred. While Bat prepared to move south into Texas, his brothers headed home to Sedgwick.

CHAPTER FOUR

ADOBE WALLS

The expedition rumbled out of Dodge in late March. Billy Dixon, to whom we are indebted for a clear and colorful account of the journey and its violent aftermath, stated that thirty heavily loaded wagons and fifty men started from Dodge. Bat Masterson, twenty years old, was the youngest. Three years on the frontier had hardened the raw youth who left his father's farm to seek fortune and adventure on the plains. Thus he was accepted by the tough buffalo hunters as an equal, wise in the ways of the buffalo and the Indian, physically, emotionally, and temperamentally prepared for anything they might encounter. He had been schooled well, and although he did not know it, he was soon to be tested severely.

Across the Cimarron, deep in the Texas Panhandle, the hunters struck a stream known to some of them as West Adobe Walls Creek and followed it to the Canadian River. Here they found the source of the creek's name, Adobe Walls, the crumbling ruins of an Indian trading post where General Kit Carson had engaged the hostile tribes ten years earlier. They stopped for the night while a scouting party looked for a permanent location.

The following day, a campsite was established on East Adobe Walls Creek, about a mile and a half from Adobe Walls. Myers and Leonard commenced work on a sod building facing east, with a picket corral extending from it and a log storehouse in the southwest corner of the corral. Just south of Myers' store, Jim Hanrahan put up a large sod saloon. Charlie Rath arrived in April to build Rath's and Wright's sod store building on the other side of Hanrahan's. William Olds and his wife, newly arrived from Dodge, opened a restaurant in the rear of Rath's and Wright's. Tom O'Keefe built a blacksmith shop of pickets between Myers' corral and the saloon to complete the little town in the wilderness.

By May, all the buildings had been finished, a number of new

37

hunters had joined the first group, and freight wagons were following a well-marked trail the one hundred fifty miles from Dodge to the village of Adobe Walls. Everyone was anxiously awaiting the coming of the buffalo. Spring was late in the Texas Panhandle in 1874, and the buffalo were slow to start their northern migration. While they waited, the hunters amused themselves with horse races, card games, and shooting matches. Bat Masterson or Billy Dixon generally took down the money in the rifle shoots. Although Bat was considered very skillful with a six-shooter, it was with a rifle that he really excelled, old-timers who saw him handle both weapons insisted. During this period, the hide bar in Hanrahan's saloon became hard and shiny as the whiskey barrels got plenty of play.

In late May, a familiar, welcome sound rolled over the plains to the assembled hunters. Billy Dixon likened it to the rumble of a train crossing a bridge in the distance. It was the bellowing of buffalo bulls, signaling the approach of the great herds. A flurry of activity swept the camp as each hunter prepared his outfit to move out and meet the first droves. By the following day, buffalo were passing within gunshot of the camp and everyone was happily taking hides.

Toward the middle of June, Joe Plummer rode to the Walls with word that his two partners on Chicken Creek, Dave Dudley and a hunter named Wallace, had been killed and scalped by Indians, their bodies horribly mutilated. Within a few days, another hunter arrived; two men in his camp had been killed. Groups of men began coming in with tales of brushes with the Indians. It was apparent from the widely scattered locations of these attacks that there was more to this business than the work of one or two disgruntled Indian war parties. The smell of full-scale Indian war was in the air.

Many of the hunters favored heading for Dodge, and some did so. But on the evening of June 26, 1874, twenty-eight men and one woman were still at the Walls, unwilling to vacate the country at the height of the buffalo season. The group was composed of businessmen like Jim Hanrahan, Tom O'Keefe, and Bill Olds, who had investments that they refused to abandon, and stubborn, reckless hunters like Billy Dixon and Bat Masterson, who were ready to fight to stay right where they were.

About two o'clock in the morning, the hunters were awakened by a loud report. "The ridgepole is breaking!" Hanrahan shouted, gazing apprehensively at the roof of his sod saloon. The men got busy throwing dirt from the roof and preparing a prop for the support. By the time they had finished, dawn was breaking in the east, so they decided to stay up. Dixon said later that he could find nothing wrong with the ridgepole. He was at a loss to explain the strange noise that aroused the men and was, in the light of subsequent events, their salvation.

Josiah Wright Mooar, who had been at the Walls just before the incident occurred, believed the whole affair was a trick played by Hanrahan. The saloonkeeper, Mooar said, had received word that the Indians were about to attack the camp. He could not inform the others of this news for fear they would all pull out and desert him and his considerable investment. Knowing that an attack, if forthcoming, would in all probability take place at dawn, he invented the story of the cracking ridgepole so that the others would be up and would not be slaughtered in their sleep. The report in the night, said Mooar, was the firing of Dixon's revolver by arrangement with Hanrahan.

Dixon and Hanrahan are the only people Mooar named as parties to the scheme, but Bat was a close friend of both men and it is unlikely that such a plan could have been hatched without his knowledge. There are many details that throw doubt on the truth of the whole story. For example, Dixon, with supposed foreknowledge of the attack, was caught in the open when the attack came and ran to Hanrahan's with his rifle, leaving all of his ammunition in Rath's and Wright's store. If Mooar's story is true, however, it is likely that Bat was a party to the scheme. It could well have been his fertile imagination that conceived the myth of the cracking ridgepole. In any event, none of the principals ever told, and the mystery of the cracking ridgepole was never cleared up.

The men were preparing their horses and equipment for the day's hunt when the clear morning air was rent with a long, savage war whoop. They looked up to see bearing down on the camp out

Billy Dixon fought Indians and scouted for the Army with Bat Masterson. To him, Bat was ''a chunk of steel.'' Courtesy Panhandle-Plains Historical Museum.

Bill Tilghman (right) and fellow buffalo hunter Jim Elder in 1873. Courtesy Denver Public Library.

of the rising sun a long, solid line of warriors, hundreds of them. They came at a full gallop, their naked bodies and the bodies of their horses splashed with multicolored war paint, their lances and rifles pointed in a bristling line at the little collection of sod buildings.

The hunters broke for the nearest buildings, grabbing for their Big Fifties. They scarcely had time to slam shut the doors and throw up flour and grain sacks for barricades before the wave swept over them. Bullets tore through windows and rifle butts hammered against doors. The Indians had expected to overwhelm the camp in the first onslaught, but they received a rude jolt. The Sharps guns were soon roaring, and deadly fire was pouring from

the buildings. The attackers milled around outside, uttering
blood-curdling cries and charging at the doors and windows, but
one after another lurched from his mount, a gaping .50-caliber hole
through his body, to fall under the churning hooves. The fourteen
professional hunters, their aim sharpened to an uncanny precision
by daily practice, dealt out death with almost every shot. The
Indians began to fall back. The buffalo guns thinned their ranks as
they galloped away.

While the Indians were regrouping for another charge, the
hunters took stock of their situation. They had suffered but two
casualties in the initial attack. The Shadler brothers, asleep in their
freight wagons, had been killed and scalped. No one within the
buildings was even scratched. Although desperate, the hunters'
position was far from hopeless. They had in each of the three
buildings they occupied plenty of weapons, ammunition, and
food. The sod construction of the stores and saloon made them
ideal for the fortresses they had become. The walls and roof, two
feet thick, were stout enough to stop any Indian bullet, and since
the sod would not burn, fire was not a threat. By luck, the hunters'
forces were fairly well divided among the three buildings. With
Jim Hanrahan in his saloon were Bat Masterson, Billy Dixon,
Mike Welsh, Oscar Shepherd, Bill Johnston, Jim McKinley, Ber-
muda Carlisle, John McCabe, and Billy Ogg. At the Myers and
Leonard store were Fred Leonard, Frank Smith, Billy Tyler,
Hiram Watson, Sam Smith, Charlie Armitage, Dutch Henry
Wirtz, Old Man Keeler, Jim Campbell, Henry Lease, and Ed
Trever. Holding the fort at Rath's were Jim Langston, George
May, Andy Johnson, Tom O'Keefe, and Bill Olds and his wife,
Hannah.

Various estimates of the number of Indians involved in the fight
have been made, some of the hunters claiming later that there were
as many as a thousand, but all hands agreed that there were at least
two hundred. When the hunters saw that Kiowas, Cheyennes, and
Comanches were fighting side by side, they knew that a big Indian
war had begun. The man who had united the tribes in an attempt to
drive the white man from the buffalo ranges was Quanah Parker,
the half-blooded son of Comanche Chief Peta Nocona and Cynthia
Ann Parker, a white girl captured and raised by the Comanches.

Stirred by the war talk of Comanche medicine man Isati (Rear End of a Wolf) and rallying to the forceful leadership of Quanah Parker, the Kiowas, Cheyennes, and Comanches, with the aid of a few Arapahoes, determined to exterminate all whites in the Panhandle country. The camp at Adobe Walls, the largest white settlement in the area, was to fall first. From the Walls, the Indians planned to range north and south, wiping out all whites in their path, but the surprisingly effective resistance of the little group of hunters dealt a blow to those plans. Quanah had to crush the party at Adobe Walls in order to maintain the allegiance of the several tribes and to hold them together as a single fighting unit. Should the attackers be repulsed here, the dissension and jealousies ever present in a large body of Indians would develop into internal bickering and strife. The great army he had assembled would degenerate into small war parties acting without central control, to be hunted down and exterminated by the soldiers who inevitably would come.

So again and again Quanah threw his warriors at the Walls. Bat recalled years later:

The red devils charged right down to the doors and portholes of the stockade but were met with a withering fire from the brave and cool men inside and had to retire time and time again. So close would they come that we planted our guns in their faces and against their bodies through the portholes, while they were raining their arrows and bullets down on us. For two terrible hours they made successive charges upon the walls, displaying a bravery and daring unsurpassed in any Indian battle known to history. So sure of victory were they, having been told by their medicine man they would win, they rode up in squads of three abreast and when at the doors whirled their horses around and tried to break down the doors by backing the horses against them. We had to support the doors with boxes of groceries, merchandise and everything we could get hold of. Sometimes the doors would be pushed partly open by the weight of the horses and at such times other Indians would shoot through the narrow openings as they dashed by. At times they drew off for a short spell to council and then come back with renewed determination it seemed to us. At one of these lulls in the fight a young warrior mounted on a magnificent pony and decorated with a gaudy war bonnet and brilliant trappings made a dash for the walls alone. He rode with the speed of an eagle and with the swiftness of an arrow came on against that side of the walls where the portholes were most numerous and danger to him greatest. He

Quanah Parker, half-blood chief of the Comanches, led the attack on the besieged hunters at Adobe Walls. Courtesy Denver Public Library.

succeeded in getting near the walls and, jumping from his saddle, ran to one of the portholes and, sticking his revolver through the opening, emptied it in the room but fortunately did no more than fill it with smoke. When he attempted to retreat he was shot from his horse which went galloping away across the prairie. He staggered to his feet but was again shot down and then while lying wounded he pulled another pistol from his belt and deliberately blew out his brains. I have never seen a bolder deed.[1]

Bat learned that the daring young brave was Stone Teeth, son of Stone Calf, one of the foremost chieftains of the Southern Cheyennes.

Indian dead littered the area, but the only hunter hit was Billy Tyler, who exposed himself at Myers' and Leonard's store and was shot through the lungs by an Indian only fifteen feet away. Tyler was a friend of Bat's and when Bat learned that Billy had been hit, he made a dash for Myers' under the fire of the Indian rifles. He found Tyler in great pain, moaning for water. Bat grabbed a pail. The well in the stockade was in full view of the Indians crouched along the pickets, but he was willing to make a try for it. Old Man Keeler stopped him at the door. Bill Keeler had been on the plains for years and was known throughout the tribes. There was a chance the Indians would not shoot him out in the open. Keeler's dog slipped out with him as he ran for the well. Bullets snapped all around him as he pumped the pail full, but, miraculously, he was not hit. The frightened dog, huddled between his legs, was killed. Keeler made it back without a scratch, but the water did Billy Tyler little good; he lived about a half-hour after being shot.

The Indian charges were signaled by a bugler in the attackers' ranks. The hunters found the bugle calls particularly annoying, and in the afternoon one of them saw an opportunity to put a stop to them. Some writers have given Bat Masterson credit for killing the bugler, who, it was discovered, was a Negro army deserter. Bat himself said, "The bugler was killed late in the afternoon of the first day's fighting as he was running away from a wagon owned by the Shadler brothers. . . . The bugler had his bugle with him at the time he was shot by Harry Armitage. . . . Armitage shot him through the back with a .50-caliber Sharp's rifle, as he was making his escape."[2]

Bat distinguished himself throughout the battle. While praising all present for their courage and skill, Billy Dixon singled out Bat for particular credit. "Bat Masterson should be remembered for the valor that marked his conduct," Dixon said. "He was a good shot, and not afraid."[3]

In the afternoon the attacks ceased and the Indians began to play a waiting game. They had killed or run off all the horses at the camp, and now they began a siege. The hunters spent a long, lonely night watching and waiting. The following day, they saw but one party of Indians, far off on a bluff. They opened fire with their long-range rifles and the warriors disappeared.

Although they were not now under direct attack, the be-leaguered defenders' situation was extremely critical. They knew there were many men back in Dodge who would gladly come to their aid, but with no horses, there was no way to send for help. Jim Hanrahan's black silk hankerchief flew from a pole atop his saloon, signaling distress.

The hunters could move freely outside the buildings now, and they used the opportunity to drag off the dead Indians and horses, which were beginning to stink in the scorching June sun. Late in the afternoon of the second day, the lookouts shouted with surprise and pleasure when they saw two teams moving toward the Walls from the south. It was Bellfield's outfit, hauling in hides from their camp down the valley of the Canadian. The new arrivals listened in wonder to the account of the battle. They had seen no sign of Indians. Later that day, the Cater brothers rode in from their camp to the north.

The hunters now had a means of sending for help, and cool, Indian-wise Henry Lease volunteered for the job. After dark he mounted one of Bellfield's horses, leaned down for a solemn handshake all around, and set out on the perilous one-hundred-fifty-mile trip to Dodge City.

Two men were dispatched to make a circuit of the other outlying camps and warn the hunters of the Indian uprising if they had not learned of it already through bitter experience. Men began to pour into Adobe Walls until, by the sixth day, a hundred or more had assembled there. One of a group that arrived the third day was young Bill Tilghman. Dutch Henry, who knew Tilghman well, gave him a warm greeting. Tilghman had a reputation as a crack shot, and Dutch Henry called Bat over. "Here's Bill Tilghman, Bat," Henry said, "and I bet he can beat you shooting."

Bat looked the newcomer over. He saw a slender youth of nineteen years, not quite six feet tall. A mass of black curly hair grew back from a wide forehead and fell to the shoulders in plainsman style. A pair of gray-blue eyes above a straight nose and well-shaped mouth looked at him with a fearless yet good-natured expression. Bat liked Tilghman on sight. He extended his hand with a lazy smile. "We'll have to have a shooting match someday, Bill," he said. In later years, Tilghman recalled the meeting and the birth of a lifelong friendship. He remembered Bat as "a handsome young fellow . . . with a reckless devil-may-care look."

He was already an experienced plainsman and a noted shot.''[4]

While awaiting relief from Dodge, the men prepared for another possible battle, cutting loopholes in the sod walls and erecting fortified lookout posts atop the two stores. On the fifth day, a scouting party of Indians was sighted. They fired a few shots, which had no effect, but their approach indirectly caused the death of one of the defenders. Bill Olds, hurrying down the ladder from the lookout on Rath's roof after the alarm was sounded, accidentally discharged the buffalo gun in his hand and blew his head off. Hannah Olds, who witnessed the tragedy, was grief stricken. The rough frontiersmen, calm and efficient in the face of an attack by screaming Indian warriors, stood awkwardly about, unable to comfort the bereaved widow.

The same unlucky Sharps gun that had brought death to its owner came very close to causing more bloodshed in the camp several days later. After a week of siege with no sign of help from Dodge, the hunters decided they had enough horseflesh and men to attempt the journey to Dodge themselves. Jim Hanrahan picked a party of fighters, including Bat Masterson and Billy Dixon, to make a run through the Indians. The evening before they were to leave, the men were gathered in the saloon, making final preparations. After Olds's death, Bat had borrowed his rifle from Hannah, preferring it to his own because of its greater range. Mrs. Olds, fearful that Bat intended to take the gun with him and, with conditions as they were, unsure that she would ever see him alive again, wrote a note to Fred Leonard, asking him to go over to the saloon and fetch the gun for her. Frank Brown, who accompanied Leonard, has left us his version of what happened then:

Batt was leaning on the bar in Hanrahan's Saloon. We went up to him and Leonard handed him Mrs. Olds' note and said, ''We came to get the widow's gun for her.''

Batt read the note, then says to Leonard, ''I have charge of this gun. You go on and attend to your own business and I'll tend to mine.''

Then I, not really knowing very much about the situation, butted in and says, ''Well, Batt, by what right do you claim the gun?'' He flew into a rage and struck at me saying, ''It's none of your business, either, you dam—— Swede. See how you like this,'' and he hit me on the jaw. I knocked him down and was getting the best of him when Hanrahan interfered and two of Batt's friends got stools and commenced lamming us with them. When they had broken the legs off the first stools, they got new ones.

They knocked Len out the door and down a steep embankment. They had me in a corner punching me in the ribs with the stool legs. I moved along the wall until I came to a window, and Hanrahan hit me on the chin and knocked me out the window.

As Brown came tumbling out of the window, two of his friends, Will Thornhill and Art Abecomb, who had been attracted by the sounds of battle, handed him a pair of six-guns. Brown started to crawl back in through the window, his "Irish fighting blood up" and a six-shooter in either hand. He had one leg over the sill when he felt the muzzle of a buffalo gun pressed to the side of his head and heard someone growl: "What do you want in here?" Very meekly Brown answered, "I want my hat."

"The saloon crowd then," said Brown, "took away both my guns and knocked me back out, but they threw me my hat."

Brown said all the hunters became involved in the dispute and that he and his friends held the saloon crowd in Hanrahan's in a state of siege for several hours, taking potshots at those who showed themselves at the windows until a white flag was waved and Mrs. Olds's rifle was produced. According to Brown, this is how the incident ended:

Before he left Batt and his partners came to me and said, "Well, Brown, how shall we settle this? With guns or with an apology from you for insinuating that I intended to steal that gun?" I says, "We'll settle it the way it began, with our fists, or you will apologize for the dirty name you called me."

He knew, without interference, I could give him a good thrashing, so he apologized.[5]

Billy Dixon's account of the affair is somewhat different:

When it was learned that we were going to Dodge, Mrs. Olds sent for her husband's gun. "Bat" sent back word that he wanted to keep the gun until morning, promising that he would promptly return it at that time. This was not agreeable to Mrs. Olds, and she sent a man named Brown to Hanrahan's to get the gun without further talk, as she feared that she might lose it. Brown made a few mistakes in his language in discussing the matter with Hanrahan, the latter having said several times that he would be personally responsible for the gun and would guarantee that it would be returned to Mrs. Olds. Brown crowded matters until Hanrahan grabbed him as a bulldog would a kitten, and then threw Brown out of the saloon, saying, "Get out of my building, you——. —— —!" Hanrahan drew his own gun and had Brown covered, ready to pull the trigger, which I believe he would have done, if several of us had not disarmed him, and then reasoned with him not to go any further, because if shooting began there was no telling what might happen, as both men had friends. Next morning "Bat" returned the gun to Mrs. Olds.[6]

The incident indicates how taut the hunters' nerves had been drawn by their week of siege. Accustomed to daily action and unlimited freedom of movement, they had become like caged tigers crowded into the confines of the three earthen buildings. It was well that the twenty-five hard-core fighters moved out the next day and relieved the congestion and tension at Adobe Walls. Frank Brown's account, set down by his daughter as he told it for years to his children and grandchildren, probably was colored and elaborated upon in the retelling. Dixon makes no mention of shots being fired, stressing instead his and others' fear of the consequences the first shot would bring. The hunters and traders were well aware of the western gun code. A man never reached for a weapon in a dispute unless he was prepared to use it on someone. Once that extremity had been reached and shots actually fired, it hardly seems likely that no one would have been killed. In Dixon's account, the main figures in the quarrel are Brown and Hanrahan. There is no mention of words between Brown and Bat on the matter. However, Bat gained far more fame in the West than Hanrahan ever achieved, and it is suspected that in later years Brown used the incident to impress his grandchildren with the story of how he backed down the renowned gunman.

Hanrahan's party struck out for Dodge, avoiding the main trail. The second day out, they reached Henry Lease's old camp and found the mutilated body of his partner, Charlie Sharp, who had not been fortunate enough to make it to Adobe Walls when the Indians made their bloody sweep of the camps. After burying Sharp, they pressed on, cutting the Adobe Walls–Dodge City trail

at the Cimarron River, and reached Dodge on July 17 without
trouble.

The whole town turned out to meet the hunters. Henry Lease had
arrived safely with word of the battle, and the citizens were eager
for more news. A relief party of forty men under Bat's old boss,
Tom Nixon, had departed for the Walls. By shying away from the
main trail, Hanrahan's bunch had missed meeting them.

Learning of the Indian trouble, hunters from far and wide were
converging on Dodge, and the town was roaring. Details of the
battle were telegraphed to Fort Leavenworth and the hide men
marked time, waiting for the Army to act. Buffalo hunting was
finished south of Dodge City until the Indians could be calmed
down, but the carefree hide men, their anticipated big season
abruptly cut short, had no time for worry or regret. While waiting
for the next development, Bat and the others swung into a time of
pleasure seeking and merriment. Like front-line soldiers on furlough, they lived each moment as if it were their last, giving the
saloons, gambling houses, dance halls, and brothels of fun-loving
Dodge their greatest play up to that time.

Bat had no idea what he would do next. Full of typical frontier
optimism, he was sure something would turn up. And, true to the
way of the frontier, something did.

CHAPTER FIVE

GUNFIRE ON THE SWEETWATER

On July 27, 1874, Colonel Nelson A. Miles received orders to organize at Fort Dodge a military force to be called the Indian Territory Expedition. He was given command of eight companies of the Sixth Cavalry and four companies of the Fifth Infantry, with orders to subdue the hostiles operating in the Indian Territory and the Texas Panhandle. Miles assigned to Lieutenant Frank D. Baldwin the task of organizing a detachment of scouts to guide the main force. On August 1, Billy Dixon was recruited into this company; five days later, young Bat Masterson signed on.

The scout company was composed of seventeen frontiersmen and twenty friendly Delaware Indians led by a seventy-year-old chief named Falling Leaf.[1] The white scouts were, as Miles wrote in his reminiscences, "expert riflemen, pioneers and plainsmen; men of courage and intelligence, and possessing the best attainable knowledge of that remote and unsettled country."[2] For this valuable knowledge and ability, the men were paid seventy-five dollars a month, with promises of fifty dollar bonuses for carrying dispatches over perilous terrain.

When the force had been assembled on the Arkansas River preparatory to moving south, Miles called his scouts together to test their sharpshooting skill. He had each man step forward in turn to take shots at branches and stones in the river. The colonel was well pleased with the marksmanship of his new men, most of them hide hunters whose shooting eyes had been sharpened by many months among the buffalo herds.

On August 11, Colonel Miles's command moved south from the Arkansas in three wide columns. After crossing the Beaver, Lieutenant Baldwin led a scouting party of forty-nine men, including Bat and Billy Dixon, west from the line of march toward Adobe Walls. At Crooked Creek they discovered the camp of a surveying crew that had been surprised by a band of Indians. Scattered in grotesque positions were the mutilated bodies of five men. The oxen and camp dog also were dead, their throats cut. After burying the dead men, Baldwin's party started again for Adobe Walls. On the night of the seventeenth, a violent windstorm struck. Wrote Baldwin: "Had a hard time preventing horses from stampeding. All the men turned out except J. H. Plummer and C. E. Jones who had to be ordered a second time. These two men will be discharged at the first opportunity."[3]

When the party reached the Canadian, Bat and Dixon rode ahead to tell the hunters still at the Walls that the troopers were coming. Baldwin was afraid that in the gathering dusk the wary hunters might mistake the cavalry column for Indians and open up with their long-range rifles. Bat and Billy received a hearty welcome from their friends, who had remained close to the Walls for more than a month. When they rode in, Baldwin's troops looked gravely at twelve Indian heads nailed atop the pickets of the corral gate, placed there, Dixon said dryly, by "some mischievous fellow."

Lulled into a sense of security by the presence of troops, the hunters began to stray from the Walls the following day. Their feeling of peace and tranquility was rudely shattered, however, when a man named Huffman was chased by a band of some fifteen braves almost to the buildings before being run through by a Comanche lance.

Next day, August 20, Baldwin's detachment and all of the remaining civilians at Adobe Walls set out to join the main force at Cantonment Creek. Heading down the Canadian River from the Walls, the scouts surprised a small war party of hostiles near the mouth of Chicken Creek. In a short engagement one Indian was killed and another wounded. "The Indian signs are fresh and a great many evidences are seen proving that they are in this vicinity in large numbers and we will probably see plenty of them before we rejoin the command," Baldwin wrote in his diary when they camped that night. "I sent McGinty and Masterson to the main command with despatches tonight. They left camp at 9 this evening and as I supposed the Head Quarters to be about 55 miles from here on Wolf Creek gave them until 12 o'clock mid-night tomorrow which I think is abundant time." When Scouts McGinty and Masterson located the command and reported seeing Indian sign almost all the way from the Walls, Colonel Miles quickly changed his line of march to a southwesterly direction.

On August 24, Baldwin's party rejoined Miles's command near the Antelope Hills. Here they were joined by Chief of Scouts Ben Clark and Amos Chapman, grizzled plains veterans who had been employed at Camp Supply. Ed Jones, Joe Plummer, and two others were discharged by Baldwin. Ira G. Wing and I. J. Robinson, two of the men from Adobe Walls, were hired as scouts. Jones and Plummer later established a trading post and ranch on Wolf Creek and blazed a route to Dodge City that became widely known in cattle-driving days as the Jones and Plummer Trail.

With his command regrouped, Miles began in earnest his pursuit of the Indians, the trail continuing generally to the southwest. He set a pace of twenty-five miles a day. The plains country was in the grip of the great drought of 1874, and both men and horses suffered in the intense heat. Water holes were few, and some had been made poisonous by gypsum and alkali deposits. Each new day found the temperature soaring to about one hundred-ten degrees in the shade. The Indians were leading the command through country which at that time of year was a desert waste.

On the twenty-eighth, scouts reported fresh Indian sign and indications of a large body of the enemy ahead. For the next two days, despite the heat and lack of water, Miles pushed his men in full pursuit. Both cavalry and infantry covered sixty-five miles in those two days, a marvelous accomplishment, considering the hardships.

Riding two miles ahead of the main columns, the scouts struck the hills bordering the Staked Plains on the morning of August 30. As they followed the Indian trail through an opening in the bluffs, they were attacked unexpectedly from the heights on both sides by some two hundred fifty warriors. The frontiersmen slid from their mounts with the first shot and took up positions in gullies and behind rocks. Their accurate fire, combined with that of the Delaware trailers, turned back the first onslaught. The other hostiles, concealed in the bluffs, rained bullets and arrows down on the detachment in the pass. The two cavalry battalions in the rear heard the noise of the battle and spurred forward. They found the Indians pinned down under the scouts' fire. The cavalry began to comb the bluffs under the cover of the frontiersmen's rifles, and by the time a battery of Gatling guns had been brought forward, the Indians were in complete rout.

The scouts and troopers pressed the retreating Indians hard, maintaining pursuit for some twenty miles. Small parties of Indians dropped back to slow the chase, but the pursuing horsemen rode roughshod over them. The remaining Indians finally fled out into the Staked Plains. Miles, seeing that his soldiers were near exhaustion and suffering so much from thirst that some were cutting their veins to obtain moisture, called a halt. White men, even the rock-hard plainsmen under Ben Clark, could not hope to keep pace with Indians indefinitely in that climate and over that terrain. The supply and ammunition train, moreover, had been left far to the rear. [4]

Although the soldiers had defeated the Indians in one sharp engagement, they had failed in their purpose to kill or capture all members of the marauding band. The renegades were still at large. Miles could not pull his forces back, for the Indians would merely follow in the wake of his withdrawal and recommence their raids on frontier settlements in Texas and on up into Kansas. Miles knew, however, that after waiting for the supply train it was hopeless to try to overtake the renegades on the waterless baked flats of the Staked Plains. He did the next best thing, ordering preparations for an indefinite encampment.

The troopers had little to do during September, but Bat and the other scouts were kept busy scouring the region for signs of Indian movement, guiding small detachments to outposts, and carrying dispatches to Camp Supply. It was on one of the latter missions that Billy Dixon, Amos Chapman, and four enlisted men engaged a band of 125 Kiowas and Comanches in what became known as the Buffalo Wallow Fight. One of the soldiers was mortally wounded at the outset of the battle, but the other five, from the limited cover of a buffalo wallow, held off the Indians from dawn until dark, when the discouraged warriors broke off the fight. All of the survivors were wounded, Chapman so seriously that his leg was later amputated, and each was awarded, upon the recommendation of Colonel Miles, the Medal of Honor.

One of the hoped-for objectives for the men of Miles's command was the rescue of the German sisters. The German family, emigrating across Kansas to Colorado, was attacked by a Cheyenne war party on September 11. Father, mother, one son, and one daughter were killed on the spot, and five daughters were taken prisoner. Another of the girls was killed before the horrified eyes of her sisters as the Indians fled south into the Texas Panhandle. The girls, aged fifteen, thirteen, nine, and seven, suffered great hardship as their captors fled. The sisters were separated; Stone Calf, the Cheyenne chief whose son had died so spectacularly at the Walls, took the two older girls, the others remaining with Gray Beard on the north branch of McClellan Creek.

On November 8, Baldwin's scouts discovered Gray Beard's camp and, with a troop of cavalry and a company of infantry, attacked. The battle was fierce but brief. The Indians pulled out for the Staked Plains again, leaving Julia and Adelaide German, aged nine and seven, huddled under a buffalo robe, quivering with fright. The two older girls were rescued when Stone Calf surrendered at the agency the following winter.

Most accounts of the recovery at Gray Beard's camp include Bat Masterson as one of the rescuers. According to War Department records, however, Bat's services as civilian scout were terminated on October 12, a month before the engagement.[5]

On November 2, 1874, Bat was employed as a teamster at Camp Supply, helping to freight in the tons of provisions required by the Indian Territory Expedition. On October 1, 1874, there was in transit between Fort Dodge and Camp Supply more than 450,000 pounds of rations, ammunition, clothing, and grain to support troops in the field. Supply trains of a dozen to fifty wagons each were being formed at Fort Dodge and heading south under military escort.[6]

Henry Raymond reported in a letter dated December 18, 1874, "I hear that Bat has got a job at camp supply, of counting mules, night and morning."[7] There was a great deal of activity at Camp Supply in December. It had been decided to establish a military cantonment on Sweetwater Creek, south of the Canadian River, near Adobe Walls. It was planned that 106 teams and wagons would haul 1,000,000 pounds of grain and 650,000 pounds of goods to the new outpost. On December 16, the first ox train departed Camp Supply but was caught in a blizzard before it had gone forty miles. Only a few wagons made it through to the new camp, and many animals perished in the storm. It was a month before another train started out, but by February 1, 1875, the new camp on the Sweetwater was rather well outfitted.[8]

The severe winter finished the job Colonel Miles's command had started; the Indians were forced to return to the reservation. Small bands of freezing, starving red men drifted in throughout the winter, and on March 6, Stone Calf led some eight hundred Cheyennes to the Cheyenne and Arapahoe Agency and surrendered. General Philip H. Sheridan, commanding the Military District of the Missouri, said in his annual report:

In the department of the Missouri, the campaign against the Cheyennes, Kiowas and Comanches was finished early in the spring, and the ringleaders and worst criminals separated from the tribes and sent to Fort Marion, Florida. This campaign was not only very comprehensive, but was the most successful of any campaign in the country since its settlement by the whites; and much credit is due the officers and men engaged in it.[9]

With the threat of Indian raids diminished and the sweet smell of spring in the air, the hide hunters moved back into the buffalo grounds in force. But there was still a need for a supply center for the hunters, so enterprising Charlie Rath, undiscouraged after his short-lived venture at Adobe Walls, planned a new store. The army decided to maintain a permanent garrison at the new cantonment on Sweetwater Creek, and in February, 1876, it was officially designated Fort Elliott. Rath, in partnership with Lee and Reynolds, the post traders, put up a hide-buying and supply store on the creek five miles from the post. His building, about fifty by twenty-five feet in size, was adobe, with a sod roof and a dirt floor. It was stocked with ten thousand pounds of flour, another ten thousand pounds of mixed groceries, fifty Sharps buffalo rifles, two thousand pounds of lead bars, and twelve hundred pounds of powder.

Shortly after Rath's store opened, Tom O'Laughlin and his wife arrived to start a restaurant and boardinghouse, and W. H. Weed showed up with a hundred barrels of whiskey to start a saloon and wholesale liquor business. A Chinese man joined the settlement and opened a laundry. Several other saloons appeared, including the most ambitious enterprise of its kind, a combination saloon–dance hall–gambling house run by Henry Fleming and Bill Thompson.

Called the Lady Gay, the Fleming-Thompson establishment was of adobe and sod construction, but the owners had freighted in from Dodge City enough wooden planking to lay a dance floor, twenty by thirty feet, in the rear of the building. They also brought furniture, gambling equipment, a billards table, and, of course, a gaggle of girls. Fleming, the saloon manager, made the necessary trips to Dodge to arrange these purchases. His partner, Thompson, who managed the gambling tables and dance hall, was a fugitive from Kansas, where he had killed Sheriff Chauncey B. Whitney at Ellsworth two years earlier.

In the winter of 1875–76, the new town, called Sweetwater, was busy and prosperous. The Rath, Reynolds & Co. store bought more than one hundred thousand buffalo hides that winter and freighted them to Dodge City. Sweetwater was a strange community, isolated in the hunting grounds. The nearest town was Dodge, two hundred miles away in another state. There was no municipal government, no law or law officer, no taxes. Mail to and from Dodge City was carried free of charge by the post ambulance, which made the trip to Kansas periodically.

The Rath store served as banker for the hunters. After opening an account with the store, the hunter could draw on his credit for his purchases at the store, the saloons, or the restaurant. His account was credited with the hides he brought in at a rate of $2.50 to $4.00 each. At the end of the season, a settlement was made with each hunter and a draft was drawn on Rath's Dodge City store for the balance due. The lowest monetary unit recognized was a quarter. A shot of whiskey, a cigar, a spool of thread, or a packet of needles cost two bits. A man named Atkins was Charlie Rath's bookkeeper at the store and kept the accounts on all the hunters who traded there. He was assisted by George Curry, a bright fourteen-year-old who had worked as a general handyman at the Dodge City store and had been at the new store on the Sweetwater since it was built.

Bat Masterson had returned to buffalo hunting that season and was a frequent visitor to Sweetwater. He sported a heavy black moustache now. His face, darkened by sun and wind, offset the blue clarity of his eyes. He was heavier, and his neck, shoulders, and arms, especially, were overlaid with thick, hard bands of muscle. His name was familiar to everyone, and he was considered an authority on marksmanship, Indian lore, and all that vast expanse of territory marked in the geography books of the time as the Great American Desert.

But he was still only twenty-one years old, and the lusty, bawdy, rollicking night life of Sweetwater drew him like a flame attracts a moth. He became well acquainted with the second echelon of the frontier fraternity, the sporting element that followed the first wave of hunters, prospectors, railroaders, and cattlemen across the prairies. Throughout the West, the pattern had been and would remain the same. Behind the trail blazers came the high livers: the saloonkeepers and barmen, the gamblers and con men, the whores and pimps. Following the smell of the fast and easy buck, they preyed on the pioneer. They hypnotized him with the spin of a wheel and the click of cards, intoxicated him with rotgut whiskey, drugged him with perfume and white female flesh — and took his money.

But the relationship of the sporting gentry to the frontiersmen, though parasitic in nature, was beneficial and necessary. The plainsmen, forerunners of a new civilization in a vast, savage wilderness, hungered for the pleasures of established society, and since they themselves necessarily had been turned half-savage by their life in the wilds, the pleasures they sought were the cruder, baser ones of the society they had known. They welcomed the gamblers and the madams with open arms and pocketbooks.

As in all of the roaring camps of the West, there arrived in Sweetwater with the sporting crowd men who had attained notoriety with their guns. Those who became well known on the frontier as experts in the art of the draw and shoot had varied backgrounds and occupations. Many, like Clay Allison and John Wesley Hardin, were cowboys by trade; some, like Bill Tilghman, were professional peace officers; career gamblers, such as Doc Holliday and Luke Short, formed a large group; and a few soldiers considered themselves expert enough with a Colt revolver to stand up against the finest gunfighters.

The most notorious of the gun-slinging soldiers was stationed at Fort Elliott that winter. He was Corporal Melvin A. King, Company H, Fourth U.S. Cavalry,[10] and he was prone to tell anyone who would listen that with a six-gun he was a match for any man alive. Twenty-eight years old, King had fought in the Civil War and was a veteran of several Indian campaigns. His extracurricular fighting included a number of saloon gun scrapes in which he was reputed to have killed several men. He got along well with the Texas cowboys, despite his blue uniform. Wyatt Earp recalled that it was King's custom to take a furlough during the cattle-shipping season and, dressed in cowboy attire, ride with his Texas friends to the Kansas cow towns where he led them on wild, drunken shooting sprees.

Earp was a peace officer in Wichita, Kansas, at this time. He told his biographer that he had trouble with the obstreperous cavalryman in July, 1875. On one of his tears with his cowboy cohorts and, as usual, looking for trouble, King was brandishing a six-shooter on the streets of Wichita in defiance of city ordinance when Earp corraled him. King was disarmed and fined on that occasion, but he did not profit by Earp's action, as later events proved. He returned to the Sweetwater cantonment as troublesome and quick on the trigger as ever.

We have it on the authority of Wyatt Earp that there arrived in Sweetwater in late 1875 a member of the elite of the six-gun fraternity. Ben Thompson, the widely known elder brother of Bill Thompson, had been in Wichita during the 1875 cattle-shipping season. In the fall, Earp said, Ben went to Sweetwater and was presiding over a faro table in his brother's establishment the following winter. Wrote Bat Masterson many years later:

Ben Thompson was a remarkable man in many ways, and it is doubtful if in his time there was another man living who equalled him with the pistol in a life and death struggle. . . . He stood about five feet nine inches in height and weighed, in later years, in the neighborhood of 180 pounds. His face was pleasant to look upon and his head was round and well-shaped. He was what could be called a handsome man. He was always neat in his dress but never loud, and wore little if any jewelry at

Nelson A. Miles was in charge of the Indian Territory Expedition of 1874. Courtesy Denver Public Library.

Ben Clark, a veteran plainsman and Indian fighter, served as chief of scouts under Miles. Courtesy Kansas State Historical Society.

any time. . . . He had during his career more deadly encounters with the pistol than any man living and won out in every single instance.[11]

Thompson, English by birth, was raised in Austin, Texas, and was apprenticed to a printer. But a reckless spirit of adventure guided him away from the tedium of the print shop. He fought the Comanches and served in the Confederate Army during the Civil War. He journeyed into Mexico with the ill-fated Shelby Brigade and fought under Maximilian until the Juaristas overwhelmed the emperor, after which he escaped to the States and took up gambling as a profession. Already a veteran of many shooting scrapes,

Ben Thompson, Texas gambler. Of all the gunfighters, Bat Masterson rated him tops. Courtesy Denver Public Library.

he found in the frontier settlements ample opportunity to demonstrate his skill. Bat, who in his time was to see the greatest of the six-gun practitioners in action, said in open admiration, "He was absolutely without fear and his nerves were those of the finest steel. He shot at an adversary with the same precision and deliberation that he shot at a target."[12] In the course of his activities, he necessarily ran afoul of some of the more notable frontier marshals, among them Wild Bill Hickok and Wyatt Earp. When Ben himself was not in trouble, he was embroiled in the difficulties of his younger brother, Bully Bill, who possessed the Thompson penchant for getting into trouble but lacked Ben's agility in getting out.

When Ben Thompson summered in Ellsworth, Kansas, in 1873 with his brother Billy, the town was in its heyday as a cattle-shipping center. The frontier sports, male and female, flocked there to partake of the cowboys' pay. Two ladies of easy virtue who answered the call of the gelt were Jennie Field and Mollie Brennan. These two soon became the darlings of the dance halls, and their services were in great demand. However, Jennie and Mollie were smitten by the color and fire of the reckless brothers Thompson. Jennie was fond of the dark, sharp-eyed Ben, and she was his favorite among the town's cyprians. Mollie's choice was Bully Billy, younger, handsomer, bigger, and louder than Ben and when soaked in alcohol, wilder and meaner. One day Bill got drunk and, in the course of some difficulty with the police force, shotgunned to death Sheriff Chauncey B. Whitney. Ben, with some friendly Texans backing him up, held off the town's irate citizens until his brother escaped. Ben left town soon afterward.

The incident had suddenly deprived Jennie and Mollie of the companionship of their dashing lovers. Ellsworth soon passed its peak as a cattle town, anyway, and the sporting element drifted on. Ben's girl, Jennie Field, headed east for Topeka, but Mollie Brennan followed Bill Thompson into Texas. In the winter of 1875–76, she was working in her paramour's dance hall in Sweetwater.

The characters were assembled for the violent drama that almost brought an end to Bat Masterson's life and drastically affected his career. Sixteen years later in another raw new frontier settlement,

Bat told a newspaper reporter: "I don't like this quiet; it augurs ill. . . . In 1875 I was in General Miles' cantonment in Texas. Along with the government employees and soldiers there were 400 buffalo hunters. Everything was quiet, like this camp, for two or three months and then things went lickety-bang."[13]

It was on the night of January 24, 1876, that "things went lickety-bang" in Sweetwater. The events have been recorded and elaborated upon by western writers for many years. Since there were no newspapers in Sweetwater, apparently no official report was ever drawn up, and since none of the principals or eyewitnesses left a written account, it cannot be determined at this late date exactly what transpired. We can only examine the various versions, weigh the source, and decide what is most credible.

Alfred Henry Lewis, Masterson's close friend and employer in later years, wrote an account as part of his article "The King of the Gun-Players":

Mr. Masterson's first gun trouble was at Mobeetie[14] in the Texas Panhandle, the theatre thereof being a dancehall called the Lady Gay. Sergeant King, a soldier and gambler, found fault with Mr. Masterson, and lay in prudent wait to take his life at a side door of the Lady Gay.

The evening was dark. A girl named Anna [sic] Brennan came up. The lurking King, giving some excuse, asked her to rap at the door, conjecturing that Mr. Masterson, who was just inside, would open it. The King conjecture was justified; Mr. Masterson did open it, and asked the girl what was wanted. At the sound of his voice, King stepped forward and, placing the muzzle of his pistol against the Masterson groin, fired. King fired a second shot, and accidentally killed the girl. Coincident with that second shot, however, Mr. Masterson's pistol exploded, and King fell, shot through the heart. The girl, King and Mr. Masterson went down in a bleeding heap; the two first were buried, while to the amazement of the surgeons at Fort Elliott, Mr. Masterson was back in the saddle by the end of eight weeks.

Observe that in this tale the Brennan girl is simply an innocent bystander, a chance victim of King's wild shooting. There is no intimation of involvement, romantic or otherwise, between the girl and either of the two men. It can be assumed that Lewis got this story directly from Bat himself. It should be noted, however, that

Bat was a married man in 1907 and Lewis may have omitted mention of sexual ramifications in deference to Bat's wife.

No one else was involved in the incident as related by Lewis. Three shots are fired in rapid succession; three bodies, a bullet in each, fall together in the dance-hall doorway; two are dead, one is not. Bat is patched up by the post surgeons. End of tale.

A second version of this occurrence was given researcher George G. Thompson on November 4, 1937, during an interview at Wichita with Bat's younger brother, Thomas Masterson, Jr. Tom was seventeen years old when, presumably, he heard this story from Bat when Bat returned home to Sedgwick a few weeks after the incident. Sixty-one years later, Tom recounted as follows:

Bat was a close friend of the proprietor of the Lady Gay. He also was very friendly with the girl, Mollie Brennan. Bat secured the key to the Lady Gay from the proprietor and was given permission to entertain Mollie there alone after closing hours. Sergeant King, who also coveted Mollie, had, in the vernacular of his cowboy friends, "thrown a brand on her." Hearing that Bat and Mollie were alone in the dance hall, he headed that way on the double, carrying a full head of steam, a bellyful of rotgut whiskey, and a loaded six-gun.

When King pounded at the door, Bat, thinking that some friend who knew he was there wanted a nightcap, unlocked the door and stepped back. King sprang inside, cursing and brandishing his six-shooter. Mollie, shrieking at King, jumped in front of Bat, but the sergeant, insane with rage, jealousy, and bad liquor, opened fire. A bullet tore through Mollie's abdomen, struck Bat, and lodged in his pelvis. The girl sank to the floor with a groan and Bat staggered backward. His legs turning to jelly under him, half-blinded with shock and pain, he managed to draw his gun and fire once. His bullet hit King squarely in the heart, killing him instantly.

The dance-hall owner and several night-prowling citizens heard the shots and rushed to the scene. They found King dead in the doorway, Mollie Brennan dying, and Bat Masterson gravely wounded. A doctor was summoned, and he announced Bat's and Mollie's chances as nil. The girl soon died, but Bat's friends sent to the near-by fort for the army physician, who removed the bullet from Bat's pelvis and cared for him until he recovered. [15]

This, then, was the story of the Sweetwater gunfight as remembered by Bat's brother. In major details, it agrees with the story Wyatt Earp told his biographer, Stuart N. Lake, shortly before Earp's death in 1929. Earp evidently got the story from Bat when, still limping from his wound, Masterson showed up in Dodge later in the year. The ingredient added to the tale in the Earp account is the part one Ben Thompson took in the action.

According to Earp, Sergeant King entered the dance hall at the height of the evening's festivities when the place was packed with soldiers, buffalo hunters, gamblers, and ladies of the night. Seeing Bat dancing with Mollie, King drew and fired, killing the girl and wounding Bat. Jerking his Colt .45 even as he crumpled to the floor, Bat shot and killed King. Many of the sergeant's friends were in the room, said Earp, and, seeing their comrade killed before their eyes, pulled their guns. It looked as if they were about to finish Bat as he lay helpless on the floor. At this crucial point, Ben Thompson intervened. Vaulting to the top of a faro layout, he took command of the room. Blue eyes snapping, legs spread wide, a six-shooter in either hand, he held King's trooper friends at bay until Bat had been moved to safer quarters. [16]

Neither of Ben Thompson's biographers places Ben in Sweetwater in January, 1876, or acknowledges this incident. It is perhaps significant, however, that Thompson's whereabouts or activities are unaccounted for during this period by William M. Walton, whose *Life and Adventures of Ben Thompson* appeared in 1884, or by Floyd B. Streeter, whose *Ben Thompson, Man With a Gun,* was published in 1957. As related by Earp, Thompson's action is entirely in character for the man. Whether Bat and Thompson were friendly before the shooting is not known, but, as we shall see, they were very friendly in later years. Even if the two were strangers in 1876, however, it is not surprising that Ben Thompson would throw himself into a fight to defend a man he did not know; that's the kind of man Ben was. He lived to fight and always took the long odds. A roomful of angry soldiers against Ben Thompson and a critically wounded buffalo hunter were just the sort of odds Ben liked. He knew Mollie Brennan very well; she had been his brother's girl. This, too, would give him reason to defend the man who had been shot down with her.

Thompson's role in the incident, if true, must have been the genesis of the peculiar friendship between Bat and the gambler. Ben was a Texan, a Confederate veteran, a hair-triggered gunman. He had the natural animosity of men of his type for Yankee peace officers in the Kansas cow towns. On more than one occasion, that dislike erupted into open gunplay. Several years later, however, when Bat Masterson was sheriff of Ford County and walked the streets of Dodge City with a star on his vest, Ben Thompson ran his game in Dodge and never once got seriously out of line.

There is one other version of the Sweetwater shootout, this provided in the memoirs of George Curry, published in 1958. Curry, it will be recalled, was the fourteen-year-old employed at the Rath store. Although he did not witness the shooting, young Curry played a minor role in subsequent events, and his is the only account we have by a person who was in Sweetwater at the time:

During one of the "dance nights" in January 1876, I was called from bed and told to ride to Fort Elliott to report to Major Hatch, Fourth U.S. Cavalry, that a soldier named King and one of the dance-hall girls had been killed and two soldiers wounded in a gunfight between Bat Masterson and several buffalo hunters on one side, and the soldier, King, and several of his buddies on the other. I rode the five miles to the Fort in fast time and Major Hatch ordered a detachment of soldiers under Lieutenant Smith, with an ambulance and hospital corps men, to come to the scene of the killing. When near the settlement, I asked Lieutenant Smith to halt his command and go into the town with me, fearing that if the troops entered in a body the buffalo hunters might open fire on them and a battle ensue. The officer agreed. Henry Fleming, owner of the saloon and dance hall, was in command of the hunters. After a brief parley he agreed that the soldiers could come in to remove the body of the soldier, the woman and the wounded soldiers. All were taken to Fort Elliott, where a brief hearing was held after which officers and civilians agreed that the killing of King was justified. Major Hatch issued an order prohibiting his soldiers from visiting our village. His order remained in effect for several months.[17]

Curry's slim narrative presents an entirely different picture of the violence that erupted in the Lady Gay. Curry describes a melee "between Bat Masterson and several buffalo hunters on one side, and the soldier, King, and several of his buddies on the other.'' If it was a general gunfight with a number of people on both sides firing, how do we know that King shot Mollie and Bat or that it was Bat's bullet that downed King? We do not know. We have only Bat's story as retold by three other men, the details differing in each instance.

Contemporary records are meager and of little help. Information in the National Archives shows that Corporal Melvin A. King, Company H, Fourth Cavalry, died at the Sweetwater cantonment on January 25, 1876, from the effects of a pistol wound received, not in the line of duty, on January 24, 1876. Almost three weeks after the incident, the *Jacksboro* (Texas) *Frontier Echo* reported the ''telegraphic news'' that ''King, of H Company, 4th Cavalry, and a woman, Molly Braman, [were] killed at San Antonio by a citizen.''[18]

Although it will never be known exactly what happened on that January night in the Lady Gay, it is from this beclouded incident that the legend of Bat Masterson, deadly, swift-handed man killer, sprang. Until that night, Bat had gained some recognition as a successful hunter and a daring Indian fighter. He had been considered a fine marksman with a rifle. But forever after the Sweetwater shootout, he would live with the reputation of gunman. As one who had ''downed his man,'' he would be admired and scorned. He would be pointed out on the street by people with fear and awe in their eyes, and in time men would write luridly of the dozens of men he had outgunned. Bat may have killed Corporal King, but if he did, he would never kill another human being.

CHAPTER SIX

"THIS MAN EARP"

When Bat arrived in Dodge City in late spring, 1876, it was no longer the rough-hewn buffalo camp he had known before he went to Texas two years earlier. The previous summer, the first significant numbers of Texas cattle had been shipped to the eastern markets from Dodge, and the talk everywhere was that in coming months the drovers would be heading their Longhorns up the new Western Trail to the railhead at Dodge. Huge loading pens were being built, and the town pulsed with excitement in anticipation of the cowboys' invasion. Wyatt Earp, who moved to Dodge from Wichita in May, has provided a concise description of the town as it looked that year:

In 1876, Dodge was mostly Front Street, a wide road running east and west just north of the Santa Fe tracks, with the principal cross-street Bridge Street, or Second Avenue, which led to the toll-bridge over the Arkansas River. For two blocks each way from Second Avenue, Front Street widened into the Plaza, with business establishments strung along the north side of the square. The depot, water-tank, and freight-house were at the east end of the Plaza, and immediately south of the tracks was the calaboose, a square, one-room building with floor, walls and ceiling of solid two-by-six timbers spiked flatsides-to, on top of which the city judge and clerk perched a light board shack they used as an office.

The Dodge House, Deacon Cox's famous hotel, was two blocks east of Second Avenue, at Railroad Avenue and Front Street — the northeast corner of the Plaza. Beebe's Iowa Hotel was at Third Avenue and Front Street. The post-office and Wright and Beverly's store, then the most important commercial establishment on the plains, were at the Second Avenue four-corners. Between the store and First Avenue were the Delmonico Restaurant, the Long Branch Saloon, owned by Chalk Beeson and Bill Harris, with Luke Short running the gambling; Ab Webster's Alamo Saloon and City Drug-Store; Beatty and Kelley's Alhambra Saloon and Dodge Opera House, a gun store, and a couple of barber shops. That was the busiest block in town. The Wright House, another popular hotel, was on Second Avenue. South of the tracks were hotels, corrals, dancehalls, and honky-tonks, the picayune gambling-houses, and a bunch of saloons.[1]

In its four-year existence, Dodge City had been visited by many frontier wild men. At one time or another, swarms of plains-hardened buffalo hunters, callous-handed railroaders, and tough army men had descended on the town. Drunken celebrations, saloon brawls, and gunfights were not new to the Dodge citizenry. They were accepted as part of life in a frontier community, to be tolerated as long as the visitors left behind their bankrolls in the merchants' coffers when they departed.

As the cattle-shipping season of 1876 approached, however, Dodge townsmen braced for a new and greater invasion. They had heard how the Texas men had tried, sometimes successfully, to take over the northern cow towns. Abilene, Newton, Ellsworth, and Wichita had all had their troubles with the Texans, who, after a lonely month or more eating the dust of a Longhorn trail herd, liked to celebrate by galloping madly through the streets, shooting indiscriminately at signs, windows, and the derby hats of townsmen. Dodge welcomed the cattle trade and the thousands of dollars' worth of business it would bring the local merchants, but the cowboy invasion was awaited with some trepidation.

On Christmas Eve, 1875, a committee of businessmen met to appoint temporary officials who were to hold office until a municipal election could be held the following April. Friction was evident at that first meeting, and it was to split Dodge City for many years to come. When someone proposed an ordinance prohibiting the firing of guns within the city limits and the riding of horses over sidewalks and into saloons, bitter debate developed. Certain businessmen hungered after the cattlemen's trade so strongly that they opposed any restrictions on the cowboys' funning in fear that the cattlemen would look elsewhere for a shipping point. In later years, any attempts to restrict liquor sales, gambling, or prostitution were fought by the same people who wanted Dodge to remain a wide-open, anything-goes playground for Texans.

Heading this group was Bob Wright, the former Fort Dodge sutler whose general store, operated in partnership with Charlie

Rath, was one of the first businesses established in Dodge City. In 1876 and for many years to come, Bob Wright was Dodge City's most prosperous businessman. Allied with Wright were James H. ("Dog") Kelley and his partner, Peter L. Beatty, proprietors of the Alhambra Saloon, Gambling-Hall and Restaurant. George B. Cox, another early arrival, always sided with the Wright forces. Cox came to Dodge from Larned in 1872 and built the thirty-eight-room Dodge House, which opened on January 18, 1873.

The wide-open-town faction was powerfully augmented on June 1, 1876, when a man named Michael W. Sutton established residence in Dodge. Sutton, a Union Army veteran who had studied law after the war, opened a practice in Medicine Lodge before moving to Dodge. A canny lawyer, Sutton was for several years the brains behind the Wright faction's political maneuvering.

These men and their followers, principally rough frontier types — buffalo hunters, teamsters, bullwhackers, Indian fighters, saloonkeepers — made up what came to be called the Dodge City Gang, a loose-knit group that wanted the town to remain as free and open as possible. Bat Masterson was friendly with most of its members. He shared their philosophy, and in time he came to be recognized as an outspoken, fighting leader of the faction.

Opposing the Dodge City Gang was a group of men who claimed to stand for law and order, led by wholesale liquor dealer George M. Hoover. Physician Sam Galland, lawyer Dan M. Frost, and livery-stable owner Ham Bell were prominent in this faction. Hoover was a Dodge pioneer, having sold whiskey to the soldiers from Fort Dodge in a tent on the townsite as early as 1871. Galland, Frost, and Bell did not establish residence until 1874, however, and early settlers Wright, Kelley, Cox, and others considered them johnnies-come-lately and resented their attempts to change the character of the town.

Peter L. Beatty was chosen acting mayor at the December, 1875, meeting of town leaders and served until April, 1876. At the first municipal election that month, George Hoover was elected mayor, heading a five-member council weighted three to two in favor of the law and order adherents. A resolution of the temporary city council to deal with "misdemeanors and punishment for same" had been agreed to after much debate at the Christmas Eve

Wyatt Earp in 1886. The highly
controversial frontier figure
made many bitter enemies, but
he had staunch friends also, the
foremost of whom was Bat
Masterson, who throughout his
lifetime defended Earp against
all detractors. Courtesy
University of Oklahoma
Library.

meeting, but during the regime of Gang member Beatty, none was
enforced. Upon his election, Mayor Hoover moved to implement
the six provisions that (1) barred animals from the sidewalks; (2)
prohibited the riding of animals into places of business; (3) prohibited the discharge of firearms within the corporate limits "other
than by those empowered to employ same, except upon Fourth of
July, Christmas and New Year's Days and the evenings preceding
these holidays''; (4) banned the carrying of firearms within the city
limits by persons other than peace officers or persons actually
proceeding into or out of town; (5) required all visitors to check
firearms immediately upon arrival at racks to be provided at hotels,
corrals, stores, and saloons and forbade the proprietors of these
establishments to return weapons so checked to owners who were
intoxicated; and (6) dealt with public intoxication and "offenses
against order and decency'' not covered by the other five.[2]

Mayor Hoover appointed as city marshal a three-hundred-pound
saloonkeeper named Larry Deger. Marshal Deger was not renowned as a fighting man, and to act in that capacity in the

enforcement of the radical new regulations, Hoover hired Jack Allen, a gunman of established reputation, as assistant marshal. According to Wyatt Earp, Allen was quickly run out of town by a gang of rampaging cowboys who proceeded to hurrah the town unmolested. Hoover then telegraphed to Wichita for Wyatt Earp to come and tame Dodge City, Wyatt claimed. He told Stuart Lake, his biographer:

> The message that took me to Dodge had offered me the marshal's job, but Hoover told me that for political reasons he wanted Deger to complete his year in office. He would pay me more money as chief deputy than Deger was drawing. I would have power to hire and fire deputies, could follow my own ideas about my job and be marshal in all but name. The marshal's pay was $100 a month, but Mayor Hoover said they would pay me $250 a month, plus $2.50 for every arrest I made. Brown and Mason were discharged from the force and I was to appoint three new deputies at wages of $75 a month, each, and make my own arrangements with them about the bonus.
>
> Bat Masterson's brother Jim was in Dodge, a good, game man who could handle himself in a fracas, and I picked him as one deputy, took Joe Mason back, and was looking for the third when Bat himself came in from Sweetwater, Texas, still limping from the leg-wound he got when he killed Sergeant King. Bat's gun-hand was in working order, so I made him a deputy. He patrolled Front Street with a walking-stick for several weeks and used his cane to crack the heads of several wild men hunting trouble; even as a cripple he was a first-class peace officer.[3]

One of Wyatt Earp's failings was his penchant for inflating his own part in any activity in which he engaged and especially exaggerating any remuneration he received. We have no record of salaries paid the Dodge City officers during that season of 1876, but records of the city council for the year 1878, when Earp again served a stint as assistant marshal, show that he was paid $75 a month, the same amount given John Brown and James Masterson, city policemen. City Marshal Charlie Bassett received $100 per month.

The *Dodge City Times* was founded in May, 1876, by the brothers Lloyd and W. C. Shinn. Nearly all issues of the town's lone newspaper for the year 1876 have been lost, however, and Wyatt Earp's recollections are the basis for most of what has been written about the town's first big season as an end-of-trail cow town. Stuart Lake supports these statements with direct quotations attributed to Bat Masterson. The quotations are undocumented; Lake does not indicate where or when, by interview, letter, or published piece, Bat provided the information.

As Wyatt told it, 1876 passed with very little gun play by the officers, mainly because of Wyatt's dictum that arrest bounties were to be pooled and shared, but only for prisoners taken alive; dead men did not count. A Dead Line was drawn at the railroad. South of the tracks, in the sporting district, almost anything went, including gunplay, but north of the line, a sportive cowboy with a gun on his hip was in for trouble. The officers informed arriving drovers that any breach of the local ordinances along Front Street would bring immediate arrest, a night in the calaboose, and a heavy fine.

Wyatt Earp was adept at handling pugnacious cowpunchers without recourse to weapons other than his two hands. Bat, who in his time was to see the greatest of prize-ring pugilists in action and who later became a noted authority on matters fistic, wrote in 1907:

> Wyatt could scrap with his fists, and had often taken all the fight out of bad men, as they were called, with no other weapons than those provided by Nature. There were few men in the West who could whip Earp in a rough-and-tumble fight 30 years ago, and I suspect that he could give a tough youngster a hard tussle right now, even if he is 61 years of age.[4]

Stuart Lake quotes Bat's description of three fights Wyatt had with tough cowboy bruisers in 1876. These champions came to town, said Bat, with a mob of supporters to humble the marshal in fist fights because they were wary of the six-gun prowess of Dodge's police force. Each time, Earp accepted the challenge, unstrapped his gun belt, handed it to Bat, and proceeded to hammer the upstart Texan into bloody insensibility. Although Bat neglected to mention it, his role at these slugging sessions was more than that of an interested bystander. Many of the cowboys who had been buffaloed by Earp bitterly resented the treatment received at his hands and doubtless would have liked to catch him with his gun belt down. Bat was there to see that Wyatt did not take a bullet in the back while fighting. Earp lived to be an old man because, although he was daring, he was never foolhardy. He made many enemies on the frontier, but he always had foresight and brains enough to surround himself with men of courage upon whom he could depend to back his play in a scrap. Of these, none ranked higher in Wyatt's estimation than Bat Masterson.

Most rambunctious cowboys were subdued by a process known as buffaloing. In general western parlance, to buffalo a man was to outdo him, whether in a business deal, card game, sporting contest, or physical combat. In Dodge City, it came to mean specifically turning a would-be bad man into a nonbelligerent by rendering him senseless with a blow on the head. Generally, the Dodge City officers used the seven-and-one-half-inch barrels of their Colt revolvers to crack the craniums of recalcitrants, but Earp says Masterson put his cane to good use for this purpose. Historian Stanley Vestal erroneously concluded that Masterson's nickname was a *nom de guerre* he acquired in 1876 when he used his walking stick to bat down cowpunchers.

Another hard-dying myth concerning the Dodge City lawmen of the time is the Buntline Special yarn. Edward Zane Carroll Judson, writer of a prodigious number of pulp thrillers under several pen names, the best known of which was Ned Buntline, supposedly came to Dodge in 1876 to gaze personally on the intrepid officers who tamed the frontier bad men and to gather material for lurid tales of the wild and woolly West. It is said that he was so impressed by the Dodge lawmen that he ordered from the Colt factory five specially made six-guns, which he presented to Earp, Bat, Charlie Bassett, Bill Tilghman, and Neal Brown. The guns, called Buntline Specials, had twelve-inch barrels, making their overall length eighteen inches. The addition of fitted walnut rifle stocks, also provided by Buntline, converted the enormous revolvers into carbines. The single word *Ned* was carved into each walnut butt.

It is a great story, one that has been repeated many times in books and periodicals, but it lacks any basis in fact. In all the records of Colt's Patent Fire Arms Company no reference can be found to a sale of twelve-inch revolvers in 1876 or to Judson's purchase of these weapons at any time. No contemporary source mentions them. None of the known written recollections of Wyatt Earp or Bat Masterson, reminiscences that dealt in great part with weapons and their uses, contains even the briefest mention of Buntline or specially designed long-barreled six-guns. None of the five guns has ever turned up, although an authenticated original Buntline Special would bring many thousands of dollars in collectors' circles today.

The entire story was a product of the fertile imagination of Stuart Lake, who set it down as historical fact in his biography of Wyatt Earp, published in 1931. For more than forty years, western writers and historians have accepted the fable, and some have even embellished it. Only in recent years have serious researchers shown the story to be another of the myths surrounding the legend of Dodge City lawmen.[5]

News of gold strikes in the Black Hills of South Dakota swept Dodge in the summer of 1876. Gold fever burned through the town, and Texas cowboys and Kansas citizens alike began to pull stakes for the rush to Deadwood. Bat caught the fever. In July, he resigned from the police force, his position being taken by Morgan Earp, Wyatt's younger brother, a newcomer in Dodge.

Bat went by train to Cheyenne, Wyoming Territory, jumping-off place for the rush to the Black Hills gold fields. He found the normal 8,000 population doubled perhaps by the flood of gold seekers who had been arriving since early winter. The town was seething with excitement. Stores, restaurants, hotels, and board-inghouses were charging outrageous prices — and getting them. Gambling halls, saloons, dance halls, variety theaters, and whorehouses were packed and turning away business. The sporting crowd had descended en masse on the Magic City of the Plains and was joyfully trimming the greenies.

"A fresh invoice of Denver gamblers and sneaks arrived yesterday," noted Cheyenne's *Wyoming Weekly Leader* on February 12. "That dying town seems to be 'taking a puke' as it were, of this class of citizen." Among the short-card artists, thimbleriggers and gold-brick peddlers were such colorfully nicknamed sports as the Preacher, Squirrel Tooth, Poker Dan, Wiffletree Jim, and the Coon Can Kid. More distinguished notables of the sporting fraternity who either headquartered in Cheyenne that season or passed through en route to the Black Hills included Denver kingpin Ed Chase; Tom Dosier of Omaha; George Devol, longtime Mississippi riverboat gambler; and John Bull, Charlie Storms, Jim Levy, and Charlie Harrison, all case-hardened veterans of a dozen boom camps. Wild Bill Hickok, the well-known frontiersman, who had turned professional gambler, was in Cheyenne in 1876 but left for Deadwood in late June, just before Bat arrived. News of his assassination reached Cheyenne about the time Bat hit town.

Cheyenne was nine years old in 1876, having been one of the hell-on-wheels track towns established during construction of the Union Pacific Railroad almost a decade earlier. A town landmark dating back to the earliest days was the McDaniels Variety Theater, a large structure housing, in addition to the theater proper, a hotel, a museum, a bar, and the Gold Room, a gambling hall first managed by Montanans Sam and Charlie Greer but presided over in 1876 by a man named Bowlby. Here and at other gambling resorts, Bat Masterson bucked the tiger, as tackling the faro dealer's game was called. The tiger smiled, and he accumulated a roll. The gambling urge was strong in Bat, and he could not leave town at the beginning of what appeared to be a hot winning streak. He decided to stay on a few days to play the streak to its limit. The winning run was lengthy: Bat was in Cheyenne five weeks. By the time he had had his fill of the gaming tables, discouraged men were beginning to return from Deadwood. That boom town was packed, they said, but all worth-while claims were gone.

Bat started back to Dodge City. At Sidney, Nebraska, he ran into Wyatt and Morgan Earp, bound for Deadwood. It was at this chance meeting, Wyatt later told his biographer, that he suggested Bat run for sheriff of Ford County at the next election. When Bat objected that he was not quite twenty-two, Wyatt replied, "You're as much of a man as you'll ever be."[6]

Wyatt Earp thus claimed credit for introducing Bat and Jim Masterson to the law-enforcement profession the previous spring and first proposing that Bat run for political office. Wyatt always had to be in the limelight; to hear him tell it, the Masterson brothers and men like Charlie Bassett, Neal Brown, and Joe Mason were handy to have around, but it was Wyatt Earp who held the lid on Dodge. Part of this attitude is understandable as it related to the

Masterson boys. Wyatt was five years older than Ed, the oldest of the Mastersons. He already had seen much of the frontier when he first met the Mastersons in 1872. He had then, and continued to have, a somewhat condescending attitude toward them, even after they were grown and had become well versed in the ways of the plains and the border towns.

Stuart Lake, while recounting the legend of Wyatt Earp's career in Dodge — much of it distorted and some of it absolutely untrue — gratuitously informed his readers that

it may be advisable to correct one error. . . . Bat Masterson never was marshal of Dodge City. There is no detraction in a statement of fact which should obviate subsequent misunderstanding. The part that Bat actually played in taming Dodge City — a not inconsiderable one — is to be ascertained from the record. It can be told here, as it is linked with the story of Wyatt Earp, by whom Bat's official career was advised and sponsored.[7]

The facts, as ascertained from the records, are that, although Bat was never city marshal of Dodge, he was for two years sheriff of Ford County, a much more prestigious and lucrative position; that both of his brothers, Ed and Jim, served with distinction in the city marshal's post during the wildest years of the cow-town era; and that none of the Earp brothers who were in Dodge during those years — Morgan, Virgil, James, or the redoubtable Wyatt himself — ever held the position of city marshal of Dodge. As we have seen, Wyatt claimed to have been the real head of Dodge's police force during the season of 1876, with City Marshal Larry Deger serving only in a titular capacity. He later claimed to have been appointed city marshal by Mayor Jim Kelley in 1877 and again in 1878 and 1879.

It is very clear from available newspapers and city records that Wyatt served on the police force in the summer of 1876 as assistant to Marshal Deger, perhaps briefly in 1877 again under Deger, and in 1878–79 under Marshal Charlie Bassett. Larry Deger was not just a political front man, wearing the marshal's badge because he was one of Mayor Hoover's cronies, as Wyatt would have us believe. When the Gang captured control of the town in April, 1877, with the election of Jim Kelley as mayor, one of his first acts was to retain Larry Deger as city marshal. Reported the *Times* of April 7:

L. E. Deger has been reappointed City Marshal, to serve under the new administration. It was thought by many that a change would be made in this branch of the government, but the Mayor and Council wisely concluded that no better man for the place could be found.

Wyatt Earp in later years exaggerated his role in the history of the Kansas cow towns and took a patronizing attitude toward Bat. On the other hand, Masterson, in his reminiscent writing, consistently praised Earp and understated his own activities. In an article on Earp written thirty years later, Bat said:

Wyatt Earp is one of the few men I personally knew in the West in the early days, whom I regarded as absolutely destitute of physical fear. I have often remarked, and I am not alone in my conclusions, that what goes for courage in a man is generally the fear of what others will think of him — in other words, personal bravery is largely made up of self-respect, egotism, and an apprehension of the opinion of others. Wyatt Earp's daring and apparent recklessness in time of danger is wholly characteristic; personal fear does not enter into the equation, and when everything is said and done, I believe he values his own opinion of himself more than that of others, and it is no good report that he seeks to preserve. . . . I have known Wyatt Earp since early in the seventies, and have seen him tried out under circumstances which made the test of manhood supreme. . . . Take it from me, no one has ever humiliated this man Earp, nor made him show the white feather, under any circumstances whatever. . . . Wyatt Earp, like many more men of his character who lived in the West in its early days, has excited, by his display of great courage and nerve under trying conditions, the envy and hatred of those small-minded creatures with which the world seems to be abundantly peopled, and whose sole delight seems to be in fly-specking the reputations of real men.[8]

Back in Dodge in the fall of 1876, Bat was approached by Bill Tilghman and Neal Brown, who wanted him to join them in a buffalo hunt. Bat's old wound scarcely bothered him any more, and he no longer carried a cane at all times. Corporal King's bullet had left him with a slight limp that he was to have for the remainder of his life, but he felt fit enough to try another hunt and agreed to team up with Tilghman and Brown.

Bill Tilghman brought along a youngster from his home town of Atchison to skin and peg out hides. The boy, Fred Sutton by name, was wide eyed at the prospect of working with the frontiersmen and peace officers. In a book relating his experiences, published fifty years later, Sutton marveled at Bat's skill with a six-shooter. During the days they spent together on the prairie, Masterson gave the youngster demonstrations of pistol artistry, with some plain and fancy hip shooting. "He would fire with the hand in any position, seldom higher than his hip or belt," wrote Sutton. "I saw him kill many a rabbit by simply pointing, without sighting, the six-shooter no higher than his hip."[9]

Bill Tilghman, no slouch with a six-gun himself, remarked on Bat's accuracy with the weapon. "I've seen Bat shoot at a tin cup thrown in the air, with his six-shooter, at twenty-five cents a shot, and make money at it," Bill told his wife, Zoe.[10] It was typical of Bat, the gambler, that he would try to make bets on his shooting ability.

As much as he may have enjoyed impressing young Sutton with his hip-shooting ability, however, it is clear from Bat's own words that he considered the sights on a weapon of great importance in an encounter with an armed adversary. In the series of articles on western gunfighters he wrote in 1907, he cited a pistol fray involving Charlie Harrison and Jim Levy, celebrated gamblers and gunmen who faced each other across a Cheyenne street and settled a personal difficulty with hot lead. Levy downed his opponent, wrote Bat, because "he looked through the sights of his pistol, which is a very essential thing to do when shooting at an adversary who is returning your fire." Another well-known western sport and pistoleer, Johnny Sherman, once emptied his revolver at a man in a St. Louis hotel room "without as much as puncturing his clothes." Sherman, said Bat, "forgot that there was a set of sights on his pistol."[11]

Further evidence that Masterson considered the sights on a six-gun to be very important is found in the records of Colt's Fire Arms Manufacturing Company. Bat ordered his first custom-tailored, personally inscribed weapon from the firm in 1879. It was a silver-plated gun with Mexican eagles carved in the pearl handles. In subsequent years, he ordered seven more Colt six-guns, either for friends or for his own personal use. In at least one letter he specifically requested that special care be taken with the front sight; the order was written on the stationery of the Opera House Saloon in Dodge and was dated July 24, 1885:

Gents
    Please send me one of your Nickle plated Short 45. Calibre revolvers. It is for my own use and for that reason I would like to have a little Extra pains taken with it. I am willing to pay Extra for Extra work. Make it very easy on trigger and have the front Sight a little higher and thicker than the ordinary pistol of this Kind. Put on a gutta percha handle and send it as soon as possible. Have the barrel about the same length that the ejecting rod is.

Truly yours
W. B. Masterson

P.S. Duplicate the above order by sending two.[12]

City elections were held in Dodge City in April, 1877, and Bat was back in town to help vote the Gang into power. The new mayor was Jim Kelley, and Bat, anticipating at least one full season of prosperous cattle trade with his pal holding the municipal reins, invested in a Dodge City business, entering into partnership with Ben Springer in the operation of the Lone Star Dancehall. This establishment, one of the largest south of the tracks, made a direct pitch for the cowboy trade, as is attested by its name. Time-tested, sure-fire entertainment for the arriving trail hands was provided. Flanking the dance floor on one side was a Brunswicke-Balke Callander mahogany bar; opposite were tables for faro, roulette, poker, monte, and chuck-a-luck. In the rear was a small stage, with space for an orchestra, where variety shows were provided occasionally. Upstairs were rooms where the dance hall girls slept and where entertainment of a more intimate nature was afforded.
    The *Dodge City Times* reported on April 28:

Dodge City is bracing herself up for the cattle trade. Places of refreshment are being gorgeously arrayed in new coats of paint and other ornaments to beguile the festive cowboy. Masterson & Springer's place can scarcely be recognized since the bar has been removed and operated upon by Mr. Weaver's brush. The graining is finely executed. Charley Lawson's orchestra are mounted on a platform enclosed by and tastefully ornamented with bunting.

Hordes of Texas cowboys poured through the swinging doors of the Lone Star that season, and on occasion they became so festive that the place turned into a roaring hell.

Charlie Siringo, later a well-known Pinkerton detective, came up the trail from Texas in 1877 and was present at one explosion in the Masterson and Springer dance hall:

> We arrived on the third of July. I drew my pay and quit the job to celebrate the glorious Fourth of July in the toughest cattle town on earth. That celebration came near to costing me my life in a free-for-all in the Lone Star Dancehall, in charge of the now noted Bat Masterson. The hall was jammed full of free-and-easy girls, longhaired buffalo-hunters, and wild and woolly cowboys.
>
> In the mixup my cowboy chum, Wess Adams, was severely stabbed by a buffalo-hunter. Adams had started the fight to show the longhaired buffalo-hunters they were not in the cowboy class. . . . I had promised Adams to stay with him until Hades froze up solid. After mounting our ponies, Joe Mason, a town marshal, tried to arrest us, but we ran him to cover in an alley, then went out of town yelling and shooting off our pistols.[13]

A month earlier, Bat had been in trouble with the city police himself. It started on June 6 when Robert Gilmore tanked up in a south-side saloon and began an alcoholic oration out on the sidewalk. Gilmore, affectionately known in Dodge as Bobby Gill, was Bill Thompson's brother-in-law. A small, inoffensive fellow, his only vice was an overweening desire to rid the town of its liquor supply by consuming it. The subject of his drunken dissertation on this occasion was City Marshal Larry Deger. A number of passers-by, including Bat Masterson, stopped to listen and laugh at Bobby's comical performance.

Suddenly the three-hundred-pound marshal hove in view and, taking exception to the remarks, started Bobby for the calaboose. The *Dodge City Times* described what happened:

> Bobby walked leisurely — so much so that Larry felt it necessary to administer a few paternal kicks in the rear. This act was soon interrupted by Bat Masterson, who wound his arm affectionately around the Marshal's neck and let the prisoner escape. Deger then grappled with Bat, at the same time calling upon the bystanders to take the offender's gun and assist in the arrest. Joe Mason appeared upon the scene at this critical

moment and took the gun. But Masterson would not surrender yet, and came near getting hold of a pistol from among several which were strewed around over the sidewalk, but half a dozen Texas men came to the Marshal's aid and gave him a chance to draw his gun and beat Bat over the head until blood flew upon Joe Mason so that he kicked, and warded off the blows with his arm. Bat Masterson seemed possessed of extraordinary strength, and every inch of the way was closely contested, but the city dungeon was reached at last, and in he went. If he had got hold of his gun before going in there would have been a general killing.[14]

Ed Masterson, who had been appointed assistant marshal the day before, made his first arrest of the season when he hunted Bobby Gill down that afternoon and lodged him in the pokey with brother Bat. After a night in the cooler with Gill, Bat confronted Judge Dan Frost in the morning. Charged with disturbing the peace, Bat was found guilty and fined twenty-five dollars and costs. Like Bat, Gill pleaded guilty, but Bobby asked the court for special consideration. Jesus Christ, he said, had died on the cross for just such sinners as he was. Judge Frost considered the point well taken and let Gill off with a five-dollar fine. A month later, Mayor Kelley, with the consent of the city council, remitted ten dollars of Masterson's fine, but the Bobby Gill incident rankled Bat and was the inception of a bitter grudge against Larry Deger that Bat was to hold for many years.

In July, Bat was appointed undersheriff for Ford County by Charlie Bassett. At a special election back in June, 1873, Bassett had been elected the county's first sheriff. He was re-elected in November, 1873, and again in November, 1875, and his term was expiring at the end of 1877. Under the Kansas Constitution, he could not hold office for three consecutive regular terms, and his position was going up for grabs in the fall election. That Bat was his choice for successor was attested by his selection of young Masterson for the job of undersheriff. Bassett had previously appointed several experienced lawmen as deputies, including Miles Mix and Dodge City Officers Larry Deger and Joe Mason. Josh Webb, Al Updegraff, and Bill Tilghman, all known as game men in a showdown, had been deputized on special occasions. But for his second-in-command in the final months of his tenure, Bassett named Bat Masterson.

Larry Deger, charter member of
the anti-Masterson faction in
Dodge City. Bat hated him
from the day Deger used his
three-hundred-pound bulk to
manhandle little Bobby Gill.
Courtesy Kansas State
Historical Society.

A one-liner in the *Times* of August 4 revealed Bat's first act in
his new office: "Marshal Deger resigned his position of Deputy
Sheriff this week, at the request of Under Sheriff Masterson."
Oddly enough, a month later, on September 17, Bat was appointed
a special city policeman by Mayor Kelley to serve under Marshal
Deger. This peculiar arrangement lasted only ten days, however,
and apparently was an emergency measure necessitated by the
large number of drovers in town.

September was a very busy month for Bat. While maintaining
his dance-hall business, he was called upon several times to act in
one of his official capacities: undersheriff or city policeman. The
Times of September 8 reported his capture of a horse thief. On the
seventeenth, he was involved in an incident that, although farcical
in its confusion and mistaken identity, nearly ended in bloody
tragedy.

It started when three buffalo hunters came into town in a wagon
and began loading supplies at Bob Wright's store. They told

Wright they needed a buffalo gun and had insufficient funds to cover their purchases and the gun, too. They then showed him an expensive gold watch and chain, which they offered to leave in payment for the rifle. Wright agreed, but after loading their wagon, the three slipped off, leaving neither money nor watch. A clerk was sent after them, but the trio refused to pay him when they found that he was unarmed. With great magnanimity, they gave him the watch.

Bob Wright asked Bat to go after the men and recover the rest of the money. Said the *Times*: "Masterson overtook them, and in his amiable manner bulldozed them out of all the money they had, amounting to about $25." The watch and chain were worth about seventy-five dollars, which, together with the twenty-five dollars in cash, almost covered Wright's bill. Bat could have taken the buffalo gun, but that would have left the hunters without the means to hunt, so he permitted them to keep it.

The strangers, it developed, were craftier than anyone suspected. The watch belonged to none of them, having been stolen a short time before in neighboring Edwards County. Sheriff Bob McCanse and two deputies were at that very moment trailing them to Dodge.

Rancher J. E. Van Voorhis of nearby Spearville had been having trouble with horse thieves. Seeing three well-mounted and heavily armed men passing his ranch, he jumped to the conclusion that they were the men who had been stealing his horses. He cut for Dodge over the back trails. Bat Masterson had just returned to the sheriff's office when Van Voorhis galloped in and told him that three approaching riders were horse thieves. He gave Bat and Deputy Joe Mason detailed descriptions of the three.

When Sheriff McCanse and his deputies rode into Dodge that night, they were prepared for trouble, but not the kind they found. They had just put up their horses at Anderson's livery when Bat and Mason, identifying them as the suspected horse thieves from the rancher's description, stepped from the shadows with drawn guns. "Masterson met one of the men, took his pistol and made him a prisoner," reported the *Times*. "Mason pointed two ivory-handled guns at another, and completely covered him. The last man they met was Sheriff McCanse. Mason seized his revolver, but McCanse did not like the idea of losing his gun, and held on to it.'' The Edwards County officer jerked loose and backed against a wall, his six-shooter leveled. Firing was about to commence when light from a saloon flare fell across his face and Bat recognized him.

The incident had a happy ending. The watch was returned to McCanse; Bat set up drinks for the officers and told them the trail taken by the three thieves. McCanse captured them several days later and returned them to Edwards County.[15]

A week later, the roar of gunfire on Front Street brought Assistant Marshal Ed Masterson and Special Policeman Bat Masterson on the dead run. A. C. Jackson, one of the more sportive cowpokes in town, was galloping his little mustang madly around the plaza, emptying his six-gun in the air. Jackson had been warned about this practice but had paid no heed. Bat shouted at him to halt, but the cowboy waved his hat in defiance and put spurs to his mount, heading for the south bridge and the bedding grounds across the Arkansas.

The Mastersons drew and fired, aiming at the cow pony. The horse "seemed to scringe" but continued on, clattering wildly over the wooden bridge and disappearing into the night. The shots had not been without effect. Two miles from town, the cowboy's horse stumbled and fell dead. Jackson had to leg it into camp, having lost a valuable animal for his sport.

Although they deplored promiscuous shooting within the city limits, the citizens of Dodge realized that most of it was done in play. The editor of the *Dodge City Times* set forth the cowboy's viewpoint:

A gay and festive Texas boy . . . like all true sons of the Lone Star State . . . loves to fondle and practice with his revolver in the open air. It pleases his ear to hear the sound of this deadly weapon. Aside from the general pleasure derived from shooting, the Texas boy makes shooting inside the corporate limits of any town or city a specialty. He loves to see the inhabitants rushing wildly around to "see what all this shooting is about," and it tickles his heart to the very core to see the City Marshal coming towards him at a distance while he is safe and securely mounted on his pony and ready to skip out of town and away from the officer.

The programme of the Texas boy, then, is to come to town and bum around until he gets disgusted with himself, then to mount his pony and ride out through the main street, shooting his revolver at every jump. Not shooting to hurt anyone, but shooting in the air, just to raise a little excitement and let people know he is in town.[16]

It is noteworthy that the Masterson brothers killed none of these playful young range riders. They could have done so on many occasions, and had they been the blackhearted, bloodthirsty killers that both contemporary and later writers have described Dodge City officers as being, they certainly would have done so.

The day after the uproar caused by cowboy Jackson, word reached Dodge that five men, believed to be those who had held up the Union Pacific at Big Springs, Nebraska, and made off with sixty thousand dollars, were heading south. The train robbers, later identified as the Sam Bass gang, were expected to cross the Atchison, Topeka & Santa Fe near Lakin. Sheriff Bassett, Bat Masterson, and Josh Webb headed west on the morning train; finding no sign of the bandits at Lakin, they returned the following day. Another report was received: five men had crossed the Santa Fe, heading south, about thirty miles west of town. Bassett, Bat, and Webb saddled up and headed southwest in an effort to cut the outlaws' trail. Meanwhile, Ed Masterson and Miles Mix headed west by train to pick up what information they could about the five riders.

In the end, the feverish manhunt availed nothing. The Sam Bass gang made good its escape to Texas. Not many months hence, however, there would be another opportunity to corral train robbers, and this time the denouement would be happier for Bat and his fellow lawmen.

CHAPTER SEVEN

"HURRAH! FOR OUR OFFICERS"

The *Dodge City Times* of October 13, 1877, carried Bat Masterson's announcement that he was a candidate for sheriff:

At the earnest request of many citizens of Ford county, I have consented to run for the office of Sheriff at the coming election in this county. While earnestly soliciting the suffrages of the people, I have no pledges to make, as pledges are usually considered before election to be mere clap-trap. I desire to say to the voting public that I am no politician, and shall make no combinations that would be likely to in anywise hamper me in the discharge of the duties of the office, and should I be elected will put forth my best efforts to so discharge the duties of the office that those voting for me shall have no occasion to regret having done so.

Respectfully,
W. B. Masterson

The Shinn brothers, owners and editors of the paper, commented on the announcement:

Mr. W. B. Masterson is on the track for Sheriff, and so announces himself in this paper. "Bat" is well known as a young man of nerve and coolness in cases of danger. He has served on the police force of this city, and also as under-sheriff, and knows just how to gather in the sinners. He is qualified to fill the office, and if elected will never shrink from danger.

Others seeking the sheriff's job were George T. Hinkle and Bat's old nemesis, Larry Deger. In late October, Hinkle dropped out of contention and threw his support to Deger.

On October 27, a "Peoples' Mass Convention" was held in the Lady Gay Saloon to nominate candidates for the county offices. Bat's name was put forward as candidate for sheriff by Peter L. Beatty, and seconding speeches were made by Mike Sutton and James Manion. All of these gentlemen were associated with the Dodge City Gang. Larry Deger's name was offered by George

Hoover, seconded by Harry Gryden, Dan Frost, and William Morphy. A ballot was taken, and Masterson was declared the party's choice for sheriff. Deger declared that he would continue to campaign as an independent.

On November 6, 1877, twenty days before his twenty-fourth birthday, Bat Masterson was elected sheriff, defeating Larry Deger 166 votes to 163. The *Hays Sentinel* commented: "Larry Deger only lacked three votes of being elected sheriff of Ford County. His successful opponent Bat Masterson is said to be cool, decisive and a 'bad man' with a pistol.''[1] Deger filed to contest the election but withdrew the suit two months later.

On January 14, 1878, Bat was officially sworn in. As sheriff, he was responsible for a vast territory. Ford County was created in 1867 and organized in 1873, but all the unorganized region west of it to the Colorado line was attached for judicial purposes. During this period, the sheriff of Ford County was the supreme law enforcement official for some 9,500 square miles, a large chunk of southwestern Kansas. To help him in this awesome task, Bat appointed three men: Charlie Bassett, his former boss, who now became his undersheriff; Simeon Woodruff, deputy sheriff; and John W. Straughn, jailer. Woodruff did not remain long and was succeeded by William Duffey, a plains-wise former Indian scout and tracker. Others whom Bat called upon as special deputies during his term of office included John Joshua Webb, Prairie Dog Dave Morrow, Kinch Riley, Miles Mix, Bill Tilghman, Wyatt Earp, and brother Jim Masterson.

It should be pointed out in this connection that as sheriff Bat was not responsible for keeping the peace in Dodge City, although, since Dodge was the county seat, he necessarily spent a great deal of his time there and was always ready to help the city marshal when the need arose.

Bat was anxious to prove himself, and less than two weeks after he was sworn in, he was given an opportunity. On January 17, word was flashed to Dodge from neighboring Edwards County that six masked bandits had twice attempted to hold up Santa Fe trains near Kinsley, thirty-seven miles from Dodge. The first attempt was made at the water tank two miles east of Kinsley, where the eastbound train out of Dodge was scheduled to stop for water, but the engineer did not halt the train at that point as the outlaws had anticipated. The gang then rode into Kinsley and reached the station before the westbound *Pueblo Express* arrived. The night operator was held up, but the outlaws failed to get two thousand dollars in the company safe. As they held the operator, a youth named Kinkade, on the platform at gunpoint, the *Express* pulled in. The nervy Kinkade suddenly leaped across the tracks in front of the braking locomotive, putting the train between himself and the bandits, and shouted a warning to the crew. Shots pierced the night as the robbers attempted to board the train but were driven back by the alerted trainmen. The engineer hurriedly started up again and pulled two miles out of town, where he stopped to ascertain the extent of damage and injury. Fortunately, no one had been hit and nothing had been stolen. The raid was a total failure.

The Santa Fe wanted no more of that sort of nonsense. Officials immediately authorized the printing of posters offering one-hundred-dollar rewards for the capture, dead or alive, of each of the outlaws. There was great excitement in Kinsley. Guns were oiled and loaded, horses were saddled, and heavily armed, grim-faced men went charging off in every direction.

Edwards County also had a new sheriff, a man named Fuller. He led one group of possemen to Fort Dodge to enlist the aid of the U.S. Cavalry in searching for the fugitives. Another posse under former Sheriff Bob McCanse trailed the outlaws to a point twelve miles from Kinsley where they had crossed the Arkansas River. McCanse lost the trail in a dense fog and returned to Kinsley after a ride of 115 miles. As the McCanse posse rode into Kinsley, yet another party of eight man hunters took the trail. Sheriff Fuller, several possemen, a scout named Calamity Bill, and a detachment of cavalry under Lieutenant Gardner left Fort Dodge and crossed the river in pursuit.

All this activity produced absolutely nothing. The desolate sand-hill country south of the Arkansas had swallowed up the train robbers. All of the Edwards County parties eventually returned empty handed.

Meanwhile, representatives of the Adams Express Company, with offices in Dodge City, had approached Bat and asked him to lead a posse in search of the fugitives. He eagerly seized the chance, deputizing three former buffalo hunters who knew the southern hill country as well as he and who, if it came to a fight, would not lack grit.

Josh Webb had seen service as a peace officer at Caldwell before coming to Dodge and acquiring an interest in the Lady Gay. Prairie Dog Dave Morrow, who got his nickname from his pointed ears, had been around Dodge from the earliest days and had served several stints as both a city and a county officer. Kinch Riley was a strapping young giant who, according to the *Dodge City Times*, "had been wounded and bruised in a number of personal encounters . . . undergone many severe trials and exposures, and made many narrow escapes."[2]

A sharp, cutting wind was blowing from the north as Sheriff Masterson led his posse into the sand hills on January 29. By the time they reached Crooked Creek, twenty-seven miles from Dodge, snow was falling, so they made camp for the night. By morning, the storm had increased in intensity, and the posse spent another miserable day and night waiting for it to abate. On the third day, they rode through intermittent snow squalls some thirty-five miles to Harry Lovell's ranch at the mouth of Crooked Creek.

Lovell said he had seen no sign of the bandits. Bat knew that they would be forced to seek shelter from the storm. Ranch houses and farmhouses were few and far between in that country, and there was a good chance that the gang would come right to Lovell's. Bat bedded his men down in a dugout some distance from the ranch house and waited. The men took turns at lookout as the storm lashed the rude building throughout the night and the following day. About five o'clock in the afternoon of that day, Kinch Riley, who was standing guard, spotted four horsemen approaching. He called to the others, and they watched through chinks in the walls as the riders came nearer. Suddenly Bat recognized two of the horsemen as Dave Rudabaugh and Ed West, both notorious criminals. The other two riders were cowhands employed by Lovell. While still some distance from the dugout, Rudabaugh and West reined up and peered ahead, apparently reluctant to ride on in. The cowboys, unaware of the identity of their companions and eager to get in out of the cold, could not understand their peculiar behavior and urged them on.

Josh Webb opened the door and stepped out into the snow. As he trudged off to meet the newcomers, he was careful to leave the door slightly ajar behind him. Dave Rudabaugh eyed him suspiciously as he walked near. He knew Josh Webb as a dance-hall owner in Dodge and wanted to know what he was doing this far from home in a blizzard. Webb described a mythical trip he was taking when the storm drove him to shelter. Chatting amiably, he walked back toward the dugout beside the horses. When the outlaws, relaxed by Webb's chatter, were almost to the building, Bat suddenly kicked wide the partly open door and leaped out with leveled rifle.

"Throw up your hands!" he snapped as Riley and Morrow scurried to his flanks with drawn guns. The startled West quickly complied with Bat's order, but Rudabaugh was a tougher customer. His hand flew from his saddle horn to his gun butt. He froze with the weapon half out of the scabbard as Josh Webb's six-gun hammer clicked behind him. Then the man whom Wyatt Earp once called "the most notorious outlaw in the range country" slowly raised his hands, and Bat told Riley to disarm the pair.

From the gun belt of each outlaw, Big Kinch extracted a Colt .45. From their saddle boots he jerked a .40-caliber Sharps rifle and a .45-caliber government carbine. He stepped back, thinking his task complete, but the sharp-eyed Bat detected a suspicious-looking bulge under Rudabaugh's greatcoat. He pulled open the coat and reached for the revolver the bandit had hidden in his waistband. Rudabaugh made one last desperate attempt to escape capture. He grabbed for the gun as Bat extricated it from his clothing, but Bat wrenched it away from him.

On February 1, Bat and his posse arrived in Dodge with their prisoners. Rudabaugh and West were held overnight in the Dodge City calaboose awaiting the arrival of a special train to transport them to Kinsley. There they were interrogated by Captain J. M. Thatcher, general agent for the Adams Express Company. Just before the prisoners were placed aboard the train on the following day, Thatcher instructed Bat to arrest a Dodge City resident suspected of being an accomplice in the attempted holdup. Bat was startled to learn that the suspect was young Bill Tilghman, his former buffalo-hunting *compadre* and part owner of the Crystal

Palace Saloon. Bat made the pinch, and Tilghman, protesting his innocence, was taken in shackles to Kinsley with Rudabaugh and West. There the three were bound over on four thousand dollars' bail. Bat then brought them back to Dodge and lodged them in the Ford County pokey. A few days later, the case against Tilghman was dropped for lack of evidence and he was released from custody.

At the height of the excitement immediately after the attempted holdup, the *Kinsley Republican* issued three extras, criticizing Bat in one story for not helping the Edwards County officers. Now that Bat's posse had lodged two of the suspects in jail, the *Ford County Globe*, a new paper in Dodge, could crow a little, even though Bat was not a political favorite of the *Globe*'s editors, William Morphy and Dan Frost:

> The *Kinsley Republican* extra of Jan. 29th, says that the failure of our Sheriff to co-operate with the Kinsley posse, in hunting the train robbers was inexcusable; and the excuse he assigned is a little "too thin." Now Mr. Republican, we don't know what you mean by his excuse, but have this to say: Our Sheriff is not in circumstances that will warrant him in incurring the expense necessary to hire horses, employ a posse of men, and pay their expenses, even to hunt train robbers whose crime was committed in a neighboring county; unless those expenses are guaranteed by somebody. We are personally not on squeezing terms with our sheriff, but when as an officer he is unjustly assailed, we feel it our duty to defend him, as well as any other officer in our county. We know that he has the stuff in his make up to be a good officer, and when he does right we will be found telling him so with the same spirit of justice that will guide us to tell him he is wrong, when we consider him so. We think that our Sheriff's hunt for the train robbers has accomplished more than the hunt of all the other posses, even if his departure was not heralded with blasts of trumpets, newspaper extras, etc.[3]

The pro-Masterson *Times*, now edited by a Dodge City newcomer, a full-bearded Missourian named Nicholas B. Klaine, was much more fulsome in its praise of the young sheriff:

> . . . The nerve, skill and energy of Sheriff Masterson and gallant posse is recorded as a brilliant achievement and is receiving just tribute for so daring a venture accomplished so adroitly and maneuvered with the skill of a warrior.

Nicholas B. Klaine, postmaster
at Dodge and editor of the
Dodge City Times. Reading
other people's mail was one of
the milder charges Bat leveled
against him. Courtesy Kansas
State Historical Society.

. . . The arrested parties are two well known desperadoes, but quailed
under the intrepid, cool and daring movements of Sheriff Bat Masterson.
Ed West, the elder of the two, is about twenty-six years old, and is a
notorious thieving character; Dave Ruddebaugh is about twenty-three
years of age, and has led a wild career in crime. . . . .
. . . The well devised and executed capture reflects credit, good
judgment and bravery upon all who engaged in it.[4]

A few days later when Bat went by train to Las Animas and
arrested "one James McDuff, a notorious character," brought him
back to Dodge charged with stealing a span of horses, and provided
him with "accommodations in the Hotel de Straughn," Editor
Klaine was again lavish in his praise of Bat, whom he called "the
right man in the right place."[5]

Ten days after his return from the hunt for train robbers, Bat
again rode out at the head of a posse in search of the remaining
members of the gang. With him went Undersheriff Charlie Bassett, Josh Webb, Miles Mix, and rancher John ("Red") Clarke

driving a wagon loaded with provisions for a long hunt. The *Ford County Globe* wished them success, saying: "No better posse ever undertook such a duty. We know every man in the party has the sand and nerve to go where any other man on earth dares to go. If the robbers are not captured it will not be for want of bravery, coolness or strategy, on the part of Sheriff Masterson or his posse."[6]

Evidently acting on a tip that Mike Rourke, reputed to be the leader of the holdup gang, had been seen in the vicinity of Lovell's ranch, Bat headed for that desolate area. When he and his posse arrived at Lovell's, they learned that Rourke and another wanted man named Dan Webster had pulled out only three hours earlier, headed south. At the camp of a man named Shepherd, fifteen miles from Lovell's, they were told that the outlaws had passed by shortly before, still heading south. Pushing on hard, the man hunters reached the Cimarron River as night fell.

Although it was impossible to track in the darkness, Bat drove on in the direction taken by the fugitives, hoping to overtake them in their night camp. At one point, certain that they were close to their quarry, he and his men dismounted and walked five or six miles along a branch of Beaver Creek. The next morning, they struck the trail again. The outlaws, aware that the officers were hot on their heels, had traveled hard all night, veering in a southeasterly direction.

The posse had far outdistanced the provision wagon and had ridden for thirty hours without rest or food. Bat was forced to wait for it to catch up. When they took up the trail again, they found a deserted camp hidden in a plum thicket. Two more men with a wagon had joined the fleeing outlaws here, according to the signs. The trail led past Kiowa and Medicine Lodge creeks, then west to the Jones and Plummer ranch on Wolf Creek. There, Rourke and his men, apparently sensing that the posse was closing on them, abandoned the wagon and struck out again on horseback. The posse followed doggedly to the Staked Plains in Texas, where the trail vanished in that trackless wilderness.

Weary and bitterly disappointed, Bat's party returned to Dodge. They had been gone thirteen days and had ridden almost six hundred miles. Ironically, after the long, frustrating, fruitless trip,

Bat was able to capture two more of the Rourke-Rudabaugh gang three weeks later — within the city limits of Dodge!

On the night of March 15 while making his rounds, Nat Haywood, a city policeman, spotted a man known as Tom Gott, alias Dugan, in a south-side gin mill. Haywood informed Bat, who quickly summoned Charlie Bassett and Ed Masterson. The trio made a tour of the joints south of the tracks looking for Gott, who was known to be a member of the Rudabaugh crowd. They were unable to locate him, but discreet inquiries revealed that he was accompanied by a man named J. D. Green, another of the gang. At Anderson's livery, the officers learned that the two wanted men had passed by shortly before, heading toward the river. The Masterson brothers and Bassett took off in pursuit and soon came within sight of the fugitives. Gott and Green started to put up a fight, but the lawmen swarmed over them. They were disarmed before a shot was fired. Shortly thereafter, the two miscreants joined their cronies in the calaboose. Editor Frost was forced to declare in open admiration: "Hurrah! for our officers! They have done well!"[7]

After questioning Gott and Green, Bat believed that all four of the at-large participants in the Kinsley holdup had been in Dodge on March 15. They had come, perhaps, to assist their partners, Rudabaugh and West, in a breakout from the Ford County jail, where the first two arrested outlaws were being held. Gott and Green had been nabbed, but Mike Rourke and a companion had slipped out of town. This sixth member of the gang was named Tillman, which accounted for the arrest on suspicion and the short incarceration of Bill Tilghman the month before.

The morning after the capture, Bat led another pursuit to the south, taking with him Charlie Bassett, Josh Webb, and young Jim Masterson. A few days later, the man hunters returned; once again Rourke had given them the slip. It was seven months before the law finally caught up with Mike Rourke. In October, 1878, he was apprehended near Ellsworth, Kansas, and a cohort named Dan Dement was mortally wounded in a gun battle with the arresting officers. The elusive Tillman made good his escape again. Rourke was sentenced to ten years in prison for his part in the Kinsley holdup.

Meanwhile, the four gang members Bat corraled had been brought to trial at Kinsley in June. Dave Rudabaugh secured his own release by turning state's evidence and testifying against the other three defendants. The *Kinsley Graphic* put it succinctly: "Rudabaugh . . . was promised entire immunity from punishment if he would 'squeal,' therefore he squole."[8] Undone by their leader's duplicity, West, Gott, and Green pleaded guilty and were given five years each at hard labor in Leavenworth Prison.

Dave Rudabaugh also testified against Mike Rourke at the latter's trial in Butler County. He showed up in Dodge City again in March, 1879, saying that his outlaw days were behind him and he was looking for honest work. It is likely that Bat enlisted him in the corps of fighting men he took to Colorado that month to defend the Santa Fe in its battle with the Denver & Rio Grande for possession of right-of-way along Royal Gorge. If so, it was probably during this escapade that the friendship between Rudabaugh and John Joshua Webb, one of Bat's lieutenants in the Royal Gorge War, developed. Webb, who had been prominent in the capture of Rudabaugh and had suffered many hardships with Bat's posses, became closely associated with Rudabaugh, whose flirtation with honest endeavor was of short duration. Although Webb was six years Rudabaugh's senior, the outlaw's influence turned the older man's career one-hundred-eighty degrees.

Later in 1879, the two went to Las Vegas, New Mexico, then notorious as the most corrupt and vicious community in the West; by Las Vegas standards, Dodge City was a model of virtue and rectitude. Miguel Otero, later governor of New Mexico, who was in Las Vegas during this period, stated that in one month twenty-nine men died violently in or around the town. Rudabaugh and Webb became policemen there, working under the auspices of a crooked justice of the peace named H. G. Neill, popularly known as Hoodoo Brown.

In March, 1880, Josh Webb was arrested and charged with complicity in the robbery and murder of a prominent cattleman. When the news reached Dodge City, a collection was taken up among Webb's old friends to help in his defense. There were forty-two donors, including Bat Masterson, who forked over twenty dollars. But in Las Vegas, Dave Rudabaugh took more direct action to aid his crony. He forced his way into the Las Vegas jail, shot and killed the jailer and took the keys from the dead man's body and threw them into Webb's cell. For some reason, Webb rejected this chance for freedom, and Rudabaugh barely managed to escape. He returned once more to the "owl hoot trail," joining Billy the Kid's outlaw gang.

Webb was convicted of murder and sentenced to hang. He received a stay of execution for refusing to break out with Rudabaugh, but he later gave up hope of a commutation and engineered a bloody mass escape in which three men died. In November, 1880, he was captured near Roswell by Sheriff Pat Garrett and was lodged once again in the Las Vegas bastille. The following month, Billy the Kid and Dave Rudabaugh were taken by Garrett at Stinking Springs. In a trial at Santa Fe, Rudabaugh was convicted of the murder of the jailer in his attempt to spring Webb and was returned to the Las Vegas jail under sentence of death.

In December, 1881, Rudabaugh, Webb, and five others tunneled out of the Las Vegas jail and escaped. Webb disappeared. It is believed that he died of natural causes several years later. Rudabaugh dodged the law for some time, finally crossing the border into Mexico. There, in May, 1886, his violent career was brought to an abrupt end. A mob of frenzied Mexicans at Parral, Chihuahua, made certain that Rudabaugh would murder and steal no more. They killed him, cut his head off, and mounted it on a pole in the town square to serve as a warning to other malefactors.

CHAPTER EIGHT

THE TROUBLE WITH ED

Sheriff Bat Masterson's conspicuous role in the apprehension of the Kinsley train robbers enhanced his prestige in Dodge City. A stranger stopped a local resident on Front Street one day, wrote Bob Wright, and asked where he could find the sheriff. Overhearing the question, a Dodge lawyer spoke up: "Look for one of the most perfectly made men you ever saw, as well as a well-dressed, good-looking fellow, and when you see such a man, call him 'Bat' and you have hit the bull's eye."[1]

As Bat was gaining fame as sheriff of Ford County, Ed Masterson was struggling to keep the lid on Dodge. In April, 1877, when Mayor Jim Kelley and the Dodge City Gang took control of the city government, Kelley, to the surprise of many, reappointed Larry Deger city marshal. In July, Ed Masterson was named assistant marshal. A few days after his appointment, he had to act as mediator in a dispute between Deger and Kelley.

The trouble started at two o'clock on the morning of July 20 when Deger arrested and jailed Charlie Ronan, gambler and staunch supporter of the Gang. Kelley braced the marshal and ordered him to release Ronan at once. Deger refused, and Kelley, white with anger, demanded the marshal's badge. Deger again refused, and Kelley sent for Ed Masterson and Officer Joe Mason, ordering them to place Deger under arrest.

Heating up under the collar himself, Deger jerked his revolver and warned his subordinates not to try. Little Ed was "placed in a doubtful position," as the *Dodge City Times* put it.[2] It was a dangerous situation in which a wrong move or a hasty word could have meant bloodshed, but Ed, with his quiet voice and calm manner, cooled the fiery Irishman and irate Dutchman and cajoled Deger into submitting to arrest and release on his own recognizance until the difficulty could be resolved at police court later in the morning. To keep things nice and even, Ed later arrested Mayor Kelley on a charge of interfering with a police officer in the discharge of his duty.

Kelley did not appear against Deger at his court hearing and the case was dropped, Judge Frost ruling that no city ordinances had been broken by the marshal. Kelley's case was continued until the following day, when a petition signed by a majority of the city council was presented, requesting that the charges against the mayor be dropped and that the marshal resume his duties. The judge so ruled. Said the *Times*: "The municipal machinery is now running smoothly."[3]

Police court at Dodge City, Judge Dan Frost presiding, could be exciting, if we can believe a *Times* description of one session:

"The Marshal will preserve strict order," said the judge. "Any person caught throwing turnips, cigar stumps, beets, or old quids of tobacco at this Court, will be immediately arranged [sic] before this bar of Justice." Then Joe [Mason] looked savagely at the mob in attendance, hitched his ivory handle a little to the left and adjusted his moustache. "Trot out the wicked and unfortunate, and let the cotillion commence," said his Honor.

City vs. James Martin. — But just then a complaint not on file had to be attended to, and Reverend John Walsh, of Las Animas, took the Throne of Justice, while the Judge stepped over to Hoover's. "You are here for horse stealing," says Walsh. "I can clean out the d——d court," says Martin. Then the City Attorney was banged into a pigeon hole in the desk, the table upset, the windows kicked out and the railing broke down. When order was restored Joe's thumb was "some clawed," Assistant Marshal Masterson's nose sliced a trifle, and the rantankerous originator of all this, James Martin, Esq. was bleeding from a half dozen cuts on the head, inflicted by Masterson's revolver. . . .

The *Times*'s jocular editor concluded his account of the court proceedings by praising the work of Ed Masterson in apprehending Martin and other miscreants:

Assistant Marshal Edward Masterson seemed to be always on time to quell the disturbance, and to bear away to the home of the friendless [the dog house] the noisy disturbers of the peace. Mr. Masterson has made a remarkable record during the month as the docket of the Police Court will bear testimony.[4]

Dan M. Frost, editor of the *Ford County Globe*. He and Bat had their political differences, but Frost let Masterson use the paper to speak his piece. Courtesy Kansas State Historical Society.

Prairie Dog Dave Morrow. Plains-wise Dave was an efficient deputy for several Ford County sheriffs. Courtesy Kansas State Historical Society.

On Monday, November 5, 1877, the day before the election that made Bat Masterson sheriff of Ford County, trouble started in that old hot bed of trouble, the Lone Star Dancehall, and Ed Masterson, as usual, was promptly on the scene. Bat was not, having relinquished his interest in the establishment when he announced for sheriff. The *Times* ran the story under the headline "Frontier Fun":

Last Monday afternoon one of those little episodes which serve to vary the monotony of frontier existence occurred at the Lone Star dance hall, during which four men came out some the worse for wear; but none, with one exception, being seriously hurt.

Bob Shaw, the man who started the amusement, accused Texas Dick, alias Moore, of having robbed him of forty dollars, and, when the two met in the Lone Star the ball opened.

Somebody, forseeing possible trouble, and probable gore, started out in search of Assistant City Marshal Ed. Masterson, and, finding him hurried him to the scene of the impending conflict.

When Masterson entered the door he descried Shaw by the bar with a huge pistol in his hand and a hogshead of blood in his eye, ready to relieve Texas Dick of his existence in this world and send him to those shades where troubles come not and sixshooters are not known.

Not wishing to hurt Shaw, but anxious to quiet matters and quell the disturbance officer Masterson first ordered him to give up his gun. Shaw refused to deliver and told Masterson to keep away from him, and after saying this he again proceeded to try to kill Texas Dick. Officer Masterson then gently tapped the belligerent Shaw upon the back of the head with the butt of his shooting iron, merely to convince him of the vanities of this frail world. . . . The aforesaid reminder upon the back of the head, however, failed to have the desired effect, and instead of dropping, as any man of fine sensibilities would have done, Shaw turned his battery upon the officer and let him have it in the right breast. The ball striking a rib and passing around came out under the right shoulder blade, paralyzing his right arm so that it was useless, so far as handling a pistol was concerned. Masterson fell, but grasping his pistol in his left hand he returned the fire giving it to Shaw in the left arm and the left leg, rendering him hors du combat.

During the melee Texas Dick was shot in the right groin, making a painful and dangerous, though not necessarily a fatal wound, while Frank Buskirk, who, impelled by a curiosity he could not control, was looking in at the door upon the matinee, received a reminiscence in the left arm, which had the effect of starting him out to hunt a surgeon. Nobody was killed, but for a time it looked as though the undertaker and the coroner would have something to do. . . .[5]

Although the *Times* editor sought to extract some humor from the incident, it is unlikely that Bat Masterson saw anything comic in the wounding and near killing of his brother.

In his book on Dodge City, Bob Wright said he remembered the scene vividly:

Someone ran by my store at full speed, crying out, "Our marshal [sic] is being murdered in the dance hall!" I, with several others, quickly ran to the dance hall and burst in the door. The house was so dense with smoke from the pistols a person could hardly see, but Ed Masterson had corralled a lot in one corner of the hall, with his six-shooter in his left hand, holding them there until assistance could reach him. I relate this to show the daring and cool bravery of our marshal, in times of greatest danger, and when he was so badly wounded.[6]

Said the *Times* in a more serious vein:

The nerve and pluck displayed by officer Masterson reflects credit both upon himself and the city, which has reason to congratulate itself upon the fact that it has a guardian who shirks no responsibility and who hesitates not to place himself in danger when duty requires.[7]

Several days later, Ed left for the Masterson home in Sedgwick to rest and recuperate but he was back within two weeks. "He is recovering from the wound received in the recent shooting affray," said the *Times*," and will soon be able to resume his duties as an officer."[8]

On December 4, the city council removed Larry Deger from office and appointed Ed Masterson to succeed him. The two most important law enforcement positions in town now were held by twenty-five-year-old City Marshal Edward Masterson and twenty-four-year-old Sheriff Bat Masterson. At the same meeting, the council voted to allow an expenditure of eighteen dollars to reimburse Ed for medical expenses incurred in the shooting. Said the *Times*:

City Marshal Edward Masterson receives the congratulations of his many friends without a show of exhultation. . . . No one accuses Mr. Masterson of seeking the position. In fact he preferred to retain his old position as Assistant, which gave him the same salary and engendered less responsibilities. As an officer his reputation is made, and it is a good one. . . .[9]

Wrote Bob Wright:

Edward J. Masterson . . . marshal of Dodge City . . . was in every way well qualified to fill this position. He was a natural gentleman, a man of good judgment, cool and considerate. He had another very important qualification, that of bravery. In those days, a man with any streak of yellow in him could have accomplished nothing as such officer in Dodge.[10]

Bat may well have had reservations about his brother, however. It was Bat's oft-quoted contention that a top-notch gunfighter had three essential qualities: courage, skill in the use of his weapon, and deliberation. There could be no question about Ed's courage; his action in the Lone Star fracas dispelled any doubt about his nerve when he was forced into a gunflight. Nor could Bat fault Ed for a lack of dexterity with a Colt six-gun. Although Shaw had his hog leg out of its holster and was waving it around when Ed entered the dance hall, Ed still was fast enough to draw and rap the troublemaker over the head. Then, when Shaw failed to drop and planted a bullet in Ed's right side, numbing his gun hand, Ed executed a gunfighter's maneuver known as the border shift. Even as he stumbled backward and fell, he instinctively threw his .45 from his right hand to his left, pulled trigger as he hit the floor, and pumped two bullets into Shaw.

Wrote Bat:

Courage is of little use to a man who essays to arbitrate a difference with a pistol if he is inexperienced in the use of the weapon he is going to use. Then again he may possess both courage and experience and still fail if he lacks deliberation. . . . I have known men in the West whose courage could not be questioned and whose experience with the pistol was simply marvelous, who fell easy victims before men who added deliberation to the other two qualities.[11]

When Bat spoke of deliberation, however, he did not mean foolhardiness. After the ruckus in the Lone Star, he may have considered his brother foolhardy. The very traits of character that endeared Ed to so many people in Dodge betrayed him in the hazardous business of law enforcement in the rough cow town. Ed was genial, easygoing, generous to a fault. He had difficulty in seeing the baser sides of the men he met. He found the free-and-easy, happy-go-lucky spirit of the typical cowpuncher to his liking and regarded the antics of the Texas youths tolerantly.

Dodge lawmen trod a narrow ribbon between life and death. They didn't want to kill, nor did they want to be killed. Most of the shooting in town was done in a spirit of fun and celebration by transient cowboys. These fellows were not killers; the taking of human life was not included in the program for their sprees. Under the influence of tanglefoot whiskey and angered by real or imagined wrongs, however, they could become extremely dangerous. For Bat, the Lone Star affair had a familiar aura. He remembered only too well another dance hall and another drunken gun wielder.

He had learned a valuable lesson that night on the Sweetwater. The question now was whether Ed Masterson had learned anything in his baptism of fire.

During the early months of 1878, more and more hard cases were swaggering down Front Street with guns at their sides. In March, there appeared in the *Ford County Globe* several editorials that were severely critical of the marshal's office for its failure to enforce the ordinance against the carrying of lethal hardware within the city limits. Still, Marshal Ed Masterson walked the streets of Dodge relaxed and unconcerned, smiling and chatting amiably with townsmen and Texans, tipping his hat to storekeepers' wives and red-light cyprians alike. From the sheriff's office, Bat Masterson watched and worried.

At ten o'clock on the night of April 9, 1878, City Marshal Ed Masterson, accompanied by Officer Nat Haywood, entered Josh Webb's Lady Gay Saloon in the sporting district south of the railroad. Alf Walker, trail boss for cattleman Oburn of Kansas City, and five of his riders were whooping it up inside. Jack Wagner, one of the Oburn hands, was whiskey wild and roaring. A six-gun was prominently displayed in his shoulder holster. Ed stepped up to Wagner and quietly explained that weapons had to be checked in Dodge. The cowboy offered no argument, docilely surrendering his pistol to the marshal. Ed then handed the gun to Walker, asking him to see that it was checked with the bartender. Walker nodded, and Ed and Haywood left the building.

The officers paused on the sidewalk, filling their lungs with the fresh, clean air of the spring night, welcome after the thick dancehall atmosphere that reeked of kerosene fumes, cigar smoke, unwashed bodies, and cheap perfume. From inside the Lady Gay came the squeal of a scraped fiddle as the interrupted dance resumed once more. Light spilled out onto the sidewalk as the swinging doors of the dance hall opened. Ed and Haywood turned to see Walker and Wagner coming toward them. Wagner staggered as he passed through the doorway, and his coat caught on the door frame. In the flickering light, Ed got a glimpse of a gun butt under the cowboy's arm.

For once, Ed was irritated. It was obvious that Walker had returned Wagner's pistol to him in defiance of the marshal's orders. He stepped close to the cowboy and tried to take the gun from its holster. Wagner resisted, and the two men scuffled. Patrons of the Lady Gay poured out to watch the fracas. Nat Haywood moved forward to help the marshal, but a gun suddenly appeared in Walker's hand and he jabbed the muzzle into Haywood's face. Haywood instinctively recoiled, his hands going to his gun belt. Walker let the hammer fall, the barrel of the gun pointing directly at Haywood's head, but the cartridge misfired.

Meanwhile, Wagner had managed to draw his pistol as he wrestled with Ed Masterson. He shoved the muzzle against Ed's right side and pulled the trigger. Ed staggered backward. The ball passed completely through his abdomen from right to left. His clothes were afire from the muzzle blast. Finally, he drew his gun and opened up. He shot Wagner through the body, and the cowboy slumped to the sidewalk. Walker, who had been holding Haywood at bay, swung his gun toward the marshal. Ed fired three times, hitting the trail boss once in the chest and twice in the right arm.

Five shots were fired: one by Wagner and four by Ed Masterson. They came in such quick succession that George Reighard, who was inside the Lady Gay, recalled later that they sounded like a Gatling gun. Reighard had started for the door when the struggle began outside, but when the first shot was heard, gun-wise Josh Webb pulled him to the floor, yelling, "You'll get hit!"

The street was a bedlam. People running from the scene crashed into new arrivals hurrying to see what the shooting was about. Wagner reeled into A. J. Peacock's saloon and fell into the arms of Ham Bell. "Catch me. I'm dying," he gasped. Bell, who had witnessed the action from Peacock's, let him slide to the floor. "I can't help you now," he said.

Walker then ran into the saloon, bloody froth on his face from a punctured lung, his mangled right arm dripping blood. He offered his gun to Bell. "Throw it on the floor if you don't want it," Bell told him. The cattleman dropped his weapon, staggered out the rear door of the saloon, and collapsed.

Ed Masterson, with a hole through his body "large enough for the introduction of the whole pistol"[12] and his clothing still smoldering, walked two hundred yards across the plaza to the north side of the tracks. Entering Hoover's Saloon, he fell at the feet of bartender George Hinkle. "George, I'm shot," he said in a hoarse whisper just before he fainted.

Ed was carried to his room, where he died forty minutes later without regaining consciousness. Walker and Wagner were taken to the rooms of Tom Lane above Bob Wright's store. The gut-shot Wagner lingered in agony until seven o'clock the following evening. He was buried on Boot Hill the afternoon of April 11. Walker, badly wounded in the lung, clung tenaciously to life.

From 1881 on, newspaper reporters, magazine writers, and book authors have credited Bat Masterson with being the agent of death who avenged the murder of his brother. In the wild tale spun to the *New York Sun* reporter by Dr. Cockrell, Bat slaughtered seven killers, his two guns spewing death from their crossed-wrist positions. This score was gradually scaled down in later versions, but as late as 1957, Richard O'Connor was still repeating in his biography of Bat the story of Bat's running to the aid of his brother and, from sixty feet away, pumping lead into the two Texans who had given Ed his death wound.

No contemporary newspaper account mentions Bat Masterson as being present at the shooting. Moreover, it is clear from these stories that a gun in the hand of Marshal Ed Masterson downed Wagner and Walker. The *Ford County Globe* put out an extra on April 10, the day after the gun battle. The story of the tragedy was told with little embellishment, but the pertinent facts are clear:

> At ten o'clock last night, City Marshal Edward Masterson discovered that a cow boy who was working for Oburn of Kansas City, named Jack Wagner, was carrying a six-shooter contrary to the City Ordinance. Wagner was at the time under the influence of liquor, but quietly gave up the pistol. The Marshal gave it to some of Wagner's friends for safe keeping and stepped out into the street. No sooner had he done so than Wagner ran out after him pulling another pistol, which the Marshal had not observed. The Marshal saw him coming and turned upon Wagner and grabbed hold of him.
> Wagner shot Marshal Masterson at once through the abdomen, being so close to him that the discharge set the Marshal's clothes on fire.
> Marshal Masterson then shot Wagner.
> About this time a man named Walker got mixed up in the fight. He, it appears, was boss herder for Oburn, and Wagner was working under him.

He also got shot once through the left lung, and his right arm was twice broken.

Marshal Masterson walked across the street to Hoover's saloon, where after telling that he was shot, he sank to the floor. He was immediately removed to his room, where in half an hour he expired.

Walker and Wagner were nearly all night insensible, and none thought that either of them could live through the night. However, morning has come and neither are dead; both are in very precarious condition and their chances for recovery very small.

The *Dodge City Times*'s story appeared in the April 13 edition. It related how Ed took Wagner's gun and

later Marshal Masterson and Deputy Marshal Nat Haywood tried the second time to disarm Wagner. While in the act Masterson was shot in the abdomen. Walker in the meantime snapped a pistol in the face of Officer Haywood. Masterson fired four shots, one of them striking Wagner in the bowels from the left side. Walker was struck three times. . . .

It is not known who started the tale that Bat shot Ed's killers. The old-timers who were in Dodge that night and who have left their recollections in print have done little to clear up the mystery.

George Reighard knew the Masterson brothers well, having hunted buffalo with them years before. In an interview with Earle R. Forrest in 1926, Reighard said Bat shot the two cowboys. "Bat got into action and . . . emptied his gun. It was the fastest gun work I ever saw and so quick it sounded like a Gatling,"[13] he told Forrest, but he later admitted that he was inside the Lady Gay, lying on the floor with Josh Webb, and was in no position to see the gun work.

Stuart Lake says Ham Bell told him he witnessed the fight from a window of the Lone Star Dancehall and that Bat cut down Wagner and Walker from a distance of sixty feet as Walker fired back ineffectively. In 1937, however, Bell told George G. Thompson that he was in Peacock's Saloon, and he either could not or would not state definitely who shot the cowboys. Thomas Masterson, Jr., assured Thompson that Bat shot both Wagner and Walker, but Tom was not in Dodge City at the time and his testimony is mere hearsay. Tom also claimed that Haywood ran away when Walker snapped a six-gun in his face.[14] This assertion, however, is not corroborated by the newspaper accounts. "The officers were brave and cool though both were at a disadvantage, as neither desired to kill the whisky crazed assailants," said the *Times*.[15]

Bob Wright's account is the most enigmatic of all:

A few minutes after Ed was shot, Bat heard of the trouble and hurried to the assistance of his brother. It took but a glance from Bat to determine that his brother was murdered. He was greatly affected by the horrible crime, and when Ed told him he had his death wound, he gathered the particulars, and, bidding his brother an affectionate farewell, hastily departed to avenge his death; and I have no doubt he made the murderers pay the penalty.[16]

Bat did go after the other four cowboys who had been in the Lady Gay with Walker and Wagner, but his actions in no way resembled those of an avenger thirsting for blood. Ed lived for a short time after the shooting — thirty minutes by one newspaper account, forty by the other. Bat stayed with him until the end. He then had warrants sworn out for the companions of the wounded cowboys and, an hour after the gunsmoke had lifted, placed all four under arrest and marched them to the calaboose. This anti-climactic arrest is the only mention of Bat Masterson in the Dodge City papers, which were full of details concerning the shootout. The four — John Hungate, Thomas Highlander, Thomas Roads, and John Reece — were released after a hearing in which no evidence that they were involved in the shooting could be produced.

Before he died, Jack Wagner admitted that he shot Ed Masterson. Because of Wagner's confession and his own grievous wounds, no charges were pressed against Alf Walker. His condition was grave for several days, and then he gradually began to recover. In May, his father arrived from Texas to attend him, and later that month he and his son started home. There is no further mention of Walker in the Dodge City papers, but Wyatt Earp says he soon died of pneumonia induced by the lung wound.

All of Dodge City went into mourning for Ed Masterson. The *Globe* extra of April 10 noted: "Every door is draped with crape; business is entirely suspended till after the funeral of Marshal Masterson, which will take place at two o'clock p.m., and will be

attended by everybody in the city.'' In its black-edged issue of
April 16, the *Globe* described the funeral:

> Everyone in the City knew Ed. Masterson and liked him. They liked
> him as a boy, they liked him as a man, and they liked him as an officer.
> Promptly at 10 o'clock in the morning of the 10th every business house
> in the City closed its doors which remained so until 6 o'clock, P.M. Crape
> draped almost every door in the City. Never before was such honor shown
> in Dodge, either to the living or dead.

Ed Masterson was buried in the military cemetery at Ford Dodge
because in 1878 Dodge City did not have a burial ground for
''respectable'' people. A year later, when Prairie Grove Cemetery
was established, Ed's body was brought back the five miles from
the fort and reinterred by the Dodge City Fire Department. In later
years, the expanding town took Prairie Grove Cemetery for a
residential area and had the bodies moved to newly established
Maple Grove Cemetery. Somehow, the location of Ed's gravesite
became lost during this move. Later still, when Bat Masterson,
then living in New York, tried to locate Ed's grave, intending to
erect a monument, it could not be determined definitely where lay
the remains of the marshal whose violent death had shocked and
saddened the entire town.

CHAPTER NINE

THE MISTRESS OF THE GAMBLERS

On April 11, Bat Masterson and his lawyer friend Mike Sutton made the sad journey to Sedgwick to tell Bat's parents the details of Ed's death and funeral. Three of the Masterson children were still living at the family homestead: Tom, Jr., George, and sixteen-year-old Minnie. Nellie had married Wichita policeman James Cairnes; Jim was off somewhere on another buffalo hunt and probably had not yet heard of his brother's death.

A week later, Bat was back on the job in Dodge, as was noted in the *Times* of April 20. This edition also reported that Charlie Bassett had been appointed city marshal to succeed Ed, at the same time retaining his position as undersheriff, and that "Assistant Marshal N. L. Haywood has resigned his office of his own accord, preferring to follow other vocations." The position was quickly filled by Wyatt Earp, who arrived in Dodge on May 8 after spending several months in Texas. On June 1, Jim Masterson, also recently returned, became a deputy marshal, so once again two Masterson boys wore the star in Dodge.

By 1878, the little city on the Arkansas had passed its heyday as the nation's major shipping point for buffalo hides. The hunters had done their work well; the vast, woolly herds were gone forever from the Kansas plains. In all that vast grassland where only five years before a man on foot ran a great risk of being trampled to death, where the earth shook when the mighty herds moved, where the bellowing of the bulls could be heard for miles, nothing but rotting carcasses and whitening bones remained. Racks of bones had replaced the stacks of flint hides which lined the Santa Fe tracks at Dodge for years.

The buffalo were gone, but the men who had killed them were not. Many of the hunters drifted back to the town in which they had reveled while awaiting the seasonal migrations. Some of the former hide men, such as the Masterson brothers, Wyatt Earp, and Bill Tilghman, became officers of the law. Others opened stores, saloons, and freight lines. Many became professional gamblers.

If Dodge no longer could call herself the Daughter of the Hide Men, she was fast becoming Queen of the Cow Towns. The year 1878 was to bring the greatest cattle drive from Texas the town had experienced up to that time: 265,000 longhorns, driven by 1,300 cowhands, came up the trail to Dodge that year. Throughout the spring, summer, and fall, the shipping pens were crowded, and bawling herds milled about in temporary camps that extended for miles along the Arkansas. As word of Dodge spread throughout the West, the frontier sporting crowd began to converge on her, and in 1878, the Queen of the Cow Towns became the Mistress of the Gamblers.

Even a partial list of the knights of the green cloth who headquartered in Dodge City that season reads like a who's who of the western sporting fraternity. In action at the tables that year were Ben and Billy Thompson, Cockeyed Frank Loving, Mysterious Dave Mather, Wyatt Earp and his brothers Virgil and Morgan, Shotgun Collins, John Joshua Webb, Tom Lane, Rowdy Joe Lowe, George Goodell, Johnny Allen, Dick Clark, Johnson Gallagher, Charlie Ronan, Kinch Riley, Colonel Charlie Norton, Joe Mason, Lon Hyatt, Charlie Bassett, W. H. Bennett, Lou and Sam Blonger, Luke Short, Bill Harris, Harry Bell, and John H. ("Doc") Holliday.

Besides the gamblers, Dodge received visitors who had distinguished themselves in other fields. Many of Texas' pioneer cattlemen came to the railhead to meet their herds. Among them were Colonel Charles Goodnight, Colonel J. F. Ellison, and Captain George Littlefield. Eddie Foy, the celebrated vaudeville performer, arrived in July and opened his review at the Comique, a new gambling house and concert hall owned by Dick Brown and Bat's former partner, Ben Springer. A delegation headed by Springer met Foy and his partner, Jim Thompson, at the train and introduced the comedians to Dodge City dignitaries. Foy was most impressed by the youthful Ford County sheriff. Bat Masterson was, as he recalled, "a trim, good-looking young man with a pleasant face and carefully barbered mustache, well-tailored

Fannie Garretson was a performer at Ben Springer's Comique, theater and concert hall, in 1878. After a stream of bullets narrowly missed her and killed the sleeping Dora Hand, she wrote: "I think I have had enough of Dodge City." Courtesy Kansas State Historical Society.

clothes, hat with a rakish tilt and two big silver-mounted, ivory-handled pistols in a heavy belt."[1]

Foy and Thompson were a big hit in Dodge, and the Comique (pronounced *com-ee-cue* by the cowboys) was crowded night after night. Commented the *Globe* on July 9: "Foye [sic] and Thompson 'lay over' anything we have seen in the Ethiopian line." Three weeks later, the paper again praised the revue:

This favorite place of resort is at present giving to its patrons the best show or entertainment ever given in Dodge. They have Billy and Nola Forrest, Dick Brown and Fannie Garretson, May Gaylor, Belle Lamont, Fannie Keenan, Jennie Morton, and that unequalled and splendidly matched team Foye and Thompson. . . .[2]

In competition with Ben Springer's Comique, Ham Bell opened a rival theater, the Varieties, with a program featuring Fannie Keenan, a beautiful singer he had enticed from the Comique. Fannie, whose real name was Dora Hand, was billed in Dodge as the Queen of the Fairy Belles. She was reputed to have come from a genteel Boston family, to have studied voice abroad, and to have sung in grand opera before heading west. At Abilene, Hays, and other border camps in which she had appeared, her physical charms, it was said, had provoked gunfights in which twelve men had died. In Dodge, she won respect on two levels of society. By night, she brought crowds of hard-bitten honky-tonk patrons to the point of tears with her rendition of sentimental ballads; by day, she mingled with staid ladies of Dodge's upper crust, led the singing of hymns in the little north-side church on Sundays, and was an energetic member of the Ladies Aid Society. Everyone was captivated by her voice and beauty.

In the fall of the year, President Rutherford B. Hayes and a retinue headed by General William T. Sherman stopped over in Dodge for a day while on a tour of the West. The president emerged from his private railroad car long enough to hear a speech of welcome by Mayor Kelley and to wrinkle his nose at the aroma that wafted from the cattle pens. Then he retired, leaving Uncle Billy Sherman to commune with the citizenry. As Eddie Foy remarked, "I don't think he very strongly approved of Dodge, anyhow, for he didn't stir from his car the rest of the day."[3]

It was during this period that Dodge achieved its greatest notoriety as a gunman's town. Sensationalists then and since have depicted it as a seething caldron of violence where the only law was the law of the gun and "a man for breakfast" was commonplace. Actually, considering the large number of characters in town with leather-slapping reputations, there was remarkably little gunplay. In June, the *Globe* proudly announced: "Three dancehalls in full blast on the South Side, stables jammed full, hundreds of cowboys perambulate daily, but two cases in police court. Who says we aren't a moral city?"[4] Eddie Foy agreed: "The majority of days passed rather peacefully in Dodge, with no killings and few fights."[5]

During the two years Bat Masterson was sheriff of Ford County, exactly seven homicides were recorded in Dodge City. Some of these were highly publicized, leading to the popular belief that violent death was a common occurrence. The gunfight in which Ed Masterson and Jack Wagner died was the first fatal episode. Three months later, another lawman was killed.

In April, U. S. Marshal Ben Simpson appointed Harry T. McCarty, a Dodge City surveyor and draftsman, U. S. deputy marshal. In July, McCarty was dead, shot with his own gun by a man the *Times* called "a half-witted, rattle-brained and quarrelsome wretch."[6] At four o'clock on the morning of July 13, McCarty was in the Long Branch Saloon, leaning over the bar in conversation with Adam Jackson, night bartender. Several cowboys from the Shiner brothers' camp were at a table in the saloon, taunting one of their number, a man named Thomas O'Haran — also known as Thomas Roach and Limping Tom — the cook for the cow camp. O'Haran, whose limited mental faculties had been diminished further by alcohol, suddenly left the table and staggered to the bar. Jerking McCarty's six-shooter from its scabbard, he "flourished it once or twice"[7] and the gun discharged, striking the deputy marshal. "The ball penetrated the right groin," the *Globe* reported, "severing the femoral artery, thence passing through the thigh, [and] lodged in the floor."[8] McCarty collapsed, bleeding profusely. A bystander instantly dropped O'Haran, creasing his side with a bullet. He "called out 'I am shot,' and dropped to the floor, thus saving himself from the immediate penalty for his crime from the leveled revolvers about him."[9] McCarty was taken to Charlie Ronan's room, where he died of loss of blood within an hour.

O'Haran was arrested and jailed. For a time in those early morning hours, there was lynch talk on the streets of Dodge. Said the *Times*:

> There is a good deal of indignation manifested over this brutal, unwarranted murder, and while it may appear in the present temper of a large class of people that law's delays and uncertainties are dangerous to the peace, life and protection of the community, we hope the sober, second thought will prevail and justice take its course.[10]

An inquest was held that morning, and at an examination in the afternoon, Judge R. G. Cook bound O'Haran over for trial at the next term of court on a charge of first-degree murder. According to the *Globe* of July 16, the examination was held as quietly as possible, "it being the desire of the officers to prevent anything that could tend to excite the already agitated crowd." There was no attempt to take O'Haran from the lawmen, however, and as the *Globe* said, "to the credit of Dodge City be it spoken, that the better council prevailed and even in the moment of excitement she determined to put herself on record as willing to submit to the law." The following January, O'Haran was tried in Ford County District Court. He pleaded guilty to manslaughter and was sentenced to twelve years and three months in the state penitentiary.

One of Eddie Foy's most vivid memories of Dodge was a shooting that occurred within two weeks after McCarty was killed. At three o'clock on the morning of July 26 Foy was performing on the Comique stage to a packed house. It was his recollection that he was calling the turns for a square dance when hell began to pop, but Wyatt Earp and Bat Masterson both say he was reciting his well-known poem "Kalamazoo in Michigan." Bat was seated at one of the gambling tables at the time. Earp, on night police duty with Officer Jim Masterson, was standing outside where he could watch the street and still hear the songs and joking patter through the thin walls.

Several cowboys rode by the Comique on their way back to the bedding grounds south of the river. Suddenly, one rider wheeled his horse and rode down the street at a gallop. As he flashed past the spot where Earp stood, a six-gun in his hand roared and three bullets tore through the plank walls within inches of the assistant marshal. "A bullet fired from a Colt's .45 caliber pistol would go through half a dozen such buildings," Bat wrote in describing this incident. "The bullets tore through the side of the building, scattering pieces of the splintered pine-boards in all directions. Foy evidently thought the cowboy was after him, for he didn't tarry long in the line of fire."[11]

Greenhorn Foy readily admitted that he looked for a hole when the fusillade began, but he protested that he was no match for the western hard cases who were present. "Everybody dropped to the floor at once, according to custom," he said. "Bat Masterson was just in the act of dealing in a game of Spanish Monte with Doc Holliday, and I was impressed by the instantaneous manner in which they flattened out like pancakes on the floor. I had thought I was pretty agile myself, but those fellows had me beaten by seconds at that trick."[12]

It seemed to the comedian that "hundreds of shots" ripped through the building, but Masterson, to whom this sort of sudden gunplay was not so new and shocking, said: "The cowboy succeeded in firing three shots before Wyatt got his pistol in action."

Earp told his biographer that he missed with his first bullet as the cowboy's mount pitched and reared. The Texan fired twice more and started at a gallop for the toll bridge across the Arkansas. Earp said he then squatted to silhouette his target against the night sky and rolled the rider from his racing pony with another shot.

In the account of the affair as reported in the *Times*, some twenty shots were fired and Earp's batteries were augmented by those of Officer Jim Masterson and others, including "some rooster who . . . perched himself in the window of a dancehall and indulged in a promiscuous shoot all by himself."[13]

The wounded cowboy, identified the next day as George Hoy and described by the *Times* as "rather an intelligent looking young man,"[14] was under fifteen hundred dollars' bond in Texas on a cattle-rustling charge. His arm had been shattered by a bullet, and when gangrene developed, it was amputated by a surgeon from Fort Dodge. On August 21, almost a month after the shooting, he died.

The reason for Hoy's sudden bombardment of the Comique is unknown to this day. Earp's story was that the cowboy was after a one-thousand-dollar bounty Earp claimed his enemies had put on his head. Wyatt told his biographer, Stuart Lake, that the cowboy confessed to that much on his deathbed but carried the names of his employers to the grave.

Eddie Foy apparently did not connect the shooting with an attempt on Wyatt's life. He said it was the result of "some argument with Springer," the proprietor of the Comique.[15]

In 1907, Bat recalled nothing of a head bounty on his friend. On the contrary, he believed that Hoy was unaware of the marshal's presence when he began firing. "The cowboy rode right by Wyatt . . . but evidently he didn't notice him, else he would not in all probability have acted as he did," Bat said. "Whether it was Foy's act that angered him, or whether he had been jilted by one of the chorus we never learned."[16]

Of the hundreds of cowpunchers who swaggered through the

streets of Dodge that summer of '78, a few became well known to the peace officers through their penchant for troublemaking and their frequent appearances in police court. One of these was young Jim Kennedy. Although he affected the dress and rough habits of the cowboys, he was no common range hand; he was the son of Captain Mifflin Kennedy, one of the wealthiest and most respected ranchers in Texas, a partner of Richard King in the operation of the tremendous King Ranch. Each year, Dodge City profited handsomely by their business. In 1878 alone, fifteen thousand head of King and Kennedy longhorns came up the trail, a figure matched only by the Littlefield and Houston outfit.

Jim Kennedy, called Spike by his cowboy friends, liked whiskey, whooping, and whoring, and as heir to the Kennedy fortune, he considered himself immune to arrest by cow-town marshals. He had been in and out of scrapes in the border towns for years. As early as 1872, he had tangled in Ellsworth with I. P. ("Print") Olive, a Texas cattleman who later had ranches in Kansas and Nebraska. Olive had a reputation as a killer, but after losing some money to him during a card game in Nick Lentz's saloon, young Kennedy angrily accused him of cheating and challenged him to fight. Olive was unarmed and told the young firebrand to sleep it off. Later that afternoon, Kennedy entered the Ellsworth Billiard Saloon, where Olive was sitting in another game, took a pistol from the gun rack at the bar, and turned it loose. Olive was wounded in the hand, the groin, and the thigh. Nigger Jim Kelly, an Olive hand who was sitting outside the saloon, stepped in and shot Kennedy in the leg. Kennedy was arrested but escaped from the Ellsworth jail the same night with the aid of friends. Print Olive recovered from his wounds and lived for many years before being killed at Trail City, Colorado, by one Joe Sparrow.

During the 1870's, Jim Kennedy headquartered in Tascosa, Texas. Hoping to make a man of him, his father had established him in the Texas Panhandle with two thousand head of cattle and a complete crew of herders. A young doctor named Henry F. Hoyt, who became friendly with him in Tascosa, wrote that "with his athletic physique, dark hair and eyes, he was the handsomest bachelor in the Panhandle." Hoyt, who was fair and had red hair, and the dark-complexioned Kennedy spent so much time together

Dodge City, 1878, as seen across the Santa Fe tracks at the "busiest block in town," Front Street between First and Second avenues. Here were the Wright and Beverly store, the Long Branch Saloon, the Delmonico Restaurant, Ab Webster's Alamo Saloon, and Beatty's and Kelley's Alhambra. Courtesy Kansas State Historical Society.

that the Tascosa cowboys dubbed them the Roulette Twins — the red and the black.[17]

For a time, Jim Kennedy seemed to have grown out of the wildness that had characterized his early years. "Kennedy conducted himself in an exemplary manner, became very popular, and his father's expectation seemed to be fulfilled," wrote Dr. Hoyt. "But, in the course of time he drove a herd to Dodge City, Kansas, sold them and, unable to withstand the temptations of the underworld there, he 'stepped out.' "[18]

On July 29, 1878, Wyatt Earp hauled Kennedy into police court for carrying a pistol. Neither the fine collected nor the buffaloing that Earp usually administered to miscreants seemed to leave any lasting impression on the young man. He was back in court again on August 17, arrested and charged by Charlie Bassett with being disorderly.

Kennedy nursed a bitter hatred for the Dodge City law officers, but he lacked the backbone to take up a personal fight with any of them. Instead, he expressed his grievances to Mayor Kelley one night in Kelley's own establishment, the Alhambra. Kelley informed him that the marshals were acting under his orders and that young Kennedy had better behave while in Dodge or prepare himself for worse treatment. Kennedy then flew into a rage and leaped at the mayor. Kelley gave the younger man a thorough beating and dumped him in the street. Kennedy was furious. Mouthing dark threats against the life of the mayor, he mounted up and rode out of town. No one in Dodge expected to see him again.

Spike Kennedy was not finished. He went to Kansas City, where he remained several weeks nursing the bruises on his face and the wounds to his vanity. He then purchased the fastest horse he could find and set out for Dodge.

Dog Kelley became ill shortly after the altercation in the Alhambra and was taken to the army hospital at Fort Dodge for treatment. While he was gone, his small two-room cottage behind the Western Hotel was occupied by Miss Dora Hand, the featured performer at the Varieties Theater, and Miss Fannie Garretson, an entertainer at the Comique.

At four o'clock on the morning of October 4, Dodge was peaceful and quiet. The peak of the cattle season had passed, and most of the cowboys who remained at the railhead had sought bedding grounds by that hour to speculate, in an alcoholic haze, on their losses at the gambling tables. The Varieties and the Comique had been closed for more than an hour, and the Misses Hand and Garretson were sound asleep in Mayor Kelley's cottage. Fannie Garretson occupied the bed in the front room, and Dora Hand slept in Kelley's bed in the room beyond.

Shortly after four, Spike Kennedy rode through the streets of a strangely tranquil Dodge. He forked a trim, beautifully proportioned race horse he was certain could outrun any animal in town. The hilt of a bowie knife protruded from his waistband, two .44-caliber Colt revolvers hung in hand-tooled leather holsters at his thighs, and a fully loaded carbine was in the saddle boot at his knee; he was a picture of a western fighting man. Dodge City residents later were convinced that Kennedy had not come back to the city to fight, however. The object of his return, they were sure, was murder.

James ("Dog") Kelley (left) with friend Charles Hungerford. At his feet is one of the hounds for which Kelley was known and which inspired his nickname. Courtesy Kansas State Historical Society.

A few moments later, the barkeep in the only saloon still open heard four shots reverberate from behind the Western Hotel. Stepping out to the sidewalk to determine the cause of the gunfire that had ripped the stillness, he saw a horseman galloping out of town, heading west. The bartender had served many a drink to young Jim Kennedy and recognized the night rider instantly.

Law officers Wyatt Earp and Jim Masterson came on the run to investigate the shooting. They heard the sound of hysterical sobbing coming from behind the Western Hotel. Beside the splintered door of the mayor's cottage, they found Fannie Garretson. Shocked and badly frightened, shivering in her thin nightgown, she could only point with horror to the interior of the building. There, Earp and Masterson found the lovely Dora Hand dead in Kelley's bed. A bullet had entered her chest cavity under her right arm, killing her instantly. Her features were still composed in the tranquility of deep sleep.

At first, the lawmen were at a loss to explain such a cowardly and seemingly incomprehensible killing, but after they had talked to the bartender, the tragedy began to make sense. They knew of the beating administered to the Texan by Mayor Kelley and of the threats Kennedy had made when he left Dodge. Since he had been gone several weeks, Kennedy could not have known of Kelley's illness and the subsequent arrangement for the two women to occupy his cottage. Wyatt and Jim reasoned that Dora Hand had been the innocent victim of Kennedy's lust for revenge. Kennedy had been seen in Dodge earlier with a companion, so the two officers arrested this man, who confirmed their suspicions but convinced them that he had had no part in the shooting. Kennedy, he said, had sworn to kill Mayor Kelley that night.

By early morning, everyone in Dodge had learned of the murder of Dora Hand. At an inquest before Judge R. G. Cook, acting coroner, a jury found that "the said gunshot wound was produced by a bullet discharged from a gun in the hands of one James Kennedy."[19] Feeling ran high. Dora Hand had been respected and admired, not only for her voice and beauty, but for her kindliness, her generosity, her great warmth of heart. A throng of volunteers was ready and eager to join a posse to pursue the suspect.

Sheriff Bat Masterson was responsible for organizing a posse.

He knew that with the start that Kennedy had, the job would call for much hard riding over rough country. It was quite possible that the fugitive would reach the Texas Panhandle before a posse could overtake him. In that event, he might have to be taken from under the guns of Captain Kennedy's hired hands. Bat needed experienced plainsmen who could ride far and fast for days, if need be, and still be depended upon if an all-out gunfight should develop. He declined many offers of help with thanks and chose for his posse City Marshal Charlie Bassett, Assistant Marshal Wyatt Earp, and Deputy Sheriffs Bill Duffey and Bill Tilghman, making up, as the *Times* put it, "as intrepid a posse as ever pulled a trigger."[20]

Wyatt said that when he went to Fort Dodge in the early morning hours to inform Dog Kelley of the killing, the mayor told him, "Bring him in alive, Wyatt. Dodge'll want to deal with him as a community."[21] But that was not Fannie Garretson's impression of the posse members' intentions when she saw them ride out that day. In an October 5 letter to a friend in St. Louis, she wrote: "The man who perpetrated this deed will never exist for a judge or a jury, as the officers have sworn never to take him alive. They were offered a big reward to get him but they declined to accept it, for they were only too well pleased to get the order to start after him."[22] The murderer, she continued, was "a fiend in human form. . . . This man has been allowed more privileges than the rest of them because he has plenty of money, and now he has repaid their liberality." She said the posse was reported within five or six miles of its quarry, adding an ominous note: "I am afraid the trouble has not ended, as some twenty of the Texas men went out after the officers and there were only six [sic] of them."

Although Fannie Garretson was understandably shaken by her experience in what she called "this wretched city" and concluded her letter by saying, "Well, I want to leave here now, while my life is safe; I think I have had enough of Dodge City," she was not entirely unaccustomed to violence. A few years earlier, she had deserted a gambler named Chaunessy, with whom she had been living in Cheyenne, to run off with Dick Brown, a banjo player and singer. Chaunessy followed the entertainers to Deadwood and interrupted their act in a hurdy-gurdy house, demanding that Fannie come back to him. Brown promptly shot him dead and, accompanied by Fannie, hastily departed the Black Hills. This was the same Dick Brown who in 1878 owned a part interest in the Dodge City Comique and was appearing in an act with Fannie Garretson at that establishment. A big fellow with a handsome black moustache and goatee, he was called Deadwood Dick after that episode.

It was two o'clock in the afternoon of October 4 when Sheriff Bat Masterson led his posse out of Dodge. Jim Kennedy had a start of almost ten hours on the hunters, whose problem was to locate their quarry in that huge prairie wilderness lying south and west of Dodge. Although Kennedy was last seen heading west out of town, the lawmen were sure that he would make for his Tascosa ranch to the southwest. They believed he would swing wide of the Jones and Plummer Trail, ford the Cimarron near Wagon Bed Springs, and head south to cut the Texas Trail in the Indian Nations. They planned to go cross country with the hope of making the Cimarron ford before the fugitive could reach it by his circuitous route.

That evening, after they had been pushing their horses hard for hours, they ran into a heavy hailstorm. Tired and battered, the men and animals huddled together under a projecting stream bank until the icy bombardment abated. Then they pressed on through sheets of drenching rain that followed the hail. All night long the rain pounded down, but the possemen slogged on without trail or stars to guide them. Only their years of experience in hunting buffalo over those same rolling grasslands enabled them to steer a straight course through that black sea of water and mud to their objective. When the rain let up at dawn, they had covered seventy-five miles and were within a mile of the ford. They examined the banks of the river closely but could find no sign of a horseman having crossed since the rain. A homesteader in a sod house at the ford told them no rider had been seen to cross during the storm, and they all felt sure that Kennedy could not possibly have made it to the river before the storm broke. So, playing their hunch to the limit, they waited for the killer to arrive.

The weary horses were unsaddled and turned out to graze so that no sign of a welcoming committee would be apparent to an approaching rider. The officers took turns watching the trail while the others ate and rested in the sod house. Bill Tilghman was on guard when a lone horseman appeared in the distance. Wyatt Earp trained a pair of field glasses on the cautiously approaching rider and grinned. The gamble had paid off; the rider was Kennedy.

In order that the homesteader and his family might be out of the line of fire if Kennedy determined to put up a fight, Bat moved his men away from the house and took up a position behind a mound of earth. When he was about fifty yards away, Kennedy spotted the posse. He instantly wheeled his mount and slashed at its flanks with spur and quirt. The Kansas City race horse, although tired and bedraggled, shot away at a hard gallop. Bat and Wyatt both shouted a command to halt, but Kennedy merely flayed his pony more viciously. The possemen turned loose a volley. Three bullets slammed into the galloping steed, dropping him in midstride. Kennedy fell, partly pinned under the dead horse, his left arm shattered by a ball from a .50-caliber Sharps. When the officers approached, according to the story Earp told his biographer,[23] the following exchange took place:

Kennedy's first words concerned the success of his murderous attack. "Did I get that bastard Kelley?" he demanded to know.

"No, but you killed someone else," Wyatt told him. "Dora Hand was asleep in Kelley's bed."

The wounded man seemed stunned for a moment. A look of seemingly genuine remorse and self-hatred crossed his face. Then, seeing the Sharps Big Fifty in Bat's hand, he snapped, "You damn' son-of-a-bitch! You ought to have made a better shot than you did!"

"Well," Bat replied in astonishment, "you damn' murdering son-of-a-bitch, I did the best I could!"

The Texan's arm had been horribly smashed by the rifle ball. Bat told Bob Wright that when they pulled Kennedy from under the horse, he "could hear the bones 'craunch.' "[24] The officers bound and splinted the arm as well as they could and started for Dodge. They apparently did not meet the twenty Texans Fannie Garretson said had ridden on their trail, and the next day they were back with their prisoner.

If Jim Kennedy did indeed kill Dora Hand, a crippled arm was to be his only punishment. For several days he lay near death from shock and loss of blood in the Ford County jail, then slowly began to recover. Three weeks later, still too weak to be moved, he was examined before Judge Cook at a hearing in the sheriff's office, adjoining his cell. In spite of his suspicious actions on the night of the murder and the testimony of the arresting officers that he had confessed his guilt at the time of his arrest, he was released for lack of sufficient incriminating evidence.

The state had freed him, but the torment in his arm had not. In December, Captain Mifflin Kennedy arrived from Corpus Christi, Texas, with Dr. B. E. Fryer, an eminent Fort Leavenworth surgeon. The elder Kennedy took his son to Fort Dodge, where, on December 16, Dr. Fryer, assisted by Drs. McCarty and Tremaine, operated on the young man's shattered arm, which had not healed properly. They removed several pieces of bone, one of them four inches in length.

As soon as he could travel, Kennedy left Dodge for good, returning with his father to Texas. It was Bob Wright's recollection that he managed to kill several more people with his one good arm "but finally met his death by someone a little quicker on the trigger than himself."[25] However, Dr. Henry F. Hoyt, one of the Roulette Twins, wrote that Kennedy was brought home to Tascosa "with a shoulder and one arm all shot to pieces." He said Kennedy never recovered fully from these wounds and lived for only a year or two.[26]

A shooting that occurred six months after the Dora Hand episode was more in the western tradition of angry men settling a personal dispute face to face with six-guns. About eight o'clock on the night of April 5, 1879, Levi Richardson, buffalo hunter turned freighter, came into the Long Branch Saloon out of a cold, windy night to warm his innards with a few drinks and soak up the heat from the potbellied stove. As he was leaving, Richardson met gambler Frank Loving coming through the door. It was well known in Dodge that there was animosity between Richardson and Cockeyed Frank over the affections of a certain dance-hall girl. When, after a few words at the doorway, Richardson turned and followed Loving back along the bar, everyone present turned wary eyes upon the pair. Cockeyed Frank sat down on the hazard table. Richardson, again standing near the stove, began to berate the gambler, his voice rising. Loving sat perfectly still. Not a trace of emotion was apparent on his boyish face, but he paled slightly.

Wyatt Earp testified:

Levi Richardson . . . was one of the best shots with rifle or pistol on the range. He had a touchy disposition that often got him into trouble, but he had the courage to back it, so was regarded as a dangerous fellow. With his plain, unvarnished style of shooting, Levi had killed several bad men in gun-fights, but then he took up gun-fanning. I have seen him on the outskirts of Dodge practicing his new tricks by the hour and on a number of occasions before this fight with Loving I saw him show off his new methods in target matches. There were few men around Dodge who could beat Levi at the targets.[27]

Bat concurred:

He was thoroughly familiar with the use of firearms and an excellent shot with either pistol or rifle. He was a high strung fellow who was not afraid of any man.[28]

On this occasion, as he baited Loving, Richardson appeared supremely confident. He stood by the hazard table like a great cat about to pounce, his right hand poised close to his gun butt. "Damn you!" he growled at Loving, "Why don't you fight?"

The young gambler eased his weight from the table, facing the other man squarely. "Why don't you try me?" he said flatly.

Richardson's .45 cleared leather with one swift, fluid motion of his right hand. His left hand flashed across the hammer of the gun with the speed of a rattlesnake's darting tongue. He fanned off five shots, filling the Long Branch with gunsmoke and one continuous roar. But as his hammer fell on an empty chamber, there stood Loving before him, unharmed except for a minor scratch on his hand. Loving raised his pistol and pumped three bullets into Richardson, who slid to the floor and was dead within a few minutes.

Richardson's death was the result of his lack of deliberation, that quality which Bat always stressed as essential in the makeup of a successful and long-lived gunfighter:

Richardson . . . didn't take sufficient time to see what he was doing and his life paid the penalty. No one, however, who knew both men could truthfully say that Loving possessed a greater degree of courage than Richardson, or that under ordinary conditions he was a better marksman with a gun. He simply had the best nerve, which is a quality quite different from courage. Courage, generally speaking, is daring. Nerve is steadiness.[29]

Bat bore no grudge against Loving, although Richardson had been a pal:

Richardson had been a buffalo hunter with me on the plains of western Kansas for several years. We were very close friends and shared our blankets with each other on a great many cold winter nights, when blankets were a very useful commodity. . . . I was the sheriff of the County at the time and refused to lock Loving up in jail, holding that he had, in killing Richardson, only acted in self defense; and permitted him to be at large on his own recognizance until his preliminary examination was held, which exonerated him, as I knew it would. I have never stood for murder and never will, but I firmly believe that a man who kills another in defense of his own life should always be held blameless and will always lend a helping hand to such a man.[30]

It is interesting to note that although Bat recalled that "Frank Loving was a mere boy at the time," the *Ford County Globe* gave his age as "about 25 years."[31] In April, 1879, Bat himself was just four months past his twenty-fifth birthday.

The last killing in Dodge City during 1878–79 hardly fit the popular conception of a cow-town gun encounter. Two Dodge residents, Barney Martin and Arista H. Webb, became involved in a drunken dispute in a Main Street saloon on the afternoon of September 8, 1879. Martin, a tailor, described by the *Globe* as "a remarkably small man, generally inoffensive and timid,"[32] was knocked down by Webb, who was not placated when Martin apologized and left the saloon to nurse his aching jaw on a bench in front of his tailor shop. As he reeled up Front Street, cursing at every step, Webb tried to borrow a pistol at F. C. Zimmerman's hardware store but was refused. He then went home, got his Winchester, saddled his horse, and returned to Main Street, Dismounting, he staggered over to the bench where Martin still sat, raised the rifle, and slammed the barrel down on the head of the little tailor. Martin sprawled on the sidewalk, his skull crushed. Webb tried to get back on his horse and escape but was restrained by several witnesses to the murder and soon was arrested by Marshal Bassett. A crowd quickly gathered and there were calls for a lynching, but Bassett and Sheriff Masterson locked up the prisoner and dispersed the angry mob. The following January, Webb was convicted of first-degree murder and sentenced to death, the execution to take place at the state penitentiary.

It is significant that noted gunfighters like Ben Thompson and Doc Holliday did not display their lethal prowess in Dodge City during Sheriff Masterson's tenure. Wyatt Earp, to whom Holliday was devoted, may be given credit for the good behavior of the deadly dentist during 1878–79, but Thompson's uncharacteristic pacifism while in Dodge can be traced directly to his friendship with Masterson.

The only recorded instance in which Thompson got out of line occurred shortly after Eddie Foy and his troupe arrived in town. The incident was memorable to Foy because the Texan's bullying antics came near to costing the actor his life. Wrote Foy:

> Ben Thompson, the Texas scrapper . . . was not highly popular in Dodge, Bat Masterson being one of his few friends. Thompson, about two-thirds drunk, blundered in back of the scenes one evening between acts. . . . Seeing me, he drew his gun and called out, "Getcher head outa the way! I wanta shoot out that light."
>
> I was seized with a sudden foolish obstinacy. . . . So, although I had turned my head to look at him, I didn't lean back, but just sat with my eyes fixed on him as impudently as I could.
>
> "Getcher head outa the way, I told you!" he yelled. "I'm gointa shoot out that light. If you want it through yer head, too, all right."
>
> With that, he pointed the gun full at me, while I still sat staring at him, hypnotized by my own stubbornness. For a long moment we confronted each other thus — and then Bat Masterson burst into the scene, threw the muzzle of Thompson's gun upward, and partly by coaxing, partly by shoving, got him out. When they had gone, I found my hands shaking so that I couldn't put on my makeup. I was limp for the rest of the evening.[33]

Ben Thompson was not given to cold-blooded killing of defenseless greenhorns, but it is quite possible that in his sodden state he might have been infuriated sufficiently by Foy's obstinacy to carry out his threat. Bat's timely intervention on this occasion may well have saved for the American stage one of its all-time great performers.

CHAPTER TEN

"CATCH 'EM AND CONVICT 'EM"

The only known instance in which Bat fired a weapon while making an arrest during his term as sheriff of Ford County was the capture of Jim Kennedy. Evidently, the lawbreakers he took into custody, daunted by his growing reputation as a quick, sure hand with a gun, submitted without a struggle. Tales of the formidable sheriff at Dodge, many of them highly colored in the retelling, spread throughout the West, and Bat must have been surprised and faintly amused to hear himself referred to by visiting cattlemen and gamblers as "that lawman who is filling up Boot Hill."

When possible, Bat employed strategy and the element of surprise to take in a wanted man. His capture of a Fort Lyons fugitive in July, 1878, was typical of the manner in which he operated. The authorities at Fort Lyons had wired to Dodge that an escaped criminal named Davis was thought to be aboard an eastbound train that would stop in Dodge. The telegram warned that Davis was armed and extremely dangerous and that care should be taken in his apprehension — but it neglected to give a description of the wanted man.

Bat was waiting when the first train from the west pulled in. He swung up on the caboose and walked slowly through the cars. His coat was carefully buttoned over the sheriff's badge pinned to his vest. He scrutinized each passenger in turn until he singled out one whose demeanor aroused his suspicions. He could not be sure whether the man he had selected was the one he wanted, but he wasted no time finding out. Walking straight up to his suspect, he said, smiling, "Why, hello, Davis. How are you?"

The stranger, caught off guard, smiled hesitantly and mumbled a flustered reply. Bat, still smiling broadly, extended his right hand, and the bewildered passenger, raking his memory to place this old friend, instinctively gripped it. Bat jerked the stranger out of his seat, slapped manacles on his wrists, and escorted the cursing fugitive to the Dodge City pokey, where he was held overnight until an officer from Fort Lyons arrived to take him back to serve a three-year sentence.

Horse stealing was a thriving criminal activity in western Kansas in the late 1870's, and hunting thieves and recovering stolen stock occupied a great deal of the young sheriff's time. Shortly after he took office, Bat arrested James McDuff in Las Animas, Colorado, on a charge of horse stealing; this capture, coming close on the heels of his snaring of two of the Kinsley train robbers, earned him paeans from Nick Klaine of the *Dodge City Times*. Acting on a tip that McDuff had stolen a span of horses from Miles Mix and had gone to Las Animas, Bat and Mix went to the Colorado town. McDuff was not readily found, but another character, known to be associated with him, was located, and Bat leaned on this fellow a little. The man talked, naming a certain parlor house, and there McDuff was found hiding under a bed. When Bat returned with his prisoner, the *Times* said: "This is but the prelude of the interesting drama on the boards, and the sequel will develop some startling characters in the clutches of the officers."[1]

A month later, the editor was giving fair warning: "Recent developments indicate that Sheriff Masterson and County Attorney Sutton will soon fasten the clutches of the law upon a band of unsuspecting horse thieves. 'Let no guilty man escape.' "[2]

In April, four men from Walnut Creek, forty miles north of Dodge, came to town in search of four horses that had been stolen the day before. They had trailed the horses to Dodge and now enlisted the sheriff's aid in finding them. Bat found two of them hidden in the brush along the river and the other two in Ham Bell's stable. The happy owners prepared to return to Walnut Creek, but the sheriff was not satisfied, and "with an eye to giving his thiefship punishment for his wrongs, made search and discovered men whom he supposed to be guilty. Swearing out a complaint himself he arrested Henry Martin and William Tilghman."[3]

This was the second time within two months that Bat had picked up his friend Bill Tilghman on a serious charge. Tilghman's arrest on suspicion of implication in the Kinsley train holdup soon had been shown to be without foundation, and this arrest apparently was based on equally shaky evidence. Martin was bound over for trial on two thousand dollars bond; Tilghman was released. If this Henry Martin was the notorious border character Hurricane Bill Martin, with whom Tilghman had been associated on the buffalo ranges, it may account for the charge. Hurricane Bill was not above horse thievery or any other kind of shady activity, and Bill Tilghman may have suffered suspicion of guilt by association.

In May, Bat gathered in a man named George Foster, wanted in Ellis County for horse stealing. Said the *Times*: "Horse thieves find hospitable reception at the hands of Sheriff Masterson. He is an excellent 'catch' and is earning a State reputation."[4]

When, in June, Masterson held two men in jail for almost two weeks on suspicion of stock stealing in the Texas Panhandle and then let them go, the *Ford County Globe* was quick to reproach him:

> W. E. Quillin and Henry Pagne, who have been held here since the 12th inst. by the arbitrary exercise of power by our county officers, were turned loose yesterday because there never existed any cause for holding them. They were compelled to pay $18 livery bill on their stock before they got it from the custody of the Sheriff who had taken possession of the same at the time they were arrested. We are surprised that the boys were not retained in custody till they paid their board during the time of their incarceration.[5]

The *Globe*'s editor also took note of Sheriff Masterson's more laudable activities. In the same issue that contained the item above was the following:

> Messrs. Sutton and Masterson compelled two of the show case institutions to disgorge some of their ill gotten gains last week, and recovered the same to the parties who had been robbed. We cannot understand how any of our county farmers can be so green as to come to Dodge and go up against those cut throat games, yet they do it nearly every day.

In the pages of the *Times*, of course, Bat and Sutton could do no wrong. "We quite agree with the generally expressed opinion that 'Judge Sutton and Bat Masterson are the right men in the right place,' " said the paper just four days after the criticism in the *Globe*. "County Attorney Sutton and Sheriff Masterson are using all fair and honorable means as officers to bring criminals to

Mike Sutton, one-time friend
and political ally of Bat
Masterson, later a formidable
adversary. Courtesy Kansas
State Historical Society.

justice. All law abiding people commend them for the honest discharge of their duties."[6]

In August, Bat and his deputy, Bill Duffey, brought in a man named James Smith, charged with horse stealing, and held him for the Ellis County authorities. Gushed the *Times* editor:

Sheriff W. B. Masterson and Deputy Sheriff Wm. Duffy are indefatigable in their efforts to ferret out and arrest persons charged with crimes. Scarcely a night or day passes without a reward for their vigilance and promptness. We do not record all these happenings, because evil doing is of such common occurrence. There is a pleasant contemplation in the fact that we have officers who are determined to rid the community of a horde that is a blight upon the well being of this over ridden section.[7]

The county officers received severe censure in September, however, when two con men fled town after being arrested by Sheriff Masterson. The pair, Harry Bell and the Handsome Kid, had been taken into custody by Bat on the complaint of a man named Markel, "an illiterate gentleman from some backwoods"[8] who claimed he had been induced to exchange good greenbacks for a fake twenty-dollar gold piece, which the *Globe* called a "gilden spiel marke."[9] Said the *Times*:

The pieces purporting to be gold were made of some base metal, plated, and did not resemble gold or the device of gold coin. A person with ordinary intelligence would not have been gulled with such a trick. It matters not, the pieces were represented to be gold, and a charge of obtaining money under false pretenses could have been sustained.[10]

Bat turned his charges over to Deputy Duffey, who, in turn, designated one "Red" to watch them. They were never locked up, apparently, and skipped town at the first opportunity. "Who is 'Red'?" demanded the editor of the *Globe*. "Does anybody know him? The only information that we can get concerning him is that he is one of the 'confidence gang.' If this is true he was evidently the right kind of man to guard his pals — from justice."[11]

At a special citizens meeting held in the schoolhouse, the whole question of confidence operators in Dodge and the officers' actions relative to them were discussed heatedly. *Globe* editor W. M. Morphy and businessmen F. C. Zimmerman and Hi Collar contended that "shovers of the queer" and goldbrick peddlers were the scourge of Dodge and that the officers had not performed their duty in driving them out. Several rose to the lawmen's defense, including City Attorney E. F. Colborn and Bobby Gill; the latter rolled his eyes heavenward and averred "that they were the best officers whom God in His wisdom had ever created."

"For which, oh, Lord, make us truly thankful," groaned Morphy in the *Globe*. He went on:

The meeting very nearly broke up in a row. . . . The officers claim that they have always lacked the support of the citizens. We cannot understand how they can expect the support of the citizens unless they show themselves more worthy of it than they have heretofore done. What Ford county needs is a complete change in judicial officers and the ballot box is the place to get it. Remember this, voters of Ford county, and vote against any and every man who has not done his duty in driving out the confidence curse from our midst.[12]

Despite Morphy's imprecation, at the elections held in Dodge City on November 5, 1878, the Gang, to which Bat belonged, captured most of the offices. Bat's term had a year to run and he did not have to stand for reelection, but Mike Sutton was reelected county attorney, Bob Wright was elected state representative, and Nick Klaine became probate judge. In a contemptuous piece, Morphy's *Globe*, on November 12, likened the Gang's sweep to the victory of a band of buccaneers:

On Tuesday a "gang" took possession of the good ship "Ford" at a well-known landing on the Arkansas river, with the intention of going upon a piratical voyage of two years. The victory of the pirates was an easy one. Some of the owners had been chloriformed, some were bought, some were scared; the true men were overpowered. . . .

Nick Klaine's *Times*, of course, continued to laud Bat's work. In late November when Bat arrested a suspected horse thief named W. H. Brown and lodged him in the Hôtel de Straughn, Klaine commented: "There are seven prisoners in jail charged with various offenses. This looks like business on the part of the officers."[13]

A week later, calamity struck. Four of the county prisoners slipped out of the jail in a mass escape. Jailer John Straughn had been directed by the Board of County Commissioners to cut in the barred door of the jail an aperture through which food could be passed without necessitating the unlocking of the door at mealtime. Straughn commenced this work on December 6, sawing partly through one of the bars. He then went to the blacksmith shop to obtain additional materials, and in his absence the prisoners managed to break off the weakened bar and squirm through the opening. Escaping were W. H. Brown; H. Gould, alias Skunk Curley, a cowboy held on a charge of assault with intent to kill; Frank Jennings, charged with horse stealing; and James Bailey, awaiting trial on a horse-theft charge. The three other prisoners, Limping Tom O'Haran, Dan Woodward, and James Skelly, were either disinclined or unable to join in the break.

When the escape was discovered, Bat, Charlie Bassett, Jim Masterson, and Bill Duffey began an intensive search. Jim Masterson captured Gould hiding in a buffalo wallow about a mile from town. "Had it not been for the approach of darkness," said the *Globe*, "the officers would probably have secured all the prisoners. They, however, continued their search through the night and the next day, but the prisoners having taken to the prairies and hills, no trace was found.[14] During the night, two men, believed to be Jennings and Bailey, attempted to steal horses from the Nichols & Culbertson corral, and a mare was stolen from a camp several miles north of town by a man answering the description of W. H. Brown.

The *Globe*, usually critical of the county officers, commiserated with them in this instance:

> The officers feel the misfortune keenly. The sheriff, whose conduct in the capture and detention of horse-thieves has been so frequently complimented of late, was greatly exercised over the news of the escape and made every effort to regain the prisoners. The feelings of the jailor can be better imagined than described, as this was the first misfortune he has had since he has held the office. He blames himself for not using more care or left some one to guard the door during his absence. While every citizen deplores this occurrence, no suspicion of complicity rests upon the officers.[15]

Echoed the *Times*:

> Our officers felt considerably hurt over the jail escapade. We believe no one censures them; and we trust that double caution will be used on the part of the jailor.[16]

It must have been with much relief that Bat learned four days after the break that two of the escapees had been apprehended in Kinsley by Officer A. D. Cronk. On December 11, he brought Jennings and Bailey back to join Gould in the calaboose. W. H. Brown remained at large and apparently was never returned to face trial in Ford County.

Bat had been embarrassed by the jailbreak, but a few weeks later he pulled off a coup that tended to make the voters of Ford County forget that unfortunate occurrence. In late December, he learned that Henry Borne, known throughout the West as Dutch Henry, the most notorious horse thief operating in the border country, was disporting in Trinidad, Colorado. Bat wired Las Animas County Sheriff Dick Wootton to arrest Dutch Henry as a fugitive from justice.

Almost two years earlier, Henry had been arrested in Ford County and charged with stealing a span of mules from a man named Emmerson. He had escaped from the jail and, according to the *Dodge City Times*, had pulled off two more escapes from other law officers since that time. Bat still held a warrant for his arrest, and on New Year's Day, 1879, after sending his telegram, he entrained for Colorado to collect the fugitive.

" 'Dutch Henry,' the man who seems to be wanted in different states and territories for a variety of crimes," said the *Trinidad Enterprise*," is rather a genteel looking man for a horse-thief, road-agent and murderer. He has black hair and eyes, black moustache, long face and Roman nose. His eyes are bright and penetrating, and indicate quick intelligence. He is dressed in a good suit of black, white shirt and other corresponding clothing."[17] Borne could pose in any border community as a prosperous professional man, which, in a sense, he was. His appearance and manner commanded respect, and it was said that his confederates were scattered throughout the frontier. Pinkerton detective Charlie Siringo testified that at one time Dutch Henry had three hundred followers.

When he arrived in Trinidad, Bat found Borne in custody, but Las Animas authorities were reluctant to give him up. He wired Mike Sutton: "Sheriff wont deliver up Dutch Henry unless I pay him $500. He says he can get that for him in Nevada." Said the *Dodge City Times*: "So Mr. Dutch Henry is high priced and the silver State can take him."[18]

But Masterson was not so easily balked. He demanded a hearing for Borne on a fugitive charge and appeared himself as a witness. The *Trinidad Enterprise* gave a sketchy account of the court proceedings held on January 4:

"Dutch Henry" . . . was brought before Judge Walker to-day, upon complaint of Sheriff Wootton, that he is a fugitive from justice in Ford county, Kansas, charged and indicted for grand larceny. The sheriff of Ford county, Mr. W. B. Masterson of Dodge City, was present as a witness. Mr. Caldwell Yeaman appeared for the prosecution, and Mr. Salisbury for the defense. We learn that in the course of the proceedings there was some sparring between one of the attorneys and the visiting sheriff from Dodge, in which the legal gentleman became considerable excited by unwarrantable mention of "unmentionable" matters by the witness. Now it is generally the witness who gets badgered and excited, and it may be well enough for gentlemen of the legal persuasion to happen upon a witness who can give them an opportunity to know how it is themselves. The result of the examination was that "deutcher Heinrich" was bound over to appear at the March term of the district court, and it was ordered that in default of bail he shall be confined in the Bent county jail. . . .[19]

The *Trinidad News* provided additional details concerning what must have been an unusual courtroom session:

Considerable merriment was created in Justice Walker's court on Saturday, during the hearing of Dutch Henry's case, by Sheriff Masterson of Dodge City, Kansas, insinuating that the attorney for the defense, Mr. Salisbury, had left Kansas under a cloud. The answer made by the sheriff was under oath, and may have caused some to believe that there was truth in it. But we happened to overhear Mr. Masterson say to a party of friends that night that there was not a word of truth in it; that he was driven into a corner by Salisbury, and had to say something to let himself out. . . .[20]

Dutch Henry was not transferred to the Bent County jail as ordered by Judge Walker. On the day after the hearing, Bat left Trinidad by train, bound for Dodge City, and the renowned horse thief accompanied him. Said the *Times*:

How Bat got possession of the prisoner without the payment of a reward and without a gubernatorial requisition, will probably be explained in one of the pages of a yellow-backed story book, which will detail the mysteries and crimes of the early settlement of this border. We are not curious to know just now. History will give us all the enlightenment we care to know. That is one of the things we hand down to posterity. . . . It seems Bat was a match for that squalid lawyer.[21]

Masterson had brought Dutch Henry back just in time to stand trial in Ford County District Court, which convened in Dodge on January 7. Borne was acquitted of the old mule-theft charge and Ford County released him, but his freedom was of short duration. A few months later, he was arrested by a deputy U.S. marshal and was taken to Arkansas to complete a prison term.

For Bat, the Dutch Henry experience had been enlightening. He had learned that a little fast talk spiced with a dash of bluster could work wonders in circumventing the cumbrous legal machinery of extradition — knowledge that he was to put to use in later years.

Of the persons tried at the January, 1879, session of the district court, Dutch Henry Borne was the only defendant to gain acquittal. Skunk Curley and Dan Woodward were convicted of assault with intent to kill; Frank Jennings, Jim Bailey, and Jim Skelly were found guilty of theft; and M. A. Sebastian and Bill Brown were convicted of stealing twenty-seven sacks of corn. All received jail sentences, ranging from two years and three months to two years and six months, with the exception of Sebastian, whose term was set at only eighteen months. Limping Tom O'Haran was given twelve years and three months for killing H. T. McCarty.

On January 11, Bat departed for the state penitentiary with a consignment of convicted prisoners. Later in the month, he delivered the others. The *Leavenworth Times* made note of his second visit and indicated that the young sheriff was acquiring a statewide reputation:

Sheriff W. B. Masterson and Under-Sheriff Bassett, of Ford County, arrived on Sunday from Dodge City with another installment of prisoners for the State Penitentiary, turning their charges safely over to the authorities of the prison. During Sheriff Masterson's term of office he has contributed liberally to the State's boarding house and has kept things as straight as a string in his county. He is one of the most noted men of the southwest, as cool, brave and daring as any man who ever drew a pistol. . . .[22]

The *Dodge City Times*, given an opportunity to toss barbs at the rival *Ford County Globe*, remarked:

The large criminal calendar suggests the "probability" of an "endeavor" on the part of the officers to do their duty. To an unprejudiced person, somebody has been making things lively. Sheriff Bat Masterson, Under Sheriff Bassett, and Deputies Duffy and Masterson, have evidently earned the high praise accorded to them for their vigilance and prompt action in the arrest of offenders of the law.

The energy of the indomitable and untiring worker, County Attorney Sutton, is manifested in the successful prosecution of these cases. Mike certainly "got to the joint" in his accustomed and able manner, and is deserving of the many good words spoken in his behalf for his efficient services in the cause of justice.[23]

And Bob Wright wrote:

When Bat Masterson was sheriff, Mike [Sutton] was prosecuting attorney, and they made a great team. It was not, ''scare 'em and catch 'em,'' as the saying goes, but it was ''catch 'em and convict 'em,'' which was nearly always sure to be the case.[24]

Sutton accompanied Bat and Bassett to Leavenworth in January, 1879, to deliver their prisoners. The three Ford County officers then went on to Topeka, where Bat accepted appointment as deputy U.S. marshal. The position at Dodge had been unfilled since the killing of H. T. McCarty the previous July. Masterson's decision to add greater responsibility to that which he already held as sheriff was prompted, perhaps, by the difficulty he had with Colorado authorities in the Dutch Henry affair. As a federal officer, he was not limited by county boundaries and could act in cases where a federal law had been broken or was likely to be broken.

On the way back from Topeka, Bat stopped at Sedgwick to visit his family; he arrived in Dodge on February 10. Five days later, two prisoners slipped away from the Ford County jail. George Holcomb and George Watkins, accused of rustling seventy-five head of cattle from the Dunham and Ward ranch, had secured a pocketknife and had whittled a hole through the pine-board ceiling of their jail cell and the floor above. Crawling through the hole, they found themselves in the office of the county treasurer, whence they escaped through a window.

Bat had one of the escaped prisoners back in custody within a week. When he received word that a man answering Holcomb's description had been seen riding freight cars west, Bat jumped on a fast passenger train in pursuit. At South Pueblo, Colorado, he enlisted the aid of Marshal Pat Desmond and soon located his quarry. George Watkins, the other jailbird, had vanished.

The insecure condition of the county jail may have led to the open break between Sheriff Masterson and the Board of County Commissioners that became evident in the following month. It was a violent disagreement that culminated in the resignation from the board of Bat's friend George Cox. "For a long time the relations of the Sheriff and the Board have not been amicable, and frequently high words have been spoken," said the *Globe* in announcing Cox's resignation.[25]

The board had done nothing to improve security at the jail even five months later when the *Times* told of still another break and reprimanded the board for its inaction:

A prisoner broke from the Ford county jail on Monday last, but was promptly captured. We are not surprised at this, for the walls of the jail are barely security against the escape of prisoners. With a board flooring above for a roof, and a dirt floor underneath, unless there is a constant and vigilant watch, the prisoners are liable to escape with little effort on their part. The prisoner on Monday escaped by digging a hole under the door. Some time ago two prisoners escaped by cutting a hole through the board floor above. The wretched and insecure condition of the jail is a matter that demands the serious attention of the Board of County Commissioners. . . .[26]

In spite of the board's failure to improve jail security, Bat continued his efforts to put more horse thieves in it. The next issue of the *Times* detailed the latest news of his continuing war:

Sheriff Masterson and officers captured in the city, Friday last, two horse thieves, who had stolen stock nine miles north of Great Bend. . . . A third person engaged in stealing with these two, managed to elude the vigilance of the officers and escaped. The prisoners gave fictitious names before their trial, thus attempting to avoid identification.

On Sunday two more persons were arrested, charged with horse stealing, and having in their possession fourteen head of horses, supposed to be stolen, which they had secreted on the range south. . . .

On Wednesday Sheriff Masterson received a dispatch from J. B. Matthews, at Fort Griffin, Texas, telling him to hold the two men arrested by him on Sunday. The prisoners' names are Charley and Jack Lyon, and they had eight horses stolen from Matthews. These horses are in possession of the Sheriff.

Horse stealing has taken a fresh start in the country, and since the wholesale conviction of thieves last winter that crime had not been on the rampage until within the past few months. The officers of Ford county are on the alert and watch with a vigilant eye every suspicious character lurking in our midst.[27]

Among the suspicious characters who came under Bat's vigilant eyes were, apparently, some he thought might be worth some money to him. In October, he wrote two letters to Kansas Governor John St. John asking whether rewards were still offered for certain fugitives. "Will you be so kind as to inform me in regard to the reward offered for one Dan Henson — alias Cherokee Dan?" he asked on October 2, 1879. "The reward was offered by Ex. Gov. Geo. T. Anthony. Amount $500.00 five Hundred Dollars. I think I can arrest him with some little Expence and if the reward is Still Standing I will make an Effort. It was for the murder of one F. U. Wyman in Commanche Co. Kansas."[28] Five days later he inquired whether a reward was still outstanding for John Scott, one of the slayers of William Taylor, a Negro restaurant proprietor, in Dodge City in 1873. There is no evidence that Bat ever arrested either of these two fugitives.

CHAPTER ELEVEN

FRONTIER FROLICS

In 1878 and 1879, Dodge City first achieved national notoriety. Newspapermen tagged the little cow town with colorful epithets, such as the Gomorrah of the Plains and the Babylon of the Frontier, and wrote reams of copy for eastern readers about the Dodge City gunfighters, who were reputed to be the fastest and deadliest of all those in the border country. Throughout the frontier, however, Dodge was building another reputation during these years. For westerners, she was to hold a distinction as unique as her claim that she was the toughest little town in America. Dodge was remembered by many of those who visited there in the late 1870's as a town of gunmen — and pranksters.

For the daredevil who came to town with a chip on his shoulder, spoiling for a fight, the warning went out: "Beware the Dodge City gunman!" Just as appropriate was the frequently heard admonition to a Dodge-bound high hat or stuffed shirt: "Beware the Dodge City prankster!"

Bat Masterson dearly loved a good practical joke, and many of the pranks in which he participated at Dodge were talked of for years in the West. A number of the men who, with Bat, had helped to establish Dodge's reputation as a gunman's town contributed to her fame as a community of jokesters. Wyatt Earp, Luke Short, Jack Bridges, Mysterious Dave Mather, and others in the sporting brotherhood were Bat's accomplices.

Greenhorns, of course, were common targets for the westerners' rough sense of humor. When Eddie Foy first hit Dodge, he minced down Front Street with what Bob Wright called "a kind of Fifth Avenue swagger and strut."[1] His second day in town, he was roped and dragged off the sidewalk. A gang of grim-faced men set him astride a pony and led it under a tree, where a rope was tightened around his neck and he was asked if he had any final words. Foy, who was not as frightened as he might have been had he not glimpsed Sheriff Masterson standing quietly on the fringe of the crowd, ready to call "calf rope" if the play got too rough, replied that anything he had to say he could say better at the bar of the Long Branch Saloon. "The whole affair ended in a laugh and a drink all around," the comedian recalled.[2]

When the Reverend O. W. Wright came to Dodge to preach the Gospel, he was surprised and pleased by the treatment he received from the sporting crowd. He needed funds, and Bat and Wyatt Earp, acting as his deacons, saw to it that the Front Street gamblers kittyed out enough in two days to erect a church. But when the Dodge City Ladies Aid Society, the backbone of the Reverend M. Wright's congregation, conceived the idea of a baby contest to raise a missionary fund, Bat and Wyatt were given an opportunity to pull off one of the town's most widely known pranks.

Dodge City–born infants under one year of age were eligible for the contest, the winner to be determined by ballots that were to sell at six for a quarter. A winner's prize of one hundred dollars in gold was donated by Luke Short, manager of the gambling concession in the Long Branch. Rivalry among the mothers of the various entrants was intense, and as the ballot sales campaign drew to a close, the men of the town were solicited at every turn by vote-peddling women. On the final day, there was a phenomenal sale. The saloon sports bought ballots in twenty-dollar lots, and the Reverend Mr. Wright and the church ladies bubbled with pleasure.

A church supper was held that evening, and the ballots were counted. The Reverend Mr. Wright rose to announce that the contest had brought more than two thousand dollars into the missionary fund. Everyone applauded, and the saloon boys in the rear seats called for the name of the winner. The mothers of the competing babies beamed in anticipation of victory from their seats of honor in the front row. The minister read the results, naming first the contestant with the fewest votes and continuing up the list toward the winner. The child of each of the confident mothers was eliminated in turn, and as Wright paused dramatically before reading the name of the victorious baby, the women stared at each other in astonishment. None of them had won!

The minister read a name unknown to any of the mothers and

Eddie Foy played Dodge during the Cowboy Capital's most colorful period. Courtesy Free Library of Philadelphia.

looked bewilderingly at the audience. ''Does anyone present know this child?'' he asked. The sports in the rear were gripping their sides to stifle their laughter. Deacons Masterson and Earp rose solemnly and announced that they knew the identity of the winning baby. If everyone would be patient, they said, they would fetch the child to the church.

In a few minutes, Bat and Wyatt were back, escorting a very large and very black cyprian from a south-side Negro dance hall. She carried a dusky cherub in her arms. Recovering somewhat from his initial shock, the Reverend Mr. Wright asked the woman if the name of the winner was that of her child. It was, she said, and where was the hundred in gold that she had been promised?

The mother of one of the losing babies evidently lacked the sense of humor of the boys in the back, who were convulsed with mirth. ''Who is the father of that child?'' she demanded angrily. ''That,'' said the Reverend Mr. Wright, awarding the sack of gold, ''is this lady's business.''[3]

When a certain Dr. Meredith, a self-styled phrenologist and specialist in the care of venereal diseases, wrote to Dodge asking if that renowned sin city would be receptive to a lecture on his particular scientific subjects, Mayor Kelley turned the doctor's letter over to Sheriff Masterson. Bat immediately dispatched a reply, assuring Meredith that the bumps on the heads of some of the camp's characters would indeed be worthy of extensive examination and that social diseases were raging unchecked. Even the ministers were not free of the scourge, Bat confided. He promised the doctor a warm reception should he choose to include Dodge in his itinerary.

Dr. Meredith hurried to Dodge forthwith and promptly engaged the Lady Gay for a night to lecture to a populace sorely in need of his services. The house was filled to capacity as he mounted the stage. Flanking the upended crate that was to serve as a lectern were Bat Masterson and Wyatt Earp. Other influential citizens of the town, who, coincidentally, were also gun hands of note, were seated at places of honor on the stage.

Bat had appointed himself chairman of the meeting, so he introduced the speaker, admonishing the audience to be polite and considerate, since the visitor was there to help many of them. The doctor arose and had scarcely begun his talk when he was interrupted by a harsh voice from the audience. Some rude fellow had called the good doctor a liar. Bat leaped to his feet and warned the crowd that interruptions would not be tolerated. He personally, said Bat, caressing his gun butt, would take charge of the originator of any further outburst. Wyatt Earp and the other gunslingers on the stage swept the audience with dark looks.

Dr. Meredith proceeded with his lecture in a taut, high-pitched voice. He paused after each quaking phrase to steal apprehensive glances at the tight-lipped citizens at his side. He had not gone very far when an obscene insult was hurled from somewhere in the crowd.

"Just at this critical moment a southside exhorter with one eye in a sling made an effort to drag the orator from the stand," reported the *Ford County Globe*, "whereupon Chairman Masterson drew from beneath his coat-tails a Colt's improved, nickel plated, size 44 shooting instrument and formed himself in a hollow square in front of the horrified doctor, determined to defend or die!"[4] Instantly the place was a bedlam. The kerosene lamps were shattered in a six-shooter fusillade. Windows crashed, tables and chairs were overturned, hoarse screams knifed the darkness. Bob Wright describes the scene:

My! what a stampede began. The people not only fell over each other, but they tumbled over each other, and rolled over, and trampled each other under foot. Some reached the doors, others took the windows, sash and all, and it was only a short time till darkness and quiet reigned in the Lady Gay. Only the smell of powder and dense smoke was to be seen, coming out of the windows and doors.[5]

When the tumult was over, Bat found an unbroken lamp and lighted it. A search was made for the distinguished scientist. He was finally found, curled up in a very undignified position, under a table. Bat helped him to his feet, and the doctor gingerly felt all sectors of his scientific person. Miraculously, he found no holes. Bat apologized profusely for the behavior of the Dodge City citizenry and assured the doctor solemnly that if he would remain overnight to deliver another lecture, things would turn out differently. Bat was persuasive and Dr. Meredith, although trembling after his close call, finally agreed.

Bat was sincere when he promised that the outcome would be different if the doctor played a return engagement. He had in mind an even more spectacular display of fireworks the following evening. Bob Wright records that certain members of the sporting crowd who were in on the joke approached him to ask whether he thought ten pounds of powder would hurt the doctor. Wright replied that a pound, if confined, would kill him. Fearful that Bat and his cronies were carrying the prank too far, Wright did a little checking and learned that the gang intended to plant a charge under Dr. Meredith's lectern. He promptly hunted up the doctor. "My friend," he said, "you don't know what you are up against. Get on the local freight, which leaves here inside an hour, and never stop until you get back to your own Illinois, because you aren't fit to be so far away from home without a guardian."[6] The doctor took Wright's advice and departed Dodge City, leaving the uncivilized denizens of that wild camp to their cranial bumps and unspeakable afflictions.

A favorite prank was the Indian Act. Some of the men who participated with Bat in the battle at the Walls had brought back to Dodge an assortment of Indian regalia that for years afterward decorated the interiors of the Long Branch and other saloons. When a new arrival to the camp boasted too loudly of his Indian-fighting ability, the gaudy trappings were taken down to teach him a lesson and at the same time provide jokesters with a little merriment.

The newcomer would be invited to take part in a hunt on the prairie west of town. As he rode out with a few of the saloon crowd — who were, of course, privy to the joke — he would be warned repeatedly to be on the lookout for roving bands of hostiles who, he was told, infested the area. The hunters agreed that if they were attacked, the only thing to do was to race to Dodge for help. "You've got the fastest mount," the stranger would be told solemnly, "so you'll make it to town first. When you hit Front Street, yell for the Gatling guns. Maybe the boys will get back in time to save the rest of us." More talk of this kind, interspersed with bloodcurdling tales of Indian atrocities, soon had the neophyte sitting stiff in his saddle, scanning the horizon with nervous eyes.

Waiting a few miles from town were several of the sporting

brotherhood, decked out in the Adobe Walls trophies, their bodies darkened with charcoal and smeared with paint. Rounding a rise in the prairie, the self-proclaimed Indian fighter suddenly would see a horde of screaming red men thundering toward him, warbonnets flying and rifles blazing. "Run for your life!" the hunters would yelp, and the little party would come tearing back to Dodge in a cloud of dust, the "Indians" whooping at their heels. Fast horse or slow, the stranger always was the first back in town, where he would go careening down the street, crying hoarsely for the Gatlings.

He would watch horror stricken as the townspeople made no move to prepare for battle but stood idly in laughing groups. Then comprehension would sweep over him as he saw the painted men ride directly into town and up to the hitching rail at the Long Branch, where there would be much slapping of backs and shaking of hands. There was nothing left for him to do but to return sheepishly to the laughing throng already forming along the bar and buy drinks for the whole gang.

Bat and his friends worked this prank many times. Among the victims were salty old John Bender, a Santa Fe conductor, and U.S. Senator John J. Ingalls.

One time, however, it backfired, an unlooked-for development that did much to bring an end to what had become a Dodge City institution. The boys plotted to pull the prank on a man named Harris, who had just opened a jewelry shop. As a precautionary measure, the pranksters had always seen to it that the victim's hunting rifle was either unloaded or filled with blanks before the party left camp; Harris' rifle was so prepared on this occasion. The jeweler, however, disturbed by talk of possible Indian trouble, unobtrusively slipped a loaded six-gun into his boot before the hunters set out. When the "Indians" attacked, Harris, to the consternation of fellow hunters and rampaging red men alike, coolly stood his ground and opened up on the onrushing tribe with his pistol. A bullet clipped feathers from the headdress of the leading chief. War whoops died in painted throats and the blood-thirsty war party scattered like chaff in the wind. Even a Gatling gun could not have been more effective in turning back an Indian raid. That day in Dodge, the drinks were on the pranksters.

When in the spring of 1879 a call went out to Dodge City for enlistees in the Royal Gorge War in Colorado, the sports rushed to join. Although this trouble between the Santa Fe and the Denver & Rio Grande, which had been brewing for more than a year, was very serious to the rival railroads, it is clear from the Dodge City newspapers that the battlers from Dodge who participated looked upon the entire affair as something of a lark.

The great silver strike at Leadville had precipitated a struggle for a railroad right-of-way into the new boom town. Freighters were hauling fifty thousand to one hundred thousand pounds of silver ore a day from Leadville and receiving eighteen dollars per ton at Colorado Springs. The railroad company that could lay track to Leadville would reap a rich harvest, and both the Santa Fe and the Rio Grande yearned for it. General W. J. Palmer, fighting president of the little Rio Grande, pulled out all the stops to lay the first steel into the silver camp. He had a formidable adversary in the person of W. B. Strong, vice president and general manager of the Santa Fe, who had pushed his line from Topeka into Colorado and was looking south and west for a route through the Rockies. Strong's main goal was a link with the Pacific Coast, but he was not overlooking Leadville and its mountain of silver ore. He ordered A. A. Robinson, his chief engineer and the man who had platted Dodge City in 1872, to lay track into Leadville whatever the cost.

The situation was complicated by the fact that there was only one possible railroad route into the silver fields, an extremely hazardous one. To reach Leadville, track would have to be laid through Royal Gorge, a slash in the mountains carved by the rushing torrents of the Arkansas River. The gorge was a narrow defile with sheer walls towering upward for a thousand feet or more; in places, they were but thirty feet apart. To build a railroad through such a chasm was a staggering problem in itself, but the Santa Fe and the Rio Grande had a primary problem to solve first. Before either could build, the gorge itself had to be won, and both companies were prepared to fight for its possession.

The battle that developed came to be known as the Royal Gorge War, a unique conflict in American history. It was fought simultaneously on two levels; legal battles raged through the state and federal courts, and violent conflicts between opposing armies occurred in the area of the gorge for more than a year.

The Rio Grande, a Colorado concern, was financially weak compared to the powerful Kansas line, and the war for Royal Gorge, like all wars, drained off a great deal of capital. In December, 1878, General Palmer, under pressure from his bondholders, was forced to lease his road to the Santa Fe for thirty years. It appeared then that the war was over and the Santa Fe had won, but in March, 1879, Palmer reopened the fight in the courts, claiming that the Santa Fe had broken the terms of its lease. At the same time, he dispatched squads of armed men to fortifications he had built overlooking the gorge. The Santa Fe rearmed its work crews and imported professional fighters to protect its holdings. The war was on again.

On March 25, 1879, the *Ford County Globe* reported:

Last Thursday evening Sheriff Masterson received a telegram from officers of the Atchison, Topeka and Santa Fe road at Canon City, asking if he could bring a posse of men to assist in defending the workmen on that road from the attacks of the Denver and Rio Grande men, who were again endeavoring to capture the long contested pass through the canon. Masterson and Deputy Duffey immediately opened a recruiting office, and before the train arrived Friday morning had enrolled a company of thirty-three men. They all boarded the morning train, armed to the teeth, Sheriff Masterson in command, and started for the scene of the hostilities.

There is no explanation here by what legal authority the sheriff of a Kansas county could deputize possemen and lead them into another state to protect the interests of a railroad company, but it is probable that Bat was acting in his capacity as deputy U.S. marshal. Royal Gorge was still legally in the hands of the Santa Fe, pending an appeal to the United States Supreme Court by General Palmer, and Masterson's job was to maintain the status quo until that court handed down a decision.

Although Bat had official status as a federal officer, the men he recruited undoubtedly were mercenaries in the employ of a private concern. J. H. Phillips, railroad agent for the Santa Fe in Dodge, authorized him to offer board and wages of three dollars a day to volunteers. Wrote Bob Wright:

Of course, the Atchison, Topeka & Santa Fe folks came to Dodge City for fighters and gunmen. It was only natural for them to do so, for where in the whole universe were there to be found fitter men for a desperate encounter of this kind. Dodge City bred such bold, reckless men, and it was their pride and delight to be called upon to do such work. They were quick and accurate on the trigger, and these little encounters kept them in good training.[7]

The sympathy of the townspeople definitely lay with the Santa Fe, which had made Dodge City possible. The *Times* reflected this bias as it praised the men who joined the posse:

Towering like a giant among smaller men, was one of Erin's bravest sons whose name is Kinch Riley. Jerry Converse, a Scotchman, descended from a warlike clan, joined the ranks of war. There were other braves who joined the ranks, but we are unable to get a list of their names. We will bet a ten-cent note that they clear the track of every obstruction.[8]

Some of the more well-known gunmen who signed on with Bat were Josh Webb, who, like Kinch Riley, had served with Bat on the posse that captured the Kinsley train robbers; Ben Thompson, the Texan who was always ready for a fresh taste of danger; and Doc Holliday, the consumptive dentist and reckless adventurer. Eddie Foy said Holliday tried to enlist him in the venture but he declined with thanks.[9]

Bat took his little army to Canon City, at the mouth of the gorge, where he found the situation very tense. A Rio Grande engineer, J. R. DeRemer, held a string of seventeen stone fortifications some twenty miles up the narrow chasm with a well-armed and determined force of fifty men. Some members of the Santa Fe party were for attacking DeRemer and driving him and his crew from the gorge, but Bat would not have it. First of all, he argued, although his men were paid Santa Fe mercenaries, he himself was a peace officer. His duty was to prevent bloodshed, not incite it. Second, DeRemer held what seemed to be an impregnable position with a superior force. A decision from the U.S. Supreme Court was expected shortly; Bat urged the restless battlers to hold off until it was handed down.

The court ruled on April 21 that the Denver & Rio Grande had prior right to construction in Royal Gorge but not exclusive right. This appeared to be a victory for General Palmer, but he still had to contend with the lease held by his rival. He took that case to the courts, endeavoring to break the lease.

The Supreme Court decision cooled the Colorado situation considerably, so Bat took his men back to Dodge. Several skirmishes had been fought, but there were few, if any, casualties. This is not surprising if the testimony, forty years later, of Nathaniel K. Hunter, one of the Santa Fe warriors, is to be believed. "We used only blank cartridges in shooting at each other in our 'battles' over the grading and right of way," he said. "The fact that the men used blanks in their guns is not generally known. . . . Of course the big bosses did not know we were using blanks. If they had, they'd have fired us."[10]

That the sports of Dodge welcomed this sort of work was proved amply two months later when Bat received another call for help from the Santa Fe. Within half an hour after receiving the telegram, he had all the volunteers he needed, and "was whirling westward with an engine and one coach containing sixty men, at the rate of forty miles an hour."[11]

W. B. Strong was marshaling his forces in anticipation of a court order abrogating the Santa Fe lease and restoring to General Palmer control of the Rio Grande. He was certain he could have the order reversed, but he was afraid Palmer would try to take over the line by force before the legal countermove could be managed. He began to fortify his stations.

Bat took his party from Dodge City on June 9. A dispatch from Pueblo to the *Rocky Mountain News* in Denver, headed "Santa Fe Arming," described deployment of the troops:

> Three extra trains came in from the south and east yesterday with the following men: Paddy Welsh and forty-five of Dick Wootton's deputy sheriffs from Trinidad; Bat Masterson, sheriff from Dodge City, Kansas, with sixty-five men; Charles Hickey, sheriff of Bent County, with eighteen men. An extra went to Colorado Springs last night with a lot of bad men from Dodge City. Bat Masterson goes to Canon City this afternoon to regulate Hadden and DeRemer. Does the governor care to hear of this?[12]

Bat was placed in charge of the railroad station and roundhouse at Pueblo, the pivotal point for the Santa Fe defense system. Pueblo controlled the tracks leading north toward Denver and west toward Canon City and Royal Gorge.

On June 10, Judge T. M. Bowen of the Fourth Judicial District at Alamosa issued the expected writ enjoining the Santa Fe from exercising control of the Denver & Rio Grande and directing the sheriffs of the counties through which the line ran to take possession of the property. That night, General Palmer tapped the telegraph wires at Colorado Springs and sat up all night listening to messages sent by the Santa Fe forces. He learned that Strong was convinced that Judge Bowen's writ would be reversed the following day. Palmer therefore determined to move, and move fast, so he issued a general order to his followers from Denver to Canon City. Sheriffs in every county down the line, armed with writs of seizure and backed by Rio Grande gunmen, were to move in on all stations at six o'clock on the morning of June 11 and wrest them from the Santa Fe.

Palmer's orders were carried out with military precision. One by one, the Santa Fe garrisons fell under the onslaught of Palmer's men. At West Denver, the general offices of the railroad were captured when the doors were smashed with a battering ram. There was severe fighting at Colorado Springs before the Rio Grande claimed all strategic points. Two Santa Fe men were killed and two wounded at Cuchara. By noon, when a passenger train was made up by the new management at Denver to proceed triumphantly southward, General Palmer's forces had taken over the entire line, with one exception.

From Pueblo came word that Bat Masterson and the Dodge City battlers had resisted all efforts to dislodge them. R. F. Weitbrec, treasurer of the Rio Grande, was in command of the besieging army at Pueblo. He huddled with Chief Engineer J. A. McMurtrie and Sheriff Henly R. Price, trying to find a means of driving the embattled defenders from the roundhouse, which had become the Dodge men's fortress. It is said that Weitbrec even considered stealing the cannon from the state armory but found that Bat had already appropriated it. The cannon was in the roundhouse, its muzzle trained on the line of attackers.

At 11:10 that morning, E. B. Sopris, inspector general of Colorado, telegraphed his boss, Governor Frederick W. Pitkin:

Sheriff Price has served the writ of injunction issued by Judge Bowen on the Atchison, Topeka and Santa Fe. They refused to deliver possession claiming Judge Hallett's court has taken jurisdiction of the case superseding the state court. The Atchison, Topeka and Santa Fe have about 150 men under arms and the sheriff 100. A collision is imminent.[13]

McMurtrie and Deputy Sheriff Pat Desmond assembled some fifty Rio Grande men in front of the Victoria Hotel at three o'clock that afternoon and issued them ammunition and rifles equipped with bayonets. These troops then made a direct assault on the telegraph office on the station platform, forced the doors, and drove the defenders out through the rear windows. Emboldened by this success, they moved on the roundhouse, the last Santa Fe bastion.

There, Weitbrec requested a personal meeting with Bat Masterson. After a short discussion, Bat ordered his men to surrender the roundhouse. The tense confrontation was over.

In an account published in 1898,[14] Cy Warman implied that Bat had been bought off by the Rio Grande treasurer. It is more probable that Weitbrec explained to Bat that he had a legal writ to take over in the name of the Denver & Rio Grande, that all other points along the line had changed hands, and that further conflict would only result in senseless loss of life on both sides. It must be remembered that there was mass confusion at all points. Bat had no contact with either Santa Fe officials or the federal authorities to whom he was responsible. Blind, emotional loyalty to one company or the other had governed the actions of most of the people involved in the war, not respect for any lawful claims by either side.

Although it was morally and legally proper, Bat's capitulation disappointed certain Dodge City folks, who, according to Eddie Foy, "had been hoping that the home boys would be permitted to wipe the Denver & Rio Grande off the map."[15] Bat's battalion had suffered one casualty. Henry Jenkins, said a biased story in the *Times*, "was shot in the back by a drunken guard of the Rio Grande force. . . . The unfortunate man was climbing out of the depot window."[16] The fighting at one point was at very close quarters, apparently, for Josh Webb lost a front tooth. The *Times* reported that a handsome gold one was inserted at Dodge to enliven Webb's dental facade but did not state whether his odontological needs were served by his compatriot in arms J. H. Holliday, D.D.S. It may have been during that particular melee that Bat Masterson, according to Alfred Henry Lewis, "smote a Pueblo railway policeman so grievously upon his skull with a six-shooter, that the latter officer, who had wrongfully assailed Mr. Masterson with a bludgeon, must be furloughed to the hospital for a month."[17]

There were minor eruptions throughout the remainder of 1879, but Bat took no personal part in them. In February, 1880, a settlement was signed in Boston. The Rio Grande agreed not to build to St. Louis or El Paso, and the Santa Fe agreed not to build to Denver or Leadville. The Santa Fe received $1,400,000 for the track it had already laid through the gorge and thereafter directed its steel south through Raton Pass into New Mexico.

CHAPTER TWELVE

COWBOYS AND INDIANS

As has been pointed out, Bat was not required by his badge of office as sheriff of Ford County to enforce Dodge City ordinances or to help members of the city marshal's office in the discharge of their duties. However, Charlie Bassett and his deputies were close friends, and Bat could not observe any of them encountering difficulties with obstreperous revelers without lending a hand. On one occasion in May, 1879, his intervention in behalf of a fellow officer came close to costing him his life.

Three roughnecks, stopping over in Dodge on their way to Leadville from their native Missouri, tanked up on ruckus juice at several saloons and then decided to "set the wickedest little city in America right square on her ear." They had not succeeded in tipping even a small corner of the town when Assistant Marshal Wyatt Earp appeared. Clamping a strong thumb and forefinger to the ear of the rowdiest member of the group, he proceeded to drag him toward the calaboose.

The other Missourians, following at a distance, evidently were unappreciative of Earp's generosity in permitting them their freedom. They secured their weapons from the saloon gun rack and closed in on Wyatt at a dark corner of Front Street with the intention of forcibly liberating their pal. Wyatt saw them coming and jerked his pistol. The would-be rescuers shouted for their arrested friend to leap clear, but Earp kept a viselike grip on his prisoner's ear. That struggling individual, unable to free himself and give his friends a line of fire at the marshal, did the next best thing and grabbed Earp's gun arm so that he could not shoot.

Wyatt Earp was not the man to lose a prisoner without a fight. Blood, perhaps his own, would almost certainly have been spilled that night had not Sheriff Masterson observed the situation from across the street. Instantly he ran to Wyatt's aid, six-gun in hand.

155

Charging up to Wyatt and his writhing prisoner, he slammed the barrel of his .45 down on the skull section next to that tortured ear. The Missourian collapsed in a heap at Earp's feet. Bat threw down on one of the attackers while Wyatt, freed of his intractable charge, covered the other. All the fight went out of the visitors as they confronted the guns of two of the West's storied gunfighters. At Bat's sharp command, they dropped their pistols and meekly submitted to arrest. Earp marched all three, this time at gunpoint, to spend a night in the cooler.

The following morning, they were fined and told to get out of town. Under Wyatt Earp's wary eye, they saddled up and rode west out of Dodge. However, these three hard cases were from Missouri and they *really* had to be shown. After dark that evening, they slipped back into town and prepared to bushwhack Bat. They were more embittered toward the sheriff than toward Earp, apparently feeling that the marshal was merely doing his duty on the previous night and Bat had butted into something that did not concern him. They gained entrance to the rear of a darkened store building, where, as they crouched by the windows, they could watch the movements of anyone approaching in the dimly lighted alley behind. They sent a little Negro boy after the sheriff with the message that a man wanted to see him in the alley.

The boy, a friend of Bat, was no simpleton. He told Masterson that three armed men were hiding in the store, waiting for him to show. Needless to say, Bat did not oblige the Missourians by walking into the trap. He posted guards at both entrances to the alley and another at the front of the store. When the bushwhackers tired of waiting for him to make an appearance and came out of their holes, he promptly slapped them back in jail.

Bat could not bring charges of attempted murder against them because they had committed no overt act. He had to be content with seeing them fined again for carrying concealed weapons within the city limits. This time, however, when he told them to git, they got. "These fellows remarked that they 'had run things in Missouri,' and believed that they could 'take' Dodge City, but admitted that they were no match for Dodge City officers," reported the *Times*, adding wryly: "Dodge City is hard 'to take.' The pistol brigands find it in a 'warm berth'!"[1]

Bat made plenty of enemies among the hard customers who drifted into Dodge during these years, but he made some friends, too. He was especially sympathetic toward the smooth-faced youngsters who poured up the trail behind the Longhorns, riding into town bug-eyed with excitement. In 1879, Bat himself was only twenty-five years old, although he looked and acted much older. He was close enough in years to the teen-aged kids from Texas, who drank themselves stupid in the saloons and threw away several months' pay in a few minutes at the gambling tables, to understand their reckless exuberance. It had not been many years since he had made just as big a fool of himself by drinking and gambling away his wages over the hide bars of the buffalo ranges.

Jim Herron, later a well-known lawman in Oklahoma, was a youngster in Dodge City at this time, and in his reminiscences he related an incident that typified Bat's treatment of rambunctious cowboys:

Bat Masterson . . . was a splendid peace officer, never took it all too seriously, and when it looked like there would be real trouble he had what it took to stop it. He was a young man and seemed to get all the fun out of living that he could. Some of them boys were like that. . . .

I recall a little episode that took place at Dodge after my return from Ogallalie. It has no importance, but shows Bat's sense of fun. There was a bunch of cowboys standing on the board sidewalk on the north side of Front Street, a half-block from the station. They were drinking and talking fight, twelve or fifteen of them, and it made it difficult for women and others to pass along the street. The boys meant no harm to others, but were just boisterous like you get when you are drinking. . . .

On one of the porch roofs directly above the cowboys' heads there were two big oak water barrels filled to the top, to be used in case of fire in the hotel lobby below. There was a twenty-foot length of two-inch hose attached to each barrel, and a spigot to turn the water off and on to empty the barrel. All you needed to do if fire broke out below was uncoil the hose, drop it off the porch, turn the spigot on the barrel and you had a little water to fight the fire. There was no pressure, just gravity fall. . . .

Well, those rannies on the sidewalk were arguing and cussing and Bat, now above the hotel lobby, signaled me from a window to step up there. I went up the inside stairs and looked out the open window. Bat was on the porch, holding the hose end.

"Step out here and hold this hose," he told me. "I'm going to cool them woolies down a bit."

I stepped out and took the business end of the hose and uncoiled it so it reached the edge of the porch above them. Bat told me to wait until he was back down on the street and had given them a talk, then to open the spigot and pour the water on them from above. It looked like real fun to me, but I was afraid of the boys, and told him so.

"Leave them to me," he said, "They'll never blame you, for they know I'm in charge of the fire department."

Well, we broke up that meeting in a hurry, with them boys pouring stale water out of their hat brims, some pretending to drink it. I was scared and left through the back door, but when I came around to the front looking innocent-like they all slapped me on the back and told me how much they enjoyed the cool bath in such hot weather. That's the way the boys were, anything for a laugh.[2]

Bill Walker, another youngster who struck Dodge in those days, has left a salty recollection of the town and its sheriff:

We unloaded at Dodge City and . . . all started out to do the town, and say! It was some town. And by the way! Dodge City was a mighty good place to stay from! You might be welcome there if you could prove your intentions were good, and your heart pure — but if they caught you with your rope a-draggin' —

It was a plumb hair-triggered country, filled to the nozzle with hair-triggered gents, totin' hair-triggered side guns. A man walked soft and light in Dodge City, or he quit walking.

I must have let my rope drag a little. Before I knew it, I found myself in the jailhouse. There had been a shooting scrape in town, and a pair of men had been gunned down. I was a stranger, fresh from the cow country, so I was a natural suspect. I languished in the bastille till morning, when court opened.

And then I made the acquaintance of the biggest sheriff of the Middle West, the one — and only — Bat Masterson. Was I spooky! I had understood that the famous lawman had a heart as hard as a tombstone, and as cold as steel.

I soon learned different. He was the judge, jury, and a whole flock of witnesses, and he decided in my favor; he turned me loose!

All I can say of Bat Masterson is, that he was plumb white.[3]

It was inevitable, however, that Bat should incur the enmity of some of the cowboys who continually poured into Dodge. As a rule, visitors who set out to raise seven kinds of hell barely got started on the first kind before they were slapped into jail to spend the night before being fined in the morning. When such miscreants returned to their home ranges, they spread lurid tales of the lawmen who had clapped a tight lid on Dodge. They exaggerated out of all proportion the gunslinging records of Masterson, Earp, Bassett & Company in an effort to minimize the ignominy of their own arrests.

The name *Bat Masterson* particularly stuck in their craws, although in all likelihood a city police officer, not the Ford County sheriff, had been responsible for their punishment. *Bat*, however, conjured up visions of the legendary vampire, a night-prowling creature thirsting for blood and preying on the unwary. Bat Masterson was depicted as a swift-handed killer who cut down innocent, fun-loving cowboys on the slightest pretext. This description, spread by word of mouth through the cattle camps south of the Arkansas, was the basis for a great deal of the trash that was written about Bat in later years. Thus we find Cy Warman in 1898 writing

of a camp called Dodge City, as rough a community as ever flourished under any flag, [from whence came] a string of slaughterers headed by ''Bat'' Masterson, whose hands were red with the blood of no less than a score of his fellow-men. In justice to Masterson, the explanation should be made that he did most of his work in daylight, with the badge of a ''city marshal'' upon his unprotected breast, and that a good majority of these men deserved killing, but had been neglected by more timid officers of the law, wholly on account of their toughness, their familiarity with firearms, and an overweaning fondness for the taking off of city marshals.[4]

Another western historian wrote:

There were nights when the main street echoed with the roaring of firearms, but, by the force of his personality and by his remarkable ability at the quick draw, Bat Masterson subdued the rebels. It came about that of what killing was done he did his full share, which greatly diminished the death list.[5]

Other writers, sympathetic to the cause of the early Texas drovers, searched newspaper and court files in a vain effort to find substantiating evidence that Bat was a cold-blooded killer. Failing in that endeavor, they came up with an incident on the basis of which they painted Bat as an even worse villain by western standards. They branded him a coward.

Clay Allison, the sullen Wolf of
the Washita who, legend has it,
"treed" Dodge and made Bat
Masterson "hunt his hole."
Courtesy Denver Public
Library.

The cowboy hero who was supposed to have made Bat "hunt his
hole" was Clay Allison, the Wolf of the Washita; the time of the
incident: October, 1878; the authority who witnessed the proceedings: Charlie Siringo, cowpuncher, detective, writer. Here is
Siringo's story as he told it in *Riata and Spurs*:

About the first of October eight hundred fat steers were cut out of my
four herds and started for Dodge City, Kansas. . . . I secured permission
to . . . accompany them to Chicago. . . .

A 25-mile ride brought us to the toughest town on earth, Dodge City. It
was now daylight, and the first man on the main street was Cape
Willingham, who . . . gave us our first news of the great Indian outbreak. He told us of the many murders committed by the reds south of
Dodge City the day previous — one man was killed at Mead City, and
two others near the Crooked Creek store.

Riding up the main street Ferris and I saw twenty-five mounted
cowboys, holding rifles in their hands, and facing one of the half-dozen
saloons, adjoining each other, on that side of the street. In passing this

armed crowd one of them recognized me. Calling me by name he said: "Fall in line quick, h—l is going to pop in a few minutes."

We jerked our Winchester rifles from the scabbards and fell in line, like most any other fool cowboys would have done. In a moment Clay Allison, the man-killer, came out of one of the saloons holding a pistol in his hand. With him was Mr. McNulty, owner of the large Panhandle "Turkey-track" cattle outfit. Clay was hunting for some of the town policemen, or the city marshal, so as to wipe them off the face of the earth. His twenty-five cowboy friends had promised to help him clean up Dodge City.

After all the saloons had been searched, Mr. McNulty succeeded in getting Clay to bed at the Bob Wright Hotel. Then we all dispersed. Soon after, the city law officers began to crawl out of their hiding places, and appear on the street.[6]

That was the way Siringo remembered it. Notice that nowhere in the recital does the name *Bat Masterson* appear, nor is there reference to the sheriff of Ford County. Allison was stalking, according to Siringo, "some of the town policemen, or the city marshal." Since Charlie Siringo was the only eyewitness to the incident who left a record, his version is particularly significant.

Certain writers have embellished this bare account and have singled Bat out as an object of Texas scorn. Dane Coolidge, one of Allison's admirers, wrote:

Bat Masterson of Dodge City . . . had been reported for some time as giving out the word that Clay Allison had better stay away. Dodge at that time was the toughest town in the world, according to the boasts of its press agents; and more than one good Texan, while shooting up the town, had been downed by City Marshal Masterson [sic]. There was a general feeling against him, especially among the trail-herders who came up from southern Texas, and when Allison announced that he was going to clean up the town he did not lack for help.

Coolidge went on to describe the proceedings, adhering closely to Siringo's account. He repeated the latter's assertion that Allison had sworn to kill the first "city police officer" he found and added:

There is no doubt that he would have done so; but the officers, one and all, had retreated to their lairs. Including the famous Bat Masterson. He was a brave man and a good officer, but a dead City Marshal was of no value to cynical Dodge. So Clay Allison made good his boast that he would come to Dodge City and make every so-and-so hunt his hole.[7]

Owen P. White, who did much to build an aura of glamour about the memory of the infamous Wolf of the Washita, said of him:

Notwithstanding his quaint joviality and his trivial way of dealing with life, Clay Allison was a man of affairs. He owned a sizable ranch, grazed a goodly bunch of cattle thereon, and was the proprietor of a bank account which gave him an assured financial standing. Everybody respected him and everybody, who knew him, liked him. He was not a bully. He was merely a light hearted, entirely fearless individual who took full advantage of his recreational opportunities and enjoyed to the uttermost the gaudy pleasures of the West.

One of Allison's "gaudy pleasures" was, apparently, the gunning of frontier peace officers, and when, according to White, Bat Masterson let it be known that Allison was not welcome in Dodge, Allison put Bat and Dodge on his list of "recreational opportunities."

White continues:

Mr. Bat Masterson, around whose austere brow there hung a perpetual aureole of six-shooter smoke which was constantly green by admiring newspaper writers, was riding a close herd on the bellicose element in Dodge City.

Standing one day in his favorite saloon, and toying with his favorite brand of liquor, Mr. Masterson remarked to a stranger, who had spoken admiringly of the prowess of Clay Allison: "Huh, that flop eared cattle rustler'd better stay out of Dodge. Just let him come a'foolin' around here and I'll sure smoke him up so that his own folks won't know what end of him to put into which end of the coffin."

The stranger, as strangers have a way of doing, rode a hundred miles out of his way to tell Allison what Masterson had said. . . .

In White's version, therefore, Clay Allison rode to Dodge not to kill "some of the town policemen, or the city marshal," as Siringo stated, but expressly for the purpose of looking up Bat Masterson. "The marshal of Dodge City," said White, referring to Masterson, had angered Allison by "taking his name in vain."

White describes what happened when Allison arrived in Dodge:

Entering town from the West, Clay Allison began at the "First Chance" and travelled the entire length of the thoroughfare, clear through the "Last Chance." He went out of one saloon and into the next, missing none and in every one inquiring most particularly for Bat Masterson.

But Bat was nowhere to be found, and neither were any of his deputies. On that day, so far as Charlie Siringo could see, and Siringo was among those present, Dodge City was an unofficered town. From one end to the other its principal street belonged exclusively to Clay Allison. No man appeared wearing a star to say him nay, and no man was on hand to interfere with him in case he became violently exhilarated.

But of course Siringo, who has written one of the versions, could not see into the darkened interiors of every up-stairs room along the main street. Had he been able to do so he would have seen a sight in one of those rooms that would have stirred him either to much merriment, or much wrath — probably much wrath.

He would have seen the great Masterson — at least so says the Masterson press agent who wrote the other version — crouched down behind the window sill, stealthily peeping along the barrel of a buffalo gun whose muzzle protruded through a small hole in the curtain. Yes, that was where Masterson was! Through a peephole in a curtain this valiant official, who had boldly told the world what he would do to Allison if Allison ever showed up, was keeping Allison covered — but at *long range*! Nowhere in the bellicose history of the southwest has any hero ever lived up more fully to the old precept about discretion being the better part of valor. According to Siringo Masterson lived up to it all day. All day, while Allison searched diligently for him in his accustomed haunts, the brave officer sat in a room with the curtains drawn on himself and his whereabouts, and with a surreptitious bead drawn on the broad back of Mr. Allison whenever the latter appeared on the street.

When the day was done Mr. Clay Allison left Dodge City and thereafter no man was ever heard to speak lightly of him or his reputation.[8]

Alfred Henry Lewis was the ''Masterson press agent'' to whom White referred, and ''the other version'' of the Allison invasion was Lewis' fictional biography of Masterson, *The Sunset Trail*. In it Lewis described a visit to Dodge by the Wolf of the Washita and related at length how Bat covered the man killer with a buffalo gun from a window as Allison, in a drunken stupor, yodeled wildly in the street. Lewis repeated the yarn in a supposedly factual article about Bat published two years later. In this version, Bat and Allison met face to face later in the day, and Allison, considerably ''simmered,'' greeted Bat cordially and agreed to check his shooting irons.[9]

Some support for the Lewis recital appears in an account by Charles Willis Howe. John Howe, the writer's uncle, was a close personal friend of Allison, and he presumably related the following to his nephew:

When Bat Masterson was sheriff of Dodge, Clay Allison heard reports to the effect that the town had succumbed to law and order under Masterson's reign, and that gun-toting was not looked upon as an innocent amusement any more. Clay decided to find out for himself. To provide a suitable setting for his experiment, he began to drink all the hard liquor in town. Between drinks he announced loudly and vociferously that he was not going to stand for having his style cramped by the law, and that he intended to engage in his favorite pastime of riding down the street with a sixshooter in each hand, shooting out windows as he went by, defying anyone to stop him. Walking finally out of the saloon, he came face to face with the sheriff. Clay Allison said, "Good morning, Bat," mounted his horse and headed back to the range.[10]

Pink Simms, an old-timer of the cattle trails who knew both Clay Allison and Charlie Siringo personally, said in 1935 that he had heard the story of Allison's invasion of Dodge from Siringo and others. It was his recollection that Clay had been aroused by the Dodge City officers' shooting of young George Hoy in July. Hoy, said Simms, had worked for or had been a friend of Allison. Simms said in a letter to Floyd B. Streeter:

It was my understanding that Allison wanted to register a protest at the needless killing, and that Bat Masterson, knowing that Allison was drinking, thought it best to avoid a meeting until he was sober. I also heard that he did meet Bat afterward and had a talk with him, and some say that he threatened to kill Earp. I do not think that he was looking for the Dodge City officers with the intention of starting a fight, though Siringo said he carried a pistol in his hand.[11]

With all this tangled assortment of tales, speculations, and acknowledged fictions concerning Allison's visit, an examination of extant records definitely is in order. Some sense can be made of the whole confused story simply by checking Siringo's account against contemporary news items in the *Dodge City Times* and the *Ford County Globe*.

One glaring error stands out in the Allison admirers' indictment of Bat Masterson: In 1878, Bat was not a town policeman or the city marshal, the officials specifically named by eyewitness Siringo as Clay's quarry. Moreover, it was not Bat's responsibility, as Ford County sheriff, to corral drunks and gunpackers on Front Street. Further, if Allison was angered by the killing of his friend Hoy, as Pink Simms alleged, he certainly would wish to vent his rage on the man who had gunned the young cowboy. Assistant Marshal Wyatt Earp, as we have seen, claimed responsibility for shooting Hoy. Indeed, Simms was told that Allison "threatened to kill Earp."

Where was Wyatt Earp on that particular morning? Where were the other Dodge City officers? And where was Bat Masterson?

In order to answer these questions, a very important fact must be pointed out. Clay Allison made at least two trips to Dodge in the late summer of '78. The first of his visits was noted in the August 6 issue of the *Ford County Globe*: "Clay Allison, one of the Allison brothers, from the Cimarron, south of Las Animas, Colorado, stopped off at Dodge last week on his way home from St. Louis. We are glad to say that Clay has about recovered from the effects of the East St. Louis scrimmage." There is no mention of misbehavior by Allison, just a simple little social note to recognize a distinguished visitor, but the date is important. Clay was in Dodge a week after George Hoy was shot. He must have heard of the gunplay at this time, and if, as Pink Simms believed, he was friendly with Hoy, he must have visited the stricken cowboy, who, it will be remembered, lingered for a month after the shooting. Allison may well have protested what he considered unnecessary gunplay by the Dodge officers. It is quite possible that he met and talked with Wyatt Earp, but if he wished to take the matter up with Bat Masterson, he may have been disappointed. On August 1, Bat left for Arkansas. "Sheriff Masterson, who has not had good health during the late hot weather, having at times been confined to his bed with attacks of something like vertigo, started last Thursday morning for a visit to Hot Springs, Arkansas, where he will remain three or four weeks," reported the *Times* on August 3. "We hope he will have a pleasant time and return restored to perfect health." Bat evidently recovered quickly at the Arkansas spa, for he was back in Dodge in less than two weeks.

Charlie Siringo, the cowboy whose account of a visit to Dodge was the basis for the Allison-Masterson tale. Courtesy Denver Public Library.

Charlie Siringo is responsible for much of the confusion that has surrounded Allison's second trip to Dodge. Siringo said he started for Dodge with a herd "about the first of October," and, although he sets no date for Allison's treeing of the cow capital, later writers have assumed that it occurred sometime during the first or second week of that month. The date has been established, however, and by none other than Charlie Siringo himself. Siringo remembered meeting Cape Willingham that morning and receiving his "first news of the great Indian outbreak." The uprising Cape spoke of was the Dull Knife Raid, the last great Indian scare for the settlers of western Kansas.

On September 9, 1878, some three hundred Northern Cheyennes under Chief Dull Knife broke out of their reservation in the Indian Nations and headed north toward their traditional native hunting grounds in the Big Horn Mountains. Unconfirmed reports of the Indians' passage had trickled into Dodge for several days, and the cow camp stirred uneasily. Their reported route would bring them within a few miles of town, and the old plainsmen of

Dodge knew that bands of marauding braves would be prowling for miles on either flank of the main body.

On September 16, one such war party struck at Meade City, a small settlement south of Dodge on Crooked Creek. Washington O'Connor, a mail carrier who was approaching the village by wagon from Dodge, was attacked and killed. Another band ransacked the Chapman and Tuttle ranch eighteen miles from Dodge. When word of these depredations reached town, a mass meeting was called. Guns and ammunition were distributed, and Dodge prepared to fight. Texas cowboys holding herds for shipment on the surrounding grasslands rallied to the call to arms. Kansan and Texan stood side by side, ready to fight the common enemy, the Indian.

At the time, only nineteen soldiers were stationed at Fort Dodge. A company of civilian volunteers from town was speedily organized to bolster the military force; reinforcements of cavalry and mounted infantry were dispatched from Fort Leavenworth to Fort Wallace. A command under Colonel William H. Lewis was in close pursuit of the renegades. Lewis sent an urgent call to Dodge for experienced scouts. Several former plainsmen responded, including Bill Tilghman and Josh Webb. The *Times* edition of September 21 describes the scene:

There has been great excitement all week over the news brought in almost hourly of murder and depredations by the straggling bands of Northern Cheyenne Indians.

Wednesday the excitement was at its highest pitch in Dodge City. The frequent arrival of couriers and messengers from off the plains, bringing accounts of the Cheyenne murder and stealing, threw the people of Dodge City into the wildest tremor, when it was reported that the Indians were seen within a few miles of the city. The ringing of the fire bell at 2 o'clock, calling upon the people to assemble at the engine house, added zest to the already highly inflamed patriot heart. . . .

At this time flames were seen issuing from the house of Harrison Berry, on an island 4 miles west of this city. It was at once rumored that the Indians had fired the house.

A locomotive loaded with civilians was at once despatched to the scene of conflagration. . . . P. L. Beatty, Chalk Beeson, Wyatt Earp and S. E. Isaacson were principals in extinguishing the flames. . . .

A large party from Dodge carried by an engine and car as far as

Cimarron, returning in the evening, but no Indians were seen along the line of the road. . . .

The party that left Dodge City Tuesday night, on Wednesday with a company of soldiers had a skirmish lasting an hour with the Indians. . . . This occurred 35 miles south of Dodge.

This was when Charlie Siringo rode into Dodge; he struck town the third week of September, not, as he said, in October. Said Charlie: "Cape . . . told of the many murders committed by the reds south of Dodge City the day previous — one man being killed at Mead City, and two others near the Crooked Creek store." Therefore, Siringo must have witnessed Allison's invasion either on the morning of Tuesday, September 17, the day after the Indians struck at Crooked Creek, or, more likely, on Wednesday, the eighteenth, the day after the people at Dodge heard of the Crooked Creek raid.

With the entire town in an uproar over the Indian scare, Clay Allison, soaked to the gills, chose this time to go officer hunting. Even drunk he could not possibly have been unaware of the tension that gripped the town. A special edition of the *Times*, printed on the seventeenth, and three telegrams dispatched from Dodge to the governor of Kansas on the eighteenth reflect the alarm of the citizenry. The telegrams pleaded for arms and ammunition to defend the town and were signed by Mayor Kelley and businessmen C. W. Willett, H. E. Gryden, D. Sheedy, H. Shinn, R. W. Evans, T. L. McCarty and J. C. Connor.

The Ford County sheriff's signature does not appear on any of these pleas for help, nor does his name appear in the *Times*'s list of civilian volunteers who rushed to the aid of the army, for during all the Indian excitement, Bat was out of town. As reported in the *Globe* of September 24, he had spent the previous week in Kansas City with other Dodge City notables: Ab Webster, Bill Harris, A. J. Anthony, Bob Wright, and Charlie Bassett.

And so it was that Clay Allison, the Wolf of the Washita, and his twenty-five Winchester-packing backers were perfectly safe that bright September morning. As Owen P. White stated, Dodge City was an unofficered town: "From one end to the other its principal street belonged exclusively to Clay Allison. No man appeared wearing a star to say him nay." With Bat Masterson and Charlie

Bassett in Kansas City and the other officers involved in the biggest excitement to hit Dodge in years, there was simply no one around to play games with Allison.

Another chapter in western mythology sprang from this incident, one that has become known as "The Day That Clay Allison Made Bat Masterson Hunt His Hole." It undoubtedly will survive in the legend of the West simply because, once it has grown, a myth is hard to kill, but for those who prefer their history to be factual rather than fallacious, the chapter should be retitled "The Day That Dull Knife Stole the Show From Clay Allison."

Bat was not in Dodge during the Indian excitement of 1878, but he became involved with the remnants of the band several months later when it was decided to try the surviving leaders in the civil courts as criminals. In November, Kansas Governor G. T. Anthony wrote to the secretary of war, asking that "the principal chiefs, 'Dull Knife,' 'Old Crow,' 'Hog,' 'Little Wolf,' and others" be turned over to civil authorities for trial "as participants in the crimes of murder and woman ravishing."[12] In December, the U.S. Army's Major General John Pope replied that he had been instructed to surrender the Cheyenne prisoners to the Kansas civil authorities and that "persons as may be needed for the identification of the criminals" be sent to Fort Leavenworth when transfer of the prisoners was made from Nebraska, where they were being held. Early in February, 1879, this transfer was completed, and John P. St. John, the new governor of Kansas, wired Ford County Attorney Mike Sutton at Dodge that the prisoners would be made available by the army upon identification.

Accompanied by Deputies Charlie Bassett, Jim Masterson, A. J. French, and Kokomo Sullivan, Bat went first to Topeka, where, on February 12, the sheriff handed Governor St. John Mike Sutton's letter introducing the party. The governor arranged train passes for the journey to Fort Leavenworth. On February 15, custodial transfer was made at the depot in Leavenworth, Lieutenant Pardee of the Twenty-third Infantry turning over seven Indians to the Ford County sheriff. There was a large crowd that was anxious to get a look at the seven "dusky demons," as the Cheyenne prisoners were described by the *Leavenworth Times*. The prisoners' names were listed as Wild Hog, Old Crow, Big

The seven Cheyenne survivors of the Dull Knife raid, who were taken from
Leavenworth to Dodge City by Sheriff Masterson to stand trial. Seated with them
on the steps of the Ford County courthouse are interpreter George Raynolds and
bearded F. C. Adams. Courtesy Kansas State Historical Society.

Head, Left Hand, Blacksmith, Porcupine, and Nosey-Walker.
   Bat put his prisoners, handcuffed and shackled, on the train and
started back to Dodge. Word of their approach preceded them, and
all along the line throngs of people turned out to see the captured
Cheyenne warriors. "At every station a mob of hoodlums assembled and made such demonstrations in their eagerness to see the
Indians that Sheriff Masterson was compelled to use physical
means in preventing his pets from being trampled upon."[13] At

Lawrence, particularly, there was a serious disturbance, during which Bat tangled with the city marshal and was himself arrested. "Sheriff Masterson says that at Lawrence he had much trouble, and was obliged finally to fight his way," reported the *Topeka Commonwealth*. "The first man he struck happened to be the City Marshal, who retaliated by taking Batt in charge. Explanations followed, and matters rightened."[14]

The Dodge City papers recounted this incident a little differently. Said the *Ford County Globe*:

At Lawrence the mob was almost overpowering, and our officers were involved in a fight which resulted in victory for Dodge City, as usual. The Mayor, City Marshal and a large portion of the able bodied braves of Lawrence undertook to capture Masterson and his outfit, but were repulsed in a very neat and workmanlike manner.[15]

At Topeka, a crowd estimated at one thousand persons met the train. The prisoners were taken by bus to the Shawnee County jail, where they were held overnight. It was thought that the Indians, if given an opportunity, might attempt suicide (Wild Hog still had not recovered fully from a self-inflicted stab wound he suffered while in the army's custody), so at the jail they were not permitted the use of eating utensils and had to "convey the fare . . . to their mouths with their dirty fingers."[16]

On February 16, the party of officers and prisoners proceeded west on the Santa Fe, encountering curious crowds along the way. "At every station, and far into the night, great crowds congregated at the depots, all eager to get a glimpse of the gentle savage," reported the *Dodge City Times*. "This was extremely embarrassing and annoying, and gave the party much trouble. The Indian took it, no doubt, as a great ovation for him."[17]

On the morning of the seventeenth, the party arrived in Dodge City and the *Times* reported proudly:

There was no demonstration in Dodge City . . . though their arrival was duly heralded. A solitary policeman . . . was the only person who welcomed the gentle savage. . . . The prisoners were taken from the cars quietly and noiselessly, and thence to quarters in the jail, where they now remain.[18]

Bat neglected to return the shackles used on the Indians during

Dodge City Kansas
Feb 20th 1879

P. S. Noble Esq
Topeka Kansas

Friend Noble
I am in receipt of your letter
this Morning and I am sorry
I was so dilatory in sending back
the Hand cuffs and leg Irons
however I have Expressed them
to your address day in a hope
you will receive them all right.
the Indians are all well and in
good spirits but want their Squaws
and papooses. Which I am in hopes
they May get

I am very respectfully
W. B. Masterson
Sheriff Ford Co.

Letter from Sheriff Masterson to Kansas Adjutant General P. S. Noble apologizing for being "dilatory" in returning the shackles used in bringing the Indian prisoners to Dodge. Courtesy Denver Public Library.

the trip from Leavenworth and had to be reminded by Adjutant General P. S. Noble that they were the property of the state of Kansas. On February 20, Bat wrote an apologetic letter addressed to Friend Noble:

I am in receipt of your letter this morning and I am sorry I was so dilatory in sending back the hand cuffs and leg irons, however I have expressed them to your address [to]day and hope you will receive them all right. The Indians are all well and in good spirits but want their squaws and papooses, which I am in hopes they may get.[19]

The seven Cheyenne prisoners were held in the Ford County jail for more than four months. Their preliminary examination was held in Dodge, but a change of venue was granted for their trial. In June, Bat was directed by Governor St. John to take the prisoners to Lawrence by train. The following October, the case was dismissed for lack of evidence.

Bat sued Ford County for several thousand dollars, claiming expenses incurred in the Cheyennes' transfer to and from Dodge City and their care while in his custody. When the Indians were released, the *Ford County Globe* snorted:

Just think of Ford county having to pay $4000 for the simple arrest of seven lousy Cheyenne Indians and that without even an effort to convict them. . . .

Masterson and Sutton made it hot for the Nations Wards whom they so cunningly conspired against, and brought to Ford County for the people to look at. They now desire to make it hot for the poor tax payers of the county, by getting them to pay the bills incurred in their innocent amusement. The Governor has gone back on them. He hasn't any funds on hand to give them so they have to fall back on the dear people of Ford county.[20]

Bat received some, if not all, of this money from the county. The *Spearville News*, which opposed Bat in his bid for reelection in the fall of 1879, reported in its issue of October 25 that "Mr. Masterson has already received about three hundred dollars on the Cheyenne Indian account, and he and some others have instituted suit against Ford county for twenty-one hundred dollars more." On January 5, 1880, the Board of County Commissioners awarded more than one thousand dollars to Bat against his Cheyenne Indian bills.

CHAPTER THIRTEEN

A NEW VOCATION

The 1879 shipping season had passed rather quietly, but the sports of Dodge livened things up a bit on September 5 in what the *Ford County Globe* called "A Day of Carnival." It began when

a slender young man of handsome external appearance . . . regaled his friends with a pail of water. The water racket was kept up until it merged into the slop racket, then the potato and cucumber racket, and finally the rotten egg racket, with all its magnificent odors. This was continued until the faces, eyes, noses, mouths and shirt bosoms of several of the boys were comfortably filled with the juicy substance of the choicest rotten eggs, compelling them to retire from the field, which they did in a very warlike manner. As the evening shades began to appear the skirmishers were soon actively engaged, and at a little before the usual hour slugging commenced all along the line. One or two "gun plays" were made, but by reason of lack of execution, were not effective. . . .

Upon the sidewalks ran streams of the blood of brave men, and the dead and wounded wrestled with each other like butchered whales on harpooning day. The "finest work" and neatest polishes were said to have been executed by Mr. Wyatt Earp. . . .

. . . It was not until towards morning that the smoke cleared away, the din of battle subsided and the bibulous city found a little repose. . . .[1]

More blood nearly flowed the very next night, if we are to believe a strange little story George Hinkle related to his son Milt. George, it will be remembered, briefly challenged Bat in his campaign for Ford County sheriff in 1877 and later threw his support to Larry Deger. In September, 1879, Hinkle was tending bar in Hoover's Saloon. On the night of September 6, as Hinkle later told it, Masterson entered Hoover's "looking for trouble and stirred up a ruckus at one of the card tables." Hinkle walked around the bar, grabbed the sheriff in his big hands and gave him the bum's rush. Masterson is said to have dusted himself off and strolled into the Long Branch next door, where he laughed off the episode as a joke.

The following night, one of Hinkle's friends ran into Hoover's with the news that Masterson and Wyatt Earp had their heads together in the Long Branch and were cooking up something. Earp was going to call on Hinkle that evening. "Yes, I have been expecting this and I am ready," Hinkle remarked coolly. Reaching under the bar, he picked up his iron, "a .44-40 with the trigger guard filed off, leaving the trigger unprotected." Easing the hammer back, he laid the six-gun on the bar, the barrel pointed forward. His right hand rested near the butt.

Sure enough, a few minutes later, in came Wyatt. He stopped short when he saw Hinkle's steely gaze and the gun on the bar.

"Wyatt, I know why you came in here and I know what your guns are tied down for," said Hinkle. "Here is my gun on the bar, so it would be best for both of us for you to leave right now the way you came in."

Wyatt sized up the situation quickly, then nodded agreement. "George, you win this time," he said. "If I had not been in the wrong, I would be the winner."

"I can still hear my dad telling the end of that tale," Milt Hinkle wrote in 1961. " 'Son, to my surprise, and was I glad, Wyatt backed out of the swinging doors of the Hoover Saloon that night and not only I but everyone took a big, long, deep breath. Son, I tell you I was in a big strain, and you know seven was always my lucky number.' It was September 7." The next day, according to Milt Hinkle, Wyatt Earp went to Mayor Dog Kelley and resigned as assistant city marshal. "On September 9, 1879, Wyatt Earp boarded a train for Tombstone by way of Kansas City."[2]

This story of Hinkle's is suspect for several reasons. The emphasis on the exact dates lends an air of verisimilitude to the tale, but a look at contemporary records casts doubt.

The *Ford County Globe* edition that was published on September 9 — the same day Hinkle said Wyatt left for Arizona — carried this single line: "Mr. Wyatt Earp, who has been on our police force for several months, resigned his position *last week* [italics supplied] and took his departure for Las Vegas, New Mexico." The discrepancy in dates, as well as destinations, is very clear. A month later, on October 7, the city council authorized payment of $13.32 to Wyatt Earp for four days' service in September. This would indicate that Wyatt resigned on Thursday, September 4, participated in the so-called carnival as a private citizen on Friday, the fifth, and left the city on Saturday, September 6, the day before his alleged staredown with Hinkle on the bartender's "lucky seventh."

We are asked to believe that George Hinkle bulldozed, on successive nights, Bat Masterson, sheriff of Ford County, and Wyatt Earp, assistant city marshal, with no help but that afforded by a mutilated six-gun. And yet, as we shall see, less than four years later, this same George Hinkle, now Ford County sheriff himself, will be thrown into a panic by the report that these same two men, no longer lawmen, are coming to Dodge on behalf of their friend Luke Short, who has been run out of town. Hinkle will organize a shotgun brigade of fifty men to watch all arriving trains and in desperation will wire the governor of Kansas for two companies of militia to preserve order.

George Hinkle was thirty-four years old in 1879. He at various times had been a cowboy, scout, soldier, hide and bone buyer, prizefighter, wrestler, railroad worker, blacksmith, teamster, and bartender. He served four years as chief law officer of turbulent Ford County. He did not lack sand, and he must have had many exciting experiences, but it appears that, to impress his young son, he concocted a story that had him running over Bat Masterson and Wyatt Earp, the most well known of Dodge's gunmen.

Before he left Dodge, Wyatt Earp told Bat that he was finished with the risky life of a frontier police officer. He intended to go into business with his brothers in Arizona. Virgil Earp had established himself with mining interests in the new boom camp of Tombstone, brother Jim wanted to open a stage depot and corral there, and Wyatt and Morgan planned to run a stage line that would link the town and the railroad. The talk was that Tombstone squatted on a mountain of silver, Wyatt said, and didn't Bat want to get in on the boom early? Bat replied that his job as sheriff would keep him in Dodge until the end of the year, and he expected to run for another two-year term. The two friends shook hands and said their farewells, but they were destined to ride together again before many months had passed.

On September 16, there appeared in the *Ford County Globe* a small item heralding the approaching election. A letter to the editor, signed "Subscriber," asked, "Will you be kind enough to let the farmers of the east end of Ford county know through the columns of your paper who the candidates are that are seeking the office of Sheriff this fall, besides Masterson? We have enough of the Masterson rule." Replied the editor: "For the information of our subscriber, we will say that as yet we have heard the name of but one man mentioned, aside from the present sheriff, and that is George T. Hinkle, of this city, who would make an excellent officer. He is not seeking the office, but would certainly make a strong candidate."

The *Dodge City Times* of September 20 carried a letter, signed by W. H. LyBrand, which defended Masterson, claiming that "diligent inquiries among farmers and settlers in this neighborhood have thoroughly convinced us that W. B. Masterson is beyond doubt their choice for the office. . . . Outside of a few soreheads, only the friends of evil-doers desire the election of a man who will as Sheriff be less dangerous to them and their associates."

The Ford County convention of the Independent party was held in Dodge City on October 18, and Masterson was duly nominated to run for reelection. The selection was lauded by Nick Klaine's *Times*, of course:

> Bat is acknowledged to be the best Sheriff in Kansas. He is the most successful officer in the State. He is immensely popular and generally well-liked. Horse thieves have a terror for the name of Masterson. He was the unanimous choice of the convention, and will be elected by a heavy majority. Every hater of horse thieves will rejoice over Bat's triumphant election; and the friends of good order and peace will contribute to his success."[3]

Candidate for sheriff on the People's Ticket was the man recommended by the *Globe*, George Hinkle. As election day drew near it became evident that Klaine's optimistic appraisal of Bat's prospects may have been a bit premature. Hinkle's backers began to spread rumors that Bat had been lavish with the taxpayers' money while in office. The word *fraud* was bandied about, and Bat's enemies began to whisper that he had been gambling with county funds. Bat did not bother to deny these charges, relying on his backers to answer the ugly talk.

Editors Dan Frost of the *Globe* and R. B. Fry of the *Speareville News*, however, made thinly veiled references to the circulating rumors, and although no one apparently had evidence or nerve enough to make specific charges against Masterson, the talk continued. Fry, in particular, bitterly attacked Bat in his paper, calling him "The Little Bull." On November 1, four days before election, he published an article stating that Bat had threatened him because of his opposition, saying, according to Fry, "I am going to make this a personal matter and follow you up and if I hear you saying any thing more about me I will shoot you through the g-ts, and when I come, you be prepared." Fry added that for lack of space and respect for his readers he had omitted Bat's obscenities.

Fry contended that he would never support "a man for an official position the second time, that during that time, has been a law breaker himself." He did not elaborate on this charge, but he did include an allegation that Masterson had charged a man named Stevenson for the return of a stolen horse. Stevenson himself put to rest this particular story in a letter printed in the *Dodge City Times* on the same day:

> I desire to inform the people of Ford County that all parties circulating the report that Bat Masterson charged me $25 or any other amount, for the finding and return of my stolen pony last fall, is telling an unmitigated falsehood as was ever uttered by any evilminded persons. My transactions with Mr. Masterson have always been perfectly satisfactory. I expect to vote for him and work for his election.

As is attested by Bat's reaction to Fry's allegations, he had become painfully aware of the type of campaign being waged against him. Election day came closer and Klaine made no effort to defend him, except for a weak note to the effect that "Bat Masterson is Sheriff of thirteen unorganized counties. Of course it costs something to run so much territory."[4] Bat protested to Mike Sutton and Klaine, saying he wanted to deny the allegations in

public print, but both Sutton and Klaine cautioned against it.
Ignore the talk, they advised; the voters knew better than to believe
that type of underhanded slander. Bat was no politician, and he
knew it. He trusted Klaine and Sutton and bowed to what he
considered their superior political acumen.

His decision turned out to be a grievous mistake. At the election
on November 4, the entire Independent slate was defeated. George
Hinkle carried all six of the county's voting districts and defeated
Masterson decisively, 404 to 268. Editor Klaine commented sour-
ly in the *Times*: "There is a good deal of speculation as to the cause
of the late defeat of the Independent ticket. . . . We conjecture the
most powerful influence was in the beer keg; and of course people
fighting for honesty and reform wouldn't use money."[5]

Bat was fuming. He thought the election results demonstrated
that most of the voters had believed the rumors that he was
crooked, and he took the whole affair as a personal affront. He was
angry with Sutton and Klaine for giving him what he considered to
be the worst sort of political advice, but he was especially enraged
at those who had spread the slime upon which he had slipped. Dan
Frost of the *Globe* and Bob Fry of the *Speareville News* were the
principal objects of his wrath.

"We hear that Bat. Masterson said he was going to whip every
s — of a b —— that worked and voted against him in the county,"
Fry wrote a few days after the election. He went on to say that "two
or three citizens" already had been "fearfully beaten" by Bat or
his friends, and asked: "If the above reports are true, how long will
the citizens of Ford County permit this to go on?" As an example
of Bat's alleged bullying tactics, Fry included a statement from one
Charles Roden:

Being in Dodge City on a visit in company with some ladies, and while
walking down Main street and in front of Col. Jones office. Mr. Jones
called me in to have a little talk. When all at once Sheriff Masterson came
in, stepping in front of me and said: "You have been doing some good
work down in the East end," and before I had time to reply, he struck me
several times; after I got out on the street, some official, I believe it was
the sheriffs brother, searched my pockets, he said to see if I had any
pistol, but did not find any. When I got ready to go home I felt in my
pocket for my pocket-book to pay my bills and found it gone. I would

advise every person from the East-end, that voted the Peoples' ticket to be on their guard.[6]

T. S. Jones, the Dodge City attorney in whose office the alleged beating took place, fired off a letter that appeared in the next edition of the *News*. According to Jones, Roden had stretched the truth more than a little in his recital of the incident, and his "incorrect report" contained statements "untrue and unjust."

According to Jones, Masterson confronted Roden in the lawyer's office and accused him of spreading lies about him before the election. The two men then "assumed the attitude of belligerents" and Roden reached for a rear pocket," evidently for the purpose of intimidating Masterson and making him believe he intended something more serious. Masterson immediately siezing him by the hand dealt him several severe blows, saying at the same time 'pull it, if you can.' Roden finally made an unceremonious exit from the scene of strife into the street." Jones acknowledged that fighting was to be deprecated but asserted that in this case Masterson had administered a "merited rebuke."[7] Jones's letter "puts a different feature on the case," Fry acknowledged, but nothing hinting of an apology to Bat was added.

Charles Roden's credibility was destroyed when, later that same month, he was arrested for thievery in Speareville; loot from several robberies had been discovered in his house. Roden posted bond but immediately skipped out, shaking the dust of Ford County from his boots forever.

Meanwhile, Bat Masterson was not letting Bob Fry go unchallenged. The November 15 issue of the *Times* carried a letter Bat wrote with a pen dipped in pure venom:

In answer to the publication made by Bob Fry of the Speareville News, asserting that I had made threats that I would lick any s — of a b —— that voted or worked against me at the last election, I will say it is as false and as flagrant a lie as was ever uttered; but I did say this: that I would lick him the s — of a b —— if he made any more dirty talk about me; and the words s — of a b —— I strictly confined to the Speareville editor, for I don't know of any other in Ford county.

It is fortunate that Bat and Fry did not meet face to face during these hectic days, for Fry, well aware that Bat was always prepared to back up his words with action, armed himself. An item in the *Times* later in the month made note of that fact, and Nick Klaine added a word of advice for his journalistic colleague: "Bob Fry, of the Speareville News, exhibited to the Hon. Nelson Adams, while on the train going west the other evening, a self-cocking pistol, that he was carrying for Sheriff Masterson. Better hitch yourself to a cannon, Bob."[8]

A week later, Bat turned on his other journalistic critic, Dan Frost of the *Globe*. Acting in his capacity as deputy U.S. marshal, Bat arrested Frost on a charge of receiving stolen government property. The complaint was sworn to and signed by W. B. Masterson, the arresting officer. It alleged that more than a year earlier, Frost had taken some government stores from Sergeant Joe Evarts of the Fort Elliott, Texas, quartermasters and that Frost had received said goods with the knowledge that Evarts had stolen them. Masterson took Frost before U.S. Commissioner R. G. Cook, who released the newspaperman under five thousand dollars' bond. In recounting the story, Frost's paper declared that "the affair is liable to cause Mr. Frost considerable trouble and expense, but his vast fortune will be poured out like water from the clouds to secure his vindication."[9] Frost was indicted by a grand jury, but after a petition — signed by many prominent Dodge City businessmen and requesting dismissal of the charges — was presented to the U.S. attorney general, the case apparently was dropped.

In December, the basis for the recurring rumors of fraud in the sheriff's office was uncovered. County Clerk John B. Means confessed to forging scrip in favor of Sheriff Masterson against the county for the conveyance of prisoners to the state penitentiary. Although the disclosure of Means's dishonesty may have cleared doubts about Bat in the minds of many, Bat himself was far from placated.

Mike Sutton and Nick Klaine kept up a pretense of friendship with Masterson for a time, but as far as Bat was concerned, friendship had ended with the counting of the election ballots. It was many years before he forgave his mentors for their poor advice. The damage to his name had been more galling to him than the loss of the election. For two years he had worked tirelessly at a demanding and very dangerous job, and he felt that his defeat was a personal rebuff by an ungrateful electorate. He was convinced, however, that had he made a frank and forthright denial of the charges going the rounds before the election, the voters would have believed him and the result would have been far different. There is no doubt that he was recalling the year 1879 when he wrote forty-two years later, only five days before his death:

> Those Kansas politicans are the limit . . . when it comes to finessing and sidestepping an issue that they suspect might have something lurking about it that would give them a political setback if they met it fairly and squarely and lost out. That's why there are so many political nondescripts found in and out of office in the Sunflower State.
>
> Kansas politicians will perhaps turn up a sneering nose at these remarks and say to hades with him. Nevertheless I had a hand in Kansas politics before many of those now ruling the roost were known, and I haven't forgotten what I then learned of the game in the land of the Kaw River.[10]

In January, 1880, Bat took two prisoners to the Leavenworth prison, his last official act as sheriff of Ford County. On January 12, he gave his badge to George Hinkle, relinquishing at this time also his commission as a deputy U.S. marshal.

Some of Bat's friends had deserted him when he needed them, but a few of the real old-timers never failed to speak up for him when his integrity was questioned. Wrote Bob Wright in 1913:

> Notwithstanding they have talked and published Bat as a robber and murderer and everything else that is vile, there is nothing of the kind in his make-up. He is a leader of men and a natural born general, always accomplishing whatever he undertook. This is the reason he was sought after by the ''gang'' and recognized as their general. He has much natural ability and good hard common sense, and, if he had got started right, Bat, today, would have been occupying a seat in the United States Senate, instead of being a reporter for a newspaper. There is nothing low about him. He is high-toned and broad-minded, cool and brave.[11]

The ''gang'' mentioned by Wright was the saloon and sporting crowd. There is in this reference an inkling of another reason for Bat's defeat in his bid for reelection. Living in Ford County were many respectable people — businessmen, merchants, farmers, and ranchers — who liked Bat personally but objected to some of his friends. They found it difficult to understand how a man sworn to uphold the law could be on close terms with known outlaws and killers, men like the Thompson brothers. They did not hold with Bat's belief that a man should not be bothered as long as he behaved himself. There were in Ford County men who could remember how Bill Thompson had gunned down Sheriff Whitney in Ellsworth and how Ben Thompson had hurrahed the town to cover his brother's escape. They did not like their sheriff's hobnobbing with this pair of Texas desperadoes.

Actually, Bat never did like Bill Thompson, but he was seen with him frequently because Bill stuck close to his older brother; Bat did have a close bond of friendship with Ben. Doc Holliday frequently was observed in Bat's company and was cited as an unworthy companion for the foremost representative of law and order in the community. In reality, Bat disliked Holliday and shunned him when possible. He tolerated him only because of his admiration for Wyatt Earp, Doc's friend and benefactor.

There was a curious relationship between lawmen and desperadoes in Dodge, one cemented by interlocking ties of loyalty and respect. The irony of the situation was illustrated later when Bat, acting out of friendship for Ben Thompson and Wyatt Earp, saved the lives of two men he disliked: Bill Thompson and Doc Holliday.

In January, 1880, Bat was twenty-six years old. He had been kicking around on the frontier for eight years and had developed skills as a buffalo hunter, Indian scout, and peace officer. During those eight years, however, a great change had taken place in the plains country he knew. By 1880, the buffalo were gone from Kansas and the Texas Panhandle. A few good herds still roamed Montana Territory, but Bat knew their slaughter was imminent. The halcyon days of the hide hunter were over, never to return. The Plains Indians were a defeated race and did not pose a threat to the white man's westward expansion. Consequently, the services of government scouts were no longer in demand. It seemed to Bat as if the frontier that had trained him had changed so drastically and quickly that at twenty-six he was already an anachronism.

Bat had learned one other skill, however, to which he now could turn for a livelihood; he was a gambler, and a good one. Dodge

City had entertained some of the most successful high rollers on the circuit in the hectic years '78 and '79. Bat had played beside these men often and occasionally had played opposite them when, as a special favor to a friend, he took a turn dealing for the house. Whether he sat on the outside or the inside, as bucking the bank or protecting it were called, respectively, he had always managed to play a good, even game. Western gamblers in the late 1870's and early 1880's were not looked upon as necessarily belonging to an underworld society. On the contrary, gambling, as Bat pointed out in writing of Dodge, "was not only the principal and best-paying industry of the town, but was considered among the most respectable." So, in February, after winding up his affairs in Dodge, Bat set out on the gambling trail.

By now two new camps had preempted Dodge's claim as Mistress of the Gamblers. Tombstone, Arizona, where Wyatt Earp had gone several months earlier, was one major port of call for the border sports. The other was the new silver camp of Leadville, Colorado, that blossoming flower for the nectar of which the Santa Fe and Rio Grande railroads had battled in 1879. Bat had been there, of course, and knew many of his friends to be there, so that was his first destination.

Leadville in 1880 was a sporting man's delight. With regard to the number of gambling games running and the stakes involved, Dodge seemed tame in comparison. Even Cheyenne at the time of the Deadwood rush did not match Leadville for a town gone gambling crazy. There was a game for every taste. Houses ranged from hastily constructed lean-tos to glittering temples of chance and featured layouts for rondo, *vingt-et-un*, poker, casino, keno, California Jack, euchre, chuck-a-luck, rouge et noir, lansquenet, and paddle wheel. But faro was king in Leadville, as it was in most western camps. Betting limits in Dodge City faro spreads had rarely been raised beyond twenty-five dollars a card; in Leadville were banks that set no limit, and bets of one thousand dollars or five thousand dollars on the turn of a card were common.

Bat visited the California Concert Hall, operated by Jeff Winney, where Kitty Crawhurst, one of the first and best of the lady gamblers, presided over a faro table; the Board of Trade Saloon, specializing in stud poker; and the Texas House, run by Bailey

Youngston and little Con Featherly, a shrewd pair of Galveston gamblers. Genial, soft-spoken John Pentland was the chief dealer at the Texas House; it was said that he won eighty thousand dollars for the house during the first few months of its existence.

All of these kingpins of Colorado gambling knew Masterson either personally or by reputation. They welcomed him to Leadville effusively and plied him with offers of jobs. Men with gunslinging reputations were employed in the gambling houses as dealers or lookouts to provide a restraining influence on those who tended to become violent when they lost. No one in Leadville carried a more formidable reputation than the former sheriff of Ford County, Kansas. Bat was offered wages substantially higher than the six or seven dollars a day run-of-the-mill dealers were receiving, but he was not yet ready to trade on his gunfighting renown. He declined all offers and limited his play to the outside.

In early March, Bat returned to Dodge to serve as a delegate to the Ford County Republican Convention. Later that month, he attended the state convention in Topeka. His luck at Leadville apparently had been good, for at the conclusion of the convention, he told friends he was going back to Colorado with the intention of investing certain capital that he had accumulated in a saloon and gambling house of his own.

Property values in Leadville had been sky high, so Bat headed for the booming Gunnison country in search of a saloon site. He explored Pitkin, Gunnison City, and Ruby City without success. When he returned to Dodge in June, he cautioned fellow Kansans against the terrors of winter in the Colorado mountain country. As late as May, he said, snow was still three feet deep in the streets of Ruby City. Commented the *Times*: "Bat does not give a glowing account of the silver state."[12]

He was still in Dodge when Ben Thompson approached him for help. Brother Bill was in trouble again, and this time it looked as if Ben were powerless to help him. Ben had just received a wire from Ogallala, Nebraska, to the effect that Bully Bill had been shot up in a row with an Ogallala citizen and was in great danger of being lynched. Ben had been outlawed in Ogallala and could not go to Bill's aid. According to the information Ben had received, Thompson enemies in Nebraska were wrought up enough to welcome a double rope party. Ben wanted Bat to go to Ogallala and see what could be done to save Bill. Bat agreed to do so.

Ogallala lay some two hundred fifty miles north and west of Dodge City. By a circuitous rail and stage route, Bat finally reached the dusty little cow town, which squatted on the main line of the Union Pacific on the north bank of the South Platte River. There were not more than thirty buildings in the whole town, most of them clustered in a one-block area along Railroad Avenue. At the Ogallala House, the only hotel, Bat found Bill Thompson propped up in bed with five shotgun pellets in him.

Thompson had come to Ogallala for the cattle-shipping season and had opened a monte game in Bill Tucker's saloon, the Cowboy's Rest. In the course of events, he and Tucker quarreled over the affections of Big Alice, a local harlot. Primed with booze in another saloon, Thompson entered the Cowboy's Rest and fired a shot at Tucker, who was behind the bar. The owner was in the act of passing a glass of whiskey across the bar to cattleman Dillon Fant. Thompson's bullet smashed the glass and neatly sliced off the thumb and three fingers of Tucker's left hand. When the saloonman disappeared from sight behind the bar, Thompson, in his alcoholic haze, turned and pushed back out through the swinging doors, believing he had killed his man. But Tucker was not finished. He emerged from behind the bar, holding a ten-gauge sawed-off shotgun in his good hand. At the doorway, he steadied the barrel on his bleeding stump of a hand and let fly at the weaving form of Thompson, hitting him in the back with five pellets. After this exchange, the combatants retired to tend their wounds, Thompson to the hotel, Tucker to his home. Bat learned that although Thompson's wounds were serious, he would recover.

"I found Thompson laid up in bed in the hotel from the effects of the several wounds he had received from Tucker," Bat wrote.[13] "I also found him under arrest with a Deputy Sheriff guarding him in his room. . . . I concluded, with a view of bringing about an understanding between the warriors, to go and see Tucker, whom I also found in bed at his home with his left hand minus thumb and fingers done up in liniment soaked bandages." Bat was convinced that Tucker and his friends intended to stretch Thompson's neck as soon as he was well enough to be on his feet, but discreet inquiries

Billy Thompson, rescued by Bat from a possible lynching at Ogallala, Nebraska. This picture was taken eight years earlier at Ellsworth, Kansas. Courtesy University of Oklahoma Library.

revealed that Tucker would let bygones be bygones — for a price. "The sum, however," Bat said, "was beyond the reach of Thompson and his friends, therefore my conference with the thumbless one was at an end."

Bat set about formulating a plan for Thompson's escape. He instructed Bill to pretend greater pain and suffering than he actually felt. There were no doctors in Ogallala and the extent of the Texan's injuries was not definitely known. Bat wanted to keep Thompson out of jail until he could work out a way to spirit him out of town. Meanwhile, Bat got on friendly terms with the guard, "a young fellow who had lately reached that country from one of the New England states. His armament consisted of a long barreled Colts 45 caliber pistol with a white handle of which he seemed duly proud."

Getting Thompson out of Ogallala proved to be quite a problem, Bat found:

Although Thompson was not as badly injured as he let on to be, he had never-the-less been sufficiently crippled to be of little use to himself in case of emergency. . . . Had Thompson been able to ride a horse, it would have been very easy for us to escape in that manner but that was out of the question. If, on the other hand, we attempted to escape by wagon, we would be easily trailed and overtaken by the posse we knew would soon be in hot pursuit. There was therefore but one avenue of escape left to us, and that was the railroad.

Some fifty miles east on the Union Pacific tracks lay North Platte, home of Colonel William F. ("Buffalo Bill") Cody. Bat had met the celebrated scout in Dodge. He knew that Cody, who was spending a rare interlude at home, was always ready for a new adventure. He figured that if he could get Thompson to North Platte, Cody would help get the wounded Texan the rest of the way back to Dodge. The eastbound flier stopped at Ogallala to fill its water tank about midnight before continuing on to its next stop at North Platte. Getting the crippled Thompson aboard that train was Bat's problem, and it was a difficult one:

It seemed as if everybody in town was watching every move I made, and from what I subsequently heard, I am satisfied that they were. I had no sooner arrived in town than the Sheriff, thinking perhaps that I might make an attempt to rescue his prisoner, issued the strictest kind of instructions to his Deputy who had been assigned to guard Thompson, to never leave the room for a moment while he was on duty and I can truthfully say that he obeyed the instructions to the very letter. One Sunday night, however, there was a dance given by the people of the town and as was the custom in those small Western hamlets in those days, everybody in the place attended the blow-out. The dance was given in the schoolhouse which was also used for church purposes whenever a preacher happened along that way. The building, which wasn't much larger than a good sized hen-coop, was situated on a little knoll about 400 yards north of the depot which was located in the center of the town. The Sheriff, who was also the town fiddler, was furnishing the music for the occasion and . . . nearly everybody in Ogallalah was at the dance. . . . This was obviously my time for getting away with Thompson.

Jim Dunn, the hotel bartender, was one of the few people who could not attend the shindig, having to remain on duty. Dunn had worked the Dodge City saloons and was a friend of Bat's, so he eagerly agreed to help when Bat asked him to join in the escape plot. Bat explained his plan, then went to Thompson's room.

Thompson's hotel room faced the schoolhouse, and as the squeaking notes of the sheriff's fiddle drifted out over the prairie, Bat, standing at the open window, remarked to the young deputy on guard: "I am sorry I'm not at that dance for they seem to be having a good time up there." The guard nodded glumly, and when Bat suggested having a drink, he readily agreed. Bat ordered two whiskey sours, which Jim Dunn delivered, winking slyly at Bat as the young deputy tossed his drink down. Bat sent Dunn back for refills. "Soon after the Deputy disposed of the second drink," wrote Bat, "he spread himself on the floor and was soon dreaming of his New England home." Jim Dunn was, as Bat put it, "an artist in his business," and the Mickey Finn was a refinement of civilization not entirely unknown even in an obscure frontier outpost like Ogallala.

Bat dressed Thompson, hoisted him to his shoulders, and carried him down the steps and across to the depot. His timing was perfect: the train was grinding to a halt as he came hobbling up. Bat stumbled aboard, and in a few minutes he and Bill Thompson "were speeding at the rate of forty miles an hour for North Platte" while the tired strains of *Turkey in the Straw* filled the empty streets of Ogallala.

When the train pulled into North Platte, Bat heaved Thompson to his shoulder, climbed down onto the platform, and looked about for the nearest saloon. It was two o'clock in the morning, but Dave Perry's saloon was ablaze with lights. Bat kicked open the swinging doors and entered to find Colonel Cody, surrounded by a ring of admirers, narrating one of his hair-raising adventures. "As a matter of course," wrote Bat, "we were given a royal welcome and were immediately taken in charge by Colonel Cody, who found a safe place for us to remain until he could outfit us for the trip across the country to Dodge City. 'The Ogallalah authorities will not take you from here,' said Cody to us that night, and we slept quite comfortably."

The following day, Bat left Thompson to go to Cody's house, "a beautiful place in the suburbs of North Platte," to arrange for a horse and rig for the journey south. When he arrived, he found Buffalo Bill out front erecting a flagpole in honor of General Hancock, who had just been nominated for the presidency by the

Democratic party. It can be safely assumed that Cody received no help from Bat Masterson, a hard-core Republican. "I may here state that Buffalo Bill is a Democrat," wrote Bat, "but that should not be held against him, for he is a splendid fellow, and perhaps regrets it as much as any genuine American could."

Cody gave Bat a big, strong Texas horse and a handsome new phaeton he had purchased recently for his wife. If Bat were willing to wait in North Platte a day or two, said Cody, he and Thompson could have company for part of their trip. General Sheridan was sending to Buffalo Bill's ranch a party of distinguished foreigners who wanted to see some of the wild and woolly West. Since 1871, when Bill had served as guide for Grand Duke Alexis of Russia and his retinue, European dignitaries had requested his services when touring the plains. Cody planned to take the visitors to Keith's ranch, a large cattle spread some twenty-five miles south of North Platte and directly on Bat's route to Dodge. He suggested that they all travel together that far. Bat was agreeable, so he and Thompson remained in town until the foreigners arrived. "There were fully twenty persons in the party," Bat recalled, "and as everybody was feeling good when we left North Platte, the trip to Keith's was a right royal one, you may be sure. I was driving a double team hitched to Cody's specially made mess wagon, which was loaded down with everything imaginable."

As noted by Bat, all members of the company were in high spirits, and their bibulous host saw to it that no one lost that fine edge because of thirst. He had arranged for periodic rest stops, during which bottles were passed freely among the convivial travelers. "The caravan would stop every little while and liquor up," Bat said, "and then go on until the next liquoring-up point was reached, when the caravan would again come to halt."

The combination of alcohol, hot July sun, and jouncing ride affected everyone, even that veteran tippler Colonel Cody himself. Bill, sagging in the saddle, finally pulled over beside Bat's mess wagon and flopped in, sound asleep. Bat was having trouble focusing his eyes on the trail ahead, and thereby hangs a tale:

We had gone only a short distance after Bill had fallen asleep when the wagon was tipped completely upside down. I was pitched out on my head in the prairie, while Cody was buried beneath the wagon and its contents.

William F. ("Buffalo Bill') Cody and his wife, Louisa Maud. Cody helped Bat and Billy Thompson escape the fiddling sheriff of Ogallala, and Mrs. Cody unknowingly contributed her handsome new carriage to the project. Courtesy Denver Public Library.

I gathered myself up as quickly as I could, and got hold of the horses by the head and held them until other members of the party came and rescued Cody, who hadn't received as much as a scratch, while I had my lower lip nearly torn from my face.

The travelers arrived at Keith's ranch without further mishap and, after cleaning up a bit, sat down together to enjoy a hearty western-style meal. After supper, Buffalo Bill, always the show-man, entertained the foreigners with feats of horsemanship and marksmanship. "The stunts he did," marveled Bat, "were nothing short of wonderful."

The next day, Bat and Thompson bade farewell to Colonel Cody and his guests and headed for Dodge City in the phaeton Mrs. Cody unknowingly had donated to them. Bat saw Buffalo Bill several years later, and the latter told him he had some tall explaining to do when he returned home and his wife questioned him about the strange disappearance of her prized carriage. Cody was making plenty of money, however, and a new and more elegant vehicle soon was purchased to replace the phaeton.

Shortly after Bill Thompson and Bat left Keith's, ominous black clouds rolled out of the west, and they were soon driving their topless vehicle through heavy rain that continued for the entire trip of more than two hundred miles. Bill Thompson and his deliverer were a sorry spectacle when they finally wheeled into Dodge. Swathed in bandages and very weak, the bad boy from Texas was huddled in a chilled, sodden ball under a buffalo robe. The former sheriff, his lip severely lacerated, held the reins in numbed hands. Both were mud spattered and rain soaked from head to foot.

Bat wanted a couple of good, stiff drinks, a hot meal, a bath, and about ten hours of uninterrupted sleep, but Thompson insisted that they first go to the telegraph office. There, Bully Bill dispatched a wire to the sheriff at Ogallala, "notifying him of his safe arrival and inviting him to come and get him in case he still thought he wanted him." Added Bat: "The fiddling sheriff made no reply to Thompson's message, and there the matter ended."

CHAPTER FOURTEEN

TOMBSTONE ·

After the Ogallala escapade, Bat headed east, stopping over a few days with his parents in Sedgwick before going on to Kansas City, Missouri. Here he remained for about six months.

Kansas City had always been a good gambler's town, and in 1880 it was at its peak; the Missouri Legislature passed the Johnson antigambling law the following year. There were thirty or forty gambling houses in town, and Bat bucked the tiger in most of them. He played the Main Street resort run by Doc Frame and the legendary Major James S. Showers, who, it was said, had once worked an establishment in Washington, D.C., where he dealt faro for Henry Clay and Daniel Webster. He was a frequent visitor at the Missouri Avenue houses kept by genteel Virginia gambler Bob Potee and Joe Bassett, brother of Bat's Dodge City crony Charlie Bassett. He tangled in high-stakes poker games with some of the best of the professionals, including Hank Teas, John Evans, Gus Galbaugh, Clay Maltby, George Frazier, and Tom Wallace.

In December, he was back in Dodge, as was duly noted in the *Times*: "W. B. Masterson, former sheriff of Ford County, spent several days here. He lives in Kansas City. Bat was welcomed by a host of friends."[1] Soon after the start of the new year, he received word from Wyatt Earp in Tombstone. Serious trouble was brewing, and Wyatt would welcome Bat's help if he could arrange to come to the new mining camp, where a job awaited him.

Bat could arrange it. On February 8, 1881, he boarded a westbound train in Dodge. At Trinidad, Colorado, he changed trains and headed south into New Mexico on the new Santa Fe line. George T. Buffum, who was aboard the same train, put a description of that trip on paper.[2] His account furnishes a vivid picture of travel in the West in those days:

People whose travelling experiences have been confined to parlor cars and common coaches perhaps do not realize how primitive and how perilous was travelling in some parts of our country even so late as the early eighties. Indeed so dangerous was a journey south and west from the terminus of the Santa Fe Railroad in the winter of 1881 that unless urged by imperitive reasons such journeys were usually abandoned, the accounts of daily scalpings by Indians being a little too realistic even for the most hardened seekers after adventure.

I was compelled to take this journey, and in the caboose attached to the construction train I found a small band of determined-looking men all armed to the fullest extent, save one fine-looking gentleman, who wore a silk hat — the first one to be tolerated in New Mexico without a few shots being taken at it — and whose only weapon was a silk umbrella. . . .

I had made the gentleman's acquaintance the evening before. . . . His name was William H. Stilwell. He had been recently appointed associate judge for the Territory of Arizona, and was on his way to his new official duties. One of the passengers was "Bat" Masterson. . . . I was glad that we were to have such a redoubtable companion on our journey. I introduced him to Judge Stilwell, and was relieved that Masterson greeted him most cordially in spite of the silk hat.

At the end of the Santa Fe steel, travelers had to transfer from the construction train to an overland coach, which would carry them through the Apache country to Deming, New Mexico, and the Southern Pacific. Wrote Buffum:

By common consent, Masterson was given the seat beside the driver as our best fighting man. I drew second choice and selected the dickey seat above and behind the driver. The three other outside seats were also decided by lot. The judge, having no weapons, was not allowed a choice. He . . . hinted to Masterson, who carried a Sharp's rifle and two Colt "navy revolvers," that if he had more guns than he could use he would relieve him of one. Bat replied most courteously that he would gladly loan the judge one of the revolvers if later he found that he could not handle them all to his better protection.

As it turned out, there was no use for the weapons. The coach continued, unmolested by Apaches, to Deming, seven miles east of the present townsite. Deming was the terminus of the Southern Pacific, which was building east toward El Paso, Texas. It consisted of several saloons and a boxcar used by the construction gangs as an eating place. Although the car provided the only available dining facilities for stagecoach passengers, the railroad men seemed to resent the travelers' intrusion into what they considered their private dining room.

Judge Stilwell managed to squeeze himself into a vacant seat at a rough plank table just before a group of gandy dancers shouldered their way into the car. One of the newcomers jabbed a grimy finger in the direction of His Honor. "See that long, lank cuss fresh from New York just filling himself as though he had been through a famine, while we railroad boys have to wait?" he roared. The room was suddenly quiet, and Stilwell's face turned scarlet. Then Bat, who had been waiting patiently with the rest, cut loose with a burst of colorful Dodge City whorehouse invective, directed at the railroaders. Wrote Buffum:

> Masterson, in great wrath and with resounding oaths, resented this insult to his friend, and ended with, "Buffum, you just take the first vacant seat and let these sons of the burro wait."
>
> The railroad men looked at one another, they looked at Masterson, they looked at his Sharp's rifle and his two Colt's revolvers, they saw his determined face as he glowered at them, and their appetites fled before that terrible presence; not a man moved when the first chair was vacated, and I seated myself.

When Judge Stilwell had finished eating, he pushed his plate back, stood up, and said politely: "I am sorry, gentlemen, to have kept you waiting, but I was very hungry." Before the construction workers could recover from their surprise, Bat strode forward. "No disrespect to you, Judge," he said, "but I will take your chair myself." The gandy dancers waited, fuming but silent.

From Deming, Stilwell, Buffam, and Masterson traveled west on a Southern Pacific work train. As a courtesy to the new judge, the railroad management hitched an old passenger car to the train; in it, Bat and his two companions journeyed as far as Benson, Arizona, where he said good-bye to his two friends of the road and swung down to catch the stage to Tombstone.

As the stagecoach tooled south from Benson into the Dragoon Mountains, Bob Paul, the Wells Fargo messenger who regularly rode shotgun on the run, told Bat the story of the Earp brothers' first year in Tombstone, a tale that was to develop into one of the bloodiest chapters in frontier history. Wyatt and Morgan, who had gone to Tombstone with the intention of establishing a stage line between the boom camp and Benson, learned when they arrived that two lines were operating and that the fat mail and Wells Fargo contracts had been grabbed up. Their plans spoiled, they took jobs as shotgun messengers on the treasure-bearing coaches that plied the trail between the silver camp and the railroad.

Before many months had passed, Wyatt was wearing a star once more. He accepted Pima County Sheriff Shibell's appointment as deputy sheriff for the Tombstone district. As usual, Virgil and Morgan followed his lead. Morgan acted as Wyatt's assistant in the deputy sheriff's office, and Virgil served as city marshal of Tombstone for a time. When Cochise County was organized, with the county seat at Tombstone, Wyatt lost his deputy sheriff's star but promptly replaced it with a federal badge; he was appointed deputy U.S. marshal by Crawley P. Dake, the U.S. marshal for Arizona.

Wyatt had acquired a financial interest in the Oriental, one of Tombstone's largest and most prosperous saloons and gambling houses. Its plush gaming rooms were jointly operated by Lou Rickabaugh, Dick Clark, and Bill Harris, three of the best gamblers in the West. Other gambling-house managers, jealous of the Oriental's popularity, had detailed a gang of ruffians to hurrah the place nightly in an effort to scare away patrons. The partners had offered Wyatt a quarter-interest in the gambling concession in the hope that his fighting reputation would daunt the hell-raising intruders. Wyatt kept peace in the house when he was there, but his other duties frequently called him away from the premises. To assist him in keeping the Oriental quiet, he had sent for Bat and Luke Short to work as dealers. Peace and tranquility would return to the gambling rooms of the Oriental, Wyatt had promised, as soon as those two began to preside over the faro layouts.

However, as Bob Paul solemnly explained to Bat, more was brewing in Tombstone than the threatened outbreak of a gamblers' war. An organized gang of outlaws from the San Simon Valley was using Tombstone as a private playground. Their operations included smuggling, rustling, and stage holdups. Worse still, the residents of Tombstone were choosing up sides for a battle royal. Siding with the outlaws were a number of their apologists, includ-

When William H. Stilwell arrived in Arizona Territory to assume his judicial duties, he was wearing a silk hat. Fortunately, he had Bat Masterson for a traveling companion. Courtesy Library, Archives and Public Records Division, State of Arizona.

ing John Behan, sheriff of Cochise County, and Harry Woods, editor of the *Tombstone Nugget*. Opposing them were the Earp brothers, backed by a law-and-order league of influential citizens the foremost of whom was noted Indian agent John Clum, who was now editing the *Tombstone Epitaph* and acting as mayor of the town.

If an all-out fight developed, the Earp faction stood to be outgunned. The outlaw element, or cowboys, as they called themselves, boasted an impressive roster of gunslingers that included Billy Clanton, Tom and Frank McLaury, Johnny Ringo, Curly Bill Brocius, Frank Stilwell, Pony Deal, Billy Claiborne, and Pete Spence. Bat nodded as Bob Paul tolled off the names; he knew some of these men personally, some by reputation. Each could be a mighty rough burr under a peace officer's saddle; organized into a gang with connections in the sheriff's office, they spelled big trouble for people who stood in their way. And that was precisely where the Earp brothers stood.

Besides his brothers, there were only two men in Tombstone of demonstrated six-gun ability upon whom Wyatt could depend to

back his play if and when a showdown came. One was Marshall
Williams, the Wells Fargo agent in town; the other was Doc
Holliday, who had followed Wyatt's trail into Arizona. Wyatt
hoped that with the addition of Bat Masterson and Luke Short to
the Earp command, the reckless cowboys would ponder a bit
before launching a campaign of bloodletting.

Bat's arrival at the Oriental signaled a Dodge City old-timers'
celebration. In addition to the three Earp brothers, Doc Holliday,
and Luke Short, Wyatt's partners were Dodge alumni, and Bat
knew them well. Lou Rickabaugh, a portly man, had played in
some high-stakes games that were talked about for years on the
gamblers' circuit. Tall, powerfully built Dick Clark had made and
lost fortunes overnight in cow towns and mining camps from
Kansas to California. Bat remembered a fabulous streak of luck
Clark had held so long in Dodge that a citizens committee had
called on him and asked him to leave. Bill Harris had located in
Dodge for years, acting as partner to Chalk Beeson in the management of the Long Branch Saloon.

The next day, Bat went to work at the Oriental. Top-notch faro
dealers like Bat Masterson were paid twenty-five dollars for a
six-hour shift in Tombstone. If the house man proved especially
popular, or if for some reason the management was shorthanded,
the dealer might be asked to work overtime. Five dollars an hour
was the standard bonus for such extra duty. The pay was good, but
the work was tedious and demanding; errors were not tolerated.
High-stakes games were played in the Oriental, and gamblers'
nerves drew taut as guitar strings as the excitement of play
mounted. Weapons were always close at hand on both sides of the
table, and an error in judgment or the slip of a finger by the dealer
could mean sudden death for one or more parties.

A shooting that took place on February 25, shortly after Bat
started work in the Oriental, may have resulted from an indiscreet
move or word by a dealer; more likely, it was an engagement in the
sporadic gamblers' war. Bat, who was indirectly involved in the
action, has furnished us with an account of what transpired, but he
fails to mention the origin of the conflict:

One morning I went into the Oriental gambling house, where Luke
[Short] was working, just in time to keep him from killing a gambler

named Charlie Storms. . . . Charlie Storms was one of the best-known gamblers in the entire West and had, on several occasions, successfully defended himself in pistol fights with Western "gunfighters."

Charlie Storms and I were very close friends — as much so as Short and I were — and for that reason I didn't care to see him get into what I knew would be a very serious difficulty. Storms didn't know Short, and . . . had sized him up as an insignificant-looking fellow, whom he could slap in the face without expecting a return. Both men were about to pull their pistols when I jumped between them and grabbed Storms, at the same time requesting Luke not to shoot — a request I knew he would respect if it was possible without endangering his own life too much. I had no trouble in getting Storms out of the house, as he knew me to be his friend. When Storms and I reached the street I advised him to go to his room and take a sleep, for I then learned for the first time that he had been up all night, and had been quarreling with other persons.

Bat took the embattled Storms to his room and tried to quiet him with peace talk. Leaving him at the hotel, Bat hurried back to the Oriental to talk to Short. He found the little gambler standing outside the Allen Street entrance to the saloon. Bat urged Luke to let the matter pass without further trouble and was attempting to make excuses for Storms's behavior when Storms suddenly appeared to plead his own cause. Wrote Bat:

I was just explaining to Luke that Storms was a very decent sort of man when, lo and behold! there he stood before us. Without saying a word, he took hold of Luke's arm and pulled him off the sidewalk, where he had been standing, at the same time pulling his pistol, a Colt's cut-off, 45 calibre, single action; but . . . he was too slow, although he succeeded in getting his pistol out. Luke stuck the muzzle of his own pistol against Storms' heart and pulled the trigger. The bullet tore the heart asunder, and as he was falling, Luke shot him again. Storms was dead when he hit the ground.[3]

As he did in the death of his friend Levi Richardson back in Dodge, Bat went to the defense of the killer of his friend Charlie Storms. He was the chief witness in behalf of Luke Short at a preliminary hearing held before a magistrate. After Bat entered his testimony, Short was freed.

The gambling rooms of the Oriental were noticeably quieter after Storms's sudden demise. Rival gamblers apparently were satisfied that the reputations of the Dodge City gunfighters were authentic, and talk of a gamblers' war subsided. But Wyatt Earp's troubles with the San Simon Valley outlaws were only beginning.

On March 15, a stage left Tombstone for Benson with a silver-bullion shipment valued at eighty thousand dollars. Bud Philpot was driving, and Bob Paul was riding shotgun. At ten o'clock that night, Wyatt received a telegram from Bob Paul in Benson. A holdup had been attempted. Paul had managed to save the Wells Fargo treasure, but Bud Philpot and Peter Roerig, a passenger, had been killed by the bandits. Wyatt wired Paul to meet him at Drew's ranch, the scene of the holdup, and, acting in his capacity as deputy U.S. marshal, immediately organized a posse to pursue the highway men. He named as deputies his brothers, Morgan and Virgil; Marshall Williams, the Wells Fargo agent; and Bat Masterson.

By midnight, the posse was riding north out of Tombstone for Drew's ranch. As they rode, Wyatt told Bat he had a strong suspicion about the identity of the road agents. Four cowhands working for the Clanton brothers had been camping for a week in an old adobe cabin on the Contention road, he said. It was Wyatt's hunch that the four — Bill Leonard, Jim Crane, Luther King, and Harry Head — had been watching the Benson stages, waiting for a chance to cop a large bullion shipment. It would be a simple matter for them to determine which coach carried treasure; only those stages laden with silver carried a shotgun messenger perched beside the driver. Wyatt suspected that the Clanton men, seeing Bob Paul in the box with Bud Philpot, had followed the stage at a distance and that while Philpot changed his teams at the Contention station, the cowboys had ridden cross country to intercept the coach and rob it.

Support for Wyatt's theory was found when the posse met Paul at Drew's ranch and examined the area of the attack in the first light of dawn. Three masked men had leaped from the chaparral, Paul said, and had thrown down on him with rifles. He could not be certain, but he thought he recognized two of them as Leonard and Crane. Philpot had kicked his horses into a gallop while Paul turned loose his shotgun. A rifle bullet fired by one of the masked men had killed the driver instantly, and Paul had been forced to drop his weapon to take the reins. As the stage pulled away, the bandits had poured a hail of fire after it. Peter Roerig, riding the dickey seat, had been hit and killed.

Seventeen spent rifle cartridges were found in the road by the Earp party. The tracks of the three bandits were traced to the spot where they had left their horses before approaching the road. Signs indicated that a fourth man had held the animals during the holdup.

Sheriff Behan and his deputy, Billy Breakenridge, arrived on the scene during the night. Behan suggested that pursuit was useless. The trail was more than twelve hours cold, he argued, and would vanish into nothingness in the desert waste. Earp disagreed. He and his brothers were skilled trackers, and Bat Masterson could read sign like an Indian. His posse was going to give chase, he told Behan, adding bluntly that if the sheriff and his deputy wanted to return to Tombstone, that was all right, too. Behan shrugged, then mounted to accompany Wyatt's posse out into the barren expanse of mesquite and sand.

The trail led east to the Dragoon Mountains, then veered sharply northwest. The highwaymen employed every trick in the fugitive's book to shake their relentless pursuers. They followed the churned tracks of cattle trails for miles, turned down dry creek beds that were floored with solid rock, doubled back on their own tracks, split up, rejoined, but the man hunters knew every trick and pushed on.

On the morning of March 19, after three days and one hundred fifty miles of arduous tracking, the posse caught up with one of the fugitives. Luther King was taken at the ranch of Len Redfield, a cattleman known to be friendly with the Clanton crowd. King denied any knowledge of the holdup at first, but finally confessed his implication. He said he had held the horses while Crane, Head, and Leonard tried to stop the stage. Sheriff Behan then claimed custody of the prisoner, arresting him for murder in the name of the county. Earp, a federal officer, could hold King only on the lesser charge of attempting to rob the U.S. mail. So Wyatt turned the prisoner over to Behan, who, with Breakenridge and Marshall Williams, started back to Tombstone.

The three Earp brothers, Bob Paul, and Bat pressed on after the other members of the gang. They followed the trail west through the foothills of the Tanque Verde, Rincon, and Santa Catalina mountains, south through the Oracles and Cañada del Oro, then east past Tucson through the Santa Cruz Valley. They recrossed the San Pedro River and once more faced the forbidding fastnesses of the Dragoons. At Helm's ranch they were rejoined by Behan and Breakenridge. Buckskin Frank Leslie came with the sheriff to help in the hunt.

Wyatt, Virgil, and Morgan Earp, Bat Masterson, and Bob Paul had been on the trail ten days and nights by this time. The fugitives had led them in a great circle for almost four hundred miles and had gained ground along the way. At isolated cattle camps in the desert, the bandits had secured fresh mounts from friendly ranchers, while their pursuers had been forced to ride the same ponies with which they had left Tombstone. The posse pushed doggedly on through the Dragoons and Chiricahuas toward New Mexico. They had traveled through the most desolate stretches of Arizona, riding at times through arid wastes where it was forty-eight hours between water holes. The hardships of the chase reminded Bat of his days as a scout with Colonel Miles during the Red River campaign in 1874.

Both men and horses suffered from fatigue and thirst, but the horses gave out first. Bat's animal fell dead under him. He was forced to give up the chase and caught a ride back to Tombstone with a passing teamster.

The other possemen went on into New Mexico to a ranch operated by Head and Leonard, but, finding the place deserted, they, too, were compelled to abandon the hunt.

"The persistent pursuit of the murderers of poor Bud Philpot is a credit to each individual member of the posse and will pass into frontier annals as a record of which all may be proud," said the *Epitaph* upon their return.[4] But Wyatt and his friends took little note of the words of praise. They were infuriated to learn that Luther King, the single prize they had to show for their long ordeal, had escaped shortly after being brought in by Sheriff Behan. Wyatt openly charged Behan with complicity in the escape, an accusation which Behan vehemently denied.

The robbery attempt on the Benson stage was one of the earliest incidents in what was to become an Earp-Clanton vendetta, a frontier feud that reached its climax seven months later in the

classic six-gun engagement of the West, the shoot out at the O.K.
Corral. Bat Masterson was not destined to participate, however.
Soon after returning to Tombstone, he received a message that sent
him hurrying back over the same route he had traversed two
months earlier. A telegram from Dodge City said his brother Jim
was in serious trouble and needed Bat's help.

CHAPTER FIFTEEN

"TOO MUCH BLOOD"

"Come at once. Updegraff and Peacock are going to kill Jim."

Thus read the telegram that sent Bat speeding back to Dodge City with guns on his hips and blood in his eye. The message had not been signed, perhaps because the sender feared Jim Masterson's enemies. If Bat ever learned the identity of the writer, he respected his wish for anonymity. "Bat showed me the message he received in Tombstone," Wyatt Earp recalled, "and it was not from his brother. It didn't say what kind of trouble Jim Masterson was mixed up in. It only said that Peacock and Updegraff were threatening to kill him. Bat had had a quarrel with Jim and was barely on speaking terms with him at the time but he took the first stage out of Tombstone to go back to Dodge to help his brother. That was the old frontier's brand of loyalty."[1]

Earp's reference to a quarrel between Bat and Jim is the first intimation we have that there was ill feeling between the brothers. Wyatt may have been mistaken on this point, but it is noteworthy that from the time of Bat's election defeat, he and Jim had traveled separate roads. There would be other indications in the future that Bat and Jim were not on the best of terms.

Quarrel or no quarrel, Jim was still Bat's brother, and that was sufficient reason for Bat to undertake a journey of almost a thousand miles to help. He had lost one brother to an assassin's bullet in Dodge just three years earlier to the very month; he did not intend to lose another if it lay within his power to prevent it.

Jim Masterson was city marshal of Dodge from November, 1879, until April, 1881. Although he lacked Bat's charisma, he apparently was an efficient lawman; Dodge was remarkably quiet during his tenure. George Bolds, who knew both brothers, was quite impressed by Jim, especially with regard to his pistol prowess:

Despite the Earp legends, as far as I'm concerned, Jim Masterson could outdraw his brother Bat and Wyatt Earp and could match them in courage. I've seen him bash a man in the face who had a gun turned on him and take that same gun and break the barrel on the bar. I've seen him in Dodge buffaloing a bunch of drunken, hooting cowhands by simply walking up, staring at them coldly and ordering them out of town.

. . . I can still shut my eyes and see him walking down the street, six-shooter under his coat, hat tilted to one side, a cigar in the corner of his mouth and his face as impassive as an Indian's. I maintain he was the most deadly man with a gun outside of Harvey Logan, the executioner of The Wild Bunch in Wyoming. If Jim Masterson had ever met Logan or that buck-toothed little Billy the Kid, my chips would have been on Jim.[2]

On April 4, Mayor Dog Kelley and his city council were defeated for reelection, and two days later, Jim and Assistant City Marshal Neal Brown were fired by Mayor-elect A. B. Webster. A letter from M. C. Ruby, agent for the Adams Express Company in Dodge, to an Iowa newspaper, the *Oskaloosa Herald*, written shortly before election and given wide circulation in Dodge, may well have been a contributing factor in this defeat. Ruby was highly critical of all Dodge City officialdom, but he singled out for special scorn Kelley, Jim Masterson, Brown, Sheriff George Hinkle, and Undersheriff Fred Singer:

The mayor is a flannel mouthed Irishman and keeps a saloon and gambling house which he attends to in person. The city marshal and assistant are gamblers and each keep a "woman" — as does the mayor also. . . . The sheriff owns a saloon and the deputy sheriff is a bar tender in a saloon. . . . No arrests are made except for killing or attempt to kill unless strangers should come in whom they think has plenty of money. They will arrest him on slight pretext and bleed him. . . . Six men were knocked down and robbed one night last week. . . . If any of your readers anticipate imigrating to Kansas, advise them to shun Dodge City as they would the yellow fever, measles, smallpox and seven year itch combined, as I think they would all be preferable in a civilized country to residence in this town. . . . However, I came here with the intention of staying a certain length of time which I intend to do if they don't raise my hair before I get ready to leave.[3]

Ruby's scalp wasn't lifted, but Kelley, Masterson, and Brown did demonstrate their displeasure with his remarks. Reported the *Times* of April 5:

The agent of the Adams Express Co., at this place, Mr. Ruby, was taken out to the railroad water tank last Wednesday, and drenched with water by Mayor Kelley and his policemen, for writing an article to an Iowa newspaper and reflecting discreditably upon said officials.

The defeat of his friend Dog Kelley and his own subsequent dismissal evidently were the final straws for Jim Masterson. Several months earlier, he had entered into partnership with A. J. Peacock of the Lady Gay Saloon and Dance Hall. Dissension plagued the venture from the outset. The main cause of trouble between the partners was Peacock's brother-in-law, Al Updegraff, whom Peacock had employed as a bartender in the amusement house. Jim did not like Updegraff, apparently for good reason. The bartender was considered a heavy drinker even in Dodge City, the Bibulous Babylon. Jim argued that Updegraff was not to be trusted, citing as an example of the bartender's dishonesty a crooked land-promotion deal in which he had been implicated eight years earlier.

Nepotist Peacock refused to discharge his brother-in-law despite Jim Masterson's objections. As Updegraff, from his advantageous station behind the bar of the Lady Gay, swilled free liquor to his heart's content night after night, Jim grew angrier. The partners quarreled openly, and the patrons of the dance hall began to take sides in the dispute. Soon the issue became a topic of argument throughout Dodge. Irresponsible charges and accusations were hurled back and forth. Then came threats. It was rumored that guns had been drawn and several shots fired without effect. At this point one of Jim's supporters thought it time to put in a call for Bat.

The journey back up from Arizona, through New Mexico and Colorado into Kansas, must have seemed interminable to Bat. He knew Dodge and the violence of its men; he had seen lives snuffed out in the twinkling of an eye in that brawling camp. He knew that if Updegraff and Peacock were gunning for Jim when the telegram was sent, his brother might well be dead and buried by the time he reached Dodge. As the hours crawled by, his fears became a conviction, a resignation.

The Santa Fe pulled into the familiar depot in Dodge City at noon on Saturday, April 16. Unsure of the situation in town and the sort of welcome he would receive, if any, Bat swung down from the train while it was still moving and walked beside it toward the depot. As the train slid by him, he looked behind the caboose and saw two men walking in the same direction south of the tracks. He recognized them at once as Peacock and Updegraff. Bat pushed his coat back from his gun butt. "Hold up there a minute, you two," he shouted. "I want to talk to you." Peacock and Updegraff knew that voice well. They took one fleeting glance at the familiar stocky figure striding toward them, spun on their heels, and ducked around the corner of the jail.

Who fired the first shot in what was to become known in Dodge as the Battle of the Plaza was never determined, but pistol bullets soon were ripping back and forth across the Santa Fe tracks. In the first exchange, Bat was at a disadvantage. He was out in the open; his adversaries had the protection of the calaboose. Bat quickly dropped behind the railroad enbankment, which at that point was some three feet high.

Bullets from the pair ensconced behind the jail snapped over Bat's head and crashed into stores along Front Street, sending strolling townsmen diving for cover; Dr. McCarty's drugstore was hit several times. As bullets ripped into the Long Branch Saloon, patrons beat a hasty retreat out the back door. Chalk Beeson, the proprietor, jerked open the door of his safe and huddled behind this improvised armor shield. George Hoover's saloon lost a window, and a bullet tore a newspaper from the hands of an idler there.

Meanwhile, Bat, firing south and east, was knocking large splinters of wood from the corner of the hoosegow, a square structure solidly constructed of heavy two-by-six timbers spiked together to form four-by-sixes. As the combatants sniped at each other, certain members of Dodge's sporting fraternity joined in the fray. Behind his rail-capped earthen parapet, Bat was receiving fire from several south-side saloons. At his rear, friendly guns opened up on Front Street. The three principals in the action suddenly found themselves in the middle of a general war raging back and forth across the tracks.

Al Updegraff abruptly pitched headlong from behind the jail, a bullet through his chest. Soon, the guns of Bat and Peacock fell silent as their hammers fell on empty cylinders. The second echelons in the saloons lifted their batteries, and peace came once more to the plaza. Mayor Ab Webster ran panting up to Bat, a twelve-gauge Fox shotgun in his hand, and placed Bat under arrest. Bat submitted quietly. His only concern, he told Webster, was for his brother Jim. When informed by the mayor that Jim was perfectly well, Bat smiled and handed over his empty six-guns. Until that moment, he had not known whether he was battling in Jim's defense or to avenge his death.

At a hearing that afternoon in police court, formal charges against Bat were brought by City Marshal Fred Singer, who had made a belated appearance. The complaint stated that "W. B. Masterson did . . . unlawfully, feloniously, discharge a pistol upon the streets of said city." Bat pleaded guilty and was fined eight dollars and costs. The *Walnut City Blade* commented sarcastically a few days later: "It costs $8.00 to shoot a man through the lung in Dodge City — such was Bat Masterson's fine."[4]

Updegraff had ben shot through the lung during the melee, certainly, but it is not so certain that Bat Masterson was the man who shot him. Updegraff, who was in serious condition for several days but slowly recovered, gave credit — or blame — for the only hit scored during the battle to an unnamed interventionist. His version of the affair was set forth in a letter to the *Medicine Lodge Index*, his hometown newspaper, and was reprinted in the *Ford County Globe*. Under the heading "The True Statement of the Shooting at Dodge City," the Peacock-Updegraff side of the case was presented:

> There having been several statements published relative to the shooting that occurred here, in which I was wounded, and as my relatives and friends live in your city, I desire to make a brief statement of the affair for the purpose of correcting the erroneous statement heretofore published, that all concerned may know that I am not entirely to blame for it all. When I arrived here from Medicine Lodge I went into the employ of Peacock & Masterson, as barkeeper. During the time I was so employed a friend of Masterson's robbed a woman of $80 by entering her room while she was absent. I advised her to have the party arrested, which she did, through the proper officers. Masterson thereupon came to me and insisted that I should make the woman withdraw the complaint, which I refused positively to do. He, Masterson, thereupon informed me that my services as barkeeper was no longer needed, and I must quit. Mr. Peacock, the

other member of the firm, thereupon insisted that I should stay, as I was right. Masterson having claimed to be a killer, then undertook the job of killing me, and attempted it on the following evening by coming into the saloon and cocking his revolver in my face. I got the best of him by a large majority, and notwithstanding his reputation as a killer, he hid out and was next morning arrested upon my complaint. He or his friends then telegraphed an inflammatory dispatch to his brother, Bat Masterson, who arrived in due time, and met Mr. Peacock and myself midway between the two front streets and without warning to us, commenced shooting at us. We of course returned the fire and soon drove Bat Masterson behind the railroad enbankment where he lay down out of range of our fire. We were then fired at by parties from the saloon doors on the north Front street, from one of which I was shot through the right lung, now six days ago. I feel that I will be around again, and will not die as the party wished me to do. The parties who participated in the affair against me were the citizens bounced out of town, and I invite anyone who doubts this statement, to correspond with any respectable man in this place, who, I am satisfied will corroborate this statement.

Respectfully yours,
Al Updegraff [5]

Bat and Jim Masterson published no statement in defense of their actions. Jim and Peacock dissolved their partnership and arrived at a mutually agreeable financial settlement. By nightfall, the Masterson brothers had departed Dodge.

Several questions might be raised in connection with the Updegraff account. First of all, there is no record of a complaint by Updegraff against Jim Masterson in the Dodge City Police Court docket for the year 1881. Second, Updegraff conveniently neglected to explain why he and his brother-in-law were walking together, guns under their coats, toward the railroad depot at the very moment a train bearing Bat Masterson was pulling into Dodge. It is quite possible that news of Bat's approach preceded him and that Updegraff and Peacock were planning a warm welcome. Bat's cautious action in dropping from the train before it pulled even with the station may well have saved his life. Finally, it is highly unlikely that if Bat, one of the finest shots on the frontier, had cut loose at the two men without warning, as Updegraff alleged, he would have failed to score a single hit.

There is little doubt, however, that many residents of Dodge

were angered by the incident and that they directed their anger at
Bat and Jim. Said the *Ford County Globe*:

A State warrant was issued later in the evening, for several parties
connected with the affair, but they were allowed to leave town, with the
understanding that they were not to return.

Great indignation was manifested and is still felt by the citizens against
the Masterson party, as the shooting was caused by a private quarrel, and
the parties who were anxious to fight should have had at least a thought
for the danger they were causing disinterested parties on the street and in
business houses.

Such was the nature of the affair that the officers thought best not to
undertake the process of criminal prosecution, although many advised it.
At any rate the citizens are thoroughly aroused and will not stand any
more foolishness. They will not wait for the law to take its course if such
an outrage should again occur.[6]

Nick Klaine's *Dodge City Times*, once Bat Masterson's staunch
champion, took up the hue and cry against the Masterson brothers,
Bat in particular:

The firing on the street by Bat. Masterson, and jeopardizing the lives of
citizens, is severely condemned by our people, and the good opinion
many citizens had of Bat. has been changed to one of contempt. The
parties engaged in this reckless affray were permitted to leave town,
though warrants were sworn out for their arrest. Bat. Masterson, James
Masterson, Chas. Ronan and Tom O'Brien were the accused, and there is
good reason to believe they will never darken Dodge City any more. We
believe the authorities were perfectly right in permitting these men to go.
If they will remain away, there will be no more trouble in Dodge City.
Should they return they will be prosecuted.[7]

Thus Masterson stock was at its lowest ebb in Dodge after the
Battle of the Plaza. Jim did not return to the Cowboy Capital for
almost eight years and then only briefly. Bat was destined to return
long before that, and the occasion of his next appearance was to be
a particularly dramatic and triumphant one.

It is clear that much of the bitterness Bat felt toward Dodge and
some of its leading citizens derived from the aftermath of this
incident and the personal censure he received from people he
considered his friends. The two most prominent were Nick Klaine
and Mike Sutton. When a report was circulated two months later

that Bat was coming back to Dodge, the sharp division between pro- and anti-Masterson people became quite clear. A letter purportedly written to Bat Masterson by lawyer Harry Gryden was published in the June 9, 1881, issue of the *Times* under the head "REACHING TO THE BOTTOM" and with this explanation: "The following letter, which was addressed to W. B. Masterson, S. Pueblo, has been handed us for publication. The contents will be well understood by the citizens of Dodge City.

Dear Bat: I am sitting in Kelley's; we have just took a drink, and Jim says to drop you a word — the damn town has been torn up over the telegram of your coming. Webster telegraphed to Sargent and the shot gun brigade was up all night. They consisted of Webster, Singer, Bill Miller, Deger, Tom Bugg, Boyd, Emerson, Bud Driskill, Hi Collar, Peacock, Updegraff and others. Nate Hudson refused to support them. Kelley and myself will be up one of these days to see you. I have an annual and have written for a pass for Kelley. Don't give away what I tell you Bat; it is damn hard for me now to stay here, because I have pronounced myself in your favor; so has Kelley and Phillips, Mose Barber, Dave Morrow and several others. You ought to hear Old Dave ROAR. Charley Powell is here, the same good fellow as of old. Kelley is looking over my shoulder and says "tell him Sutton is at the bottom of it all, damn him."

Yours as ever,
H. E. Gryden

The letter created a minor sensation in Dodge. "As there was considerable demand for the paper and we were unable to supply the call for extra papers," said the *Times* the following week, "we reproduce the letter with a paraphrase in rhyme, written by a well-known bard who was present last week." Under the line " 'Better Walk 100 Miles to See a Man than Write a Letter' — Van Buren" appeared the rhymed parody of Gryden's letter:

Dear Bat: I am sitting in Kelley's
And we are filling our bellies
With something to drink:
That is fair, we think.

Jim says to send you word,
For we have just now heard
That the damned town is humming

With the news of your coming;
They say that "the shot gun brigade" —
(Kelley bring me a lemonade,)
Was up all the night;
It was a hell of a sight
To see Webster, Singer and Bugg
Each biting off the very same plug,
And Deger, Boyd and Miller,
Fill up their glasses and swill'er
Down, while Driskill, Peacock and Collar
Were enough to make you holler.

Nat Hudson I know does not belong,
You hear me sound my gong.
I'll try my best to be up some day,
And from the looks of things I'll come to stay;
I'll get a pass for Kelley to ride on,
As sure as my name is Harry Gryden.

It's damned hard for me to stay here,
At night, by day in constant fear —
Have to stand them off for beer,
And the shot guns are always near,
And you may bet your belly
That I and Kelley,
And I state it flat,
Are for you, Bat;
And so is Morrow,
To his own sorrow;
And there is Barber,
They will not harbor,
Because he is sound and true
For truth, freedom and you.

It would make you sore,
To hear old Dave roar.
Let's have some beer;
Charley Powell is here,
He is not wise as he becomes older;
Kelley looks over my shoulder,
And says to send you a kiss,
And tell you, at the bottom of this,

Is that sinner and glutton,
Whom you know as Mike Sutton.

So be kind to yourself and clever,
And I am, Gryden, as ever.[8]

Either the rumor of Bat's imminent return to Dodge was un-founded or he changed his mind; he avoided the cow town the rest of that year. During the ensuing months, he toured the Colorado mining camps, bucking faro banks wherever he found them, from resplendent houses that rivaled Tombstone's Oriental to rude lean-tos on distant railroad sidings. Everywhere he went, his reputation had preceded him and men viewed covertly from the shadow of their hat brims the renowned gunslinger from Dodge. When he turned up in a town, whether it was Trinidad or Denver, Gunnison or Aspen, Silverton or Buena Vista, the tales of his exploits would circulate again, to be colored and elaborated upon in the retelling.

Then came the story spun by Dr. Cockrell to the correspondent for the *New York Sun*, which was widely reprinted, and this was quickly followed by the equally fatuous "interview" with Master-son in the *Kansas City Journal*.

If Jim Masterson saw the story in the Kansas City paper, he must have been astounded to learn that he had been killed by Peacock and Updegraff. He would have been taken aback also to read that Bat, upon hearing of the killers' remark, "The Mastersons were born to run," traveled eleven hundred miles back to Dodge be-cause it "infuriated him more even than the death of his brother." It was some comfort to know, however, that if Peacock and Updegraff read the story, they would learn that they, too, were both dead, victims of Bat's smoking guns.

Jim Masterson, of course, was not shot during the Battle of the Plaza; it is far from certain that he was even a participant. Peacock was not hit. The wound Updegraff received was not fatal, and it is evident from his published letter that he did not believe the shot that felled him had been fired by Bat but thought it came from someone firing from the saloons along Front Street. Alfred Henry Lewis and Wyatt Earp include Updegraff among Bat's supposed six-gun victims and have been followed in this by most later writers. Walter Noble Burns quotes Wyatt as saying that Updegraff lingered for two months after the Battle of the Plaza and finally died of the lung wound, which had been complicated by pneumonia.[9] Actually, the bibulous bartender lived for two years after the ruckus with the Masterson boys. He died in 1883 at Dodge City, a victim of smallpox.

The reference in the *Journal* article to Bat's "reported run-in with soldiers in Texas" undoubtedly concerned the Corporal King fracas in Sweetwater. Lewis and Earp credit Bat with King's death, but Bat may or may not have fired the shot that killed King in the general melee described by George Curry.

"Bat Masterson was a brave man," Burns quotes Wyatt Earp as saying. "As a peace officer he deserved all the celebrity he ever had, but as a killer his reputation has been greatly exaggerated. Old stories credit Bat with having killed twenty-seven men. The truth is, he never killed but four in his life."[10] These four, said Wyatt, were King, Wagner, Walker, and Updegraff. To this list, Lewis added the name of Jim Kennedy.[11]

Here is what available contemporary records show:

(1) King probably was killed in a general melee. Bat's gun *may* have fired the fatal shot.

(2) Wagner suffered a death wound from a shot fired by Ed Masterson after Ed was fatally wounded.

(3) Walker was wounded by Ed Masterson but recovered.

(4) Kennedy was wounded by one of several bullets fired at him by Bat's possee. It *may* have been a bullet from Bat's rifle. He did *not* die as a result of this wound.

(5) Updegraff suffered a wound from a shot which *may* have been fired by Bat. Updegraff himself did not think it was. This wound was *not* fatal.

(6) There is only one recorded instance after 1881 in which Bat unlimbered his gun and burned powder. It occurred sixteen years later in Denver. Bat was acting in an official capacity and one slight injury resulted.

Hence the sum total of Bat's victims is one dead, maybe; one wounded, certainly; two wounded, perhaps. Indians he may have shot as a hunter and scout are excluded, but even in the battles in which he participated he had no confirmed kills.

On November 17, 1881, two days after the write-up in the *Kansas City Journal*, the editor of the *Atchison* (Kansas) *Champion* gently chided his newspaper brethren for their cupidity and, in an amusing editorial, demanded an audit of Bat's sanguinary score:

TOO MUCH BLOOD

The **Champion** is the last paper to discourage any citizen in a worthy pursuit, or to deprive any Kansan of the fruits of his honest toil, or of honors earned; but really the newspaper correspondents east and west credit some of our people with more bloodshed than rightfully or reasonably belongs to them. We do not stickle about a few tubs full of gore, more or less, nor have we any disposition to haggle about a corpse or two, but when it comes to a miscount or overlap of a dozen, no conscientious journalist, who values truth as well as the honor of our state, should keep silent. To credit unjustly a man with having killed thirty or forty people when his accomplished bookkeeper, with the undertaker to check off, can only find two dozen has a tendency to bring Kansas statistics into disrepute, and also to discourage some humble beginner in the field of slaughter who has yet sent only four or five to act as foundations for the daisies.

Somebody out at Pueblo, in a letter to the New York **Sun**, started the story that ex-sheriff "Bat" Masterson, of Dodge City, had killed twenty-six men, and was as yet only twenty-seven years of age, with a long life of usefulness before him. Two of the men were Mexicans, whom Mr. Masterson bagged at one hunt, and whose heads, we are informed, he cut off and carried to Dodge City to sell for whatever the market price was at that time. Mr. Masterson being in Kansas City since, in company with the celebrated romanticist, Mr. Harry Gryden, a Kansas City paper comes out with the **Sun**'s story greatly renovated, repaired and generally beautified. Mr. Masterson is represented as modestly disclaiming the statement that he decapitated the two Mexicans. The reporter had got ahead or, rather, two heads of him there, but, while he wished no public reception, brass band, or anything of that sort, he **was** the bright and morning star that had shown on twenty-six graves, besides a fight with a fragment of the United States army, which had led to Gen. Sherman's earnest request for more men.

Now this may all be so, but we "allow" that twenty-six men is a good many. They would make a string about one hundred and fifty feet long, or well on to half a cord. Incorporated, they would make a city of the third class in Kansas, and the crowd largely outnumbers the Democratic vote in some counties, though not much "deader" than that party in some localities. Twenty-six, two dozen with two "brought forward!" It may be all right, but it seems too much for a small man only twenty-seven years of age, and we call for a recount.

In all of his writing about the events and characters he had seen and known on the frontier, Bat never mentioned his supposed killings. But neither did he ever deny them in print, which at first blush might seem surprising for a man who was known for hating sham and pretense. Bat's reason for allowing the legend to grow during the early years can be surmised. He was a professional gambler and sometime lawman. A reputation as a swift-handed death dealer was useful in the world in which he moved. Notorious gunfighters were in demand as dealers in border gambling houses and as peace officers in frontier towns. Contrary to the idea, developed by western writers, that well-known gunmen were constant targets for eager youngsters seeking instant reputations, a man known as a fast gun, a survivor of many six-shooter duels, was much less likely to be braced by toughs and roughnecks in saloons and gambling halls than other men. Bat must have reasoned that if, as was the way in much of the West, a man's courage and fighting ability was to be measured by his contributions to Boot Hill, he would allow the twenty-six to be claimed for him.

In a letter dated February 4, 1890, and addressed to Frank D. Baldwin, his commander during the Indian campaign of 1874, Bat commented on the notoriety he had attained:

> The newspapers both East and West have devoted a great deal of space to me, and it seems that when they run out of a subject upon whom they can appropriately devote a column or two, their minds revert to me. They do it with such a recklessness and with such utter disregard of the truth that I make no kick — just let them go ahead. I have concluded that they can't do me any harm.[12]

In his later years, the tale must have appealed to Bat's strong sense of humor.

Wyatt Earp related a story illustrating this element in Bat while explaining to his biographer that the notching of gun butts to tabulate killings was a highly overpublicized practice.:

I never knew a man who amounted to anything to notch his guns with "credits," as they were called, for men he had killed. . . . I have worked with most of the noted peace officers—Hickok, Billy Tilghman, Pat Sugrue, Bat Masterson, Charlie Bassett, and others of like caliber — have handled their weapons many times, but never knew one of them to carry a notched gun.

Strange how such wild tales become current. I know the start of one, about Bat Masterson's "favorite six-gun with twenty-two notches in the butt." Bat's sense of humor was responsible. . . .

Some rapacious collector of souvenirs pestered Bat half to death with demands of a six-gun that Bat had used on the frontier. The collector called on Bat in his New York office and so insistently that Bat decided to give him a gun to get rid of him. Bat did not want to part with one that he had used, so he went to a pawnshop and bought an old Colt's forty-five which he took to his office in anticipation of the collector's return. With the gun lying on the desk, Bat was struck with the idea that while he was providing a souvenir, he might as well give one worth the trouble it had caused, so he took out his penknife and then and there cut twenty-two "credits" in the pawnshop gun. When the collector called for his souvenir and Bat handed it to him, he managed to gasp a question as to whether Bat had killed twenty-two men with it.

"I didn't tell him yes, and I didn't tell him no," Bat said, "and I didn't exactly lie to him. I simply said I hadn't counted either Mexicans or Indians, and he went away tickled to death."[13]

Apparently, the naïve gun collector was none other than Fred Sutton, the lad who had skinned buffalo hides for Bat when he went on his last hunt with Bill Tilghman and Neal Brown in 1876. "Bat had killed aplenty," said Sutton in his book of reminiscences, adding proudly: "I have his best six-shooter in my collection, and it is pretty well covered with notches."[14]

CHAPTER SIXTEEN

THE DEADLY DENTIST

Early in 1882, Bat Masterson journeyed to New Orleans to witness the first of the many heavyweight title fights he was to see in his lifetime. Paddy Ryan, recognized by the *National Police Gazette* as the American heavyweight champion, was scheduled to meet a young upstart from Boston who had badly battered a series of opponents in his swift ride to eminence in fistic circles. Ryan and the Boston Strong Boy, John L. Sullivan by name, were to fight on February 7 for the right to the title and a side bet of twenty-five hundred dollars.

On February 6, about a thousand fight enthusiasts from all over the country assembled in New Orleans, but on the eve of the battle, it was learned that Louisiana authorities were not going to permit it to take place. A special train was chartered forthwith and the entire gang — fighters, handlers, and followers — rode in twelve coaches over the state line into Mississippi. At Mississippi City, a small town on the Gulf, a ring was set up on the front lawn of the Barnes Hotel, and preparations were made to stage the battle in open defiance of a hasty proclamation issued by Governor Lowry of Mississippi forbidding prizefighting in that state. From the train poured a heterogeneous throng.

As he shouldered his way through the crowd in search of a good position from which to view the proceedings, Bat may have recognized such unlikely spectators as Joe Jefferson, William H. Crane, and Nat Goodwin, all prominent actors of the day; Dan O'Leary, the renowned peripatetic; and Henry Ward Beecher and T. DeWitt Talmadge, a pair of eminent divines who, presumably, had come to be properly shocked at the primitive gladiatorial combat, the better to denounce such activity from their pulpits. It is less likely that as Bat brushed past a young man who spoke with a strange accent and was dressed in a beaver-collared greatcoat with a sunflower in the lapel he would have recognized Oscar Wilde, recently arrived in the United States for a lecture tour. Red Leary, a notorious bank robber, was among those present, as were Frank and Jesse James, the latter but two months away from his date with death at the hands of Bob Ford.

All of these diverse characters, linked only by their mutual love for the ring, anxiously awaited the appearance of the principals of the occasion, Ryan and Sullivan. The odds favored Ryan two to one, and betting was brisk. How Bat fared in the wagering is unknown, but, win or lose, he was privileged in seeing, according to prize-ring legend, the first knockout in pugilistic history. Billy Madden, Sullivan's trainer, reportedly coined the term after the great John L. leveled Ryan with a right-hand smash in the ninth round. Sullivan became the bare-knuckles heavyweight champion of America, and a new era in boxing had begun.

From New Orleans, Bat headed back to the western country. On February 14, he stopped off for a day in Trinidad, Colorado, on his way to Raton, New Mexico. Trinidad, a city of 6,500 situated in southern Colorado at the gateway to Raton Pass into New Mexico, was a prosperous cattle and mining center called by its inhabitants in their more ambitious moments the Pittsburgh of the West. Here Bat found many members of the sporting fraternity who had left Dodge and taken up residence in Trinidad. Brother Jim was well established and was serving on the police force under City Marshal Lou Kreeger. Charlie Ronan was involved in the Battle of the Plaza the previous year and had been ostracized with Bat and Jim, was there, coughing out his life in the last stages of consumption. He would be dead within six weeks at the age of twenty-six. Frank Loving and John Allen were dealing faro in rival establishments; P. L. Beatty, Jim Kelley's former partner in Dodge, was managing the Grand Central Bar; and George Goodell, who had served on the police force at Dodge in 1880, was on hand.

Gambling was brisk in Trinidad, Bat was told. Among the establishments were the Imperial Saloon, where John Allen ran the faro game; Collier and Gilman's Bank Exchange; Dave Blubaugh's Tivoli Saloon, featuring "Handsome and Orderly Club Rooms"; Mac's Place; the Boss Saloon, managed by Dutch John Butz; and Jake Emick's Brunswick, where A. J. Vaughn conducted the keno and highball games. At all of these, the action at the tables was often interesting and sometimes profitable. However, most of the high-stakes games were to be found in the Bonanza Saloon, presided over by W. J. ("Billy") Martin, veteran Cheyenne high roller and circuit follower. "The faro game at the Bonanza ran way up in the 'C's' last night," a Trinidad paper had noted a few days earlier.[1]

Bat went on to Raton as planned, but nine days later he was back in Trinidad checking out the prospects. "Bat Masterson, the good looking brother of Officer Masterson, is taking in the sights about town," noted the *Trinidad Daily News*.[2] Evidently liking what he saw, Bat stayed on. The Democrats had control of city government at the moment, but a municipal election was only five weeks away, and Republican John Conkie, who was running for mayor, told Bat that if he were elected he would push for Bat's appointment as city marshal.

Louis M. Kreeger, the current city marshal, was a popular man in Trinidad. He was born in North Carolina, served with Quantrill's Guerrillas during the Civil War, and had been early on the scene at Trinidad, coming to the infant town in 1867 from Taos. He had served ably on the city police force, his most dramatic exploit having been a gunfight with two cowboys less than two months before Bat arrived. In this battle, he downed one adversary after two bullets had ripped through his clothing.

The sheriff of Las Animas County, of which Trinidad was the seat, was Juan Vijil, a prosperous Mexican-American who was returned to office in election after election by a county constituency that was half Spanish-speaking. Vijil held himself aloof from the dirty, dangerous business of frontier police work, spending much of his time on the large cattle spread he owned with his brother or looking after his mining interests. He delegated the daily routine of the sheriff's office to Undersheriff M. B. McGraw, a hard-nosed Irishman with a fiery temper. When McGraw needed help, he enlisted the services of one or more of the former officers and experienced fighting men in the city. Jim Masterson, Jose Alirez, H. E. Hardy, Dave Wilkins, and George Goodell all served at times as deputy sheriffs.

Jim Masterson had attained a certain level of popularity and respect as an officer, often being singled out for commendation by the press, as in January, when the *Daily Times* said he had "commenced a good work Thursday night by 'running in' five of the numerous vags and bunco steerers who are hanging around town."[3] But Jim was criticized for his lack of patience with some miscreants and the alacrity with which he would apply the barrel of his six-gun to their craniums. An indictment for one such incident already had been filed against him when he went into Mac's Place one evening in March with Lou Kreeger to break up a fight among several miners. According to the story in the *Daily News*, one of the belligerents objected to arrest and "squared himself off for a fight. . . . Officer Masterson, without many words, struck him full in the face with his .45 and the men were marched to jail without any further trouble."[4]

When Jim again was accused of brutality for this action, he was defended by Marshal Kreeger and Olney Newell, editor of the *News*. "The man was drunk and surrounded by a drunken party," Kreeger was quoted. "He was getting ready for a fight in which his companions would have joined. The only thing to do was to drop him. Masterson was nearest to him and hit him. If he had not done so I would."[5] Said Newell: "If a man resists arrest we say bring him to time, and if it is necessary to hit him, hit him hard."[6] The following April, the case against Masterson for assault with intent to inflict bodily injury was dismissed in the county court, with all costs being assessed against the prosecuting interests.

Jim may have had an eye on the city marshal appointment himself. In February, a few days after Bat took up residence, Jim complained to Olney Newell that he was "playing in hard luck lately . . . missing chances to show his nerve."[7] When John Conkie was elected mayor the first week in April, however, it was Bat Masterson's name that was mentioned as being in the running for the job. Reported the *News*:

There is considerable wire pulling over the nomination of the city marshal. The office pays ostensibly $75 per month drawn from the city but it is said to be worth at least $125. Naturally this neat little income is worth fighting for and the candidates are various and many. Kreeger, the present marshal, wants to hold his place if he can and Bat Masterson is being strongly pushed forward. Dick Wootton would be quite willing to accept the position and several others are lying quiet as a dark horse.[8]

The first meeting of the new city council was held on Monday, April 17, when appointments of city officers were to be made. By far the greatest topic of interest in town that Monday morning, however, was the gunfight that had occurred the preceding evening between Frank Loving and John Allen. Cockeyed Frank Loving, it will be remembered, was the young gambler who shot and killed Levi Richardson, Bat's old buffalo-hunting companion, in the Long Branch Saloon in Dodge three years earlier. Bat was impressed by Loving's coolness and later used his performance as an example of the quality of deliberation Bat considered essential to survival in a showdown gunfight. Allen had served briefly as a law officer in Dodge but left ignominiously in the spring of 1876.

On Sunday, April 16, Allen wounded Loving mortally in a gunfight that began in the Imperial Saloon and ended in the street outside Hammond's hardware store next door. Allen was arrested by Marshal Kreeger and Jim Masterson. After a preliminary hearing, he was released on bail pending his appearance before the grand jury.

In September, Allen was cleared, the grand jury having brought no true bill against him. He was congratulated by the *Trinidad Democrat*: "Mr. Allen has a host of friends — not only sporting, but among business men [and] all are gratified."[9] When Allen left town, headed for Dodge City, the editor said it was "the wish of his many sporting friends in Trinidad that he 'live long and prosper.' "[10] Bat Masterson apparently was not one of those who wished him well. He wrote some years later, with more than a trace of bitterness: "Allen, soon after his acquittal for the murder of Loving, became a street preacher and of course all has been forgiven."[11]

Under the heading "Turbulent Trinidad," a correspondent for Denver's *Rocky Mountain News* provided details of the Allen-Loving fracas in its April 21 issue, adding:

Trinidad is having her annual Spring boom and the city is unusually lively. No attempt is made to suppress gambling and that it is becoming the sporting men's stronghold is painfully apparent, and from early in the evening to the small hours of the morn, the sonorous voice of the dealer is heard at the numerous resorts, as he ropeth in the unwary and sometimes the wary, for verily "high ball" and "monte" and "keno" are not always with the "swift," and the experienced rounder often "goes broke," and pawneth his diamond stud and calla-lily scarf pin to secure a new stake.

This is the third shooting affair that has taken place here in the past four months. They *will* occur, in spite of the Argus vigilance of the well organized police force, and, in consequence, Trinidad is establishing a reputation that is anything but enviable.

At the first meeting of the new city council, Mayor Conkie, as promised, offered the name of Bat Masterson for appointment as city marshal and asked the council to confirm it. Four of the six councilmen voted for Bat, the other two casting their ballots for Uncle Dick Wootton, the old pioneer and plainsman, who also had been nominated. Lou Kreeger and Feliciano Vijil were appointed city policemen to serve under Bat. Salaries were set at $75 per month for the marshal and $60 per month for the other officers. "City Marshal Masterson sports a handsome silver star engraved with his official title," proclaimed the *Daily News*.[12] A few days later, the *News* editor, aware of the unsavory reputation the town was developing, inserted the following item:

Two shooting affrays were nipped in the bud Sunday. The guns were drawn and fired but no one was hurt and the matter is hardly worth noticing. Why? Because it does not need a great deal more of this kind of business to hurt the town immeasurably and if no one is hurt or arrested it don't count.[13]

In another edition, Newell growled, "If the killings hold out as they have begun since the new year, the office of coroner will be looked upon hereafter as something more than a sinecure."[14]

The usually uproarious months of April and May passed with little violence to report in the Trinidad periodicals. On May 3, Newell praised the new marshal for closing down a particularly rowdy whorehouse:

Bat Masterson deserves credit for breaking up a gang of harlots that located on West Main Street. Their quarters had for some nights been the scene of disgraceful orgies that aroused the attention of the neighborhood and made it a public disgrace until Masterson served his written notice to vacate.

In early May, Bat received a visit from an old friend. One day, Wyatt Earp swung down from the northbound Santa Fe. With him were his young brother Warren, Doc Holliday, and four hard-eyed Arizona gunmen.

During the winter of 1881–82, Bat had followed closely in the newspapers the developments in Arizona's long-smoldering Earp-Clanton feud, which had at last burst into open warfare. Communiqués from the Tombstone front told how Wyatt, Virgil, and Morgan Earp and Doc Holliday had shot it out at the O.K. Corral with a force of San Simon cowboys composed of Tom and Frank McLaury, Ike and Billy Clanton, and Billy Claiborne. Both McLaurys and Billy Clanton were killed, and Virgil and Morgan Earp were wounded. Later dispatches told how Virgil was ambushed outside the door of the Oriental and crippled for life by a double load of buckshot. Several months later, unseen assassins murdered Morgan Earp and narrowly missed Wyatt.

Wyatt Earp then began as cold-blooded a manhunt as ever was staged in all the western country. With his deputy U.S. marshal's commission and a handful of warrants issued by Judge William H. Stilwell, Bat's silk-hatted railroad acquaintance, Wyatt organized a posse that included Warren Earp, the kid of the fighting Earp clan; Doc Holliday; Sherman McMasters; Dan Tipton; Texas Jack Vermillion; and Turkey Creek Jack Johnson. At the railroad depot in Tucson, Wyatt, accompanied by his ubiquitous shadow, Doc Holliday, shot and killed Frank Stilwell, believed to be one of Morgan's murderers. Florentine Cruz, a half blood commonly known as Indian Charlie, was apprehended by the Earp posse at a ranch near Tombstone and, after confessing to participation in Morgan's killing, was cut down by Wyatt. Within ninety-six hours after Morgan Earp's death, two of his assassins had fallen victim to Wyatt's wrath. The posse scoured the Arizona wastelands for the rest of the outlaws. At Iron Springs in the Whetstone Mountains, they came face to face with a hideout band led by Curly Bill Brocius. Earp claimed to have killed Curly Bill in the sharp engagement that followed, and although Sheriff John Behan and Wyatt's enemies vociferously denied that the ringleader of the San

John H. ("Doc") Holliday. Bat did not like him, but Wyatt Earp did, and that was reason enough for Bat to go to Doc's aid. Courtesy Kansas State Historical Society.

Simon outlaws was dead, it is significant that he was never seen again in the Tombstone country.

Wyatt led his posse in one more swing through the outlaw bailiwicks in a futile search for other members of the gang, then headed north for Colorado. The man hunters sold their horses in Silver City, New Mexico, and continued by stage and train to Trinidad, where Wyatt disbanded his posse. McMasters, Johnson, Vermillion, and Tipton headed south for New Mexico and the Texas Panhandle. Holliday went north with Trinidad gamblers Texas George and Sam Osgood to try his luck at the gaming tables of Pueblo and Denver. Wyatt and Warren remained with Bat a few days in Trinidad before starting for the Gunnison country. "Messrs Wyatt and Warren Earp are still with us," reported Olney Newell on May 5. "Their brothers [sic] went south Wednesday morning. Again the *News* takes pleasure in saying they are all 'way up' boys — gentlemen of the first water."

While in Trinidad, Wyatt explained to Bat that a grand jury in Tucson had brought in a murder indictment against Doc Holliday

and himself in the death of Frank Stilwell. Sheriff Behan held
Cochise County warrants for all members of the Earp posse for the
slaying of Indian Charlie. He would be willing to return to Tucson
in Pima County, where his old friend Bob Paul was sheriff, Wyatt
said, but he was convinced that once back in Arizona, Behan
would claim him. If he or any member of his posse were delivered
unarmed into Behan's clutches, Wyatt said grimly, he would be
killed in cold blood.

Within a few days, Bat had an opportunity to do a favor for his
old friend. Doc Holliday was arrested in Denver and was being
held for the Arizona authorities. Wyatt could do nothing to help,
but Bat Masterson could — and did. As in the rescue of Bill
Thompson, Bat's distaste for an individual did not prevent him
from taking unusual steps to aid that individual if by so doing he
was helping a friend. As has been said, Bat did not like Holliday
but tolerated him on Wyatt's account. He made his dislike clear in
an article on the fast-shooting dentist:

Holliday had a mean disposition and an ungovernable temper, and
under the influence of liquor was a most dangerous man. . . . I have
always believed that much of Holliday's trouble was caused by drink and
for that reason held him to blame in many instances. While I assisted him
substantially on several occasions, it was not because I liked him any too
well, but on account of my friendship with Wyatt Earp who did.

Holliday had few real friends anywhere in the west. He was selfish and
had a perverse nature — traits not calculated to make a man popular in
the early days on the frontier. . . .

Physically, Doc Holliday was a weakling who could not have whipped
a healthy 15-year-old boy in a go-as-you-please fist fight, and no one
knew this better than himself, and the knowledge of this fact was perhaps
why he was ready to resort to a weapon of some kind whenever he got
himself into difficulty. He was hotheaded and impetuous and very much
given to both drinking and quarreling and, among men who didn't fear
him, was very much disliked. . . .

He was slim of build and sallow of complexion, standing about five
feet ten inches, and weighing no more than 130 pounds. His eyes were of
a pale blue and his mustache was thin and of a sandy hue. . . . It was
easily seen that he was not a healthy man for he not only looked the part,
but he incessantly coughed it as well.[15]

The close friendship that developed between Holliday and

Wyatt Earp certainly must be recognized as one of the strangest in the annals of the frontier. Wyatt apparently saw — or thought he saw — in Doc's character qualities that completely escaped Bat Masterson. In explaining his friendship with the unpredictable dentist, Wyatt said:

> With all of Doc's shortcomings and his undeniably poor disposition, I found him a loyal friend and good company. . . .
> To sum up Doc Holliday's character as I did at the time of his death; he was a dentist whom necessity had made a gambler; a gentleman whom disease had made a frontier vagabond; a philosopher whom life had made a caustic wit; a long, lean ash-blond fellow nearly dead with consumption and at the same time the most skillful gambler and the nerviest, speediest, deadliest man with a six-gun that I ever knew.[16]

As for Doc's devotion to Earp, Masterson testified:

> His whole heart and soul were wrapped up in Wyatt Earp and he was always ready to stake his life in defense of any cause in which Wyatt was interested. . . . Damon did not more for Pythias than Holliday did for Wyatt Earp.[17]

Wyatt was a lucky man; in addition to the devotion of Doc Holliday, he had the deep friendship of Bat Masterson, which was a rare friendship indeed. Bat was ready to go to great lengths to save Holliday from what Wyatt said would be sure death in Arizona. Wyatt's certainty on that score was echoed by Holliday in an interview with a reporter from the *Denver Republican* after Holliday's arrest. Said Doc:

> If I am taken back to Arizona, that is the last of Holliday. We hunted the rustlers and they hate us. John Behan, Sheriff of Cochise County, is one of the gang, and a deadly enemy of mine, who would give any amount of money to have me killed. It is almost certain that he instigated the assassination of Morgan Earp. Should he get me into his power my life would not be worth much.[18]

Doc was arrested in Denver on May 15 by a man named Perry M. Mallan, who said he was an officer from Arizona. Bat was in Denver at the time and, upon learning of it, acted immediately to secure a writ of habeas corpus.

Interviewed by a reporter who was at the police station covering the story, Bat scoffed at the reports that Holliday was a vicious desperado. Said the May 16 *Denver Tribune*:

Masterson said that Holliday was a responsible man, a Deputy United States Marshal, and for a time Deputy Marshal of Tombstone, and that the cowboys only wanted to assassinate him as they had Virg and Morgan Earp. It was feared that he would be taken from the jail last night and murdered. . . . At 3,30 o'clock this morning, a writ of habeas corpus signed by Judge Elliott was served upon Sheriff Spangler, ordering him to hold the prisoner until he could be brought before the Court this morning.

Bat's next move was to wire City Marshal Jamieson of Pueblo, who soon arrived in Denver, armed with a warrant for the arrest of one John Henry Holliday, D.D.S., and together the two marshals tried to snatch Doc from the capital before extradition papers arrived from Arizona. In his 1907 article on Holliday, Bat said the trumped-up charge against Doc was for a holdup:

I had a complaint sworn out against Holliday, charging him with having committed a highway robbery in Pueblo. . . . The charge of highway robbery made against Holliday at this time was nothing more than a subterfuge on my part to prevent him from being taken out of the state by the Arizona authorities.

The years had dimmed Bat's memory on that point, apparently, for the *Rocky Mountain News* of May 19 stated that Marshal Jamieson wanted Doc for running a bunco game: "The warrant charges Holliday with being an operator in a confidence game at the place above named, by which a 'sucker' was relieved of the sum of $150." The *News* went on to explain how Bat's brash attempt to whisk Doc quickly out of Denver failed:

While Marshal Jamieson was sitting in the Sheriff's office Deputy Sheriff Charles Linton brought in "Doc" Holladay [sic]. It is said that the Marshal showed his warrant and asked to immediately take Holladay along with him, when Sheriff Spangler refused to let him do so, saying that Holladay was already held on one charge and that he could not be taken to Pueblo unless a writ of Habeas Corpus was granted by Judge Elliott. . . . Sheriff Spangler says the arrest by the Pueblo parties is a put up job to secure Holladay's release. He says that . . . he shall hold Holladay till the arrival of officers from Arizona, but that he shall not deliver him to them unless they show they have the proper authority.

Although his first try had failed, Bat continued to work diligently to free Doc. The Denver papers were full of wild tales concerning Holliday's lurid past. Said the *Republican*:

> Doc Holliday, the prisoner, is one of the most noted desperadoes of the West. In comparison, Billy the Kid or any other of the many Western desperadoes who have recently met their fate, fade into insignificance. The murders committed by him are counted by the scores and his other crimes are legion. For years he has roamed the West, gaining his living by gambling, robbery and murder. In the Southwest his name is a terror.[19]

Bat buttonholed a reporter from the *Republican* and vehemently denied that Doc was the blackhearted scoundrel that he had been painted. "I tell you," he was quoted as saying, "that all this talk is wrong about Holliday. I know him well. He is a dentist and a good one. He . . . was with me in Dodge, where he was known as an enemy of the lawless element."[20] In emphasizing Doc's good behavior in Dodge, Bat failed to mention his more characteristic proclivity for troublemaking in other border camps.

Bat was never content to remain on the defensive in any issue, so he launched an attack on Perry Mallan, who was becoming something of a hero in Denver. Said the reporter for the *Republican*: "Masterson . . . claims that Mallen [sic] is a fraud and a friend of the cowboys, whose only object is to get Holladay back in order that he might be killed." The following day, Bat confronted Mallan in the sheriff's office and took some of the wind out of his sails in person. "Part of the conversation between the officers last evening," reported the *Republican*, "was in relation to Mallen's claim that Holladay was the man he had hunted for seven years for killing a man back in Utah. Masterson asserted positively that Holladay had never been in Utah, and Mallen finally acknowledged that he might have been mistaken."

By branding Mallan a fraud, Bat had struck closer to the truth than perhaps he himself realized. Some time after the Doc Holliday case had disappeared from Denver headlines, an enterprising writer for the *Republican* did a little checking on the overnight celebrity and found that Mallan held no commission as a peace officer in Arizona or anywhere else. He was, in fact, nothing but a petty swindler. Trading on his sudden fame, Mallan had conned a couple of Denver citizens out of money. "These two cases," said the paper, "will cause Perry's forcible return to Denver should he be found anywhere, but it is probable that his face will never be seen here again. What is our gain is some one else's loss."[21]

While the legal battle for custody of Holliday was going on in Denver, another contest for the same prize was being waged in Arizona. John Behan, sheriff of Cochise County, and Bob Paul, sheriff of Pima County, had both petitioned Governor Tritle for extradition papers with which to secure custody of Holliday. The Arizona governor presented the papers to Paul, much to Behan's anger. Sheriff Paul entrained for Denver to claim the prisoner, but he was forced to wait several weeks in the Colorado capital. Frederick W. Pitkin, governor of Colorado, had to sign the extradition papers before they were effective, and Pitkin was out of town.

The extradition hearing had been set for May 30. Late in the evening of the twenty-ninth, Bat learned that Pitkin had returned to the capital. Direct and resolute as always, Masterson was determined to see the governor in person to plead Doc's case. He needed help, however, someone who could get him close to the gubernatorial ear. He went to see E. D. Cowen, Capitol reporter for the *Denver Tribune*, a man well known and respected in local political circles. "Bat Masterson . . . made a plea for assistance in the *Tribune* editorial rooms," wrote Cowen in recalling that visit. "He submitted proof of the criminal design upon Holliday's life. Late as the hour was, I called upon Pitkin."[22]

The nature of the "proof" Bat offered to support his claims and the arguments he used during his audience with the governor were never disclosed. Bat himself disposed of the meeting and its consequences with one simply worded sentence: "I was in Denver at the time, and managed to secure an audience with Governor Pitkin who, after listening to my statement in the matter, refused to honor the Arizona requisition for Holliday."[23]

For the record, Pitkin denied extradition on two grounds. The first was faulty legal terminology in the drawing up of the extradition papers; the second was the warrant for Doc that Bat had fabricated in Pueblo. The governor's action was not without repercussions. The *Rocky Mountain News*, which led the journalistic crusade for Holliday's return to Arizona, commented bitterly:

Frederick W. Pitkin. The
Colorado governor listened to
Masterson's appeal, and Doc
Holliday escaped the Arizona
warrants. Courtesy Denver
Public Library.

The excuse upon which he allowed the alleged murderer to go free has
not impressed the Sheriff's force with a high opinion of his candor, they
claiming to know of a case in which a requisition from the same Territory,
with the same defect, was honored by him. Neither does the expression of
opinion that "Doc" should be taken to Pueblo for trial give general
satisfaction. . . . There does not appear to be any doubt that the Pueblo
charge was trumped up solely for the purpose of taking "Doc" out of the
hands of the Denver Sheriff's force.[24]

On the same day Pitkin denied the Arizona requisition, Doc
Holliday was taken to Pueblo by Marshal Jamieson to face the
bunco charge. Bat went as far as Pueblo with Doc, then went on to
Trinidad. There is no record that he ever saw Doc again.

As expected, Holliday was troubled little by the Pueblo matter.
He "always managed to have his case put off whenever it would
come up for trial," Bat said, "and, by furnishing a new bond, in
every instance would be released again."[25] Tuberculosis finally
brought an end to the wayward dentist's career, a feat that several
top-notch gunmen had been unable to accomplish. When Doc died
at Glenwood Springs, Colorado, in 1887, he was still under bond
for Bat's rigged indictment in Pueblo.

CHAPTER SEVENTEEN

THE JAIL OF TRINIDAD

"Marshal Masterson, who has been in Denver for some time past interesting himself in the release of Doc Holliday, is home again," reported the *Trinidad Daily News* on June 2. Oddly enough, there was no word of censure for the city marshal who had absented himself from Trinidad for more than two weeks to engineer the liberation of a notorious gambler and gunman wanted for murder. Perhaps this was because Trinidad had been so peaceful, with or without the presence of the chief law officer. On May 1, H. E. Hardy, a popular former officer, had been appointed to the force, and during Bat's absence, Lou Kreeger, Feliciano Vijil, and Hardy had managed very well to hold things level.

Hardy stayed on the force for only two months, then took a job herding cattle on the Sam Doss ranch. Punching cows evidently did not agree with him, for within another month he was back in Trinidad with an appointment as deputy under Sheriff Vijil.

The *News* of July 6 noted the opening on Marshal Masterson's staff: "Since Officer Hardy has resigned his position, the council should be looking for a man to fill his place. As the streets have become orderly and quiet it should be kept so." Then was appended a gratuitous recommendation: "George Goodell is the best man for the place."

When the vacant position had not been filled by July 9, the paper applied some pressure by means of an open letter addressed to "Our Marshal and Police," deploring the conditions on the streets which had been "orderly and quiet" only three days before:

There is a grand howl on the part of Commercial Street people on account of the fact that the ruffians are holding high carnival there with perfect freedom from arrest. A respectable gentleman informed the *News* that he saw three fights there yesterday afternoon within as many hours and not a single arrest was made. These fellows who have flocked here from the lower country appear to think that in Trinidad they are licensed to do as they please. . . . Unless something is done soon the indignation of the people may assert itself in a way that means business.

The "fellows from the lower country" were a crowd of tinhorn gamblers, bunco artists, and saloon ruffians who had been run out of Raton in a general crackdown. Most of them had come to Trinidad, twenty miles north, to set up their swindle games and sucker traps again.

The council was quick to react, and, as Olney Newell of the *News* had suggested, George Goodell was soon on the force. "Officer Goodell issued his mandates yesterday to ten or fifteen of the gamblers to leave town at once. They asked until Monday to settle their bills and pack their pie boxes," reported the *Democrat* on July 15, adding a few days later: "Officer Goodell looked too utterly too yesterday in his new uniform."[1]

Included in the roundup of undesirables by Marshal Masterson's police were some familiar characters of the frontier towns, con men and crooks who had worked their skin games in railheads and mining camps from Wichita to Leadville and had been outlawed in cattle towns from El Paso to Ogallala. Johnson ("Cornhole Johnny") Gallagher, who had plied the gambling trails for fifteen years and in palmier times had been associated with high-rolling hotshots like Dick Clark and Luke Short, encountered evil days and was arrested as a common vagrant. Fined twenty-five dollars and costs by Judge Bransford, Gallagher was unable to pay and was put to work on the chain gang, shoveling up horse manure in the streets.

The most notorious character gathered in, however, was John Jefferson Harlan, known throughout the West as Offwheeler, who was arrested on July 22 as a vagrant, fined one hundred dollars, and sentenced to thirty days by Judge White. Offwheeler, so called because he seemed to have the strength of a mule, was the leader of a gang of confidence men who had been operating around the depot. He and two other men were accused of robbing a resident named Krille.

Four months earlier, Harlan had been run out of tough Las Vegas, New Mexico, by a vigilance committee. Notices appeared in Las Vegas on March 24 directed to "Thieves, Thugs, Fakirs and

Bunko-Steerers, Among Whom Are J. J. Harlin, alias 'Off Wheeler;' Saw Dust Charlie, Wm. Hedges, Billy The Kid, Billy Mullin, Little Jack, The Cuter, Pock-Marked Kid, and about Twenty Others,'' advising them that if they were found within the city limits after ten o'clock that evening they would be invited to a "Grand Neck-Tie Party" catered by "100 Substantial Citizens."[2]

A Pueblo paper described Harlan as "a man of medium height but extraordinary breadth, having shoulders like those of a buffalo bull. He has a pleasant, good-humored countenance, which has won him many a friend among his class. He is not only an 'Off-Wheeler' but a whole team when it comes to shrewd planning and decided execution."[3]

A few weeks after the crooks and sharpers had been given the bum's rush out of Trinidad, a few of them sneaked back into town. "Officer Goodell fired a noted crook by the name of Fox yesterday on a 24 hour notice," reported the *News*. "There are three or four more remaining of that stripe, who were run out of town several weeks ago and have had the audacity to return again." Then Newell called for the direct action that had apparently worked in Las Vegas: "Our citizens will yet have to make a telling example to such thugs by a necktie festival of some of them, some of these nights during the 'wee small' hours."[4]

Newell favored strong, forceful action against miscreants, especially when George Goodell was involved, Goodell being a particular favorite of the editor. While making an arrest one day, Goodell was bitten on the finger by his prisoner. Enraged, he slammed the man over the head with his six-shooter and "he fell like he had been hit with a pile driver." Newell defended Goodell and frontier lawmen in general, saying necessity compelled them to be very tough:

A mind with the tenderest feeling would not accept the position of a marshal or police officer in a town containing more or less tumultuous characters. Men are required for these positions who are willing to take their lives in their hands and who expect not only to get hurt, but to give hard knocks.[5]

J. J. Harlan and those arrested with him did not serve their thirty-day sentences. Shortly after they were incarcerated, they somehow escaped and skipped town.

The calaboose at Trinidad belonged to the county, and the prisoners were the responsibility of Sheriff Juan Vijil. The city of Trinidad paid him monthly for guarding and caring for persons deposited there by Marshal Masterson and his deputies. On the morning of August 11, Olney Newell published an editorial entitled "Escaping Prisoners," in which he took the county officers to task for "carelessness and negligence" in the operation of the jail. It elicited no response from Sheriff Vijil, but Undersheriff M. B. McGraw was quick to retort by means of a card published in the *Democrat*, a new paper edited by A. K. Cutting: "Olney Newell . . . all you have said I think was intended for me; but I am like the man that the ass kicked — I consider the source."[6] Thus were fired the first shots in a battle that was confined to the pages of the newspapers for a week before it erupted into an angry confrontation, drawn guns, and blood spilled on a Trinidad street.

Since McGraw had chosen to take on Newell, the editor directed his criticism at the undersheriff and challenged him to answer specific charges relating to the management of the Las Animas County hoosegow. McGraw replied through the pages of the *Democrat* with increasingly heated cards. It soon became apparent to McGraw that Newell was being fed information that McGraw found embarrassing. Furious, McGraw sought out the *News*'s editor and demanded the name of his informant. When Newell refused to divulge his source, the lawman, by means of the *Democrat*, invited him into the street:

> In regard to the articles that Olney Newell has published about me, all I wish to say is that they are a lot of *cowardly* and *willful lies*; and if he refuses to give me the name of the author, I consider him, Olney Newell, a *cowardly*, *malicious liar* and the author of the articles referred to is a dirty low-bred *pimp* and a coward, and now if you are any part of a man, put on your "fighting clothes" and come to the front and take your part.[7]

Newell calmly replied in his next edition that "the editor of the *News* has no time for street broils but is generally to be found doing business in the old stand where he will be pleased at any time to see people who have matters to settle."

By this time, McGraw had learned that Officer George Goodell was Newell's informant, and in his next card, he blasted the city policeman:

Sir — In regard to the cowardly and malicious lies that have been published in regard to myself in the News, the author of which has been unknown to me until yesterday morning, I find a willful lie sworn to by one George Goodell. Now, all I wish to say about the matter is first, to give the character of George Goodell, the originator of the cowardly lies that have been published. He, George Goodell, lived in Dodge City previous to his coming to Trinidad, and for one year he acted as a pimp for his own wife, and, I am told, by good authority, that he has done the same thing here in Trinidad; and after his wife would make money in that way, he [George Goodell] would take the money and gamble it off. This is the true character of George Goodell. I do not ask anyone to take my word for it but let Mr. Goodell come forward and demand the proof and I will furnish it. I will state further that the first time I was satisfied of these facts was the day I discharged him from the Sheriff's office.[8]

M. B. McGraw was a very reckless man. A few months earlier, when most Trinidad citizens were breathing easier because several weeks had passed without shooting, he had been quoted in the paper as saying, "There has been no one killed for a long time but there are lots of them that ought to be."[9] What he had now spat out in public view about Goodell, whether true or not, was an open invitation to fight. More than an invitation, it was a demand.

During all that week of charge and countercharge, accusation and bombast, City Marshal Bat Masterson had been out of town, on one of his frequent trips to Denver. Whether he could have done anything to head off the showdown between his deputy and the county officer is doubtful. At any rate, when he stepped off the train in Trinidad on the morning of August 19, he found the town in a state of great excitement.

At 9:10 that morning, Officer George Goodell was standing in front of Jaffa's Opera House watching Undersheriff M. B. McGraw walking resolutely toward him. McGraw stepped up close, snarled a few words, and, putting his right hand on his gun butt, slapped Goodell in the face with his left. Goodell jerked his pistol and brought the muzzle up just as McGraw's weapon was clearing the holster. Goodell's first shot smashed into McGraw's upper right arm, and the undersheriff's pistol fell to the sidewalk. Goodell fired again, hitting his man in the body. McGraw stumbled and fell into Jaffa's open doorway. "For God's sake, hand me my gun!'' he screamed. Goodell pumped two more bullets into him, hitting him in the left arm and breast.

Deputy Sheriff Hardy, who had come on the run with the first shot, reached Goodell and threw both arms around him. But George Goodell at that moment was a man gone kill crazy. Dragging Hardy, he lurched to the gutter, stooped, and picked up McGraw's gun. Swinging around, a pistol in each hand and Hardy on his back, he fired twice more at the prostrate McGraw, hitting him once, before Hardy managed to bring him under control.

Hardy placed Goodell under arrest. McGraw was carried into the Ritenburg House. He was like a sieve. There were ten holes in his body where .45-caliber bullets had entered and exited. He was still alive, but the doctors gave him little hope. Two days later, on August 21, he died. On the same day, a coroner's inquest found that ''M. B. McGraw came to his death by pistol shot wounds inflicted . . . by one George Goodell, and . . . that said shooting and killing was not done with felonious intent.''[10]

Obviously a little stunned by events, Olney Newell wrote: ''Human life is a sacred thing and the *News* looks upon the ending of the controversy as most lamentable and may be said to be traceable to the unwillingness of men to recognize the fact that Trinidad is no longer a lawless frontier settlement, but a busy, thriving city where intelligence and law has superceded the revolver and the mob.''[11] This was written by the same man whose paper that very month called for ''a necktie festival . . . some of these nights during the 'wee small' hours'' as an example to the thugs in town.

A. K. Cutting of the *Democrat* was criticized severely for publishing McGraw's inflammatory cards in his paper. Several subscribers demanded that he discontinue publication. ''One of them had quite a skeleton in his own closet a year or so ago,'' Cutting remarked casually.[12]

George Goodell remained on the police force at Trinidad until the middle of October, when he resigned and departed for Dodge City. With Goodell safely out of town, Cutting began inserting slanderous items about the former officer, calling him a murderer and thief and intimating that he had an accomplice in the ''murder'' of McGraw, a charge that had not been made, by Cutting or anyone else, at the time of the killing. "It is said by knowing ones," he announced in his issue of October 18, "that George Goodell — one of the murderers of Under-Sheriff McGraw — left Trinidad several hundred dollars ahead, from fines collected and not turned over to the proper authorities. His accomplice will count ties when he skips." Nothing ever came from the unsubstantiated charges, and by the end of the year, Cutting was through as a publisher in Trinidad. The *Democrat* was taken over by Dr. Mike Beshoar and E. M. Bogardus and renamed the *Trinidad Daily Advertiser*.

Trinidad was unusually quiet in the weeks following the Goodell-McGraw gunfight. "Police matters for the past few days have been remarkably dull, said the *Democrat* in September, "so much so that Judge Bransford has a severe case of ennui. This indicates stirring times before long, if we should judge from the saying that 'there is always a calm before a storm.' "[13]

The biggest excitement in town that fall was caused by the arrest of a sneak thief named Charles Miller, who was charged with breaking into the house of E. N. Post and stealing some jewelry. When arrested, he had in his possession a ring that belonged to Post and eighty dollars in cash, which he claimed to have won gambling. He was convicted of petit larceny and paid his fine and court costs with the eighty dollars. After his release, he was spotted on the street by several "leading citizens," who pursued him, bent on horsewhipping him. Miller ran back to the jail and begged for protection:

> Marshal Masterson came up and took him out, saying he would see that he got out of town without hurt. Mr. Masterson led him around our streets for some time, trying to get him away from those who were bent on whipping him. . . . After the would-be whippers quieted down, Miller kept himself secluded until dark and skipped out of town.[14]

It was Wyatt Earp's recollection that in April, 1881, when Bat went from Tombstone to Dodge City to help Jim Masterson, the two brothers were alienated, having quarreled at some time. Although there is no direct evidence of fraternal estrangement during the Trinidad period, no open argument or public display of animosity by one brother toward the other, it is significant that the two

Lou Kreeger, city marshal of Trinidad. It was common knowledge that he was an expert with the six-gun, but Bat thought him more agile as a spoonwielder. Courtesy Old Baca House–Pioneer Museum, Colorado State Historical Society.

experienced lawmen never served together during this time. Jim had been on the city police force under Lou Kreeger, but when Bat took over, he found himself out of a job. Kreeger, Feliciano Vijil, Hardy, and Goodell were appointed during Bat's regime, but Jim Masterson was always passed over.

After Bat was appointed marshal, Jim took a job as bartender in P. L. Beatty's Grand Central Bar. Finally, in late October, he again pinned on a badge, this time as a county officer. "Jim Masterson is fully clothed with the power and authority of constable," reported the *Trinidad Weekly News*. "He was invested with these honors by the board of commissioners."[15] A month later, the *Democrat*, noting that with the departure of George Goodell the city police force was a man short, pushed Jim for the job: "Now that there is a vacancy on the police force, it is to be hoped Mr.

James Masterson will be remembered by our worthy mayor. Jimmy has proved himself worthy of the position."[16] But it was not to be. "Jose Y. Alirez has donned his policeman's uniform," recorded the *Democrat* three days later.[17] Jim Masterson would have to wait for a new city marshal to get back on the force; he would not, or could not, work for his older brother.

Bat was involved in a few rough-and-tumbles while making arrests late in the year. In light of the fiction that Bat got his nickname by hitting troublemakers on the head with a cane in Dodge City, it is amusing to note this item in the November 9, 1882, issue of the *Democrat*: "Marshal Bat Masterson received a severe bat on the head from a cane in the hands of a drunken man yesterday whom he was in the act of arresting." A month later, the paper reported: "Bat Masterson, our city marshal, in a scuffle to arrest a man on Sunday evening, lost a valuable diamond ring for which he will reward the finder if returned to him."[18]

The city police were censured soon after the start of the new year 1883. On January 9, the *News* berated them for not having "vags" clean up the streets and not making

more arrests of men who violate the city ordinances by committing nuisances on the street and using profane and vulgar language on the streets, especially Commercial Street. . . . We do not say that our policemen are not watchful, but they are not sufficiently so for the good of the peace, decency and dignity of a fast growing city like Trinidad.

The new paper in town, the *Daily Advertiser*, joined in on the seventeenth:

There were more saloon brawls in town on Monday night than for a month previous. . . . The city councilmen say that these saloon brawls must be stopped, even if the saloons have to be closed and the officers of the city removed. This is as it should be, for the rough element is getting too much of the upper hand here.

Border drifters and saloon bums had indeed begun to show up more frequently in town, and Bat methodically went about rounding them up again. " 'Slapjack Bill' and Herman Larson got into a little ruction last night and Bat Masterson took them up and put them in the cooler," duly noted the *News*. Two familiar barflies from Dodge City, Bobby Gill and James Dalton, were collared and

Juan Vijil was sheriff of Las
Animas County when Bat was
city marshal of Trinidad.
Courtesy State Historical
Society of Colorado Library.

given a ticket-of-leave: " 'Bobby, the Gil' and 'Jimmy, the Dalt'
have been a little too 'fly' recently, and Bat Masterson gave the
gentlemen a polite invitation to walk out of the city at the earliest
convenient moment, and Bobby went this morning and Jimmy
goes this evening."[19] Bat always had a certain affection for the
utterly worthless but completely harmless Bobby Gill, and when
he saw the derelict shivering on the road, he relented. "Bat
Masterson, seeing Bobby the Gil exposing himself to the cold air
last night, took compassion on him and run him into the county
hotel to keep him comfortable," said the *News*.[20]

   In February, Bat became involved in a controversy that for a few
days provided copy for newspapers in three states and one territory
and ultimately brought forth from Bat's pen one of the vituperative
epistles for which he became known. The story, as first detailed in
the pages of the *Trinidad Daily Advertiser*, concerned a man
named O. L. Hale, alias J. H. Conway, alias Elias Conway, who

was a fugitive from Iowa, where he had broken jail six years earlier while awaiting trial for forgery. Hale had made his way to Salida, Colorado, where he had been charged with murder. He somehow slipped out of Colorado and went to New Mexico, settling first in Albuquerque and later in Silver City. Sheriff Joe R. Landes of Lucas County, Iowa, acting on information that Hale was in Silver City, went there and arrested him on the old Iowa fugitive warrant. At Wallace, Hale's friends tried to take him from the sheriff. The attempt was unsuccessful, but the story reached the Colorado papers. Said the *Advertiser*:

On Sunday there arrived in Trinidad, registering from Salida, two men named Miles Mix and Jesse Brown, who came down for the purpose of arresting Elias Conway on the charge of Murder. They had heard of the prospective passage of Conway through this place and telegraphed the officers to hold him, should the train bearing him come along before they did.

Miles Mix, who had worked with Bat in Dodge, and Brown were sheriff's deputies from Chaffee County, Colorado, and held a capias warrant for the arrest of Hale, alias Conway. The *Advertiser* story continued:

Sunday evening the two men from Salida, accompanied by a couple of officers from this place, met the east bound train on which were Sheriff Landes and his prisoner and demanded the surrender of the prisoner to them as they held a warrant for him on the charge of murder. Landes refused to give up the prisoner, when a lively scuffle ensued, and the prisoner was forcibly taken from the sheriff and turned over to the Colorado officers. Yesterday morning Mix and Brown, accompanied by Conway, left for the north. Sheriff Landes remained here all day yesterday awaiting word from the governors of Colorado and Iowa to whom he telegraphed for instructions, but went east by last evening's train. . . .

The effrontery practiced upon Sheriff Joe R. Landes . . . was something seldom excelled in the West and . . . entirely took him by surprise and force too. . . .

It is commonly regarded that the affair of Sunday night was but a ruse of Conway's pals to release him from the clutches of the law, and it is supposed that he is now again at liberty. Be that as it may, Landes is short one prisoner for whom he searched long and patiently, for whom a large amount of money has been spent in an endeavor to bring him to justice in an Iowa court.[21]

The *Las Vegas* (New Mexico) *Gazette* picked up the story, comparing the Trinidad and Salida officers to swindlers:

There may be some sharp bunkomen down in New York or Boston who can come a game over unsuspecting mortals like Oscar Wilde and Charles Frances Adams, but for nervy impudence commend us to the men of the "perfesh" in the breezy west. The capture of the prisoner from the Iowa sheriff at Trinidad was an artistic piece of work which eastern bunglers would find difficult to imitate.[22]

In a letter to the *Denver Republican*, Miles Mix defended the action of the Colorado officers:

I will state that I am no bunkoman and that none of the men who assisted me were to my knowledge. I went to Trinidad armed with a capias issued out of the district clerk's office of Chaffee County, Colorado, and secured the assistance of W. B. Masterson, marshal of Trinidad, and a policeman and with their assistance took charge of Conway as I believed then and yet I had a right to do, and brought him here and delivered him to the sheriff of this county. He is now in jail and will be arraigned in court today on the charge of manslaughter.[23]

Over in Dodge City, *Times* editor Nick Klaine had long since ended his pretense of friendship with Bat Masterson and was taking editorial jabs at him whenever he could. The Conway story was just to his liking; in the *Times* edition of February 8, he wrote:

Bat Masterson rescued a prisoner who was in the hands of an Iowa officer, at Trinidad, some days ago. Bat tried the means of false papers, but failing in that, he took the prisoner by force. There are some people in this city who would like Bat to return. We think Trinidad is more congenial to him.

Bat had ignored the stories in the other papers, but he lashed back at Klaine with a vengeance. The letter below was published in the *Ford County Globe*:

Editor Globe: — Sir:
Having noticed a short squib in the last issue of the Dodge City Times in reference to myself and as it was evidently written with a view of doing

me a malicious and willful injury, I deem it as a duty devolving on me to refute the malicious statement contained in that short paragraph. I am actuated in writing this explanation of the rescue referred to by the editorial nonentity of the Times in order to give what friends I have left in Ford County who read the Times an opportunity to judge for themselves whether my statement or that of the Times is correct.

I am accused by Old Nick of the Times of having rescued a prisoner from the custody of an Iowa sheriff by force and that I first tried to get possession of the prisoner by means of false papers and finding this could not be done, I resorted to force, which is as infamously false as it is ridiculous. I will dispose of the whole statement by saying that I had no false papers of any kind, and that I did not demand the prisoner from the Iowa sheriff or attempt to take him by force; and furthermore had nothing whatever to do with the prisoner, but simply went to the train in company with Miles Mix, a deputy sheriff of Chaffee County, Colorado, who had a capias warrant for the arrest of the prisoner on a charge of murder committed in Chaffee County two years ago. I was solicited by Mix to accompany him to the train which I did as a matter of friendly courtesy and nothing more.

Mr. Klaine can ascertain the truth of this statement by referring to any official in this place, or to Sheriff Landes of Iowa, if he feels so disposed, but I am satisfied he has no desire to do so, as he has never been accused of either telling or writing the truth by anyone who knows anything of his Missouri or Kansas reputation. He concludes his scurrilous article by saying that some residents of Dodge City are anxious that I should return but adds that Trinidad is a more congenial place for me. To this I will say that I have no desire to return to the delectable burg, as I have long since bequeathed my interest in Dodge City and Ford County to the few vampires and murdering band of stranglers who have controlled its political and moral machinery in the last few years. In conclusion I will say that Dodge City is the only place I know of where officials have taken people by brute force and without the sanction of law, and that on all occasions the officials who committed the unlawful act never failed to receive a laudatory puff from the long-haired Missourian who edits the Times.

Respectfully,

W. B. Masterson, Trinidad, Colorado

Feb. 12, 1883[24]

Bat's literary outburst is interesting from several standpoints. First of all, it reveals the depth of his anger with his enemies in Dodge. Nick Klaine had written and published the article that

incurred the Masterson wrath and consequently bore the brunt of
the epistolary attack, but Bat went on to lambaste the "vampires
and murdering band of stranglers" in league with Klaine in Dodge.
Although, aside from Klaine, he mentioned no names, Mayor A.
B. Webster, City Attorney Mike Sutton, City Marshal Fred
Singer, and erstwhile Marshal Larry Deger knew full well to whom
he was referring.

Bat's outraged denial that he had, as Klaine suggested, rescued a
prisoner unlawfully is amusing in the light of Bat's record as a
deliverer of personal friends (or friends of friends) in legal distress.
No one knew better than Nick Klaine how Bat had snatched Bill
Thompson from under the nose of Ogallala's fiddling sheriff and
how he had contrived Doc Holliday's rescue from the Arizona
murder rap. Neither of these actions — although highly unethical,
to say the least — was ever denied by Masterson, for he felt
justified on each occasion by the peculiar circumstances involved.
To have been accused of yet another illegal deliverance by anyone
other than Klaine or one of his cronies probably would have
bothered him little; during his career, he had been accused of
everything from brutal murder to petty thievery. However, the
unfounded story written by "Old Nick" infuriated him.

A third point of interest is the style of Bat's letter. By 1883, he
seemed to have acquired a command of the language, and there
were indications that he was maturing, to some extent, as a writer.
Three years earlier, it will be remembered, he had composed a
vitriolic missive denouncing Bob Fry of Spearville for publication
of certain charges against him. At that time, Bat could do little with
a pen to express his resentment other than to call Fry a liar and a s—
of a b——. By February, 1883, he was beginning to reveal a
facility with the written word that was to create a new sphere of
fame for him in a later day when the pen replaced the six-gun as his
tool of trade.

From time to time, the Trinidad papers inserted items of interest
to the sporting folk in town. Frank Jackson, "a first class boy and
well known among the sporting men of this part of Colorado as one
of the finest faro dealers in the state," had gone to Wichita for the
summer; or John ("Shotgun") Collins was a visitor in town; or
Buck Foster, Nat Haywood's former saloon partner, had been

killed in Raton by Jim Blackwell; or Nat Haywood had departed Raton and was tending bar at the United States Hotel in Trinidad; or a local faro bank had ''gone by the boards,'' a gambler tapping it for three hundred dollars, and the bank had ''closed for repairs.''

In January, 1883, Billy Martin celebrated the opening of an addition to his Bonanza Saloon with a gala free-lunch night. Lou Kreeger, renowned as a voracious eater, was expected to take all prizes at the free-lunch table, and Olney Newell of the *News* advised everyone to attend just ''to see Kreeger wield the big spoon.'' Fellow Officer Jack Alirez might furnish some competition, said Newell, and Bat Masterson would be in attendance and there was an outside chance he would ''get away with the cake.''[25] A month later, the *Advertiser* reported that ''pools are selling in favor of Masterson in the pool tournament tonight at the Bonanza. Eight poolists have entered the contest.''[26] But the paper did not say whether the favored ''poolist'' was Bat or Jim Masterson, nor did it report the winner.

The annual municipal elections were scheduled for April 3, 1883. A change had been made in the selection of city marshal. In 1882, the position was appointive, the marshal being chosen by the mayor; in 1883, candidates were required to stand for election. Bat was nominated on the Citizens' Ticket; H. E. Mulnix was the candidate for mayor. Opposing them on the Democratic ballot were Louis M. Kreeger for city marshal and D. L. Taylor for mayor.

Throughout the year he had served as Trinidad city marshal, Bat Masterson had been active in his other occupation, gambling. He had maintained a faro bank almost constantly in the Bonanza or one of the other Trinidad gambling establishments and had been available for high-stakes poker games when they could be arranged. No mention of this was made in the press until March, 1883, about a week before the spring municipal elections.

Mike Beshoar, editor of the *Daily Advertiser*, announced that he would support neither slate in the coming election, feeling that the electorate should choose the best man for each office. In late March, however, he began to toss barbs at Bat Masterson regarding his faro bank and his status as a professional gambler:

Mr. Masterson has the advantage over Mr. Kreeger of being a bank president.

There are now two bankers running for city offices — one on each ticket — Mr. Taylor of the Las Animas County bank, and Mr. Masterson of the bank of Fair O. Both have large numbers of depositors — the one of time depositors and the other receives his deposits for keeps.

Mr. Masterson is a professional gentleman and stands high for proficiency in his profession. It is for the voters to say — professional or non-professional.[27]

When *The Squelcher*, a political pamphlet backing the Citizens' Ticket, defended Bat, contending that it required brains to be a successful faro banker and therefore Masterson was the better man for marshal, Beshoar retorted:

If it takes the kind of brains a marshal requires to deal faro, how much cerebral matter is required to buck the tiger? . . .

The mechanics and working men who cater to and spend some of their money at the games are the gamblers who lose and those who preside over the layout are the gentlemen who win. How does this statement of the situation suit *The Squelcher*? . . .[28]

Let each voter scrutinize the character and ability of every man for whom he casts his ballot, for surely the men chosen to make and execute the laws should themselves be lawabiding citizens. . . .[29]

If all our people outside of the churches gamble, it only remains to be ascertained how many are outside and how many inside to know which is uppermost in the city — the gamblers or the churches. If the gamblers, they will win and the churches lose, and vice versa. . . .[30]

The Democrats scored an overwhelming victory over the candidates on the Citizens' Ticket, winning the contests for mayor, treasurer, clerk, attorney, and marshal and electing three aldermen with ease. Lou Kreeger defeated Bat by the lopsided vote of 637 to 248. At that, Masterson did slightly better than his party's candidate for mayor, who was defeated 650 to 241.

The Trinidad election was Bat's third experience as a candidate for office on a general ballot. His record with voters was dismal. In 1879, he had been elected sheriff of Ford County by the slim margin of three votes. Two years later, he was soundly beaten by George Hinkle. Now, in Trinidad, he went down under a landslide. It was the last time he would lose in a general election. He would never enter another.

On April 8, five days after the election, a much ballyhooed footrace was run in Trinidad, matching a New Mexico racer named Maxwell and Corteze D. Thompson from Denver. Maxwell was a local favorite and Trinidad residents plunked down their money on him to win, but the smart money, including Bat Masterson's, backed Thompson heavily and by race time the Denver runner was favored in the odds. Bat knew that Cort Thompson had been running races in Colorado mining camps for six or seven years and at the distance to be run, sixty yards, he was almost invincible. Cort was a gambler and the "solid man" of Denver's leading madam, Mattie Silks. He was fast, but he was also crooked and had been known to throw races.

Bat stationed himself near the finish line and kept a wary eye on Thompson. An instant before the gun sounded to start the race, Thompson bent down to tie his shoelace. At the shot, Maxwell jumped off to a good lead. Thompson ran hard, but he was still behind as the runners approached the wire. It was plain that he would not overtake Maxwell. Suddenly, Bat's foot shot out and Maxwell tumbled to the ground, just short of the finish. Thompson flashed over the line first. As might be expected, complete chaos resulted. Gesticulating, shouting bettors crowded around Masterson, Maxwell, Thompson, judges Shaw and Evans, and McEvery, the referee. The race result was finally voided by the judges because of a foul and the race was rescheduled for the following day.

Bat was still city marshal, the newly elected officers not yet having been sworn in. That night, he secured warrants for Thompson, Maxwell, and Billy Martin of the Bonanza, who was the stakeholder for the race, and arrested them on a charge of obtaining money under false pretenses. Martin was forced to return the money wagered on Thompson. That fleet gentleman was not to be found; he and McEvery had skipped town. The next morning, Maxwell showed up for the race. When Thompson did not appear, Maxwell tried to claim victory on a forfeit, but Bat would have none of that and promptly rearrested the New Mexico runner. The race was never run, and all bets were canceled. "The action of

Sheriff Lou Kreeger (left) and deputies in front of the Las Animas County jail in 1893. Courtesy Old Baca House–Pioneer Museum, Colorado State Historical Society.

Masterson is applauded by the sporting fraternity,'' wrote a *Rocky Mountain News* correspondent who covered the race for the Denver paper, ''while the better class pronounce the act cowardly. There must have been at least $15,000 bet on the race.''[31]

The new City Council held its first meeting on April 16. Lou Kreeger became marshal once again, and Jose Sylvester Raymond and Jim Masterson were appointed policemen to work under him.

Bat Masterson, dandified frontier highroller. Courtesy Kansas State Historical Society.

Bat was not around to see his subordinate take over and his brother move back onto the payroll: five days earlier, he had departed Trinidad. The *Advertiser* gave him one line: " W. B. Masterson left this morning for Denver."[32]

Leaving Trinidad represented no great strain for Bat; he had never put down any real roots. It was reported years later that he had made a thousand dollars a month while serving as marshal at Trinidad, but if he ever made that much money in one month — or in six months — while there, it came across the painted oilcloth of his faro table and not from the city treasury. He never attained the popularity in Trinidad that he once held in Dodge, the kind of popularity that Lou Kreeger had and would continue to have for many years to come. Kreeger served the town or county as a peace officer for thirty years, until his death in 1913.

In January, 1884, Bat remarked on the exalted status of his former deputy in a letter to the *Trinidad News*:

It would be next to impossible for me or anyone else to say anything that would be accepted by the average Trinidadian as a reflection on the official competency of Kreeger. He is recognized by them as their official "demi-god." Therefore, it would be absurd for me to say anything derogatory to his well established character as a brave and efficient officer in the community. In the estimation of a Trinidadian no country can produce Kreeger's equal. As a gormandizer — I am of the same opinion.[33]

CHAPTER EIGHTEEN

THE LUKE SHORT RESTORATION

In February, 1883, Bat said in a letter to the *Ford County Globe* that he had no wish to return to the ''delectable burg'' of Dodge City, but later in the year there transpired events that precipitated a visit by him. Once again he was called upon for help, and once again he dropped everything to rush to a friend's cause. This time, it was Luke Short who enlisted Masterson's aid.

Shortly after Bat's departure from Tombstone, Luke Short and Bill Harris left also, returning to Dodge City. Harris and his partner, Chalk Beeson, owned the Long Branch Saloon, and Short managed the gambling concession in this establishment. In February, 1883, Beeson sold his interest to Short. This ownership change was made at a time when Dodge was undergoing one of its periodic political struggles and set off a chain of events that culminated in the celebrated Dodge City War.

The Long Branch was one of a string of saloons and gambling houses on Front Street. Its neighbor on one side was George M. Hoover's retail and wholesale liquor store; on the other was the Alamo Saloon, owned and operated by Ab Webster, the mayor. Luke Short, himself a Texan, was very popular with the trail hands from the Lone Star State, and after he took over at the Long Branch, Webster, Hoover, and other competitors for the cowboy trade noticed a definite loss of business. Webster was, as Bat put it, ''a stubborn and strong-willed man'' and was not above using his political office to further his personal investments. He set out to break Luke Short.

In March, a slate of candidates for city offices was selected at a mass meeting of voters. Luke's partner, Bill Harris, was the choice for mayor on a ticket backed by the remnants of the old Dodge City Gang, led by former Mayor Jim Kelley and the *Ford County Globe*. A few days later, an opposition slate was chosen by the

BIRD'S EYE VIEW OF
DODGE CITY, KANS.
COUNTY SEAT OF FORD COUNTY
1882
POPULATION 1200

1. Court House.
2. School House.
3. U. S. Signal Service Office.
4. Odd Fellows Hall.
5. A. T. & S. F. R. R. Depot.
6. Post Office, Lloyd Shinn, P. M.
7. Dodge City Grist Mill, H. F. May & Co., Prop's.
X—Methodist Episcopal Church.
A—Presbyterian   "
B—Roman Catholic   "
C—Union

D—Dodge City Times, N. B. Klaine Ed's and Prop.
E—Ford Co. Globe, Frost & Shinn, Ed's and Prop's.
F—Dodge House, Cox & Boyd, Prop's.
G—Iowa   "   W. C. Beebe, Prop.
H—South Side House, South end of Bridge,
                    (Wm. Stales, Prop.
J—Great Western Hotel.
K—Wright House.

Bird's-eye view of Dodge City, 1882. Courtesy Kansas State Historical Society.

anti-Gang group headed by Mike Sutton, Nick Klaine, and Webster; its candidate for mayor was Larry Deger. This faction was ostensibly reformist, which apparently explained Webster's decision not to run again. Webster, a Dodge resident since 1872, had operated a dry-goods store, a grocery, and a lumber business, but when he took over the Alamo Saloon in 1883, he felt that his new role as saloonkeeper was incompatible with his position as reformist mayor. He therefore stepped aside in favor of his close friend Deger, who could be counted on to implement any reform activities without hurting Webster.

The campaign was short but bitter, with vitriol generously dispensed by the antagonistic *Times* and *Globe*. On April 3, Deger defeated Harris, 214 to 143.

Within a month, the new mayor and city council enacted new legislation against prostitution and vagrancy. Ordinance No. 70, "An Ordinance for the Suppression of Vice and Immorality within the City of Dodge City," provided for fines ranging from five to one hundred dollars for anyone convicted of keeping a "brothel, bawdy house, house of ill fame, or of assignation," or of being an inmate or resident of such establishment, or of "plying or advertising" the business of such establishment. "The general reputation" of such houses or inmates was to constitute "prima facie evidence of the character of such houses or persons."

Ordinance No. 71, "An Ordinance to Define and Punish Vagrancy," passed the same day, set fines of ten to one hundred dollars for anyone convicted of "loitering, loafing or wandering" in the city without lawful vocation or visible means of support. Keepers of brothels or gambling houses and those "engaged in any unlawful calling whatever" were subject to prosecution under this law.[1]

On April 28, two days after the ordinances went into effect, City Marshal Jack Bridges and City Clerk L. C. Hartman, the latter wearing a special policeman's badge, entered the Long Branch and arrested three women, euphemistically called singers, charging them with prostitution. Luke Short shrugged. As a professional gambler for many years, he was familiar with the practice in frontier communities of levying fines periodically in order to enrich the coffers of the city treasury. An ordinance prohibiting games of chance had been on the books in Dodge City since 1878, although it had never been strictly enforced. It had been enacted as an emergency measure to secure badly needed municipal funds and was used for that purpose five years. Gambling-house entrepreneurs had paid the city regular monthly sums called fines, but they were actually taxes. Philosophical Luke figured that the new blue laws were just another tax gouge and that all the saloon and gambling-house proprietors who allowed girls in their places — and this would include almost all of them — would have to endure it as another cost of doing business.

When Luke was told several hours after his singers were caged that no women had been arrested in any other saloons or gambling places, he took a walk next door to Webster's Alamo and looked in. The two girls who worked the Alamo were perched on patrons' laps, plying up a storm. In relating the tale, Bat allowed as to how "Luke then smelled a mouse."

Luke Short was a little fellow. He was about five feet, six inches tall and weighed less than one hundred and forty pounds. "It was a small package," said Bat, "but one of great dynamic force."[2] Some people had tried to push Luke around only to learn, to their regret, that he was not easily pushed. Strapping on his hardware, he now headed for the city jail, where the girls from the Long Branch were being detained. City Clerk Lou Hartman, the special officer who had assisted in the girls' arrest was standing on the plank sidewalk near the jail as Short approached. Seeing the diminutive Texan walking toward him with a brace of six-guns displayed prominently, Hartman suddenly remembered Short's reputation as a deadly killer when aroused. Some referred to Luke as "the undertaker's friend" because he usually dispatched his victims with a clean shot through the head, thereby minimizing the mortician's labor.

Hartman jerked his gun and threw lead at the oncoming Short. He fired hastily, and his shot merely kicked up dust behind Luke. The little gambler, surprised but cool and calm as always, drew and returned the officer's fire. But even as Luke pulled trigger, Hartman was running. In his anxiety to depart the vicinity, he tripped over his own feet and pitched headlong off the high sidewalk into Front Street as Luke's shot whistled past his ear.

Short thought he had killed Hartman and went directly back to the Long Branch. Loading a shotgun, he barricaded the door of the saloon and refused to submit to arrest. Larry Deger could talk no one from the marshal's office into going into the saloon after Luke, and the gambler stood his ground throughout the night. The following morning, an emissary sent by Marshal Bridges explained to Short that he had not killed Hartman, only scared him half to death, and that if Luke would surrender his weapons and go peaceably to police court, he would be allowed to plead guilty to a charge of creating a disturbance and would be released after payment of a small fine. Luke agreed. He put aside his guns and started out the door. He had no sooner stepped, unarmed, into the street than two officers closed in on him and marched him to jail, where he was

Luke Short, "a small package, but one of great dynamic force." Courtesy Kansas State Historical Society.

A. B. Webster. He ran Luke Short out of town, thereby precipitating the Dodge City War of 1883. Courtesy Kansas State Historical Society.

locked up and charged with assault. He was released on two thousand dollars bond but was rearrested the following day with several others. Fellow saloonman and gambler Tom Lane and circuit gamblers W. H. Bennett, Doc Neil, Johnson Gallagher, and L. A. Hyatt joined Luke in the calaboose. When they demanded to know the charge against them, they were told they were undesirables.

Short averred in a formal complaint against city officials that he was denied access to counsel while locked up. When Harry Gryden attempted to see him, Luke claimed, he was turned away and threatened if he persisted. Bill Harris wired Larned for attorney Nelson Adams, who hurried to Dodge by train. Mayor Deger and a party of armed men met Adams at the depot and told him to stay out of Dodge.

Finally, Short and his fellow gamblers were taken from the jail by a large body of men and marched to the train station. Included in this party were Deger, Marshal Bridges, Assistant Marshal Clark

Chipman, Undersheriff Fred Singer, Special Policemen Bob Vanderburg and L. C. Hartman, and saloonmen Tom Nixon, Brick Bond, and A. B. Webster. Some twenty-five others, armed and menacing, tagged along. At the depot, the gamblers were offered a choice of trains out of Dodge: east or west. Luke Short chose the eastbound train for Kansas City.

The Webster-Deger combine had succeeded in running Luke out of Dodge, but he was not ready to surrender to the enemy as yet. His pride had been injured, but of even greater importance was the substantial financial investment he had in the Long Branch, for which no settlement had been made. Realizing that the forces arrayed against him in the cow capital were too powerful to tackle alone, he decided to seek help. Of course, the first man he thought of was Bat Masterson. "I was in Denver at the time," Bat said, "and he wired me to come to Kansas City at once, which I did."[3]

At the Marble Hall, a plush Kansas City gambling casino run by Colonel Ricketts and Joe Bassett, Luke Short and Bat discussed the situation. They were joined in their conference by old Dodge hand Charlie Bassett, who was dealing for his brother Joe at the Marble Hall. Bat, no doubt remembering his successful appearance at the governor's mansion in Colorado on behalf of Doc Holliday, suggested that Short pay a visit to Governor George Washington Glick in Topeka. Meanwhile, Bat said, he would line up some muscle to be used if it came to a showdown with the ruling clique. Accordingly, Luke headed for Topeka and Bat started back to Colorado.

On May 10, Short filed a petition addressed to Governor Glick, airing his grievances and asking protection when he returned to Dodge City. The truth of the charges in Short's complaint was attested by W. F. Petillon, court clerk of Ford County, whom Glick had summoned to Topeka. The governor then wired Sheriff George Hinkle at Dodge for a report on the problem there. Hinkle said there was no problem in Dodge:

I showed your message to Mr. Deger who requests me to say that the act of compelling the parties to leave the city was simply to avoid difficulty and disorders. Everything is as quiet here as in the capital of the state and should I find myself unable to preserve the present quiet will unhesitatingly ask your assistance.[4]

Glick was obviously displeased with both the content and the tone of Hinkle's answer. In a long letter to Hinkle on May 12, he made it clear that conditions would change in Dodge City or he would definitely interfere:

The accounts of the way things have been going on there are simply monstrous, and it requires that the disgrace that is being brought upon Dodge City, and the State of Kansas, by the conduct that is represented to have occurred there, should be wiped out. Your dispatch to me presents an extraordinary state of affairs, one that is outrageous on its face. You tell me that the mayor has compelled several parties to leave the town for refusing to comply with the ordinances. Such a statement as that if true, simply shows that the mayor is unfit for his place, that he does not do his duty, and instead of occupying the position of peace maker, the man whose duty it is to see that the ordinances are enforced by legal processes in the courts, starts out to head a mob to drive people away from their homes and their business.

After lecturing Hinkle on his responsibility as sheriff to uphold the law impartially for all citizens, Glick offered assistance in the form of arms or the state militia if necessary.

I ask . . . that you call together the good citizens of Dodge City, lay this matter before them, ask them to come to your assistance. . . . If they offer to furnish you assistance, and will respond to your call, I will order a sufficient amount of arms and ammunition into your custody, so that you can have any assistance that you require.

If this is not sufficient, a company of troops will be at once ordered to Dodge City, and placed under your command and control, so that you shall have full authority and full power to preserve the peace and protect every individual that may be in the city. If this is not sufficient, proceedings will be commenced, for the purpose of at once installing officers in power who will discharge their duties honestly and faithfully to the public. Please give me a full, careful and correct statement of the condition of affairs now, and say to me whether people who have been driven away will be permitted to return to their homes. Use the telegraph freely at my expense, as I have a train ready to go to your city on a moment's notice. . . .[5]

Hinkle's answer indicated a complete lack of understanding of the point at issue:

I will continue to do all in my power to preserve order in the community

yet I cannot become responsible for the actions of any individual. Mr.
Short's expulsion from the city is the direct result of his own action and
the feeling of the people generally is very strong against him. The city is
as quiet now as it has ever been but I fear that if Mr. Short returns trouble
will ensue. . . .[6]

By this time, the story of Luke Short's difficulty was in newspapers all over Kansas, and soon papers as far away as New York and
Chicago were carrying the daily details of what was being called
the Dodge City War.

When Bat returned to Kansas City a day or two later, the *Kansas
City Journal* took note of the appearance of ''Bat Masterson . . . one of the most dangerous men the West has ever produced,'' saying he headed a roster of gunslingers that included
Wyatt Earp, Rowdy Joe Lowe, Shotgun Collins, and Doc Holliday. Dire consequences were predicted when this elite six-shooter
corps descended on Dodge: ''This gathering means something,
and it means exactly that these men are going to Dodge City.
. . . For the good of the state of Kansas, it is hoped the governor
will prevent violence.''[7]

When the news of the gathering clan reached Dodge, something
closely akin to panic struck the Webster forces. Sheriff Hinkle
fired off a frantic telegram to the governor: ''Are parties coming
with Short for the purpose of making trouble? Answer quick.''[8]
Glick's answer, if he sent one, has not been preserved. Someone
started a rumor that the Short platoon was approaching Dodge on
the Santa Fe's *Cannonball*. Hinkle wired the governor the following day: ''Agreeable to your message I was at train with fifty armed
men. No one came. Shall I hold these men in readiness for use?''[9]

Glick must have thought Hinkle had lost his head over the
excitement. He knew that Short and Masterson were in Topeka, for
they had arranged with the governor for another interview. Wrote
Bat:

> The Governor denounced the conduct of the Dodge City authorities but
> said that he could do nothing, as the local authorities at Dodge had
> informed him that they were amply able to preserve the peace and didn't
> desire state interference. We stated to the Governor that we believed we
> were able to rehabilitate ourselves in Dodge, but didn't care to run afoul
> of state authorities, in case we concluded to do so. The Governor told us

Fred Singer, Dodge City fighting man of note, sometimes sided with, sometimes against the Mastersons. Courtesy Kansas State Historical Society.

George Hinkle. The office of Ford County sheriff did not fit him any better than his coat. Courtesy Kansas State Historical Society.

to go ahead and re-establish ourselves, if we could; that he would keep off, and wished us luck.[10]

It is a revealing sign of the free-and-easy conditions prevailing in Kansas in the 1880's, this interview between the governor of the state and a pair of circuit gamblers. Although Short complained of the high-handed treatment he had received from city officials in Dodge, Glick certainly knew that the root of the trouble lay in a competitive struggle for saloon control there — and a law prohibiting the manufacture and sale of intoxicating liquors had been on the statute books of the state for three years!

A few days later, Luke entrained for Caldwell and Bat headed for Colorado again. Wyatt Earp had not followed him to Kansas City, as was reported in the papers, nor had Holliday, Rowdy Joe, or Shotgun Collins. The *Dodge City Times* mistakenly concluded

Governor George Washington Glick. Bat and Luke simply wanted his assurance that he would not interfere with their plans. Courtesy Kansas State Historical Society.

that the Short-Masterson separation indicated a disintegration of their forces and smugly intimated that the planned invasion had been aborted:

Bat Masterson went west Monday night, passing this city on the cannon ball train. Some of the citizens of this place went on the train but they could not gain access to the sleeping car which contained the redoubtable Bat. . . . Few people believed the statements in the Kansas City papers about the proposed action of the gang. And the chief shall flee into the mountains of Colorado, where the lion roareth and the Whangdoodle mourneth for its first born.[11]

Bat was not fleeing, however. He was off to Silverton to marshal the warriors. A few days later, Luke, Bat, Wyatt, and their friends were meeting in Caldwell in a council of war.[12] Wyatt, whose prestige in Dodge had diminished little since he left there four years earlier, was chosen to enter Dodge first. Luke and Bat waited at Kinsley, while Wyatt, backed by four experienced gunslingers — Texas Jack Vermillion, Dan Tipton, Johnny Millsap, and Johnny Green — moved in on the cow camp.

As Wyatt related the story to his biographer, Stuart Lake, when he (Wyatt) arrived at the depot, he came face to face with Prairie Dog Dave Morrow, who was wearing on his vest the badge of a special policeman. Dave greeted Wyatt cordially and nodded sympathetically when Wyatt explained his reason for coming. "Luke got a dirty deal," Dave acknowledged. Wyatt said he thought it would be a good idea if he and his four friends were deputized so that they could wear their guns openly in town. After a brief glance at the cold eyes and determined faces of the five gunfighters, Dave agreed. So, without a great deal of thought about the legality of the move, Special Policeman Morrow appointed Earp and his friends city police officers right there on the depot platform. Wyatt then posted the four at strategic points along Front Street in preparation for a showdown meeting with Mayor Ab Webster. Several other Short cohorts, including Charlie Bassett, Shotgun Collins, and Frank McLain, drifted into Dodge unobserved about this time. Wrote Bat:

It finally became whispered about that Wyatt Earp had a strong force of desperate men already domiciled in town in the interest of Luke Short. . . . When Mayor Webster learned that he had been trapped by Earp, he hunted up the sheriff and prosecuting attorney and sent a hurry-up telegram to the governor, which was signed by all three of them, requesting him to send with as little delay as possible two companies of militia, assuring him that unless that was immediately done, a great tragedy would surely be enacted on the streets of Dodge City.[13]

In his recital of the story twenty-four years later, Bat consistently errs in calling A. B. Webster mayor of Dodge, although he was correct in representing him as the dominant leader of the anti-Short faction. The telegram alluded to here actually was signed by Mayor L. E. Deger, Sheriff George Hinkle, Postmaster N. B. Klaine, Councilman George Emerson, County Commissioner Bob Wright, and merchant F. C. Zimmerman. Dated 8:23 A.M., June 6, 1883, and addressed to Governor Glick, it read:

Our city is overrun with desperate characters from Colorado, New Mexico, Arizona and California. We cannot preserve the peace or enforce the laws. Will you send in two companies of militia at once to assist us in preserving the peace between all parties and enforcing the laws.[14]

Glick did not dispatch militia to Dodge. He sent his attorney general, Thomas Moonlight, and asked Dodge authorities to keep him advised concerning the situation. Bat describes what happend next:

When it became known in Dodge the sort of reply the governor had sent back to the appeal for militia, something of consternation took possession of the mayor's followers. Those who had lately been the loudest in their declarations of hostility to Short were now for peace at any price.

Webster, himself no coward, saw that the yellow streak he knew was in the makeup of his followers was giving unmistakeable signs of recrudescence. He knew that when the time came he would have to fight the battle alone. . . . It was at this stage of affairs that Webster concluded to send for Wyatt, and if possible bring about a settlement of the difficulty without an appeal to arms. In making this move the mayor acted both wisely and timely; for had the case gone over to the next day there would have, in all probability, been bloodshed on both sides.

At the meeting with the Webster faction, Earp presented his demands: Short and Masterson were to be permitted to return to town, and Short was to resume business at the Long Branch unmolested. Webster and his cohorts expressed full agreement with this proposal, and Earp gave his personal guarantee that there would be no conflict. Wrote Bat:

Wyatt immediately notified Short and I by wire of the complete backdown of the enemy, and when we reached the city next day we were cordially received by our friends. The enemy, not being sure that Wyatt could control the situation, kept in the background until he had received assurances from both Luke and I that the peace terms made by Earp would be faithfully lived up to by us.[15]

Although Bat neglected to mention it, at least one of the Webster gang kept so far in the background that he backed clear off the stage and hightailed it out of Dodge.

The *Ford County Globe* described the triumphant return of Luke and Bat:

As soon as Bat Masterson alighted from the train on his late arrival into this city, Mike Sutton started for his cyclone building on Gospel Ridge, where he remained until a truce was made. . . .

On the return of Luke Short and his friends, it didn't take Mike long to arrive at the conclusion that Kinsley was a much healthier locality, and that town is now his abiding place. . . . When Dodge becomes too hot for Mike Sutton, h — l itself would be considered a cool place — a desirable summer resort.[16]

A letter from Bat appeared in the June 9 issue of the *Daily Kansas State Journal*:

I arrived here yesterday and was met at the train by a delegation of friends who escorted me without molestation to the business house of Harris & Short. I think the inflammatory reports about Dodge City and its inhabitants have been greatly exaggerated and if at any time they did "don the war paint," it was completely washed off before I reached here. I never met a more gracious lot of people in my life. They all seemed favorably disposed, and hailed the return of Short and his friends with exultant joy. I have been unable as yet to find a single individual who participated with the crowd that forced him to leave here at first.

All was quiet on the western front when Attorney General Moonlight arrived from Topeka to see what all the fuss was about. Moonlight helped organize a quasi-military organization called the Glick Guards, composed of men from both sides in the recent confrontation. Pat Sughrue was named captain; Dog Kelley was second lieutenant; a Webster backer, Dr. Sam Galland, was appointed surgeon. In the ranks were Luke Short, Neal Brown, Clark Chipman, W. H. Harris, W. F. Petillon, Print Olive, Bill Tilghman, John Sheridan, and Charlie Springer, a mixed bag of Short and Webster adherents.

One of the most well-known photographs in western history was made in Dodge that second week of June, 1883. Luke Short and the more celebrated of his gunslinging friends posed together. The June 14 *Times* noted the event: "The photographs of the eight visiting 'statesmen' were taken in a group by Mr. Conkling, photographer. The distinguished bond extractor and champion pie eater, W. F. Petillon, appears in the group."[17] With Short and Petillon in the picture are Bat Masterson, Charlie Bassett, Bill Harris, Wyatt Earp, Frank McLain, and Neal Brown. Someone long ago labeled this group portrait, perhaps facetiously, "The Dodge City Peace Commission," and the story went that the group ruled Dodge for ten days and dictated new police officers for the town. Contemporary accounts do not confirm this. Jack Bridges remained city marshal until the following year; Clark Chipman had

The Dodge City Peace Commission. Standing (from left): W. H. Harris, Luke Short, Bat Masterson, W. F. Petillon. Seated (from left): Charle Bassett, Wyatt Earp, Frank McLain, and Neal Brown. Courtesy Kansas State Historical Society.

been replaced as assistant marshal by Mysterious Dave Mather just before the gathering. The county officers — Sheriff George Hinkle and Undersheriff Fred Singer — were active in their official capacities until the end of 1883. Of the group, Bat Masterson, for one, was not in Dodge for ten days; he arrived with Luke Short on the seventh of June, and on the tenth he and Wyatt Earp, their mission fulfilled, left town, heading west. The *Garden City Irrigator* reported on the fourteenth that "Bat Masterson and Wyatt Earp alighted from the westbound train Sunday and had a confab with Marshal Earp [Newton, Wyatt's half-brother, city marshal of Garden City]. They were on their way to the recently discovered silver mines at Silver City, N.M."

Dodge returned to its hectic normality. Reported the *Globe*:

Our city trouble is about over and things in general will be conducted as of old. All parties that were run out have returned and no further effort will be made to drive them away. Gambling houses, we understand are again to be opened. . . . A new dance house was opened Saturday night where all the warriors met and settled their past differences and everything was made lovely and serene. All opposing factions, both saloon men and gamblers met and agreed to stand by each other for the good of their trade.[18]

Later the editor reported that "the gambling gentry smile and are again happy, since they are allowed to spread their layouts again. All games were in full blast early yesterday morning."

As might be expected, Nick Klaine of the *Times* carried on an editorial barrage against the men who came to Dodge in defense of Short's interests, centering his attack on Bat Masterson. The editor of the *Trinidad News*, who had been following with interest the goings-on in Dodge, rose to Bat's defense in an article that was reported in the *Globe*:

Out in the wild, wild West, journalism has a breezy sweep which is in fresh contrast to the effete writing of the Eastern press. The Dodge City *Times* at the arrival of Luke Short and his friends contained an announcement that Shot Gun Collins, Dynamite Jack, Dirty Shirt Tom, Cyclone Bill and other notorious characters had come in to "down the town." One of the characters referred to in this bitterly sarcastic manner was Bat Masterson of Trinidad, Colorado, and his home paper, *The News*, resented the slur cast by the *Times* with energy and force. The *News* maintained that the editor of the *Times* had stolen horses in Clay County, Missouri, and was obliged to swim across the Missouri River to escape. He is, said the Trinidad *Addison*, a vile creature. Dirty Shirt Tom, forsooth! The editor of the *Times* had not washed himself for eleven years when he knew him. He used to stand out in the sun and the flies would gather round until the city council condemned him as a nuisance and ordered that he be washed by the police at the expense of the city. This is good old fashioned English. There is no innuendo, no sarcasm, but simple, plain straightforward charges. We await the reply of the Dodge City *Times* with interest.[19]

CHAPTER NINETEEN

"THE DELECTABLE BURG"

The role Bat Masterson played in the Short-Webster difficulty was important not only to Luke's restoration in Dodge but in returning Bat himself to favor in the cow town as well. Many of his old friends who, rightly or wrongly, had been angered by the sudden gunplay that had marked his return to the city in 1881 welcomed him warmly in 1883. Bat's attitude softened in turn, and he spent much time in Dodge during the next several years.

Bat went to Colorado with Wyatt Earp after Dodge was again calm, but in September he was back. The *Ford County Globe* made note of his arrival and mistakenly announced: "We understand that he will engage in the mercantile business at this place."[1] Bat, of course, had no such prosaic intention. He had come to Dodge because county election time was approaching, and he wanted to help some of his friends who were campaigning for office. Pat Sughrue, an old pal, was running for sheriff against former City Marshal Fred Singer. Singer was supported by Mike Sutton and Nick Klaine, and that was enough for Bat; he used all the influence he could muster in the county on Sughrue's behalf.

Bat argued the Sughrue cause so vociferously that it was reported he was to be Pat's chief deputy if Pat won the sheriff's office. In a letter published in the *Globe*, Sughrue denied the rumor:

Some of the opposition, or Singer faction, are circulating a report among stockmen that in the event I am elected sheriff, W. B. Masterson will be my undersheriff, which I positively assert is false; not that Mr. Masterson wouldn't be fully competent and acceptable to a great many people in this county, but he is not a resident of this state and has no intention of becoming such. I am sure, however, that he would reflect as much credit to the office as Mysterious Dave who will be Mr. Singer's right hand man. Respectfully P. F. Sughrue.[2]

Bat's political enemies definitely were unnerved by his presence in Dodge. They next accused him of dictating editorial policy to the *Globe*, the newspaper backing Sughrue's ticket. Said the November 1 *Times*:

Col. Bat Masterson, a well known character in the west, has discarded his former illegitimate business and has adopted newspaper writing as a profession. While Col. Masterson's literary effusions do not have moral or religious tendencies, they are chaste productions in a literary way. The fine artistic style in which Col. Bat wields the pen is adding fame to his already illustrious name. Col. Masterson is now associate editor of the Ford County Globe, and the last number of that paper bears ample evidence of that statement. The Globe has long needed a brainy editor, and the substitution of brains for adipose tissue is certainly commendable, and must be highly appreciated by the readers of that journal. As a newspaper writer Bat is gaining distinction.

When Bat went back to Trinidad shortly before election, editor Frost of the *Globe* commented, tongue in cheek: "As Mr. Masterson has left the city, the *Globe* will be rather a tame paper this week."[3]

Bat reappeared in Dodge on election day, bringing with him Wyatt Earp. Together they watched contentedly as the citizens of Ford County voted Pat Sughrue into office. "Their presence about the polls that day," said the *Globe*, "had a moral effect on our would-be moral element that was truly surprising."[4] A few days after the election, Bat left for Texas with Luke Short. The diminutive gambler, having won the bloodless Dodge City War, had decided to quit the town after all. Bat accompanied him to Fort Worth, where Short bought an interest in the White Elephant Saloon.

From Texas, Bat went on to Trinidad, where he stirred up a controversy with City Marshal Lou Kreeger. In late December, Kreeger went to southwest Kansas after a man named Ed Hibbard, alias Ed Lee, who was wanted for a murder near Trinidad. Accompanied by John Meagher of Caldwell and Fred Singer of Dodge City, Kreeger located Hibbard at his parents' home near Wauneta. Kreeger returned, with Hibbard under arrest, to lavish acclaim in the Trinidad press.

Bat penned a sour-grapes letter to the *News*, contending that

Pat Sughrue. Bat and Wyatt Earp returned to Dodge to help him become sheriff of Ford County. Pat had a twin brother, also a Kansas lawman, and it was difficult to tell them apart. The powder burns on Pat's face, left by a gunfight, helped. Courtesy Kansas State Historical Society.

Fred Singer actually made the arrest and escorted Hibbard to the state line, where he was turned over to Kreeger. As a Colorado officer, Bat said, Kreeger had no jurisdiction in Kansas. He also was ignorant of the law, did not know a requisition from an acquisition, or a habeas corpus from a hocus pocus. When Kreeger attempted to defend himself in the press, Bat wrote another letter:

Kreeger . . . may not be able to express himself as intelligently as some people and possibly knows very little about a habeas corpus or a requisition, but in Trinidad where such little defects are not considered as essential in the constitution of an officer, he stands preeminent in his business. . . . [5]

The jousting in the Trinidad papers was watched with some amusement in Dodge City. Said the *Democrat*:

The . . . Trinidad News contains some letters signed W.B.M. and a reply from City Marshal Kreeger concerning the arrest of the alleged murderer Hibbard. We are informed by under sheriff Fred Singer that the statement of facts made by W.B.M. are verbatim et literatum, true. Yes, says Fred, and more too. But we enter our protest, and hope the News will chastise "Bat" for his deplorable carelessness in spitting out the truth about the "great and good." It was his great fault here and made him enemies, but the predominating streak in Bat's corporosity is that, like Jim Bloodsoe, "he wouldn't lie and he couldn't flunk, I reckon he didn't know how."

Further on in the paper, the editor remarked:

> In a controversy through the Trinidad press, "W.B.M." shows himself almost as adept with the pen as he undoubtedly is with the six-shooter — a dual accomplishment much appreciated on the frontier.[6]

In late January, 1884, Wyatt Earp and Johnny Green stopped in Trinidad from a gambling swing through Texas. Wyatt went on to Salt Lake City, but Green remained in Trinidad, probably serving as lookout for Bat's faro game. Bat was in Dodge City for the township elections on February 5. "Col. Bat. Masterson . . . dropped down from Trinidad on election day," reported the *Dodge City Democrat*. "Bat looks as smooth, pretty and guileless as of old, and was heartily welcomed by his innumerable friends."[7]

Bat went back to Trinidad after the election, remaining only a few days before returning to Dodge. "Bat Masterson and John Green have gone to Dodge City for the summer," said the *Daily Advertiser* on February 20. A few days later, the *Democrat* offered a possible reason for Bat's change of base:

> The genial ex-sheriff, Bat. Masterson, is down amongst us. He was, we understand, drawn as a member of the Grand Jury, soon to convene at Trinidad. Bat, who is constitutionally opposed to secret inquisition and condemnation courts, avoided serving as a juror by a visit to old Dodge. Better come to stay, Bat. What a genial City Attorney or rare old Police Judge you would make, eh?[8]

Bat apparently accepted the invitation to remain in Dodge, for by May he was helping to organize a baseball team and was acting as its vice president. He also participated in a football scrimmage, which left him a bit worse for wear, according to the *Democrat*: "Bat Masterson has the reputation of being able to face a six-shooter without flinching, but when a football pasted him a gentle reminder under the left ear last Tuesday evening, he gracefully retired."[9]

For the big Fourth of July celebration, which was to feature a genuine Mexican bullfight, Bat served on the footrace committee. He and Bill Tilghman acted as judges for a race held June 21 for a thousand-dollar purse. More than three hundred spectators turned out to see a white man named Sawyer and a black man named Hogan run three hundred yards. Hogan won in a close finish, and a great deal of money changed hands in the betting. Said the *Globe*: " 'Bat' and 'Til' were the judges, therefore everything was on the square, and no grumbling was heard by the losers."[10]

There was much grumbling after a close horse race judged by Bob Wright and Drs. Cockey and Chouteau on July 2. In what probably was his first attempt at written description of a sporting event, Bat reported on the race in a letter to the *Topeka Commonwealth*. Wright had not seen the order of finish quite like the two doctorial judges did, and Bat agreed with his friend. With typical directness, he called the doctors "foptailed nonentities" and submitted that although they might be efficient in rendering relief to the afflicted, their heads were too small for judges on a race track.[11] The races held at Newton a few days later apparently were more to Bat's liking. The *Dodge City Democrat* reported on July 19 that he and gambler Walter Hart cleaned up two thousand five hundred dollars during the Newton runnings.

A man named A. J. Howard, who had been around Dodge City for several years, tangled with Bat in September. Howard claimed to be an attorney but never practiced law in Dodge. He had been a clerk in the Great Western Hotel, which was owned by Dr. Sam Galland, one of Bat's enemies. At the time of the altercation reported in the *Kansas Cowboy*, he was a short-order cook in a Front Street restaurant. "Determined to make mince-meat of Mr. Bat. Masterson," said the *Cowboy*, "he selected as a very appropriate instrument for that purpose a carving knife from a foot to eighteen inches long." Howard found Bat in a saloon, and as he opened his assault, someone yelled a warning. "Then the stalwart form of Masterson rose in its majesty."

The paper reported that Bat was unarmed and that he seized a chair and decked Howard. It is unlikely that Bat ever appeared in public without a sidearm during these days. More probably, when he saw Howard approaching with a blade, he used the handiest object to protect himself. Had Howard chosen a gun for his ill-advised attack, Bat's response undoubtedly would have been in kind. As it was, witnesses intervened after Bat knocked Howard down but before he used the chair to administer a fearful beating.

Arrested and taken before Judge Cook, Howard was admonished and fined twenty-five dollars and costs. "But for the want of the requisite funds, Esq. Cook 'cooked the goose' of the cook by sending him to the lockup to work out the fine."[12]

Bat was still deeply embroiled in the politics of Dodge City, Ford County, and the state of Kansas. In July, 1884, the *Dodge City Democrat* reported gleefully that "Sheriff Sughrue, Judge R. G. Cook, Bat Masterson and a dozen others, the backbone of the Republican party in this county" would support Democratic Governor George W. Glick in his bid for reelection. Nick Klaine commented in the Republican *Times*: "We regret that the 'backbone' has become weakened by this bolt. If the party can worry through the summer with a weak backbone probably a November breeze will stiffen the demented anatomical member."[13]

Perhaps Bat may have considered backing Glick because of the sympathetic treatment he and Luke Short received in the governor's office during the Webster-Short confrontation the previous year, but, as Klaine predicted, before the November breezes blew, Bat was safely back in the Republican fold, supporting John A. Martin. At the Ford County Republican Convention at Dodge City in October, Bat was named to the committee on permanent organization.

Later that month, the *Globe* published a piece attacking certain Republican candidates for county office, including R. E. Burns, E. D. Swan, and Nick Klaine. The article was signed *Coal House*. In the next issue of the *Times*, Klaine averred that Coal House was none other than Bat Masterson, whom Klaine dubbed "The Boss Gambler of the West." Masterson countered in a letter to the *Globe Live Stock Journal*:

I see by the last issue of the Dodge City Times, that I am accused of being the author of the article signed Coal House, which appeared in your last issue, and also that I am honored with the title of being the "boss gambler of the west."

As to the article I have this much to say, that any time the good (?) deacon of the Times or any of his scurvy outfit feel desirous of refuting any of the statements contained in Coal House's article I will consider it as an imperitive duty, to sustain every allegation contained therein by the affidavit of every responsible man in Dodge City, and if I fail to do this, I will write an apology to every individual named in said article, and cause the same to be published in all the papers published in this city. There was not anything said in the article referred to that cannot be proven, and if Deacon Klaine, Burns, Schmoker, Swan, or the pestiferous cur who adorns (?) the editorial tripod of the Clipper, don't think I can furnish the necessary amount of documentary evidence to sustain my position in the matter, let them turn their monkey loose, and see whether or not I will be forthcoming.

As to being the "boss gambler of the west," I will say, that I have no desire to usurp a title that the sapient scribe at the Times office bestowed upon one of our worthy citizens, a long time before he became a defaulter in Dodge City.[14]

Always on the lookout for a weapon with which to smite his enemies and having more to say than could be crammed into the letters-to-the-editor section of the *Globe Live Stock Journal*, Bat took up a new cudgel in the form of a special-edition newspaper called *Vox Populi*. A more accurate name for the paper would have been *Vox Masterson*; Bat was publisher, editor, and reporter, and he expounded on the frailties of his foes with great gusto. In a salutation, he declared that the purpose of the paper was to expose the moral character of some of the candidates in the forthcoming election. The paper's "political warfare upon those whom it opposed will be bold and untrammeled. It asks no favors and will give no quarters," promised the editor.

In a lead article, Bat described a "grand collection of living and fossil relics." There was a rare curiosity known as "Klainus Homo, a species of former man now extinct, but the only fossil remains of which we have secured at great cost. . . . It was first discovered buried in mud in one of the valleys of the State of Missouri. When the natives beheld it such terror was spread among them that it was swiftly transferred to the borders of civilization in Kansas."

Bat then pictured "a peculiar kind of winged thing . . . like unto a bird the ancients worshipped, called the Swan. Said bird has been known to take valuable papers from one Ferrier in Spearville, and appropriate them to a fraudulent use."

Next was "a marvelous amphibious creature known as Sutton-a-cuss Gymnatus or the electrical. To whatever object it comes in contact, it transmits a shock such that the victim seldom recovers (in his purse)." In a deft reference to Mike Sutton's defection from the saloon forces in Dodge to the prohibition element, Bat said the creature "is also allied to the chamelion, changing its color to correspond to the object it approaches. It has been known to be one day red like wine and on the next allied to water."

To this remarkable list Bat added "a species of Badger, prowling by night and having a fang of chemical properties, by the use of which the hardest iron is softened and it has even been known to open a safe in a mill by that means" and "the greatest of living wonders, a cross between the Chimpanza and Baboon — nature recoils at such an object."

The paper was interlarded with slanderous statements and accusations:

E. D. Swan would be a nice man to have charge of the poor widows and orphans of Ford County, after turning his aged and decrepit father out upon the streets to die of starvation.

Let Burns go back to Naperville, and tell the people there, who were generous enough to purchase him a paper ticket to Dodge City that the people here don't want him.

Ford County does not want the scum and filth of other communities for county attorney, such is Burns the Republican candidate.

Vote for Milton and Crumbaugh and force the crawling reptiles who are their opponents, to crawl in their holes.

Old Nick Klaine has repeatedly been branded as a thief, liar and murderer, yet he never whimpers, or attempts to deny any of the accusations. We expect that proof of his being a rapist, barn burner and a poisoner of his neighbors horses could be obtained without much effort.

If old Nick Klaine would pay as much attention to the speedy distribution of the mail as he does to the reading of postal cards that come through the postoffice, there would be not so much kicking.

And Bat certainly must have been thinking back to the sheriff's election of 1879 as he composed this final shot: "A candidate is certainly out of luck that has old Nick Klaine supporting him. One puff from the columns of his foul sheet would defeat the best man in Ford County for any office that he would be an aspirant for."[15]

Masterson's diatribes were marked by a certain journalistic talent that was recognized and commented upon by the editors of both the *Globe Live Stock Journal* and the *Trinidad News*. Said the *Journal*: "We are in receipt of the first number of the Vox Populi, W. B. Masterson, editor, which in appearance is very neat and tidy. The news and statements it contains seem to be somewhat of a personal nature. The editor is very promising; if he survives the first week of his literary venture there is no telling what he may accomplish in the journalistic field."[16] The editor of the Colorado paper agreed: "Bat is an easy and graceful writer and possesses real journalistic ability. The News will be glad to hear of his making a howling success."[17]

The only howls heard at the time emanated from the targets of Bat's attacks. All of the candidates bombarded by *Vox Populi* were defeated, and a slate of men friendly to Masterson was elected.

Having accomplished its editor's purpose, *Vox Populi* was allowed to die after its single edition, and Bat, except for occasional letters to other papers, permitted his budding literary talents to lie dormant for the time being. He had learned, however, that, when expertly wielded, the pen was a mighty weapon that could bring a cry of anguish almost as quickly as a blow on the head with the barrel of a six-shooter. He learned also that a fearless, aggressively written assault, if presented honestly, could win many friends for its writer and bring consternation to his enemies.

Bat announced his paper's demise in a letter to the *Globe*.

The Vox Populi is no more. Its mission in this world of progress and usefulness is performed. While its existence was comparatively of short duration, the wonders it performed were simply miraculous. The blows it dealt to the venomous vipers whom it opposed had a telling effect as the returns from the different voting precincts has indicated. . . . The Vox Populi said nothing that it is sorry for, and with this declaration it says good day.[18]

In retaliation, Nick Klaine had to content himself with a *Times* story concerning Bat Masterson as the victim of confidence operators. Two young men appeared in Dodge, said the story, with a farm wagon drawn by two mules. A third mule was hitched behind the wagon. The men gave the impression of being the greenest yokels, "wandering apparently aimlessly about the town with mouths open and a smile that was childlike and bland." They met and fell into conversation with Bat Masterson. The talk came around to the pulling power of mules in general and the mule hitched to the wagon in particular. Masterson "was induced to make a bet as to the pulling powers of the greenie's mule. The preliminaries were arranged, the mule was hitched to the load and walked away with it as easy as its green (?) owner did with our enterprising fellow citizen's money."

Klaine then entered into a tongue-in-cheek denunciation of the sharpers who had skinned the man he had recently called the Boss Gambler of the West:

> If green horns are allowed to come in here, and swindle our unsophisticated people out of their money what are we coming to? What do we keep policemen for? If it is not to protect our citizens from being fleeced by the superior abilities of the country green horns. This fellow knew that Mr. Masterson's business had been of a financial nature nearly all his life, and that he knew no more about the pulling powers of a mule than the mule did of the ten commandments. The city has been disgraced, the character of one our business men smirched and the perpetrator of the vile deed is still at liberty — Let him be hunted down, and let his fate be a warning to every granger that Dodge City will protect its citizens from the avaricious greed of the settlers, even if the Glick Guards have to be called out.[19]

Bat let that one pass, but shortly thereafter, when Klaine attempted to embarrass him again, Bat turned the tables on the editor. A woman in Iowa had written to the postmaster at Dodge City asking to be referred to a minister in the town because she was considering a move to the area. Postmaster Klaine answered her inquiry and recommended that she contact the Reverend W. B. Masterson. The innocent woman followed Klaine's suggestion. Bat's answer to her letter appeared in the *Globe Live Stock Journal*:

> My Dear Madam: On my return from Kansas City last night where I had been for ten days, I found your letter awaiting me. I was somewhat

astonished to find that you had addressed me Rev.; unfortunately, perhaps for me, I have not the honor of being a member of the clergy, and there is probably no man in this part of Kansas farther from it. I am a gambler by profession, and our esteemed (?) Post Master knew this to be so when he referred you to me. Our P.M. in doing what he thought a very smart trick, only demonstrated what has long been accepted as a fact in this community, relative to himself; (to-wit), that he lacks many of those elements that constitute a gentleman; he should at least, in my judgment, have considered you a lady and treated your letter of inquiry with the consideration that a lady is entitled to from a gentleman.

The name of our Post Master is N. B. Klaine, he is also editor of a nasty sheet published here, under the caption of Dodge City Times. He is a blatant prohibitionist, and a deacon in the Baptist Church. A strictly moral man and a gentleman, as his letter refering you to me would indicate. There are several first class physicians here, all of whom are gentlemen, and any one of whom he could have referred you to with a greater degree of propriety than myself. I herewith send the names of our most prominent physicians: T. L. McCarty, C. A. Milton and T. J. Wright. By addressing either of the above named gentlemen you can undoubtedly obtain the desired information.[20]

The *Globe Live Stock Journal* said it plainly: "Bat Masterson has his failings like other white folks, but he is a gentleman and does not sail under false colors."[21]

Two of the men who played important roles in Bat's early years on the frontier came to sudden and violent ends during the year 1884.[22] On a March night, Ben Thompson entered the Vaudeville Variety Theater in San Antonio with King Fisher, another noted Texas desperado. Ben had killed a man named Harris, a part owner of the establishment, on a previous visit, and Harris' partners, Joe Foster and W. H. Simms, either out of lust for vengeance or in fear for their own safety cut loose on Thompson and Fisher without warning. Wrote Bat:

Thompson . . . and King Fisher were killed from ambush by a number of persons who were concealed in the wings of the stage, and neither ever knew what happened. Ben was hit eight times by bullets fired from a Winchester rifle, and King Fisher was hit five times. All the shots were fired simultaneously and both sank to the floor dead as it is ever possible to be. It was a coldblooded, cruel and premeditated murder, for which no one was ever punished by law.[23]

Mysterious Dave Mather wearing an assistant marshal's hat during one of his stints as a Dodge City officer. Courtesy Kansas State Historical Society.

Bill Tilghman as he looked when he lived in Dodge City during the 1880's. Courtesy Denver Public Library.

In Dodge City on the night of July 21, Mysterious Dave Mather shot and killed Tom Nixon. In 1884, Old Tom was acting as a deputy city marshal. A few days before the fatal gunplay, he had had hard words with Mather, who, according to Bob Wright, "had more dead men to his credit at that time than any other man in the West."[24] Sheriff Pat Sughrue, despite his slurring reference to Mysterious Dave before the election, had sworn the secretive gunslinger in as his deputy. Nixon and Mather were both wearing badges, therefore, when they came face to face outside the Opera House Saloon. There was a roar of gunfire, and Old Tom lay sprawled in a bloody heap on the board sidewalk.

Sughrue had the unpleasant task of arresting his own deputy for the killing. Mather submitted peaceably and was held in the county jail on a charge of premeditated murder until he was released on bail. Among the prominent citizens of Dodge who furnished bond were a quartet of Bat's political and personal enemies: Larry Deger, Fred Singer, Mike Sutton, and Nick Klaine.

Bat was among the witnesses called to testify at Mather's preliminary examination on July 31. Like most testimony given by first-hand observers to a sudden and dramatic happening, the various accounts were conflicting and confused, but the consensus seemed to be that Mather confronted Nixon, declared that he was going to kill him, drew, and fired immediately. Nixon, most witnesses agreed, made no move for his weapon. He probably never had a chance against the lightning draw of the redoubtable Dave. Although Bat did not see the actual shooting, he was an early arrival at the scene of the tragedy and, presumably, his experience in such smoky matters was considered valuable.

Mysterious Dave was bound over for trial, which was held in Kinsley, Edwards County, the following December. The jury was out only twenty-seven minutes before bringing in a verdict of not guilty, and Mather returned once more to the gamblers' circuit. The western code that made a man wearing a gun fair game for anyone had been upheld again.

Masterson was called to testify at the Kinsley trial, and he took umbrage at some of the remarks made by Sam Vandivert, assistant prosecuting attorney, so he fired off one of his vituperative epistles on January 2 to get the new year of 1885 rolling right. According to Bat's letter, published in the *Kinsley Graphic*, Vandivert had characterized some of the Dodge City visitors as "pimps and prostitutes." The attorney's remarks were not to be taken too seriously, however, said Bat, since he was but recently arrived from Missouri, "that sweet and verdant land that gave birth to the Fords and Liddells"[25] and the comments were "the utterances of a coarse, vulgar, and untutored mind." Although Vandivert was probably considered a good lawyer in Missouri, continued Bat, "it doesn't require much material to gain a distinction there. . . . This frequent allusion to pimps and prostitutes would lead the ordinary person to believe that he possessed a greater knowledge of this class than he did of law, for he scarcely ever referred to the latter." Bat closed by advising the "insipient diciple [sic] of Blackstone . . . to pay more attention to law, and less to blackguardism" and wished the citizens of Kinsley a Happy New Year.[26]

Albert Griffin came to Dodge
City to close down the saloons.
But for the intervention of Bat
Masterson, the sports of Dodge
might have closed down Mr.
Griffin. Courtesy Kansas State
Historical Society.

By 1885, Bat had taken up semipermanent residence in Dodge
City, but he put down no real roots there. He sought no public
office, invested in no business property. He carried on his vocation, gambling, acting as chief house dealer in the Long Branch,
the Opera House Saloon, the Lone Star, and other familiar establishments. He was always ready to pick up and leave at a moment's
notice. He did accept appointment as a deputy sheriff under Pat
Sughrue in 1885 and again in 1886, but both appointments apparently were of short duration when Bat was asked to handle a
particularly difficult situation.

The first crisis developed from a visit to Dodge by a man named
Albert Griffin, editor of the *Manhattan* (Kansas) *Nationalist* and
president of the Kansas State Temperance Union. Griffin delivered
a lecture in which he denounced the saloonkeepers of Bibulous
Babylon. He was shocked, he said, by the wide-open conditions
and the utter disregard for the five-year-old prohibition law.

Although it was true that saloons ran openly in Dodge in violation of state law, one oft-repeated tale concerning the town had no
basis in fact. Reputed to have been posted at a conspicuous site on
Front Street was a notice to this effect: "$1,000 in cash has been
placed in bank for the widow of the man who informs on any
person violating the prohibition law." In a newspaper article on
Dodge City written some years later, Bat scoffed at the yarn,
saying, "I personally know that nothing of this kind happened."[27]

Griffin stated in his lecture that he was going to Topeka and
would bring back state officials to close the saloons forcibly. Upon
his return. he promised, he would stay "until every viper engaged
in the sale of liquor was crushed from existence." Wrote Bat:
"This peroration was emphasized by a stamp of the foot, convey-
ing the impression that it was intended as a threat."[28]

Several weeks passed with no sign of the temperance crusader,
but he continued his attacks on Dodge in the editorial pages of the
Nationalist:

> The population of the city is a little over 2,000, and I am told it contains
> about sixty professional gamblers and nearly fifty houses of ill repute,
> three of them located immediately across the street from the public
> school. . . . I do not believe there is another place this side of hell, of
> which a similar statement can be made![29]

Finally, on June 29, Griffin returned, bringing with him Colonel
A. R. Jetmore, representing the attorney general of Kansas. Word
of their approach had preceded them, and some three hundred men
were waiting at the depot when the train pulled in. Griffin and
Jetmore hurried to Dodge's sole temperance hostelry, Dr. Sam
Galland's Great Western Hotel, where preparations were being
made for a public meeting to be held that evening. Tension
mounted along Front Street throughout the day. Late in the afternoon, an angry mob, resentful of the invasion of the Topeka dries,
began to form in the street outside the hotel.

Bat Masterson, of course, had no use for Griffin. He was
convinced that he had been invited to the city by ardent prohibitionists Klaine, Galland & Company. He would have been
delighted to see Griffin ridden out of town on a rail, but the anger
that was sweeping Dodge portended a more violent fate for the

The interior of Ham Bell's Varieties in Dodge City. The bartender has been identified as George Masterson, youngest of the brothers. Courtesy Kansas State Historical Society.

temperance man. When a nervous Pat Sughrue asked Bat if he would accept a deputy's badge and help to hold things level, Bat agreed and offered to visit Griffin and Jetmore in their rooms and warn them of the possible consequences of their proposed meeting.

While Bat was in the room, Dr. Galland and gambler John Sheridan, a leader of the crowd outside the hotel, got into a violent argument. Galland struck Sheridan, and the gambler knocked Galland down. This incited the crowd, and a rush was made for Griffin's room. Bat stood in the doorway and ordered the mob to disperse. Although Griffin had repeatedly characterized Masterson in his Manhattan paper as "one of the most disreputable characters of the west" and a "leader of the lawless elements of Dodge City," he later acknowledged that it was Bat Masterson who saved his bacon that day:

Bat Masterson . . . had voluntarily called on us and stated that neither Colonel Jetmore nor myself should be molested, and when the assault was made on Dr. Galland, he went out and ordered the mob to go across the street. . . . Bat Masterson stayed in front of our room for half an hour or more, and sent the men back as they attempted to come and they finally retreated across the railroad. So far as I know, Mr. Masterson steadily did all he could to prevent any attack being made upon us, but said to me that he would not be responsible for what would happen to the citizens of the place who had taken a prominent part in the movement for the closing of the dram shops, against whom he also evidently entertains the bitterest of feelings.[30]

The resolve of Griffin and Jetmore to launch an attack on Dodge's saloons was shaken considerably by Bat's arguments and their close call. The public meeting was canceled, and the prohibition party caught the train east on the following day.

Any gratitude Griffin may have felt for Bat's action that day was forgotten within a week. On July 10, he was writing in his paper:

Bat Masterson is a professional gambler who has killed two or three men and shot several others. He is smart and has many elements of a leader, but is unquestionably a vicious man. He did not want Assistant Attorney Jetmore or myself killed, and the reason he is said to have given his associates was that "they could not afford to bring down upon themselves the vengeance of the State government and the State Temperance Union." We had never had any personal intercourse, and he supposed we were simply operating as a matter of business. . . . He probably felt no enmity toward us individually, and as he had already "made a long record" he had nothing to gain and everything to lose by permitting an attack on us.

Nevertheless, we would, in all probability, have been killed but for the accidental fact that he happened to be in our room when the mob made its rush for our quarters. While he was with them the rioters obeyed him implicitly, but when out of his presence they were ready to follow any ruffian who proposed to *do* something. I do not suppose Masterson is one of those human tigers whose chief delight is shedding blood, but no one who knows his history and studies his face would feel safe to have in his power a friend against whom he holds a grudge. The very fact that he has the qualities of "good fellowship," "occasional generosity," "steadfastness to friends," "fluency of speech" and "cool courage," make him all the more dangerous a man in such a community.[31]

Several weeks later in a letter to the *Kansas Cowboy*, Bat spoke his piece concerning Griffin and Jetmore and the Dodge City politicos he said had invited them there:

Griffin and Jetmore . . . both have stated that the town on their arrival was in the hands of an infuriated mob and have repeatedly spoken of reputed leaders of that mob. Now the only leaders of a mob that I saw on that day were Griffin and Jetmore. The only individuals in this community that were ever engaged with a mob were those who were following Griffin and Jetmore. Sutton, Galland, Swan, Bullard, Emerson, Deger, et al have always been members of a mob, and the dirtiest and most villianous mob that ever went unhung. . . . Mr. Griffin came here at the solicitation of Sutton, Dr. Galland, N. B. Klaine and E. D. Swan. We will not put Bullard in this category, for the very good reason that he is too contemptable and dirty to even entitle him to a place with this galaxy of stranglers. We will, to commence with, deposit $100 with the bank of Dodge, to be donated to any charitable institution in this state if we fail in the proposition we are about to submit, to wit:

1st. that I can get twelve of the most respected citizens of the county, (when I say respected citizens I mean business men and tax-payers) that will go upon the witness stand in the district court and swear that they would not believe any of those parties I have named under oath.

2nd. that I can prove each and every one of them to be purjured villians, and

3rd. that I can prove this whole outfit to be thieves and aiders and abettors of midnight assassins.

This proposition I am willing to let stand until the crack of doom. Now, if this is not true, there is a law against malicious libel, and I am amenable to the law and ready for the fray. . . .

Mr. Griffin says he will not desert those people here in their adversity, thereby intimating that he intends to come again. I say for the benefit of Mr. Griffin that he better stay away. . . . The people here feel justly indignant at the wholesale way they have been lied about by this sniveling, hypocritical, political paltroon, and will not tolerate his detestable presence again.[32]

Neither the "paltroon" from Manhattan nor any of the Dodge City notables referred to by Bat in such scathing language seemed inclined to dispute his remarks, either in court or in the street, and Albert Griffin took heed of Bat's advice to stay away. He was seen no more in that wild and woolly locale. In July, 1910, Bat wrote with obvious satisfaction: "The last heard of Albert Griffin he was working for twelve dollars a week in a printing office in Topeka and . . . those who took an occasional drink of rum are still at it."[33]

S. S. Prouty, editor of the *Kansas Cowboy*, commented after the visit of the temperance men:

They [Griffin and Jetmore] had seen enough with their own eyes and heard enough with their own ears to convince them that if prosecutions were commenced, hell would break loose and the devil would be to pay. . . . It ought to be evident to everybody familiar with the scenes in Dodge City last Monday, that the time is not ripe for an attempt to suppress the saloons in this place.[34]

In the summer of 1885, Bat's reputation in Dodge City reached its zenith. At the Fourth of July festivities, a vote was taken to determine "the most popular man in Dodge City." Ballots were sold for ten cents each. Bat won hands down, receiving 170 of some 300 votes cast, and was awarded a gold watch chain and a gold-headed cane worth twenty dollars.

One of the reasons Bat was so admired was his frequent display of generosity and his compassion for those who were down and out. A story in the *Dodge City Democrat* of October 17, 1885, typified this aspect of Masterson's character. A former soldier in the last stages of "galloping consumption" turned up in Dodge. It was obvious that he was near death, and he was trying to make it to his home in Flint, Michigan. He was penniless, however, and was surviving on the whiskey he could beg from saloonkeepers. Bat heard of his plight and began a canvass of the sporting element. Within half an hour, enough funds had been raised for the veteran's ticket home. The man broke down when Bat turned the money over to him. "It was a touching sight," said the *Democrat*, "one that will not soon be forgotten."

Even as Masterson reached the pinnacle of his popularity and unofficial power in Dodge City, however, the last grains of sand in the town's time as the Cowboy Capital were running out. Every month brought more and more dirt farmers into western Kansas. A bill was passed prohibiting the entrance into Kansas, between the months of March and December, of Texas cattle "capable of communicating . . . Texas, splenic or Spanish fever." Prohibition pressure from Topeka was constant.

Bat Masterson about the time Nick Klaine dubbed him "the boss gambler of the West." Courtesy Denver Public Library.

Then there was the continuous struggle between those with opposite views of the town they wanted Dodge to be. Bob Wright, Bat Masterson, and the remnants of the old Dodge City Gang wanted Dodge to remain a wide-open, sporting man's town catering to what was left of the cattle trade. The prohibitionists and most of the merchants, led by Mike Sutton and Nick Klaine, felt that the future of Dodge lay in selling gingham and hay rakes, not whiskey and .45-caliber ammunition. Increasingly, this faction looked to Topeka for help in the fight.

An incident involving Masterson that would not even have received mention in the papers a few years earlier touched off a controversy in late October, 1885, that reached all the way to the governor's mansion. A Dodge City gambler named Phelps ran a game at Kinsley during the Edwards County Fair. On the last day of the fair, he left town and returned to Dodge without paying his licensing fee. Edwards County Deputy Sheriff, Terry was dispatched to Dodge to arrest Phelps, but, according to a report sent to Governor Martin, a mob took Terry's prisoner from him and sent Terry back to Kinsley empty handed. Dodge City was described to the governor as being completely lawless. Martin considered state intervention until he learned that the mob who had taken Terry's prisoner was composed of only one man — Bat Masterson. At the depot, where Terry was awaiting the train to Kinsley with Phelps, Bat approached the Edwards County officer and tried to arrange a financial settlement so that Phelps would not have to go back to Kinsley. While Bat and Terry were engaged in conversation, Phelps walked off.

Governor Martin learned the facts of the incident before making himself look foolish by dispatching militia to Dodge City, but he did write Mayor Bob Wright beseeching him to clean up the town:

Visitors inform me that the saloons are increasing, not only in numbers, but in depravity; and that thieves, desperadoes, gamblers and criminals generally, are multiplying. It is also alleged that these lawless characters dominate in the city; that they have terrorized all the better elements of society; that they openly and defiantly flaunt their viciousness and depravity; and that they appear to think there is no power or authority that can reach or punish them. . . . Sooner or later you know that Dodge must reform or perish. Why not reform it now? Why cannot all decent citizens of Dodge unite in a determined effort to make Dodge an orderly, peacable [sic], decent and prosperous city?[35]

Wright replied:

Governor, you have been imposed upon by a lot of soreheads of this town. This gang only consists of about a dozen who breed all the trouble here & continually keep things in hot water, they are public disturbers & agitators & are a curse to any community — who want every one to think & do as they say — who if they cant rule want to ruin, who do not hesitate to lie & prevaricate to gain their selfish ends, who pretend to be Moralists but are wolves in sheeps clothing, in short they are hypocrites of the deepest & darkest kind. Such even is M. W. Sutton N. B. Klaine . . . & a few others of this kind. . . . I know them and I know well their dirty black hearts, which never beat with a single generous thought for their fellow man. Sutton is a good lawyer & I admire his ability, but I know his motives. He pretends to be a great temperance man & he drinks more whiskey in a week than I do in a year. Now Governor these are the men who have cought your ear & I assure you I have not pictured them half as mean & contemptable as they really are.

Wright implored the governor to maintain a hands-off policy and to let Dodge guide itself through this critical transition period:

You must recolect [sic] that our situation is diferent [sic] from that of other Towns in the Eastern part of the State, which have always enjoyed the benefits of churches, schools & other civilizing influences. We have always been a frontier Town, where the wild & reckless sons of the Plains have congregated, their influences are still felt here, but we are rapidly overcoming them, let us alone & we will work out our own salvation in due season. I flatter myself that I know how to handle the boys, they cannot be driven. . . . Please do not borrow trouble Governor about the conduct or management of Dodge City.[36]

Martin did not follow Wright's admonition, however, and on November 24, Attorney General Bradford arrived in Dodge to close the saloons. While the state officer remained in town, the doors of the watering holes stayed closed. Bradford left Dodge on the twenty-sixth; on the morning of the twenty-seventh, the saloons reopened.

That night, a fire of mysterious origin started in an upstairs room over the Junction Saloon, next door to the Opera House Saloon. It was soon out of control, and a whole block on Front Street, including the Junction, the Opera House, the Long Branch, and Bob Wright's brick storehouse, burned to the ground. Even as hundreds of men fought to contain the raging fire, the rumor spread that prohibitionists had started it. At four o'clock in the morning, while flames still licked at his demolished store, Mayor Bob Wright pumped three shots into Mike Sutton's house. Wright later claimed that many threats had been made that awful night against Sutton and others and that he had been at the house to protect Sutton's family. He fired, he said, at a prowler.

An uneasy truce prevailed in Dodge's political and social war during the winter that followed. The citizens had other problems. On New Year's Day, the first of a series of blizzards howled down out of the Rockies, driving snow in gusts of forty miles an hour. A week later, a second storm struck Dodge, with winds reaching forty-four miles an hour, more snow, and bitter cold. The temperature dropped to sixteen below zero. More snow and cold followed throughout the month of January, 1886. Twenty inches of snow covered the ground, and drifts were ten feet deep. Trains could not get through; the town was snowbound. Several lives were lost, and frostbite resulted in the amputation of many hands and feet. Economic losses were staggering. Cattlemen in the area estimated their losses at 20 to 100 per cent.

With the coming of spring, the adversaries in Dodge's continuing internecine war began their sniping. Then, on March 10, came a real thunderbolt: The saloons of Dodge were shut down tight. This feat was accomplished not, as might be expected, by a company of militia from the capital, but by a single man: Bat Masterson.

The *Dodge City Democrat* reported the story with a trace of incredulity:

Deputy Sheriff Bat Masterson has filed complaints with the county attorney against all of the saloon men and druggists in the city. . . . Warrants have been issued and the parties have been arrested. The saloons are all closed now and the prohibitory law apparently enforced. How long this state of affairs will continue to exist is hard to tell and the object of the move will probably develop in the near future.[37]

A Dodge City correspondent quoted in the *Trinidad News* felt that Bat had jumped on the prohibition wagon:

The saloon men have all been arrested and are under bonds; nearly all the saloons are closed. W. B. Masterson, a sporting men of considerable notoriety, . . . has suddenly become converted to prohibition and to attest his sincerity has filed complaints against them. He bids fair to develop into a Sam Jones on the prohibition side. Mr. Masterson is a fearless fellow, and has buckled on his six-shooter and is making it as lively for the saloon men now as he did for Griffin and Jetmore last summer while they were in this city on their expedition against the saloon.[38]

Wily old Nick Klaine of the *Times* knew that there was more to the story. A few days before Bat's unexpected move, a petition had been circulated asking A. B. Webster to become a candidate for mayor. A number of saloonmen, suffering from Dodge's depressed economic condition and disenchanted with the Wright regime, had joined the temperance people in signing the petition. Said the *Times*:

The saloons of Dodge were closed yesterday morning, complaints against the saloon-keepers having been made by W. B. Masterson. This step was produced by the candidacy of A. B. Webster for Mayor. Several saloon men signed the petition calling upon A. B. Webster to become a candidate for Mayor, and in consequence of this some feeling has been engendered. If Mr. Masterson will carry out his prohibition movement successfully he will have the gratitude of a generous public.[39]

More than an act of reprisal against the saloonists who had strayed from the fold, Bat's closing of the saloons was a form of blackmail, according to Mike Sutton. On March 10, the same day Bat swore out his warrants, Sutton wrote a letter, marked "Private and confidential," to Attorney General S. B. Bradford, "A very remarkable state of affairs exists in this city now," he said, "and as I promised to keep you posted I shall endeavor to make matters plain."

There were in Dodge, said Sutton, three factions. The prohibitionists, the group to which he belonged, favored strict enforcement of all laws. The saloonists, led by A. B. Webster, favored enforcement of all laws except those prohibiting gambling and drinking. The third faction, led by Bob Wright and Bat Masterson, was composed of "thugs" who respected no laws. The Wright-Masterson "Gang" had been in control of the town and had been "the worst element that ever infested a place." Outrages in the form of confidence swindles and holdups had become so frequent that the saloonmen had formed a coalition with the prohibitionists to bring about a change. The dries agreed to back saloonkeeper Webster for mayor on the condition he would drive out the Wright-Masterson crowd. Wrote Sutton:

> Masterson . . . has made complaint against whiskey men right and left. . . . The saloons are closed and prohibition reigns supreme. Now this break of Masterson is to force the saloon men to accept his man for mayor and drive Webster off the track. So soon as he accomplishes this feat he will withdraw his complaints. The Co. Atty. will consent and the affair will be ended. The game can only be defeated by your appearing on the field and informing the Co. Atty. that the cases must stand. The complaints must be pushed. [You] get to be the atty. of record, and let the courts know that the cases must not be dismissed. General, now is the opportunity. We pray you come next train.[40]

Bradford did not go to Dodge again, but, as it developed, Sutton did not need him. Bat's complaints resulted in hung juries, and Ab Webster was elected mayor. Bat's ploy had failed, and the reform element was in the saddle.

So, for the second time, Bat Masterson quit the "delectable burg." Nick Klaine's *Dodge City Times* announced warily on April 1: "Bat Masterson and his gang went west on the afternoon train of Sunday. Where the next base of operations will be made we are not informed."

CHAPTER TWENTY

FROM SODA TO HOCK

Despite prolonged sojourns at Tombstone, Trinidad, Dodge City, and other frontier oases, Bat Masterson evidently thought of Denver as home after 1880. In a letter to Frank Baldwin written from the mile-high city in February, 1890, he said, "I have resided here for the past ten years and like the country and its people very much. . . . This is a delightful climate and a beautiful city."[1] The next ten years would change that opinion; in 1900, Bat would be quoted in a Denver paper as saying, "I hope nobody thinks I have been living in this rotten place because I loved it or because I was making money here or because I had no other place to go."[2]

In the middle and late 1880's, however, Denver was his favorite port of call as he plied the gamblers' circuit. By nature and by choice, he became a floating gambler, a frontier high roller, a border sport, always on the move, always on the lookout for a livelier camp, a bigger game. It was during this time that his stocky, nattily clad figure and his distinctively brisk, slightly halting gait became familiar in towns and cities scattered throughout the West. "Masterson," said the *New York Times* at his death, "was said to have been the best known man between the Mississippi and the Pacific Coast."[3]

In January, 1886, he showed up in Reno, Nevada, according to a story told by Joe Forsythe, manager of a hotel there, and capriciously signed his name *Bartholomew Masterson* on the hotel register. Arriving in town on the westbound express after a blizzard had dumped eighteen inches of snow, Bat, carrying two valises and decked out in patent-leather shoes, a plug hat, and a sealskin-trimmed chinchilla ulster that almost reached the ground, walked the block from the train station to Forsythe's hotel through a barrage of snowballs thrown by a gang of sports who wanted to knock the hat from the head of an eastern dude; when he finally entered the hotel, he was covered with snow where he had been pasted, but his plug hat was still intact. Masterson, described by Forsythe as a "compactly-built man with grayish hair and a serious countenance," removed his hat and peeled off his ulster and the cutaway beneath it with one motion. Rolling up his sleeves, he went back outside and began pelting the sports with accurately thrown snowballs of his own. After a wild exchange, Bat tired of the game and returned to sign the register and go to his room to clean up. When the local yokels trooped into the hotel to ask the name of this strange tenderfoot, they were thunderstruck to learn that they had been having fun at the expense of Bat Masterson. "The crowd went up to Masterson's room," said Forsythe, "dragged him out by main force, and there was nothing in the town too good for him for twenty-four hours. They would hardly consent to let him attend to the private business that had brought him to Reno, and you can gamble that no snowballs were chucked at his plug hat when the gang escorted him in a body down to the station a couple of days later."[4]

As a professional gambler, Bat undoubtedly had his ups and downs at the tables, but he was conceded to be one of the shrewdest and most consistently successful of the circuit's followers. In his letter to Baldwin from Denver, Bat wrote:

I can't say that I have been prosperous, although I have not suffered much from adversity. . . . I have been connected nearly all the time since coming here in the gambling business and have experienced the vicissitudes which has always characterized the business. Some days — plenty, and more days — nothing, this may all be greek to you. . . . I came into the world without anything and I have about held my own up to date.[5]

A tale that found its way into print some years later reveals how Bat could exploit the slip of a gambling opponent to offset the normal vagaries of Dame Fortune. A gambler identified only as an "old-time faro player" was quoted in the *Denver Times* as saying:

The shrewdest men in the business are caught playing off base once in a while. I was to Denver one winter when John Hapenny had about the best game in town. . . . I wandered into the place when on my way to my hotel late one bitter cold night, and found the game on its last legs.

. . . Hapenny was alone, his associate dealers having gone home a short time before. Bat Masterson was among the few players, and as Hapenny spilled out what he denominated the last turn of the night, Masterson began to relate a story of his experience in Leadville, which won the undivided attention of the company. Hapenny at once became absorbed in the narrative to such an extent that he left the cards in two piles, just as they had fallen from the deal. As the story progressed, however, he mechanically picked them up and placed them in a box without even the suspicion of a shuffle, all the time keeping his eyes firmly fixed on Masterson, while his interest grew with the recital.

Just as Masterson was concluding . . . in walked a party of young fellows . . . anxious to play the bank, and so Hapenny concluded to give them a game. They all bought chips, Masterson with the rest, and to the latter's intense surprise, he saw that Hapenny was going to hand out the bunch just as he had placed them during the story telling. Glancing hurriedly at a tab, which contained a record of the last deal, he got a bet down to a topper, but it lost. Then he made another earnest scrutiny of the tab and got down two more bets, both of which won.

Well, sir, he had solved the run of the pasteboards and his luck (?) after that was little short of criminal. He would lose a bet here and there, just for decency's sake, but every time he pressed them up, he won. . . . Masterson's stacks were growing from dollars to hundreds, and all eyes were riveted on his play. The spectators knew what he would do to a faro bank when he got away with his right foot foremost, and as he pressed his bets they looked forward to something positively spectacular when the turn should be reached.

But they never arrived at that point, for Hapenny, who was fairly writhing under the positive conviction that he was "up against" something, cut the proceedings short. As had been anticipated, Masterson was pluming himself to simply earthquake the turn when Hapenny, with a weary yawn, turned the box over carelessly, remarking: "I guess that will do for tonight, boys."

. . . Masterson's keen eyes were the only ones to detect Hapenny's blunder, and it was the "cinch" of a lifetime, as he sat there reading the deal as an open book.[6]

Masterson also participated in a celebrated poker game, according to another of the players, Charles ("Rusty") Coe, a longtime professional gambler. Coe's story, written for him by Hugh Walters, was published in 1902 under the title *My Life as a Card Shark*.[7] In August, 1885, said Coe, there gathered in Luke Short's

Photograph taken June 18, 1886, at John Kine's training quarters at Beloit, Wisconsin. From left are Bat Masterson; John F. Clow, heavyweight champion of Colorado; Charlie Mitchell, English prizefighter; and John Kline. Courtesy Denver Public Library.

White Elephant Saloon in Fort Worth, Texas, five of the cleverest gamblers in the West. Besides himself and Short, there were in the game Bat Masterson, Wyatt Earp, and Jim Courtright. Bat had been backed by cattleman Jim Devine in the amount of nine thousand dollars. The game, which had been building larger and larger pots, finally came down to a showdown between Short and Coe. Short showed a full house and Rusty Coe raked the pot with four kings. Coe said Bat later asked him to "go partners" with him in a Dodge City gambling house and that he and Bat looked over property, but prices were not to their liking and the venture never came off.

Little note was taken in the chronicles of the period of the shifting fortunes of the devotees of Lady Luck, however, and it is through Bat's frequent excursions into his three main other fields of interest — politics, pugilism, and police work — that we are able to follow his trail during these years.

By 1885, he had achieved sufficient stature as a pugilistic expert to be called upon to serve as referee in an important prizefight. In July of that year, he was in Denver, where a pair of well-known western heavyweights named Clow and Hands, their handlers, and the usual assortment of ring followers were gathering for a major bout. John P. Clow was the recognized heavyweight champion of Colorado and was putting his title up for grabs. The Colorado authorities, however, frowned upon the notion of fisticuffs in their state, so the entourage moved across the border into Wyoming. At Rawlins, a little cow town on the main line of the Union Pacific, the fight was pulled off on August 1, Clow winning by a knockout in the sixth round. According to the *Ford County Globe*, wagers on this fight amounted to "not less than twenty thousand dollars." The *Rocky Mountain News* published a full account of the proceedings, its correspondent remarking that "Masterson makes a ready umpire."[8]

Clow spent several months in Kansas with Bat after the fight. In October, they took in the races at the Edwards County Fair, and in December, Bat arranged for an exhibition match with an English fighter named Ed Smith at Medicine Lodge in Barber County. Bat was quoted in the *Barber County Index* as saying that Medicine Lodge was the best town he had ever struck in Kansas. The *Index*, complimentary in turn, found Bat to be a "plain, unassuming young man, with lots of horse sense and a very pleasant conversationalist."[9]

On this and other junkets, Bat formed many of the friendships that were to affect the course of his later life. In Kansas, he met a pair of young brothers from Ohio who stared in wonder at him, hanging on his every word as he spun tales of wild times on the border. The brothers' names were Alfred Henry and William E. Lewis. Alfred, known as Hank on the frontier, was a working cowhand on a Kansas ranch when Bat first knew him, and William was an energetic cub reporter for the *New York Sun*. Bat's stories were the basis for many of the Wolfville novels for which Alfred Henry Lewis later became widely known. Embellished as they were by the fertile Lewis imagination, there was little left for Bat to

Bat Masterson (left) and Charlie Mitchell at Minnehaha Falls near Minneapolis. Courtesy Denver Public Library.

recognize when they finally appeared in print. William E. Lewis, sent to Kansas by his paper to write feature stories of "Western color," found Bat Masterson a veritable storehouse of information concerning frontier characters and their doings.

On one of his trips north into the Dakotas, Bat met a stocky, powerfully built New Yorker, some five years younger than himself, who was having a try at ranching on the raw frontier. The young man's name was Theodore Roosevelt, and he and Bat established a bond of friendship that grew stronger with the passing years. Although their backgrounds were worlds apart, their personalities were quite similar in many respects. Both were extreme individualists who held firm convictions and were ready at all times to fight in defense of their beliefs, both were full of a love of adventure and were utterly fearless, both deplored sham and pretense in any form, and both were staunchly Republican in their political outlook.

Early in 1887, Bat's rambling led him south to the booming towns of Texas. He described Luke Short's White Elephant in Fort Worth as "one of the largest and costliest establishments of its kind in the entire southwest."[10] Fort Worth was a wide-awake town, the White Elephant's business was booming, yet little Luke was unhappy when Bat found him. Jim Courtright was giving him trouble, Luke explained. Courtright, known as Longhaired Jim, wore his guns low and loose and had established a reputation in Texas and New Mexico as a swift-handed killer. He had scouted and fought Indians a bit and had even done odd jobs as a peace officer. But of late, said Luke, Courtright had taken to running a protection racket in Fort Worth. Trading on his notoriety as a killer, he had opened what he called the T. I. C. Commercial Detective Agency. He had approached each of the Fort Worth gambling-house operators, offering his services as a "special policeman" to preserve order. Thinly veiled hints as to the calamitous consequences that might befall an operator who declined his services brought each one into line — all, that is, but Luke Short. Luke thanked Courtright for his offer of help but stated flatly that he had all the men on his payroll that he needed and he was sure he himself could handle any trouble that might arise.

Longhaired Jim left on that occasion, muttering imprecations.

Luke knew that he would be back, and he was awaiting the return visit when Bat blew into town. At eight o'clock on the evening of February 8, Bat and Luke were sitting together in the billiards room of the gambling hall, discussing the problem of the pestiferous Courtright, when word came that the subject of their discussion was waiting outside to see Short. According to Bat, Courtright's visit was not in the cause of peace:

> He brought along no olive branch, but instead a brace of pistols, conspicuously displayed. It was not a parley that he came for, but fight, and his demeanor indicated a desire that hostilities open up forthwith.
>
> No time was wasted in the exchange of words once the men faced each other. Both drew their pistols at the same time, but, as usual, Short's spoke first and a bullet . . . went crashing through Courtright's body. . . . By the time his lifeless form reached the floor, Luke had succeeded in shooting him five times.

In his recital, Bat glossed over the aftermath, saying only that Luke was arrested, spent a night in jail, and was never tried for the shooting because a grand jury refused to indict him.[11]

According to Alfred Henry Lewis, there was a dramatic sequel to the shooting that Bat modestly neglected to mention. After Luke submitted quietly to arrest and was lodged in the lockup, some of the friends and admirers of the late Jim Courtright began talk of a lynching. Bat got wind of the proposed necktie party and promptly went to the jail and talked the sheriff into allowing him to spend the night in the cell with his friend. For his night of voluntary incarceration, he took with him a pair of six-guns for himself and an additional pair for Short. Marveled Lewis:

> Friendship such as Jonathan's would have hesitated at so desperate a step! It turned out well, however, for the would-be lynchers, told by the sheriff that Mr. Masterson and Mr. Short were together in the jail, and each with a brace of guns, virtuously resolved that the law should take its course, and went heedfully home to bed.[12]

The fight with Longhaired Jim was the last of Luke Short's shooting scrapes, according to Bat, "with the exception of a little gun dispute three years later at Fort Worth which had no fatal results." It was also the last of Short's adventures involving Bat Masterson. Luke died of dropsy at Geuda Springs, Kansas, in 1893.

After his stint as city marshal of Trinidad, Bat did not accept police work for extended periods, preferring to feel free to move on as the notion struck him. He did, however, undertake short-term assignments as a troubleshooting peace officer in various frontier communities during the 1880's.

When Silverton, Colorado, was raw, rough, and roaring in the middle years of the decade, the saloon and sporting-house gang ran the town pretty much as it pleased. On Blair Street alone, when the mining camp was at its peak, were thirty-seven saloons, the doors of which were never closed. In front of one of them one night, Clayton Ogsbury, a town constable popular with the sporting crowd, was riddled by a pair of fugitives from Durango. A drunken mob roamed the streets for hours in search of the murderers; failing to find them, it strung up an innocent Negro. This outrage galvanized Silverton's decent element into action. A band of vigilantes was organized, and, under its prodding, the town council sent for Bat Masterson. Acting as a special city marshal, Bat spread the word to the worst of the troublemakers that Silverton was no longer healthy for them. Most of these men knew Bat and realized that when he spoke, he meant business. The undesirables cleared out without Bat having to touch his gun butt.

At Buena Vista, a Colorado mining camp that in its heyday rivaled Silverton for lawlessness, Bat was present when another lynch mob was lusting for blood. According to Alfred Henry Lewis, Bat rescued the prisoner and brought him before a judge for legal sentencing. But, records Lewis,

when the magistrate, in sympathetic league with the lynchers, would have committed the man to the local jail, where the mob could get at him, he, Mr. Masterson, tore up the commitment papers in the face of the court, and carried the man off to the Denver jail, where subsequently he was sufficiently yet lawfully hanged.[13]

Bat and other circuit gamblers frequently took on jobs as man hunters during their travels, working as agents for insurance companies, railroads, express companies, detective agencies, and sometimes the United States government. As he crisscrossed the Southwest on these junkets, Bat often ran into old pals and on occasion enlisted their aid. In her account of her life as Wyatt's wife, Josephine Earp recalled Bat's dropping in on them at their home in San Diego about 1885. He was on his way to Enseñada, Mexico, to pick up an army deserter who was reputed to be a tough hombre. Bat asked Wyatt to accompany him. "That made sense to Wyatt," wrote Josephine. "This careful approach, so characteristic of both these men, may account for their survival to a ripe old age despite years in a dangerous business that claimed the lives of many. Neither of them took unnecessary chances."[14]

With the influx of thousands of immigrants into western Kansas in the 1880's, several new counties were chartered, and town promotions flourished. Speculators, hoping to realize tremendous profits on small investments, bought up cheap prairie land, platted lots and streets, and fought for the recognition of their newly formed towns as county seats. Naïvely confident that with the capture of the seat of county government their towns would prosper and property values would skyrocket, the boomers resorted to rigged elections, intimidation, and even murder to achieve their coveted goals. This led to the Kansas County Seat Wars.

When elections were held to determine where the county seat was to be located, rival towns hired gunmen to decorate the polling places. Gun hands of demonstrated ability suddenly found their talents in great demand. A few, like Charles Coulter and Ed Prather, were cold-blooded killers, hired by unscrupulous promoters to scare away opposition voters. Others, like Bill Tilghman, Neal Brown, and Ben Daniels, were employed as special deputies to maintain order at the polls.

Bat Masterson has been named frequently in later writings as an active participant in the county-seat wars of western Kansas. Some of these stories may have derived from a dispatch to the *New York Sun* in early 1887. The rival towns of Leoti and Coronado were contesting for the seat of Wichita County, and a booster for Leoti warned that Bat Masterson had been enlisted to head a cadre of Dodge City gunmen employed to ensure Coronado's victory at a special election:

The fact that he and his crowd are to be imported by the people of Coronado has caused intense excitement here, and every body is preparing for the worst. No man now goes out without his guns, and even the farmers go around with rifles and revolvers strapped to them. The election will be a bloody one if Bat takes part in it in the style which has made him celebrated at Dodge City.[15]

The Leoti supporter's fears were unfounded as far as Bat was concerned. He did not put in an appearance in Wichita County, but blood flowed freely anyway. Before the Wichita County war ended, three men had been killed and five wounded.

Nor was Bat Masterson present during the fight between Hugoton and Woodsdale for the seat of Stevens County. In 1888, four men were wantonly murdered there in what was called the Hay Meadow Massacre.

According to a Kansas historian, when feeling ran high in the rival towns of Eminence and Ravanna as the time drew near for a special election to determine the county seat of Garfield County, C. J. ("Buffalo") Jones, representing Eminence, summoned Bat to guard the polls. Bat is said to have arrived with twenty deputies, including Bill Tilghman, and the election was held without trouble on November 8, 1887. In spite of the preelection protests of some of its supporters that Bat's platoon of gunmen would ensure an Eminence victory, Ravanna carried the election. The writer quotes Garfield County old-timers as saying that the presence of the Masterson six-shooter corps was "the only thing that prevented the worst gun battle that ever took place between citizens of a state."[16]

In fact, Bat Masterson had no part in this contest. About two weeks earlier, on October 23, he had checked into the Delmonico Hotel in Dodge City, giving Lamar, Colorado, as his home city.[17] He was still in Dodge on the day of the election, November 8, and on the following day wrote a letter denying the reports of his participation:

To the Kansas City Times,

Dodge City, Kan., Nov. 9 — In reply to a special telegram sent to the Times from Cimarron, Kan., on November 7, and appearing in the Times of November 8, where it is made to appear that I was taking an aggressive part in the Garfield county seat fight, I wish to say that I was not in Garfield county, and have taken no part, directly or indirectly, in the county seat election in said county.

W. B. Masterson[18]

In Gray County, just west of Dodge City, Cimarron and Ingalls vied for recognition as the county seat. Asa T. Soule, a millionaire from the East who had amassed his wealth from the sale of a panacea called Hop Bitters, was promoting Ingalls. At an election held in Cimarron in October, 1887, he employed Bill Tilghman, Ben Daniels, and several other Dodge City worthies, including one Eat-Em-Up-Jake, as special Ingalls representatives to see that no skulduggery was carried out by the Cimarron partisans. Cimarron won the election, but Soule, charging fraud, obtained a court order preventing certification of the vote and took the case to court.

The Gray County war dragged on for more than a year, with skirmishes fought in both the courts and the towns. It was climaxed by a dramatic coup scored by Soule mercenaries. On January 12, 1889, a bright, brisk Saturday morning, a gang of Ingalls men pulled up in front of the temporary Gray County courthouse in Cimarron and proceeded to steal the court records, the symbols of sovereignty, from under the noses of the peacefully sleeping Cimarron citizenry. Several of the company carried the records from the courthouse while the rest stood guard over the wagon in which they had arrived. Before their mission had been completed, however, an early riser discovered the theft of the records and, like a plains Paul Revere, rushed through the streets to spread the alarm. A gun battle ensued, aroused Cimarron men spilling out into the street in nightshirts to take potshots at the Ingalls trespassers. Several of the mercenaries were hit, and a prominent Cimarron citizen was killed. Finding the locality suddenly too hot for them, the invaders piled into the wagon on top of what records they had collected and careened out of town.

From this incident, the Battle of Cimarron, grew one of the Bat Masterson legends, a colorful tale that has been given the weight of established fact by eminent chroniclers of western history. Clyde B. Davis recounted the battle in his book, *The Arkansas*, and identified the two Ingalls men who sacked the courthouse as Bat Masterson and Three-Fingered Jim Marshall, later a noted lawman in Cripple Creek and other rough Colorado mining camps. When the guards at the wagon tore out of town, wrote Davis, they left Bat and Marshall stranded in the courthouse "in a very embarrassing position." Throughout a full day and night, the two carried on a

gun battle with their besiegers. Ammunition exhausted, they surrendered the following morning and were tried for murder before a
hastily organized court. Their defense was inspired: They could
not be guilty of murder because they did not know the dead
Cimarron resident, and he had just been unfortunate enough to get
in the way of one of their bullets.

This seemed reasonable to the Cimarron jury and the jurymen brought
in a verdict of acquital with two qualifications. First, Masterson and
Marshall must pay for the window glass the Cimarron boys had shot out
of the courthouse. Second, neither of the defendants must ever set foot in
Cimarron, Kansas, again under penalty of immediate hanging.

So Jim Marshall and Bat Masterson left not only Cimarron, but the
state of Kansas. [19]

William MacLeod Raine narrated substantially the same yarn in a
sketch of Masterson's life that he wrote for his book *Guns of the
Frontier*. In this version, however, there is no mention of the
Cimarron jury's unique verdict, Raine stating only that Bat and
Marshall were tried for murder and acquitted.[20] Although based on
an actual occurrence, this diverting tale is, unfortunately, pure
myth. Unlike most others, however, it can be traced to its source.

Clyde Davis made it clear that he heard the story directly from
Jim Marshall when he wrote in his account:

One of the principals of that affair was a friend of mine — a picturesque old gunfighter named Jim Marshall. I knew Jim Marshall in his
closing days, when he was a deputy sheriff in Denver — a dignified,
handsome old fellow with a white Vandyke and stiff-brimmed Stetson.

Davis concluded his narrative by quoting Three-Fingered Jim
himself:

"By God and by Jesus," drawled Jim Marshall, pawing his white
Vandyke with the stub of his trigger finger, "there wasn't a doubt that
Cimarron jury meant just what it said. Their verdict went right down in
the county records — if Bat Masterson or Jim Marshall ever showed up
in that town again there was to be a necktie party.

"I was willing to believe 'em. So was Bat Masterson. Even when Bat
Masterson went back to New York he went out of his way to keep from
going through Cimarron. Didn't even want to go through there on a
train."

W. M. Raine, who was a resident of Denver, undoubtedly got the details of the yarn from the same "picturesque old gunfighter."

Both writers, it seems, were taken in by Three-Fingered Jim. Many later writers, including Richard O'Connor in his 1957 biography of Bat Masterson, have repeated the tale. Jim Marshall was not present at the Battle of Cimarron, and neither was Bat. There was a Masterson involved, however: Bat's brother Jim.

CHAPTER TWENTY-ONE

"A BROTHER OF BAT MASTERSON"

During the 1880's and 1890's, Jim Masterson was a participant in some of the most dramatic episodes on the frontier and became a familiar figure in wild border towns in Colorado, New Mexico, Kansas, and Oklahoma. Although he was recognized as a tough and courageous fighter, a formidable enemy, and a valuable friend, Jim never was able to emerge from the shadow of his more widely known brother. Perhaps it was because of Bat's colorful nickname, or perhaps it was because Bat was facile with a pen, which Jim was not, but Jim's older brother early acquired a notoriety that never attached itself to Jim. How many times Jim must have bristled to see his name in print followed by the inevitable appendage, ''brother of the famous Bat Masterson.''

In late 1884, Jim became involved in the latest battle of the long war over the Maxwell Land Grant in northern New Mexico. It had raged for years in and out of the courts and would continue to do so for many more before it was settled by a decision of the U.S. Supreme Court. The managers of the Maxwell Land Grant Company laid claim to nearly two million acres, encompassing all of Colfax County and part of Taos County in New Mexico and part of Las Animas County in Colorado. They were opposed by the people who had settled the area, who argued that the boundaries of the Spanish grant had been vastly extended by means of a fraudulent survey and that the original grant had been for no more than one hundred thousand acres.

The disputed survey had been approved by a Republican Congress and a Republican president and had been bitterly opposed by the Democrats. When a Democrat was elected president in 1884, enemies of the land-grant company were jubilant. New Mexico, a territory, was administered by officials appointed by the president; Grover Cleveland would surely appoint men sympathetic to the antigranters. There was wild talk of driving all the scoundrels out of the Territory. Smelling trouble, hard-case gunmen began showing up in Colfax County. In those days, when trouble brewed, demand was great for the services of proven gun hands.

George Curry, who had been at Sweetwater, Texas, when the King-Masterson gunfight took place, was living in Raton, New Mexico, in 1884. He was now a strapping six-footer, twenty-three years old, and, as he tells it in his memoirs, was working in the grocery department of D. W. Stevens' general store.[1] Stevens was chairman of the Board of County Commissioners and a determined foe of the Maxwell Land Grant Company. Miguel A. Otero, later governor of New Mexico, had known George Curry since 1873, when Curry was a small boy. It was his recollection that in 1884 Curry was running a chuck-a-luck table in the Raton saloon of an antigrant fanatic named Whitlock.[2] There may be no inconsistency here. Curry was an intelligent and ambitious young man; he may have been holding down both jobs. At any rate, George Curry and his brother John were soon deeply embroiled on the side of the settlers in the Colfax County land-grant troubles.

The Curry brothers were not gunmen, but there were among their associates some very tough and hardened gun slicks. Foremost of these was a Texan named Dick Rogers. Others were Tom South, Sam Staley, Red River Tom Wallington, Ed King, and John Dodds. On October 20, 1884, Rogers shot up a joint in Chihuahua, the Mexican section of Raton. Before he had finished, a citizen named Miller lay dead. Rogers skipped. Reports of other depredations by the gunman reached Raton. He was said to have killed two men in Trinidad; a railroad section hand fell before his smoking iron a few days later.

On November 22, John Hixenbaugh, sheriff-elect of Colfax County and staunch land-grant adherent, heard that Rogers was back in Chihuahua. He had, said Hixenbaugh's informant, hidden his horse in a graveyard near by while he slipped into a dance hall to sample the charms of the Mexican girls. Hixenbaugh and a deputy stole into the cemetery and waited. When Rogers appeared, Hixenbaugh stepped into the open and ordered him to raise his hands. Rogers chose to go for his gun, and Hixenbaugh fell, a bullet in his leg. The sheriff and his deputy both fired, but Rogers escaped. Hixenbaugh eventually lost his leg, and the land-grant forces lost one of their best men.

Managers of the Maxwell Land Grant Company prevailed upon Governor Lionel A. Sheldon to authorize creation of a militia company at Raton to prevent a total breakdown of law and order. Sheldon obliged and, at the suggestion of the petitioners, named Jim Masterson captain of the unit. Jim was empowered to recruit thirty-five militiamen. The antigrant partisans bitterly opposed this move, charging that the members of the militia were, with few exceptions, nonresident gunmen and gamblers. Jim Masterson himself was considered an outsider, having just come from Trinidad, where he had lived three years. Trinidad was only twenty miles from Raton, but it was in Colorado, which might as well have been another country. Jim was appointed undersheriff of Colfax County; according to George Curry, he also was given a commission as deputy U.S. marshal and was handed eviction notices to serve on some of the more militant settlers in the Maxwell grant.

On January 30, 1885, the Dick Rogers gang took over a dance hall in Raton. Rogers, South, Staley, Wallington, and King burst into the place with drawn guns and backed employees and patrons against the walls. It may not have been entirely by chance that they chose this particular time for the raid, for Jim Masterson was one of the patrons and they had great sport humiliating the newly appointed captain of militia. Jim was made to dance a jig in the middle of the hall as .45-caliber slugs ripped splinters from the boards beneath his feet.

Governor Sheldon put a thousand-dollar reward on Dick Rogers' head, and a few days later, there arrived at the express office in Raton two cases of arms and ammunition addressed to James Masterson, Captain, Company H, Territorial Militia. Colfax County was tense. Citizens braced for full-scale war.

On February 21, J. C. Holmes, editor of the *Raton Independent*, arrived in Santa Fe with a petition, signed by eighty-eight Raton residents, requesting disbandment of Masterson's militia unit. In a statement to the governor as he presented the petition, Holmes declared:

The first we knew of the organization of a militia company, was when several cases of arms arrived at the depot addressed to one James Masterson. The organization of this company is going to injure our town. It is not in the hands of the right kind of citizens. . . . Masterson himself is a pretty hard man, being a brother of the notorious "Bat" Masterson . . . and the signers of the petition object to him as the head and front of this new militia company. We have no fear of Rogers. . . . But we all fear . . . that the organization of Masterson's militia company will be the cause of more bloodshed.[3]

Later in the day, editor Holmes met with Attorney General Bartlett, who assured him that Raton and Colfax County had nothing to fear from Masterson and the militia company and that Captain Masterson was under his personal direction. The matter of the petition, he was told, would be taken under advisement by the governor. Holmes returned to Raton and the situation simmered.

Several days later, Captain Masterson was ordered to take his company to Cimarron and await further orders. Suddenly, on March 1, there came from Santa Fe instructions to disband Company H. According to Miguel Otero, this word reached the anti-grant forces before it reached Masterson. While the militiamen were enjoying themselves in a Cimarron dance hall, a party of men led by George Curry confiscated their weapons and ammunition and returned to Raton. They called on all their partisans to assemble for the purpose of organizing a vigilante group to rid Colfax County of their enemies once and for all. Curry's story is slightly different, with no mention of stealing the territorial armament. He wrote that the vigilance committee was armed with rifles and revolvers taken from a Raton hardware store.

When Jim Masterson learned that Company H had been deactivated and its arms cache had disappeared, he headed for Raton with a group of his followers. Seething with anger, he began looking for those who had signed the petition to the governor, certain they could tell him who had taken the weapons and where they were. It was later claimed that he pulled a gun on J. E. Herndon and orally abused him. D. W. Stevens, Curry's employer and mentor, fared worse. Masterson is said to have struck Stevens with the barrel of his six-gun when the storekeeper denied having knowledge of the weapons.

Meanwhile, Curry assembled his vigilante company from the

surrounding ranches and rode into Raton. The former members of
Company H were hunted down, disarmed, and held under arrest.
Jim Masterson and two sidekicks took refuge in the Moulton
Hotel, barricaded the doors, and prepared for a siege. Finally, a
parley was arranged, and George Curry personally guaranteed the
safety of the three if they came out. Jim and his pals emerged, and
Curry proved as good as his word. "A little later," he wrote,
"when an attempt was made to kill Masterson by several of the
settlers whom he had abused, I was able to protect him."[4]

The former militiamen were taken to a skating rink, where a
mass meeting was being held to organize the vigilante company.
Six hundred rabid antigrant partisans were on hand, including the
outlawed Dick Rogers and his gang. The word *militia* was in
disrepute at that particular time in Raton, but the vigilantes were
organized as a military unit. The man with a price on his head,
Dick Rogers, was elected captain, Charlie Hunt, first lieutenant,
Tom Gable second lieutenant, and George Curry first sergeant.
After the election of officers, the question of what to do with the
prisoners was taken up. It was decided that they should be walked
up Raton Pass to the Colorado line and warned to stay out of New
Mexico on pain of death. Jim and his cohorts trudged the ten miles,
every step of the way uphill. "To the best of my knowledge,"
testified Curry, "none of them ever set foot in New Mexico
again."[5]

"We have a report that seems to be more than idle rumor," said
the *Trinidad Daily Advertiser* of March 3, "that Dick Rodgers and
associates captured Jim Masterson and his militia company at
Raton today and started northward with the prisoners. It is supposed that they will camp about the Colorado-New Mexico line
tonight." The following day, the Trinidad paper reported simply:
"Mr. James Masterson of Raton, undersheriff of Colfax County,
N. M., is in the city." That the expelled militiamen were boiling
mad there can be no doubt, but one of them, Ed Stone, must have
been particularly distraught; the newspaper editor advised, "If you
want to get paralyzed, just ask Ed. Stone how far it is from here to
Raton by wagon road." By March 6, it was apparent that Masterson's crew was not going back. "The Raton 'Walking Militia'
pitched their bivouac here in time for the city election," said the

Advertiser. "Some of them are citizens of Trinidad from 'away back' and can swear the others in."

Otero writes that Masterson's "gunmen and gamblers" were not the only people to depart Raton after the vigilante sweep. Some prominent businessmen and officials, including Henry Whigham, T. A. Schomberg, and District Attorney M. W. Mills — all associated with the Maxwell Land Grant Company — fled to Trinidad in fear of their lives. These men returned, however, when conditions had cooled somewhat.

George Curry had one more confrontation with Jim Masterson, and it occurred several months after Jim was exiled from New Mexico. Curry and Bob Lee were hired to drive a herd of horses to a ranch between Trinidad and La Junta, Colorado. They delivered the horses and entrained for Raton. There was a thirty-minute stop for lunch at the Harvey House in Trinidad, and as they were eating, someone spotted them and passed the word to Jim Masterson that two members of the bunch that had driven him from New Mexico were in town. Shortly after the two returned to their coach, a crowd began forming at the depot. Curry recognized Jim Masterson and several others who had been forced to walk those ten uphill miles to the Colorado line. He asked the other passengers to move to another car, and he and Bob Lee, armed with Winchesters, took up positions at either end of the car. When the gang outside attempted to enter the coach, shots were fired, several windows were broken, and one man was wounded slightly by a bullet from Curry's rifle. Curry said the train was held up for more than an hour before officers arrived to disperse the crowd.

Soon after this episode, George Curry moved to Lincoln County, New Mexico, where he held several offices, including that of sheriff. During the Spanish-American War, Governor Otero appointed him captain of a cavalry company that became a part of Theodore Roosevelt's Rough Riders. Curry later served with distinction in the Philippines, and in 1907 was appointed governor of New Mexico Territory by President Roosevelt.

Taking the embattled Colfax County settlers at their word, Jim Masterson stayed clear of the Territory after March, 1885. Trinidad, Colorado, was again his base of operations for several years, and then, in the late eighties, when the county-seat wars flared in western Kansas, he turned up again in Dodge City. Bill Tilghman and Neal Brown, two of his buffalo-hunting partners from a decade before, were still in Dodge, and Jim became closely associated with them.

Jim may have been employed as a special deputy to guard the polls at several of the hotly contested county elections. Bill Tilghman and Brown definitely took on these assignments, and there were reports during and after several of the struggles that a Masterson had been involved. In at least one instance, as we have seen, Bat Masterson made a point of publicly denying participation. In the Ingalls-Cimarron fight to become the seat of Gray County, it is clear from contemporary records and the reminiscences of George Bolds, one of the participants, that it was Jim Masterson who was actively involved, not Bat, as has been often repeated.[6]

The raid on the Cimarron courthouse (January 12, 1889) was instigated by Asa T. Soule, the Hop Bitters King, and it has been said that he put up one thousand dollars to be split among the mercenaries employed to carry off the court records. The key to Soule's plan was Newt Watson, Gray County court clerk and strong Ingalls man. Buffalo Joe Reynolds, sheriff of Gray County, was a Cimarron sympathizer. When he became incapacitated as the result of a wound he received in a gunfight with rustlers, Soule had Watson appoint Bill Tilghman temporary sheriff with authority to pick the deputies he needed to get the court records. Tilghman deputized Jim Masterson, Neal Brown, Ben Daniels, and Fred Singer, all former Dodge City officers. George Bolds, Billy Allensworth, and Ed Brooks, younger Dodge spirits of nerve and daring, joined the entourage. Newt Watson was the official in charge, and Charlie Reicheldeffer, an Ingalls coal dealer, was enlisted to drive his team and wagon, the gunmen inside, from Ingalls to Cimarron.

When the alarm was spread that the records were being taken and the gun battle commenced, Watson, Jim Masterson, Fred Singer, and Billy Allensworth were in the two-story brick building that was serving temporarily as the courthouse. When the sniping began, Tilghman and his guards outside returned the fire but found their exposed positions on the plank sidewalk extremely hazardous. They raced for the wagon, but the thin sideboards afforded little protection from the increasing fusillade laid down by the embattled Cimarron citizenry. Ed Brooks crumpled, a bullet in his belly. George Bolds went down with a bullet in his leg, struggled to his feet, and was dropped again as two more slugs ripped into his body. Bill Tilghman took a shot through the calf of his leg.

On the seat of the wagon, Charlie Reicheldeffer fought to control his frightened team until a bullet slammed him backward into the wagon bed. The horses bolted, jerking the wagon down the street. Suddenly deprived of their scant cover, the bloodied Ingalls fighters hobbled after the wagon, snapping shots as they went. A block away, Reicheldeffer regained control of his team. Tilghman's gunmen all managed to reach the wagon and careened out of town with rifle bullets whining after them. Miraculously, all of the wounded recovered.

The four other Ingalls men left in the courthouse prepared for a siege. Bullets tore through the upstairs windows as the townspeople concentrated their ire and their fire on the trapped mercenaries. Checking casualties, the Cimarronians counted J. W. ("Will") English dead and Ed Fairhurst and Jack Bliss badly wounded. Asa Harrington had a thumb shot away, and Frank Luther, recovering his derby hat after it was shot off, found it contained two bullet holes and a lock of hair that had been clipped neatly from his head.

Several attempts were made to dislodge the warriors. A determined rush for the stairway was turned back by fire from above, and when a ladder was raised to a rear window, Jim Masterson kicked it away. Shots were fired blindly through the wooden second floor, but the besieged quartet climbed atop the steel safe and filing cabinets to avoid the bullets. Finally, after six hours, Jake Shoup, acting as spokesman for Cimarron, stepped into the street and waved the white flag of truce. If the Ingalls foursome would surrender, he said, they would be allowed to leave town and no one would harm them. Masterson insisted that they be allowed to keep their guns. Shoup finally agreed, and the four were escorted to the depot and permitted to leave on the train.

George Bolds said the safe-passage decision was made when a wire arrived from Bat Masterson in Denver, warning Jake Shoup that if his brother and the others were not allowed to leave immediately, he would "hire a train and come in with enough men to blow Cimarron off the face of Kansas." Bat had learned of the battle when the editor of the *Cimarron Jacksonian* telegraphed the exciting news to the *Kansas City Star*, which in turn put it on the national press wires. A newspaper friend in Denver had hurried to Bat, prompting his ultimatum.[7]

Six months later, on June 10, 1889, Jim Masterson, Newt Watson, Billy Allensworth, Fred Singer, Neal Brown, and Ben Daniels were tried for the murder of J. W. English and acquitted. Four years later, in 1893, another election was held to determine the Gray County seat. Cimarron won, and the court records were quietly returned from Ingalls.

Long before the Ingalls-Cimarron conflict was settled, however, Jim Masterson had left Kansas for the new excitement in Oklahoma. For years white men had cast covetous eyes on the Unassigned Lands, some three million acres in Indian Territory that had been set aside by the federal government for the relocation of nomadic western tribes but had never been used. Boomers moved onto the land illegally and were evicted by federal marshals and, at times, military forces. A growing clamor for public opening of the lands territory finally caused Congress to act. President Benjamin Harrison proclaimed that on April 22, 1889, the Unassigned Lands would be opened for settlement. Immediately, thousands upon thousands of homesteaders and speculators began gathering at the border to make the run. They would race for about 10,000 quarter-sections of virgin farmland on foot, on the backs of horses, mules, and jackasses, and in every conceivable type of conveyance. The Santa Fe, which had completed a line across the Territory in 1887, would bring in thousands. On the day of the opening, fifteen trains were scheduled to start from the Kansas border town of Arkansas City. Jim Masterson was making the run from there, and among the throng he recognized many people he had known on the buffalo ranges of western Kansas a dozen years earlier. Bill Tilghman was present, as were Neal Brown, Fred Sutton, and Henry Garris.

At high noon on April 22, the signal was given and the great run began. Jim took one of the Santa Fe trains to Guthrie, which before the opening consisted of nothing but a water tank for the railroad and a land-office shack. But 320 acres had been set aside for a townsite, and by nightfall of the first day, ten thousand people were scrambling to claim lots. The federal government had provided for a townsite, but no survey had been made. In the chaos of milling men and animals, railroad-delivered construction materials, tools, provisions, and store goods of all descriptions, no one knew whether his tent was pitched on a lot or in the middle of a street. Movement within the city was possible only by means of labyrinthine pathways through the maze of tents.

Within a few days, a provisional city government had been set up, with D. B. Dyer acting as mayor. His first order of business was a survey and the location of streets. This accomplished, he issued a proclamation that all persons encamped upon the rights-of-way would have to move by a certain day. Those affected by this edict took a very dim view of the procedure. Many fingered their shooting irons, expressed imprecations, and refused to budge. Dyer sent for Bill Tilghman and Jim Masterson. The streets had to be cleared, he said, forcibly if necessary. Would they take on the job? They would.

Two huge logs were dragged to the crest of a hill where Oklahoma Avenue was to start. The logs, chained together, stretched the width of the street. Four mules were hitched to either end of this immense broom, and ahead of the mules rode Jim Masterson and Bill Tilghman. Wrote Frank Greer, editor of the *Daily Oklahoma State Capital*:

Each was mounted with a rifle on his saddle and two sixes showing on each side of his belt. Each made speeches to the people saying that the streets had been fairly surveyed, that no town could be without streets, that they were going right down Oklahoma Avenue and were sending men down the street to tell the people to get their tents and luggage out of the way before the mules rode over it.

There were great mutterings. Men stood with their Winchesters and revolvers in hand, saying that they had the same right to their lots in the street as others who were lucky enough not to locate in the street and that no one could drive them out without suffering the consequences.

At the appointed time Tilghman, Masterson, the mules and the logs started. In an hour, there was not a tent or piece of luggage in Oklahoma Avenue and for the first time since the occupation of Guthrie you could stand on the hill and look straight down the avenue to the Santa Fe station.[8]

From 1889 on, Jim Masterson called Guthrie home. He served as a deputy sheriff of Logan County and followed his gambling vocation, dealing in Fred Sutton's Turf Exchange Saloon and other establishments.

In 1893, President Grover Cleveland established a new U.S. marshal district, with Guthrie as headquarters. E. D. Nix, Guthrie wholesale grocer and partner in the HX Bar Ranch, was appointed marshal. Nix was not a fighting man, but he was an able administrator, and he soon deputized as fine a group of law enforcement officers as ever was assembled in the West. Bill Tilghman, Neal Brown, John Hale, Chris Madsen, Heck Thomas, Bud Ledbetter, Frank Canton, Tom Houston, John Hixon, Orrington ("Red") Lucas, and Jim Masterson were among them, and the story of the war these men waged with the organized outlaw gangs of Oklahoma has enriched the history of the Great American West. Masterson's most well-known exploit as a federal officer in Oklahoma was his participation in the bloody gun battle at Ingalls, an outlaw rendezvous in the Cherokee Strip.

On October 2, 1892, the Dalton gang was shattered in an abortive attempt to rob two banks simultaneously in Coffeyville, Kansas. An embattled citizenry killed outlaws Bob and Grat Dalton, Bill Powers, and Bill Broadwell and wounded and captured Emmett Dalton. Survivors Bill Dalton and Bill Doolin quickly organized a new gang, enlisting some of the hardest cases in Oklahoma Territory, which was swarming with vicious thieves and killers. Recruited were George ("Bitter Creek") Newcomb, Tulsa Jack Blake, Roy ("Arkansas Tom") Daugherty, Charlie Pierce, George ("Red Buck") Waightman and Dan ("Dynamite Dick") Clifton. During 1893, the Doolin-Dalton gang pulled several lucrative jobs. It was especially active in the Dodge City area, staging a bank holdup in Spearville and robbing the Santa Fe express at Cimarron.

Acting on a tip that the gang was using as a hideout the tiny village of Ingalls, some thirty-five miles northeast of Guthrie near the border of the Creek Nation, Deputy U.S. Marshal Red Lucas

This picture, taken in front of the marshal's office at Guthrie, Oklahoma, in the town's first days, includes some of the Territory's most celebrated lawmen. Jim Masterson waves a hat. Flanking him are Bud Ledbetter (left) and Heck Thomas (right). Chris Madsen is the bareheaded man third from the right, front row. Courtesy Robert Cunningham, Stillwater, Oklahoma.

went undercover in the summer of 1893 to check out the report. Posing as a dim-witted catfish peddler, Lucas pitched a tent in Ingalls and soon gained acceptance by the inhabitants, who catered to the well-heeled gang members during their periodic visits. Lucas sent word that the outlaws were slipping in and out of town at odd times and with no apparent pattern. A large, heavily armed force of officers might make a haul if it were to hit the town at the right time, he thought.

In late August, Marshal Nix assembled a posse of a dozen tough deputies under the leadership of John Hixon. Jim Masterson was named Hixon's second-in-command. The possemen headed for Ingalls in two canvas-topped wagons, representing themselves as a party of hunters, which in fact they were. In the wagons they carried a large store of provisions and a prodigious arsenal. At a prearranged location not far from Ingalls, they camped to await word from Lucas. He appeared on September 1. The entire gang was disporting in town at that very moment, he said. Most of them would be in the Ransom Saloon, but he warned that gang members might be anywhere in town, that any building might hold a desperate killer.

Jim Masterson took one of the wagons and circled the town to enter from the opposite side. With him were Deputy Marshals W. C. Roberts, Henry Keller, Hi Thompson, George Cox. H. A. Janson, and Lafe Shadley. The second wagon approached from the west. Deputy Dick Speed was up front on the seat. Hidden in the back under the canvas were Deputies John Hixon, Red Lucas, Tom Houston, Steve Burke, and Ike Steel. With the addition of Lucas, thirteen officers in all moved in on Ingalls that morning, a figure that might have given the superstitious among them something to ponder.

As Speed's wagon rolled slowly into Ingalls, the deputies dropped over the tailgate to hide themselves in the brush at the edge of town. When the wagon was empty, Speed drove on, finally stopping in front of a livery stable.

From the saloon up the street, Bitter Creek Newcomb saw the wagon come into town. Suspicious, he stepped outside to investigate. He mounted his horse at the saloon's hitch rail and rode slowly toward the wagon. Seeing the approaching rider, Speed asked a young boy who happened to be passing the stable who the rider was. The boy, Dell Simmons by name, waved an arm toward the horseman. "Why, that's Bitter Creek Newcomb," he said. Bitter Creek, intently watching the stranger and the boy, saw the gesture in his direction. Instantly he reined up and pulled his Winchester from its scabbard. Dick Speed raised his own rifle and fired. With that shot, the ball began. The Battle of Ingalls was on.

Speed's bullet smashed into Newcomb's rifle, driving fragments of wood and metal into the outlaw's body. Newcomb dropped the useless weapon and wheeled his horse around in the middle of the street. Speed leveled his rifle for a killing shot.

On the second floor of the Pierce Hotel, Arkansas Tom Daugherty heard that first rifle report and looked out the window. Below he saw a man aiming a rifle and Bitter Creek Newcomb, swaying weakly in the saddle, attempting to flee. Arkansas Tom steadied his weapon on the window frame and fired, levered, and fired again. Speed crumpled, dead when he hit the ground. Newcomb, hunched over the neck of his horse, made the timber at the edge of town.

The opening shots caught the possemen out of position. Now they had to seek cover where they could find it as five guns inside the saloon laid down a withering fire and the sniper in the hotel snapped off shots at any deputy who became exposed. The officers unlimbered their Winchesters and began to riddle the saloon. Soon, Ransom, the saloonkeeper, and Murray, his bartender, were hit. On the street outside, the boy Dell Simmons lay dying, struck by an outlaw's bullet.

Suddenly, Bill Doolin burst from the saloon. Crouching low, he dashed for the Ransom stable down the street, where the outlaws had their horses. Making the stable doorway safely, he set up a heavy barrage to cover Bill Dalton and Red Buck, who followed. The three then maintained a fusillade as Tulsa Jack and Dynamite Dick ran, ducking and dodging, to the stable.

Deputy Lafe Shadley ran into the street and took up a position behind the body of a horse that had been killed by an errant bullet. From this spot he poured lead into the doorway of the stable. Deputy Tom Houston also maneuvered for a better spot and in so doing became visible to Arkansas Tom, the sniper in the hotel.

Arkansas Tom fired twice and Houston went down, gut shot. "I'd like to see the man who shot me," he moaned as he lay dying.

Meanwhile, the outlaws in the stable had saddled their horses. On signal, Doolin and Clifton rode out the rear door as Dalton, Waightman, and Blake charged out by the front. An officer's bullet struck Dalton's horse in the jaw. The crazed animal dropped its head and whirled like a dervish. Another bullet broke its leg and it stumbled and fell. Dalton leaped clear and raced after the other outlaws, who had pulled up their mounts at a wire fence. He had gone but a short way when he remembered that the only pair of wire cutters were on his saddle. Turning back, Dalton spotted Lafe Shadley crawling to a new firing position. He pumped three bullets into the lawman. Securing his cutters, Dalton ran back to the fence, cut an opening, and then swung up behind Bill Doolin's saddle. The five outlaws galloped out of town and rode hard for the timber.

Having no horses of their own, the officers were unable to pursue. They had to settle for the capture of Arkansas Tom Daugherty, who was still winging shots from the hotel. The officers riddled the upper floor of the building with bullets, but for an hour Daugherty kept up the fight. Finally, Jim Masterson produced two sticks of dynamite and called to the outlaw to come out or he would "blow the house into the middle of next week." Arkansas Tom, not yet twenty years old, decided the game was over and walked out of the building with his hands high. In shackles, Daugherty was led to the dying Tom Houston, who stared at him blankly. He had been granted his dying wish, to look upon the face of his slayer, but somehow it did not seem to make dying any easier for him.

The Battle of Ingalls was over, and it seemed that the outlaws had won a great victory over the deputy U.S. marshals. Dick Speed, Tom Houston, and Lafe Shadley, three fine officers, were dead, a terrible price to pay for the capture of one member of the gang. But this gunfight in September, 1893, spelled the beginning of the end for the Doolin-Dalton gang. Marshal Nix's deputies mounted a determined, relentless manhunt.

Arkansas Tom was sentenced to fifty years in prison for killing Tom Houston. He survived by many years the other outlaws who escaped the raid on Ingalls.

In May, 1895, Tulsa Jack Blake was killed by a posse led by Deputy Chris Madsen.

Two months later, Bitter Creek Newcomb and Charlie Pierce were trapped and killed by a party of marshals led by Heck Thomas.

Shortly thereafter, Dynamite Dick Clifton was waylaid by Deputies Steve Burke, W. M. Nix, and W. O. Jones, shot three times and captured. He died in prison.

Bill Dalton was killed in September, 1895, by Deputy Loss Hart.

Red Buck Waightman was cornered and killed in October by a party of deputies led by Chris Madsen.

Bill Doolin, the cunning and daring leader of the gang, was captured by Bill Tilghman and taken to Guthrie. He managed to escape, but in August, 1896, he was found by Heck Thomas, who ended the outlaw's career with a blast from a double-barreled shotgun.

Jim Masterson was not around to help by that time. Nineteen months after the epic Ingalls raid, he was dead. He expired on March 31, 1895, at the age of thirty-nine, the victim of a type of tuberculosis popularly known as galloping consumption, the quickly fatal form of the dread disease. Frank Greer's *Daily Oklahoma State Capital* carried the story of his passing on the front page of its April 1 edition:

Jim Masterson, a first day settler of Guthrie and a well known figure about town, died last night about 11 o'clock. The cause of his death was quick consumption. He was conscious to the last. He was even out Saturday; but last night about 10 o'clock he called to have some of his friends come to see him, and died an hour later.

The deceased was at one time a well known figure in western Kansas. He was one of the marshals at Dodge City during its cowboy days and was reputed to be a brave man. He came to this city the first day and has been acting as deputy marshal since. He was considered here the bravest of the marshals. Whenever a big raid was to be made on any stronghold of outlaws, like that at Ingalls, he was always asked to be one of the party. When every man would flinch, he would still be found in the front rank. Every man has his virtues and his faults. Jim Masterson was a man who never went back on a friend, and never forgot an obligation. He never pretended to keep up the conventional social amenities; but yet there was a man whom money could absolutely never make break a trust, and who would have done a kind act to a man on the gallows after all the world had given him the cold shoulder, and where there was no chance of any personal reward. Many who walk the conventional paths of social life are not as honorable in their obligations to their fellow man as he was. He was so proud that in his last moments he would not let his condition be known to his relatives. He is a brother of Bat Masterson, a man of national reputation as a backer of athletic sports, and quite rich, but he would not apply to him for aid.

The body will be shipped to relatives in Wichita in the morning for interment.

Even in the story of his death, which attempted to justify Jim's life as a sporting man and to emphasize his redeeming qualities of loyalty, compassion and courage, it will be noted that Jim was again identified as "a brother of Bat Masterson." The appellation had followed him to the grave.

It should also be noted that although Jim Masterson had for twenty years been directly involved in some of the most violent episodes in the history of the wild border towns of the West, there is no evidence that he ever killed a man. Like Bat, Jim was no killer.

CHAPTER TWENTY-TWO

FRIENDS, CONCUBINES, WIVES

Bat Masterson's amorous adventures have been greatly neglected both in the accounts of contemporary writers and in the reminiscences of old-timers who knew him. Although many remarked on his handsome features and impeccable dress, references to the women who were attracted to him were conspicuously absent. This seems particularly odd when it is remembered that one of the earliest tales that went into the making of the Masterson legend was a reported battle over the affections of a dance-hall girl. That there were women, perhaps many of them, with whom he had relationships of varying degrees of intimacy can scarcely be doubted; Bat did not keep his trousers immaculate, his moustache carefully barbered, and his shoes shined just to impress the faro dealer in the next gambling hall.

Bat moved in a masculine world. Females were scarce in the cow towns and mining camps he frequented, and scarcer still were women of the type a man would choose for a wife. Being a gambler, Bat necessarily spent most of his time in saloons, honky-tonks, and hurdy-gurdy houses. Most of the women with whom he came in contact would hardly inspire an intelligent young man to protestations of undying love and affection. There were a few female gambling professionals and many who professed to be entertainers and waitresses, but the large majority of women who frequented the saloons were unabashed whores. During hard times, the lady gamblers, waitresses, and entertainers often fell back on the older profession for a living.

Most of these heroines who first brought femininity to the frontier camps lived and died in obscurity, but the names or nicknames of some of these who worked the towns Bat frequented have survived. Aside from a young blade's natural reluctance to hooking up with a known hooker, the nicknames of some of the girls indicate they were anything but raving beauties. Included among the nymphs of Dodge were Hop Fiend Nel, Little Dot, Scar-faced Lillie, Emporia Belle, and Miss One Fin. In the Colorado mining camps were Slanting Annie, Lulu Slain (called the Mormon Queen), Marie Cantassot, and Rose Vastine, who, because of her six-foot-two elevation, was known as Timberline. In Arizona, the reigning queens of the demimonde were Madame Mustache, Crazy Horse Lil, and a pair of Katherines renowned for their generous proboscises, Big-Nose Kate and Nosey Kate.

The few contemporary references we have to women in Masterson's life are tantalizingly brief. There is Henry Raymond's German notation in his diary in February, 1873, about Bat and Ed "sleeping with friends." In a social item in a June, 1878, issue, the *Dodge City Times* reported that "Sheriff Masterson and lady" were among those present at the grand opening of the Summit House in neighboring Spearville. "There was gayety and beauty there, the staid bachelor and the festive young man, the buxom lassie, the comely maid and the village belles. A sumptuous board was spread to which the guests responded with alacrity and avidity — especially those from Dodge City.''[1] At a grand masquerade ball given by the Dodge City Social Club on Christmas Night, 1878, in attendance, according to the *Ford County Globe*, were "W. B. Masterson and Miss Brown."[2]

The tenth federal census, taken in Dodge City in June, 1880, listed W. B. Masterson, age 25 years, occupation laborer. We are then treated to a juicy piece of intelligence: Masterson was reported living with Annie Ladue, "a 19-year-old concubine." This same report listed James Masterson, city marshal, age 24, as living with Minnie Roberts, "a 16-year-old concubine." For what it is worth, it should be noted that the enumerator of this census was Walter C. Shinn, who with his brother Lloyd founded the *Dodge City Times* and who was always critical of the Masterson brothers in Dodge.[3]

It was a practice of some of the frontier journalists, however, to lend respectability to certain recognized cohabitational arrangements. In November, 1877, when Ed Masterson came back to Dodge after being winged in the Lone Star Dancehall, the *Times* reported: "Assistant Marshal Masterson returned from Wichita the first of the week. He is recovering from the wound received in the recent shooting affray, and will soon be able to resume his duties as an officer.'' On another page, the editor noted: ''Ed Masterson's wife has returned, she came from Hays on a horse.''[4] Apparently, Ed's ''wife'' had gone to Hays while he went to his parents' home to recuperate. When he came back to Dodge, she returned also. This reference to a wife undoubtedly was a euphemism; Ed Masterson was never married.

Whether called friends, concubines, or wives, the girls who warmed the beds of the brothers Masterson are as dark stars now; we know they were there, but we know little else about them. Even of the woman Bat eventually married, little is known. Her name was Emma Walters, and she was said to have been raised in Philadelphia, where her father had the distinction of being the first Civil War veteran to be buried in that city.[5]

Emma was a blonde song-and-dance performer, four years younger than Bat, whom he reportedly met and married in Denver. Tom Masterson, Jr., told George Thompson that the date of the marriage was November 21, 1891.[6] This would have been five days before Bat's thirty-eighth birthday, when Emma was thirty-four. However, there is no record in the files of either Denver or Arapahoe County that this marriage was performed on that date, and other evidence indicates that Bat and Emma were living together as man and wife as early as 1889.[7]

In his letter to Frank Baldwin dated February 4, 1890, Bat wrote: ''I am a benedict, having married some eight years ago.'' This would indicate a marriage about 1882, or during the time he was city marshal of Trinidad. In her reminiscences, Josephine Earp recalled going with her husband to the Coeur d'Alene mining district in the late winter of 1883–84 and taking with her a pet canary that had been given to her by ''Bat Masterson's wife.''[8] The first known contemporary reference to Bat's wife is a brief item in the July 5, 1884, issue of the *Dodge City Democrat* reporting that ''Olney Newell, of the Trinidad *News*, and his two children, were guests of Mr. and Mrs. Bat Masterson.''

No official record of the marriage has been located, but it is believed that Bat and Emma were married in the early 1880's, perhaps in Kansas. Milt Hinkle, son of George Hinkle, has written that his mother and Emma Walters were close friends and that his parents met in Topeka, Kansas, where his mother was working. [9] George Hinkle married a Miss A. C. Robinson on May 7, 1879; Milt was born on October 15, 1881. There is the possibility that Bat and Emma Walters lived together during Bat's stays in Denver and that the common-law arrangement was formally legalized on the 1891 date furnished by Tom Masterson.

If Bat and Emma were married during the 1880's, however, an escapade by Bat in 1886 must have shaken the marriage to its foundation. Because of its scandalous and sensational nature, the story was given a big play in the *Rocky Mountain News*.

Denver in the mid-1880's was rapidly changing from a little frontier town to the metropolis of the West. Top-flight variety shows and vaudeville acts from the East were presented regularly at several theaters. Bat spent much time at these theaters on his visits to the city, frequenting especially the California Hall and the Palace Theater, the latter managed by Ed Chase and Ed Gaylord, two of the leading lights of the Denver gambling fraternity.

Showing at the California Hall in September of 1886 was a minstrel review featuring a popular black-face comedian of the day, Lou Spencer. Bat attended every performance. He was drawn, however, not by the talents of Mr. Spencer, but by those of the comedian's wife. While Spencer was cavorting on the stage, Bat was cavorting with Mrs. Spencer in a box in the wings. The lady, a well-known performer in her own right, went under the name of Nellie McMahon. As a singer she had appeared previously in Denver as a member of the Kate Castleton Opera Company. It is possible that Bat had met her during her earlier visit. At any rate, their friendship had progressed to a remarkable degree when it was discovered by Spencer.

For the details of what then took place, we have Spencer's story as told to a reporter for the *Rocky Mountain News*:

The trouble commenced Saturday night. I saw my wife sitting on Bat Masterson's knee in a box during the performance. I went to the door and called her out, and asked what she was doing. Masterson spoke up and said that if I had anything to say to the lady I might tell it to him. I reminded him that the lady was my wife, when he struck at me with his pistol, and I struck back with my fist. Then we were arrested and taken down to the station, where we were both released and I went back to work.

For the next two days after the incident, said Spencer, Nellie McMahon pleaded with him to forgive her for her indiscretion and played the part of the penitent wife. The following Tuesday, however, Nellie suddenly filed suit for divorce, charging her husband with nonsupport, brutality, and habitual drunkenness. The *News* reported the divorce action, adding: "The case was made very sensational last evening by the discovery that . . . Nellie McMahon had eloped with W. B. Masterson. The couple left the city in the afternoon, and are now supposed to be located in Dodge City, Kan."

Spencer's version of the events leading to the split were given with the observation of the reporter:

Spencer does not seem much put out because his wife has run away "with a handsomer man." . . . Nellie McMahon is a beautiful woman, with a fine wardrobe and a sweet voice. Her singing has made her famous to some extent. . . . W. B. Masterson is well known in this city. He is a handsome man, and one who pleases the ladies. The affair has been sufficient a sensation to create a great stir about California Hall.[10]

It must also have created something of a stir around the Masterson household.

Bat headed for Dodge City, where his arrival was duly noted in the September 28 issue of the *Globe Live Stock Journal*, but if the beautiful singer was with him, the paper carefully avoided reference to her. The Nellie McMahon affair was, apparently, a brief interlude that ended as spontaneously as it began; Nellie's name was never again linked with Bat's, and, so far as is known, Bat never again involved himself in extramarital peccadilloes.

In November, 1888, Bat Masterson was thirty-five years old. For almost a decade, his restless energy and love of excitement had kept him on the move. He had prowled the length and breadth of the frontier, bucking the high-stakes games, rushing to the aid of friends, troubleshooting a semblance of law and order into border sin sinks. His luck at the tables had run from hot to cold and back again many times, but gradually he had accumulated a sizable

The Palace Theater in Denver. The Very Reverend Henry Martin Hart called it ''a death-trap to young men, a foul den of vice and corruption.'' Courtesy Denver Public Library.

bankroll. As he wearied of drifting, he looked about for a likely spot in which to settle.

When Ed Chase and Ed Gaylord, overlords of ''square'' gambling in Denver, let it be known that the Palace Theater, their finest property, could be had for a price, Bat asked the price and met it. In buying the Palace, Bat became the owner of a building that had developed into a Denver landmark.

The Palace Variety Theater and Gambling Parlors, the official name of the new Masterson property, was a large brick edifice on the corner of Blake and Fifteenth streets. Chase and his former partner, Hub Heatley, had opened it twenty-three years earlier, and over the years, millions of dollars had passed back and forth across the elaborately carved gaming tables. The bar and gambling rooms in the Palace were second to none in the West. A gigantic gas chandelier in the barroom dazzled patrons with reflected light from five hundred glass prisms. A sixty-foot continuous mirror behind the bar reproduced the full glory of the elegant lighting fixture. The gambling room, operated by twenty-five dealers, could accommodate two hundred players. There were layouts for any game that might strike a gambler's fancy, from hop and toss to over and under seven.

The theater, bedecked with tapestries and heavy velvet, had a capacity of seven hundred fifty. Boxes flanking the stage were heavily curtained to provide privacy for those who desired it. Food and liquor were served in the boxes; a bottle of beer sold for one dollar. A midnight lunch, served free to all, had been a tradition of the house, and the policy was continued during Bat's tenure. Among the delicacies provided for these nocturnal feasts were roast pork and beef, venison, antelope cutlets, breast of prairie hen, and sundry salads and sandwiches.

Some of the finest vaudeville performers in American show business played the Denver Palace during the eighties. Bat's old friend, Eddie Foy, appeared there many times. Other top acts were Lottie Rogers (known as the Leadville Nightingale), Cora Vane, Ettie Le Clair, Effie Moore, Donnelly and Drew, Ed Conley, Ben Collins, and the Holland Sisters.

Managing the barroom and overseeing the gambling spreads in his new establishment posed no problems for Bat; he had had a wealth of practical training in those lines. But booking performers for his theater was a new experience. He set about it in his usual forthright manner. He drew up a set of rules, which he had published in vaudeville trade papers. Here are a few typical examples:

Performers writing to this house for an engagement will state the quality and quantity of their wardrobes and the amount of salary they will work for, not what they want, for we make all the allowances for a performer's gall. We care nothing about how they "split 'em up the back at Grand Rapids," or "How they knocked 'em silly on the coast."

Variety ladies with more than three husbands need not write to this house for a date.

The proprietor doesn't care whether the performers worked one or thirty seasons with Tony Pastor, all he expects of you is to please the hoboes of Blake Street.[11]

When he wed Emma Walters, who performed a song-and-dance number at the Palace, Bat followed the example of the former owners. In the early 1880's one of the theater's featured acts was performed by two sisters, Frances and Addie Barbour. In 1880, Ed Chase married Frances; two years later, Gaylord took Addie as his wife.

The Masterson marriage was childless. Throughout it, Emma remained a shadowy figure. She was, apparently, as reserved as her husband was aggressive. Few of Bat's many friends ever knew her. There is no reason to suppose that she was ever anything but a loving and devoted wife.

Shortly after Bat assumed ownership of the Palace, a wave of moral reform swept Denver. Led by the Very Reverend Henry Martyn Hart, dean of the Episcopalian Cathedral of St. John in the Fields, irate reformers decried the wide-open conditions prevailing in the city. From his pulpit, Dean Hart stormed against gambling houses and brothels in general and, for some reason, the Palace in particular. He called it a "death-trap to young men, a foul den of vice and corruption."[12] Bat sold out to Billy DeVere, who remained open for a time by throwing lavish private parties for city officials, featuring bevies of chorus girls and "possum and sweet 'tater suppers," but the pressure from Dean Hart and his followers became too great and the Palace Theater finally was padlocked.

After selling the Palace, Bat ran a saloon on Larimer Street for a time. In late '91, when the rush to a new silver camp at Creede began, Mart Watrous of the firm of Watrous, Benniger & Company offered Bat the gambling manager's job at a combination restaurant, saloon, and gambling house the company had built in the raw new town. Soured on Denver and the reform movement, Bat decided to take one more crack at a newborn western boom camp.

CHAPTER TWENTY-THREE

THE LAST BOOM

"It is day all day in the daytime, and there is no night in Creede," wrote Cy Warman, editor of the town's newspaper. Here, to the latest in a long string of storied frontier towns, flocked the men and women who, like Bat, thrived on the peculiar excitement inherent in a freshly spawned bonanza center. Almost overnight, Creede blossomed from a few rude miners' shacks into a city of ten thousand. At the height of the boom in 1892, an estimated thirty thousand fortune seekers were on hand at the diggings.

Mart Watrous' amusement house, called the Denver Exchange, was from the start the most popular hangout in Creede. It was a far cry from the Palace or the California Hall back in Denver; nonetheless, it stood in regal splendor amid the tents and jerry-built lean-tos of early Creede. "It was a big place," recalled a Colorado pioneer, "and run on the square and thoroughly businesslike principles. Anyone who ever knew Masterson will know that that is the only sort of thing he would have."[1]

Twenty-four hours a day, the Denver Exchange was packed with free-spending miners. A newspaperman covering the story of the new boom camp for a St. Louis paper reported that the bar receipts alone averaged six hundred and fifty dollars a day.

There is no telling how much they rake off the gaming table every twenty-four hours. Every gambling device known to the West is carried on in their house, and every table is literally full night and day. Masterson walks around the house about sixteen hours out of twenty-four, and knows everything that is going on.[2]

A photograph of Bat taken at this time reveals that he was no longer the dashing young stripling who ran the Lone Star in Dodge City's infancy. He was much heavier, and his hairline had receded noticeably from his forehead. His moustache, once full and dark, had been trimmed short and was streaked with gray. Bat was

In an 1894 issue, *Illustrated
Sporting West* called Bat "one
of the best judges of pugilists in
America." Courtesy Denver
Public Library.

beginning to show signs of age, but the pale eyes beneath the heavy
black eyebrows were as clear and sharp as ever. Whether because
of his maturing years or his new status as a married man, Bat
dressed less flamboyantly in Creede than he had in other border
towns. The newsman said he customarily appeared in a corduroy
suit, soft white shirt, and plain black string tie, unadorned by
jewelry. The corduroy suit, however, was a rich lavender in color.

Manager of the saloon and restaurant sections of the Denver
Exchange was Billy Woods, who claimed to be heavyweight
champion of Colorado. Saturday-night bouts were a regular feature of the establishment, Woods taking on all comers and Bat
acting as referee. Later on, Woods and a gambler named Frank
Oliver quarreled over a girl named Ella Diamond. Oliver killed
Woods and was arrested by Marshal Jack Pugh. Another officer,
Peter Karg, later shot and killed Pugh. Lillian Shields, Pugh's
mistress, got into the act by killing a former lover named Rum-
ridge.

All of this gunplay took place late in the boom town's history; there was surprisingly little shooting during the early days of its existence. In February, 1892, a reporter asked Bat for a comment on this strange situation. Replied Bat:

I don't like this quiet; it augurs ill. I have been in several places that started out this way and there were generally wild scenes of carnage before many weeks passed. . . . It only needs a break to raise Cain here. The same thing happened in other notorious camps. It seems as though there must be a little blood-letting to get affairs into proper working order.[3]

More than one boom-town veteran who was on hand during those early days in Creede believed that the presence of Bat Masterson had a pacifying effect on ruffians in the camp. The St. Louis newspaperman remarked on this:

Bat Masterson is generally recognized in the camp as the nerviest man of all the fighters here. He has a record for cool bravery unsurpassed by any man in the West. . . . There is no blow or swagger about him. He is of unusually pleasant address, and his language is that of a man of uncommon education. His deportment and bearing are such that, despite the fact you know his record, you could never summon hardihood enough to ask him about some of his escapades. But all the toughs and thugs fear him as they do no other dozen men in camp. Let an incipient riot start and all that is necessary to quell it is the whisper, "There comes Masterson."[4]

If one story about Bat in Creede is true, he set a fine example of self-control and judicious restraint under extreme provocation. While having a friendly drink at the bar of the Denver Exchange one evening, the story goes, Bat suddenly was confronted by a drunk who struck him in the face without warning. Immediately, the place was like a tomb. "The silence was so great we could hear the electric light sputter in the next room," said a witness. Bat looked the drunk over and broke into laughter. He quietly told the man to go home and sober up. If he still wanted trouble, he could always come back. He himself would be there, Bat said.[5]

A Chicago newspaperman must have had reference to this incident when he wrote from Creede in February: "Masterson . . . has been known to take a slap in the face from some drunken fool who didn't know his record, and not resent the insult; but woe betide the fellow who offered him an affront in cold blood." He described Bat as "a man of 38, of muscular build and pleasant face. He is quiet in demeanor and sober in habit. There is no blow or bluff or bullyism about him. He attends strictly to business." He also credited Bat with being the chief force for peace in the camp:

It is probably owing to Masterson's presence here, as much as anything else, that we have had no bad breaks as yet. He is here in the interest of peace, having a commission from certain Denver parties to maintain order in their gambling places. It is believed he will be made city marshal when the towns are organized. No better man could be selected for the office, since his very name in this community carries with it a degree of order and security which is associated with none other.[6]

Added a writer for the *Colorado Sun*:

It is thought that Governor Routt, when he arrives at Creede this afternoon, will be somewhat coldly received. He goes to sell the lands and demand order and peace. It is believed that Bat Masterson is a bigger man than the governor for the peace part of it.[7]

An example of the way in which Bat kept peace in the Denver Exchange by means of a sharp look and a few well-chosen words is furnished by Charlie Meyers, who worked for Bat at Creede in 1892. The incident involved Jefferson ("Soapy") Smith, a bunco artist. Soapy, owner and operator of the Orleans Club, was rapidly becoming a leading figure in western criminal circles and was generally conceded to be the sinister power behind Creede's newly formed municipal government. Although not recognized as a gunslinger himself, he was known to have a formidable roster of gunmen in his employ, and few persons in Creede dared cross him. The Denver Exchange was said to be the only amusement house in town from which Soapy did not collect a weekly tribute. This was the man who stepped into Bat's place one evening to play faro. Charlie Meyers describes the scene:

Jeff Argyle was dealing and Tom Crippen was lookout. A row started, during which Soapy yanked out his gun and yelled, "Argyle, you're through as dealer in this game. You pull that card and you'll pull the next one in hell! I want a change of dealers."

There was no yellow in Argyle. He looked Soapy square in the eye and said, "If Bat Masterson tells me to pull, I'll pull it." I ran over to Bat, and he came to straighten things out just in time. Peg Leg Charlie Adams, who helped rob the Denver & Rio Grande Express, had piped up and said, "Soapy's right, and anybody who says he ain't is a damned liar." Nobody cared to dispute Peg Leg because he was wearing six-guns, had a derringer in his vest pocket and another in the palm of his hand.

About that time, Bat reached the scene. He was a friend of both Jeffs, so he sized the situation up for a second and then said, "Now, look here. You're both friends of mine, and I won't stand for this, Be a couple of good boys and stop quarreling. You, too, Peg Leg. What's the use of getting excited? You all know Jeff Argyle's a fair, square dealer or I wouldn't have him here. And we all know Jeff Smith's a square shooter. Two square guys have no call for any gun play with each other. Just remember that. Now, how about it?"

Bat usually had his men sized up right, and he proved it again this time. Soapy grinned and put up his gun. "Guess you're right, Bat," he said, and the game went on.[8]

Bat Masterson, it seems, had fed Jeff Smith some of his own soft soap.

As Creede mushroomed and more and more hair-triggered roughnecks arrived to brush shoulders in the jampacked saloons, the bloodletting Bat had predicted began in earnest. Killings became a routine nightly occurrence. The most well known of the camp's assassinations took place on the afternoon of July 8, 1892, when a bedraggled border drifter named Ed O. Kelly stepped into a tent saloon managed by Bob Ford, slayer of Jesse James. A shotgun in his hands, Kelly said softly, "Ho, Bob," and as Ford turned, he emptied both barrels into the chest of the onetime Missouri bandit, thereby achieving a kind of immortality as "the man who killed the man who killed Jesse James."

Creede's most renowned gunfighter took part in none of the town's revolver frolics. Bat's reputation daunted even the boldest of the troublemakers, and the Denver Exchange remained unclouded by gunsmoke. Although Bat was never called upon to prove his prowess as a gun hand, he did have an opportunity while in Creede to add another credit to his secondary reputation as a practical joker.

Bat was standing at the bar of the Exchange one evening,

watching contentedly as the whiskey barrels and gambling tables received exceptionally heavy play. He was approached by a gaunt, wizened party in a tattered frock coat and battered derby. This ludicrous personage Bat recognized as Parson Tom Uzzell, self-appointed carrier of the Gospel and familiar figure in Colorado mining camps for many years. Reminding Masterson that the day was Sunday, Parson Tom requested permission to preach a sermon to the assembled celebrants in the saloon.

For an instant, Bat hesitated. At the rate the hard money was crossing the bar and tables, a delay of even half an hour would cost the house almost a hundred dollars. Then, smiling at the sad-faced preacher, he nodded assent, saying that he guessed a little sermon wouldn't hurt the crowd any. Rapping sharply on the bar with a whiskey bottle, he gained the attention of the patrons and asked for quiet and a removal of hats. Then he turned the floor over to Uzzell.

Parson Tom chose for the subject of his sermon the prodigal son's return. Not a wheel turned and not a glass was lifted as he solemnly unfolded the story. At its conclusion, he led the gathering in an off-key rendition of *Rock of Ages* and closed with a benediction. He then replaced his dusty derby on his head, signifying that the services had ended.

The members of the impromptu congregation, many of whom had never heard an honest-to-God sermon before, were noticeably subdued. Harry Taber leaned across a faro table and asked Dick Bradshaw what he thought of the tale of the prodigal. "I think," said Bradshaw in a hushed voice, "that the fatted calf got a damned bad break."

Parson Tom was making for the door when Bat stopped him, suggesting that a collection was appropriate. Bat nodded to Big Dan Butler, the bartender, and Dan passed among the crowd with his huge bowler. The hat was delivered to Bat heavy with cash. Bat turned the money over to Uzzell, who stuffed it into his pockets, repeatedly expressing his gratitude. The contributions would all go toward the construction of the first church in Creede, he vowed. With a final wave of his hand in a gesture of blessing, he jingled out into the night.

Play dragged after that. The men could not seem to get the

picture of the dried-up old preacher out of their minds. Several expressed regret that they had not kicked in more when the hat went around. Somebody asked Bat how much the parson's kitty had totaled, and he replied that he did not know. He had never thought to count it, he said. Joe Palmer slammed his fist on the bar. Whatever the amount had been, he said, it certainly had not been enough. Someone else expressed the belief that the amount should have been doubled. There were grunts of agreement from all corners of the room.

Bat's dark eyebrows were pulled tight with thought for a moment. Then, smiling, he suggested that they do just that: double the parson's money. Dan Butler glanced questioningly at his boss. They couldn't double the collection when they didn't know what it was, he objected. They could count it, Bat said. Then he laid his plan before the assembly.

Parson Tom was staying in one of the tents that Brainard and Beebe had thrown up behind their hotel to accommodate an overflow of guests. It would be a simple matter to cut the canvas and steal the parson's pants while he slept. Back at the Exchange, the money could be counted and an equal sum added. The mischief of his youth dancing in his eyes, Bat suggested that the pants be kept until Uzzell awoke. Thinking he had been robbed, the parson would set up an awful howl.

It was agreed. Joe Palmer, one of Soapy Smith's henchmen and no tyro in the art of thievery, and two confederates were commissioned to purloin the pants. In a short time, the deed was done and Palmer was back. The money, spilled out on the bar and counted, totaled three hundred and forty six dollars. Another collection was held, and the boys chipped in enough to bring the parson's take to $700 even. Bat deposited the silver-laden trousers in the saloon safe, and all hands settled down to await the dawn.

Parson Tom arrived with the sun. Storming into the Exchange attired in derby, frock coat, and knee boots, his face almost the color of the long red underwear that flapped loosely about his skinny legs, he called down the wrath of God on those he had blessed the previous night. When Bat inquired innocently as to the cause of the outburst, the parson roared that some blackguard had stolen his pants and the church money.

As the saloon sports roared in a paroxysm of mirth, Parson Tom's face changed from red to purple. Bat decided it was time to put an end to the prank. Stepping behind the bar, he swung the safe door open and brought out the missing trousers. Uzzell listened in wonder as Bat explained what the boys had been up to. Pulling the heavy garment over his bony knees, he once more profusely expressed his gratitude. Then, remembering that a big winner at the gambling tables always bought drinks for the house, he called for all hands to order, and the stampede to the bar began.

CHAPTER TWENTY-FOUR

FIGHTING, RINGWISE AND OTHERWISE

Not long after the Prank of the Parson's Pants, which became a frontier classic, word reached Bat that a heavyweight title bout was shaping up between John L. Sullivan and a brash young boxer from the West Coast named James J. Corbett. The participants were scheduled to meet in New Orleans on September 7, 1892, and already sporting gentlemen from all over the nation were heading for the Gulf city. Bat promptly served notice on Mart Watrous that he was quitting as manager of the Denver Exchange and hastened southeast toward Louisiana.

From the year 1889 until the day of his death, there was scarcely a heavyweight prizefight of major importance in the United States that Bat Masterson did not witness. During the 1890's, his role was frequently more than that of a mere spectator, however; he was often directly involved in the promotions.

In 1889, he served as special bodyguard to Jake Kilrain and Charlie Mitchell when Kilrain arrived in New Orleans to meet John L. Sullivan for the title. Mike Donovan, onetime middleweight champion of America, and Mitchell, a tough English pugilist recently arrived in the States after cleaning up most of his opposition in Europe, accompanied Kilrain to New Orleans, where they were to act as his seconds. Bat met the party at the railroad station in the Louisiana city. He had been summoned by George Washington ("Pony") Moore, Mitchell's father-in-law and manager. Moore, a former circus man, minstrel-show end man, and theater manager, had become acquainted with Masterson during the latter's term as manager of the Denver Palace.

"Gunmen were an important part of the pugilistic picture in those rough-and-ready days, when fair play was best maintained by a judicious display of force on both sides," writes Nat Fleischer, America's foremost authority on ring warfare.[1] For this encounter, Bat Masterson personified the Kilrain party's show of force. Kilrain and Mitchell were never out of his sight before the bout, and Mitchell himself carried two pistols during his sojourn in the South.

When the sporting crowd converged on New Orleans, city officials decreed the fight could not be held there, so a special train was chartered to transport fighters and entourage to a secret site. The Kilrain party paraded to the railroad station in two ornate carriages. Donovan and Johnny Murphy, another of the challenger's handlers, rode in the first; Kilrain, Mitchell, Moore, and Bat in the second. The fight train chugged over the state line to Richburg, Mississippi, where a lumber magnate and ring patron named Fisk had hastily thrown together a wooden arena.

On July 7, 1889, John L. Sullivan and Jake Kilrain met in the last bare-knuckles fight for the heavyweight championship. Once Bat had escorted the challenger to ringside through a milling, clamoring throng, the stopwatch replaced the six-gun as his tool of trade; he was to act as official timekeeper for Kilrain during the fight. John Fitzpatrick, later mayor of New Orleans, was the referee, and William Muldoon, former wrestling champion and lifelong friend of Bat Masterson, was in Sullivan's corner.

The Great John L. was hailed by many as the best fighter of all time, but Kilrain was highly respected, and a report had circulated that Sullivan had been weakened by a recent illness. Immediately before the opening bell, betting was at even money. The gladiators clashed at high noon under a blazing Mississippi sun. In round after round they fought on almost equal terms, but gradually Kilrain weakened before the bull-like charges of the champion. For seventy-five rounds and two hours and sixteen minutes, the magnificently conditioned body of the challenger was battered and beaten by Sullivan's sledgehammer fists; when it became obvious that Kilrain had nothing left but his courage, Donovan threw in the towel.

The Kilrain handlers took their fighter back to New Orleans and bedded him down at the Southern Athletic Club. In addition to the damage inflicted by Sullivan's fists, Jake had been burned severely by the torrid sun. Every movement he made was agonizing. Johnny Murphy remained with him at the club while Mitchell,

Donovan, and Bat went to the St. Charles Hotel, where most of the sporting brotherhood were gathering. At the hotel there occurred an incident that might well have developed into a bloodier spectacle than any the fight fans had witnessed that day. Mike Donovan, who disliked Mitchell, describes it:

Mitchell was posing around the hotel rotunda, treating people in a superior and patronizing manner, Bat Masterson following him like a shadow.

As I stood watching him I was approached by a young friend of mine named Reynolds. After chatting a few moments he pointed at Mitchell and said, "I'm going to kill that Englishman tonight."

"My Lord! What are you going to do that for?" I asked aghast, knowing he was a "killer" and would be as good as his word. "Didn't I second Kilrain against Sullivan today as well as he?"

He replied that I was all right, but it made him mad to see Mitchell strutting around putting on airs.

I told Reynolds I thought that a small excuse for killing a man, adding, "Don't you see Bat Masterson with him? He might kill you."

Quick as a flash he replied, "Well, then, I'll kill him, too."

I saw that if I didn't get Reynolds away quickly he would make trouble, so I induced him to go downstairs to the other bar of the hotel to talk things over. I did my best to get him to say he would not do as he threatened, but he was obstinate and finally insisted on returning to the rotunda. When we got upstairs I found, much to my relief, that Mitchell and Masterson had left the place.[2]

Soon after this near tragedy, Bat saw his charges off on a north-bound train.

Kilrain's defeat was for Masterson a bitter disappointment. He had been certain that his man would win and had wagered heavily on him. There were many who said after this fight that Sullivan was invincible and that no man living was a match for him. Bat was convinced, however, that the ravages of wild times, whiskey, and women would bring ruin to the amazing Sullivan physique and that in time the champion would be brought to his knees.

Bat was back in New Orleans again in September, 1892, this time in the corner of Gentleman Jim Corbett as he challenged the Great John L. As predicted, the years of dissipation had taken their toll. The champion was but a flabby caricature of the Boston

Strong Boy whom Bat had seen bludgeon Paddy Ryan into submission ten years before. In contrast, Corbett was trim, sharp, and bursting with confidence. Bat wagered every dime he had on Gentleman Jim, whom the legend of Sullivan's invincibility had made the underdog in the betting. For twenty-one rounds, Sullivan stalked a dancing, slashing wraith named Corbett. When finally, a bleeding wreck of the once truly great John L. crashed to the floor, even Bat was saddened. The shattering of a legend is not a pretty thing to see, even if one does not believe in the legend.

In late 1893, Bat was with Charlie Mitchell as the Englishman readied himself for a crack at the heavyweight championship crown now worn by Jim Corbett. Mitchell and Pony Moore had arranged a match in Jacksonville, Florida, on January 25, 1894, for a $25,000 purse and a side bet of $5,000. Masterson and Australian middleweight Jem Hall were to act as Mitchell's seconds.

Charlie Mitchell's recorded weight for his shot at the heavyweight title was 168 pounds, but Bat wrote that the Englishman scaled no more than 150 when he entered the ring. At thirty-three years of age, the veteran ring campaigner was well beyond his prime from a pugilistic standpoint. Aware that he would be at a disadvantage in the vital matters of age, weight, and reach when he faced the strong young champion, Mitchell, Moore, and Bat planned to offset these drawbacks as much as possible with an old trick of the ring. Corbett's forte, they knew, was his almost impregnable defense. He was a skilled counterpuncher who coolly drew his opponent into awkward leads, then cut him to pieces with lightning jabs. The Mitchell strategy was to infuriate the champ and make him lose his head. By slugging with Mitchell, Corbett would be fighting the Englishman's type of fight, and it was hoped that this single factor would decide the issue in the challenger's favor.

Before the fight was held, Mitchell insulted Corbett repeatedly to newspapermen. When the fighters met in the ring with Honest John Kelly, the referee, the Englishman again berated the champion. At the bell, Corbett rushed from his corner, his face a mask of hatred, and began throwing wild haymakers at the smaller man. Bat, Moore, and Jem Hall, huddled together in Mitchell's corner, exchanged smiling glances. The scheme was working; the rest was up to their seasoned battler.

Mitchell took the first round easily, handling the madly charging Corbett like a baby and cutting up his handsome features. In the second round, however, the Englishman grew careless, and one of Corbett's churning gloves caught him flush on the chin. Mitchell went down, and as he staggered to his feet, Corbett climbed all over him. Mitchell managed to survive that round, but in the third he was knocked cold by the vengeful champion.

Some years later, Jack Johnson, then heavyweight champion, carried on a running feud with Jim Corbett and, among other things, accused the former title holder of running up a string of victories with fixed fights. He mentioned the Mitchell bout as one in which Corbett's opponent "laid down, according to pre-arrangement." With reference to Johnson's allegation, Bat wrote:

> I happened to be identified with Mitchell in that fight and know positively that there was no fake about it. . . . The battle was on a winner-take-all basis and Corbett got all the money. . . . I do not believe that it was possible for Corbett and Mitchell to engage in a fake fight. Both hated each other bitterly, and I believe both would have gladly entered the ring and fought each other with axes had they been allowed to do so. . . . I doubt very much if the prizering ever produced a better fighter than Corbett was that day at Jacksonville.[3]

Illustrated Sporting West featured Bat in its issue of February 23, 1894, saying he was one of the most widely known sporting men in the West, was "considered one of the best judges of pugilists in America," and could "pick the winner in nine cases out of ten when any of the top-notchers" met. The Corbett-Mitchell bout had been the tenth case, apparently, and Bat found himself dead broke. He had backed the Englishman with every cent he had. With the philosophical shrug of the born gambler, he headed back to Denver and to work.

Work for Bat during the middle years of the Gay Nineties was in the capacity of dealer or manager for one of the many gambling houses operating in Denver in defiance of the still-active reformists. Curtis, Larimer, and Seventeenth streets, the heart of the sporting district, were liberally dotted with houses of chance. On

Curtis Street, where Bat and Emma Masterson made their home for several years, were situated Ed Chase's Inter-Ocean Club; the Morgue, managed by Gavin and Marshall; and the colorful Hog Wallow, owned by Bill Gates. On Larimer were the Arcade, the Missouri House, and the Chicken Coop.

There were many familiar faces among the sports of Denver. Sam and Lou Blonger, gamblers and con artists, had operated in Dodge City many years before. Rowdy Joe Lowe, whose Wichita dance hall was known as the toughest joint in Kansas in the early seventies and who had seen service in Dodge, was also on hand. Wyatt Earp dealt faro for a time in Denver during these years. And Soapy Smith and his brother Bascom, whom Bat met in Leadville and later came to know well in Creede, were very prominent in Denver.

Soapy Smith was a sort of genius in the gambling and sporting world he frequented. Highly intelligent and completely amoral, he had the great con man's disarming smile, warm handshake, and gift of gab that made it impossible to dislike the man. He was a born leader, but his great fault was the inability to distinguish between leading and dominating. In Creede, he had got a taste of power and found it agreeable. He tried to run the show in Denver and was run out of town. Finally, during the rush to the Klondike, he found a town where he could develop his skinning operations unchecked. At Skagway, he was the unchallenged kingpin of vice, and he and his gang waxed fat until he and a mining engineer named Frank Reid killed each other in a shootout.

Although Bat Masterson was always considered by the fraternity to be a square gambler and Jeff Smith was of the sure-thing breed, the two were friends for many years. When Smith was exiled from Denver, Bat wrote to him from time to time, keeping him abreast of affairs in the city's sporting world. A short note dated January 24, 1897, reflected Bat's disgust with conditions: "Everything is running open here, but the play is very spotted. It has got to be a piking game all over town."[4] Another letter, undated, apparently was a reply to an inquiry from Soapy about his brother Bascom:

I have not seen Bascom since he was released after completing the year's sentence.

I have heard of him, however, as always in some kind of trouble. He has been arrested twice of late for disturbance and for discharging firearms down in the neighborhood of Twentieth and Market Streets, and you know the kind of people who frequent that locality.

If I were you, I would advise Bascom to leave here, as it is only a question of time until he will get a "settler," and every time the papers speak of him they always say he is the brother of Soapy Smith who was last heard of skinning suckers in Alaska.[5]

For a time, Bat managed the Arcade, owned by Pete and Charlie Persson. It was from this establishment that he was reputed to have led the Denver chief of police by the nose. The *Denver Post* reported many years later:

Pioneers recall that the chief sent word to Masterson that he wanted to see him. Masterson routed the subordinates and the chief himself went after the "bad man." Masterson listened to the chief for a minute, then calmly reached out two fingers, twined them about the official's nose and escorted him from the hall.[6]

In other versions of the tale, it was the mayor who received this undignified treatment from Bat.

In June, 1895, Bat saw service as a bodyguard, this time for a client who was altogether different from the pugilists he had squired on other occasions. George Gould, heir to Jay Gould's fabulous railroad empire, was receiving threatening letters from a "supposed lunatic" and appealed to New York City Chief of Police Thomas Byrnes for protection. Remarking that the situation called for "a sure shot, a quick shot, and one who could be counted on not to hit the wrong person,"[7] Byrnes wired Denver for Bat Masterson. Bat hurried to New York and glued himself to the railroad tycoon.

It was a great job while it lasted. Bat wrote to Denver pal Frank Quay that he was acting as a confidential adviser on sporting matters to George Gould and that Gould had given him five thousand dollars to play the horses. He had won four thousand five hundred the first day at Gravesend, Bat said, but had lost it back the next. "Went down the other day fishing with the Goulds on their yacht," he remarked offhandedly. He did "not hanker for the light air of Colorado," he said, and expected to stay in New York indefinitely. Bat's Denver cronies squirmed with envy. "By George!" exclaimed a gambler to a *News* reporter, "Bat has at last fallen into a dead easy game!"[8] But it was too good to last. The poison-pen scrivener was soon captured, and Bat returned to the mile-high city in Colorado.

The only known time Bat was involved in any gunplay during the Denver years was in 1897. Occasionally during his residence in the Colorado capital, he was called upon for duty as a special deputy sheriff of Arapahoe County. He was acting in such a capacity when he approached the polling booth at Eighteenth and Larimer on April 6, municipal election day. Charles Davis and James Doyle were engaged in a close contest for city alderman, and it had been reported to the sheriff's office that challengers representing Davis, the Taxpayers' candidate, had been evicted from the Third Precinct polling place. When Bat arrived, according to the story in the *Denver Post*, he found the ballots spread out on a table and Doyle partisans busily counting.

> Masterson . . . insisted that no votes should be counted until the matter of allowing the Taxpayers' challengers to take their places had been decided upon.
> "You can keep the challengers out until the matter is settled," exclaimed Bat, "but you can't count any more votes."
> The judges failed to heed his admonition — began to count and as a result Bat began to shoot. Pandemonium at once reigned. . . .[9]

As Bat set about cleaning out the polling place, he was opposed by booth official Tim Conners, a man of nerve who later served as a Denver city detective for many years. According to Alfred Henry Lewis, Conners "applied his pistol, intending the destruction of Mr. Masterson." Bat shot the weapon from Conners' hand, said Lewis, and "let him live to apologize for his murderous rudeness."[10] That Bat fired close to Conners is certain; twenty-four years later, the detective told a reporter for the *Rocky Mountain News* that he still recalled vividly how "a bullet from Bat's shooter zipped past his face during a friendly argument as to who should control a polling place at Eighteenth and Larimer streets."[11]

The only person hit during the ruckus was C. C. Louderbaugh, proprietor of the Wentworth Hotel, whose hand may have been too close to a suspiciously bulging pocket. "Masterson . . . kicked in a side door and showed a gun ahead of him," Louderbaugh told a *News* reporter the day after the incident. "Tim Conners . . . sprang to the weapon and seized it. The gun went off and as I was rushing to Tim's aid, the bullet landed in my left wrist." Louderbaugh displayed a pocketbook which had belonged to his late wife and which he always carried in a hip pocket. In it were "several pieces of jewelry, mashed and twisted out of shape by a wicked-looking bullet which ploughed its way into his wrist and his hip."[12]

There were no legal repercussions to this affair. It was the first time Bat had fired his gun in anger since the fight with Peacock and Updegraff in 1881, and it was the last known time he pulled trigger.

Bat did not hesitate, however, to threaten the use of firearms when it served his purpose. In 1898 at a bout in New Orleans, according to a story in the *Rocky Mountain News*, he climbed into the ring as a second to Denver Ed Smith in his fight with champion Joe Goddard. Protruding from each hip pocket was the handle of a derringer. The guns were to intimidate Denver Ed Smith, Bat's fighter, who was almost petrified with fear of Goddard. But he was more afraid of Masterson and his guns, since he had been told that the instant he did not carry the fight to the champion, death would result. Said the *News*: "Denver Ed Smith would have jumped over the ropes a dozen rounds before he was forced into victory had it not been for Masterson and his hip pockets."[13]

Masterson was dealing faro at the Central, a gambling house owned by Chase and Gaylord, when William MacLeod Raine first met him. Raine, later to become the dean of western novelists, was at that time a young reporter for the *Denver Republican*. "I had been sent out by the city editor of the *Republican*," he recalled, "to report a cricket match between Denver and Omaha teams, and an English friend had induced Bat to attend for an hour. He thought it very tame, and by way of sarcasm inquired whether cricket or croquet was the British national game."[14] Raine was impressed by what he called Bat's "cold blue eyes." "It was a notable fact," he said, "that all the frontier bad men had eyes either gray or blue, often a faded blue, expressionless, hard as jade."[15] Bat was, Raine testified, "a local celebrity in the city, an authority on the train-end towns and on more-up-to-date sporting matters. If you wanted to find out what had become of 'Dutch Henry,' the famous horse-thief, or how many rounds the Sullivan-Kilrain fight went, you had only to consult Masterson."[16]

No job could hold Bat in Denver when a big fight was in the making. In February, 1896, he was off again to attend what proved to be one of the most bizarre heavyweight promotions in the colorful history of pugilism.

Jim Corbett had retired as undefeated champion and had named Peter Maher his heir apparent. The admirers of Ruby Bob Fitzsimmons raised a storm of protest. Fitzsimmons held a victory over Maher, and his supporters contended that he should be the logical recipient of the crown. To determine the rightful champion, a fight was arranged between Maher and Fitzsimmons by Dan Stuart, the foremost promoter of his day and a close friend of Bat's. Stuart planned to stage the battle in Texas, but, since that state had an antiprizefight statute on its books, he had to resort to a bit of intrigue.

On February 20, fight fans convened in El Paso and were duly informed by the authorities of that city that fisticuffs would not be condoned. Captain Bill McDonald and Company B of the Texas Rangers were on hand to enforce the ban. Dan Stuart, however, had anticipated the El Paso restriction. He had arranged for a special train to carry the fighters and their followers, some two hundred strong, to a secret rendezvous where preparations for the battle were under way.

The train stopped at Sanderson, and all hands poured out for lunch. Bat is reported to have had a brush in the station dining room with Ranger Captain McDonald, who had accompanied the excursionists.[17] According to the tale, Bat was irked by the clumsiness of a Chinese waiter and picked up a table caster as if to strike the man.

McDonald gripped Bat's arm, saying, "Don't hit that man."

"Maybe you'd like to take it up," Bat snapped.

Replied McDonald quietly, "I done took it up."

A hush fell over the railroad hash house. Here, indeed, was an explosive situation: Bat Masterson, for twenty years one of the most feared gun hands of the frontier, facing Bill McDonald, the toughest officer of the storied Texas Rangers. Sitting tensely near Bat were a number of his friends, many of them armed; backing McDonald were several hard-eyed Rangers. A false move on either man's part at that moment could well have precipitated the goriest gunfight in border history.

But Masterson and McDonald were not of the hot-headed breed. Bat smiled and sat down without a word, and McDonald moved on. The tension drained from the room. Thus was avoided what might have become known in western annals as the Battle of the Bungling Chinaman.

On the afternoon of February 21, the train pulled into Langtry, Texas, a tiny settlement on the Mexican border presided over by the notorious Judge Roy Bean, the self-styled Law West of the Pecos. Bean had assured Dan Stuart that the fight could be held in his bailiwick without fear of interference by Texas authorities. *He* was the law in Langtry, bragged the bearded old reprobate. However, Stuart was in for a shock when he led his congregation from the train. Assembled in a ragged skirmish line extending the length of the Langtry depot were twenty-six Texas Rangers. Behind them, a number of deputy U.S. marshals and assorted peace officers formed a second line of defense. It was plain that these stalwart defenders of Texas decorum were going to prevent two grown men from flailing each other with hands encased in five-ounce gloves if they had to shoot some people to prove it.

Stuart called a hasty conference with Judge Bean. Others attending were Joe Vendig, the promoter's lieutenant in charge of ticket sales; Tom O'Rourke, a New York sporting man who was carrying the ten-thousand-dollar purse; and Bat Masterson, O'Rourke's bodyguard. Bean insisted that he could arrange an understanding with the posse leaders. While the fighters and their entourage crowded into Bean's Jersey Lilly Saloon for refreshments, he affably assured the grim-faced Rangers that no Texas statute was in jeopardy of fracture. This high-spirited throng merely wanted to cross the Río Grande into Mexico, he said. What possible harm could be found in that? The law officers mulled the problem for a time, then granted grudging approval.

If the two hundred sports had been keyed up and boisterous upon alighting from the train, their sojourn in the Jersey Lilly, sampling Bean's most potent wares, had in no way tranquilized them. They were a roaring, ripsnorting bunch as Bean led them through the chaparral to the bank of the Río Grande. For seventy-five yards they wallowed through knee-deep silt before reaching a pontoon bridge that spanned the river into Mexico. Many a pair of carefully tailored pegged pants was ruined and many a Prince Albert coat and brocaded vest were ripped by cactus, but for this select corps of fight followers, these were minor matters. A heavyweight championship was at stake; for them, nothing was of greater import.

On the Mexican side of the river, a ring had been thrown together and a canvas enclosure erected around it. Joe Vendig stationed himself at the entrance to the impromptu arena and began to collect admissions at twenty dollars a head. Beside him stood Bat Masterson, his coat thrown back over his holster and his hand resting carelessly on the butt of his old six-gun. There were no gate-crashers.

George Siler was the referee for the Maher-Fitzsimmons encounter. When all the spectators had entered the enclosure, the bell sounded and Siler waved the combatants forward. The battle was on at last. Ninety seconds later, it was all over. After some preliminary sparring, Maher led with a wild left. Fitzsimmons stepped back nimbly and crossed with the powerful right that was to make him famous. Maher collapsed in a heap, and that was that.

Martin Julian, Fitzsimmons' brother-in-law and manager, strode to the center of the ring after Maher had been carried off and began an oration to the effect that Fitzsimmons was now undisputed champion and was prepared to take on all challengers. He was interrupted by a hue and cry from the riverbank. The pontoon bridge was straining at its moorings and was in great danger of being washed away at any moment by the swift current. All hands made a rush for the river and regained the American side without incident.

Despite Julian's claim that Ruby Bob was undisputed champion, recognition by the ring fraternity was slow in coming. The general feeling was that no man could rightfully call himself champ until he had licked Gentleman Jim.

A year later, Corbett did indeed come out of retirement to meet

Fitzsimmons in a title fight scheduled for Carson City, Nevada. On February 8, 1897, on his way to the site, Corbett stopped in Denver and was met at the train depot by a delegation of admirers that included Bat Masterson, Billy Woods of Creede fame, Joe Woods, Tom Clark, Three-Fingered Jim Marshall, and a euphoniously cognomened sport named Otto C. Floto. With the regal hauteur befitting his exalted status as undefeated heavyweight champion of the world, Gentleman Jim invested Floto with the right to make up a train of Denver aficionados for the trip to Carson City. Floto was elated, predicting that two hundred would be aboard the special.

Masterson was not to be one of them. On February 25, there appeared in the *Rocky Mountain News* an editorial asserting that money had been used to influence one or more state senators relative to a bill pending in the Colorado Legislature. When challenged to document his charges, editor T. M. Patterson revealed that he had secured his information from W. B. Masterson. A special investigating committee of the Senate was appointed immediately, and subpoenas were issued for Patterson and Masterson to testify before the committee on the twenty-sixth. The *News* editor appeared, but W. B. Masterson was not to be found in Denver. The officers sent for him reported that he had departed the city sometime during the night and was believed to have left the state.

Patterson testified that Bat had been hired by "certain wealthy Colorado Springs people" to lobby against a controversial bill that would divide El Paso County, which included the rich Cripple Creek mining district. When he was not paid the sum he had been promised, he had threatened to reveal details of "a corrupt deal between the Colorado Springs people and a certain senator." When his money still was not forthcoming, Bat had gone to Patterson and had given him enough information for the editorial — without naming names. After the editorial was published on the morning of the twenty-fifth, Bat appeared in the editorial rooms of the *News* and said the parties in Colorado Springs had got in touch with him and had guaranteed his payment on condition that he leave the state until the legislature adjourned. The official report of the investigating committee concluded that the charges could not be substantiated and severely rebuked Patterson for publicizing the unsupported allegations of "Mr. Masterson, a man of admittedly ill repute."[18]

Two days later, Bat was interviewed in Salt Lake City, Utah. He said he was on his way to the Corbett-Fitzsimmons fight in Carson City and had just started "a little earlier than expected." When he arrived in Carson City, Chief of Police Kenney placed him in charge of a squad of officers assigned to the fight. On March 17, Bat watched as Bob Fitzsimmons' celebrated right uppercut, which had cost him a victory in the Sharkey imbroglio, landing solidly on that previously unpublicized sector of anatomical vulnerability, the solar plexus, and Gentleman Jim Corbett collapsed, his comeback dreams shattered by that single punch.

It was at the bout in Carson City that Harry Tammen, co-owner of the *Denver Post*, came to know Otto C. Floto and hired him as sports editor simply because, Tammen always claimed, his name was so beautiful. Strangely enough, that engagement was to have a profound effect upon the course of Bat Masterson's life.

Otto Floto was a two-hundred-fifty-pound Californian who claimed to be the grandson of Friedrich von Flotow, composer of the opera *Martha*. Like Masterson, he had been kicking around frontier towns most of his adult life without finding a profession. At one time or another, he had been everything from a bill poster to a saloonkeeper. He shared with Bat a love for the ring and had seen most of the major fights since the Sullivan-Kilrain battle of 1889, when he had been John L.'s timekeeper. He managed Bob Fitzsimmons' theatrical tour and accompanied Peter Maher on a trip to England. Gene Fowler, whose name stands high on a long list of Denver newspapermen who achieved distinction in the literary field, began his career as assistant to Floto at the *Post*. "Otto Floto was a big man in every way," said Fowler. "He was a merry man much of the time, but when offended had the mien of an archbishop who had just heard the confession of Gyp the Blood."[19] Floto married a girl named Kitty Kreuger, who, before her marriage, was a bareback rider in a circus, where she was billed as the Girl in Red.

In late 1898, Bat and Floto were discussing the fight situation in the West and deploring the lack of facilities in which matches could be held when it occurred to them that they could establish a

Otto Floto vied with Bat for
control of boxing in Denver.
Courtesy Denver Public
Library.

fistic club of their own in Denver. Presenting the idea to several
other sports-minded Denver citizens, they received enthusiastic
encouragement and promises of financial backing. They then
sought out some well-known fighters whose names would add
prestige to the project.

In Denver at the time was a tough young welterweight named
Norman Selby, better known as Kid McCoy. He had knocked out
Tommy Ryan to gain the welter title in 1896 and was generally
recognized as one of the flashiest, best-drawing men in the business. Also in evidence was Patrick ("Reddy") Gallagher, a pugnacious Irishman from Cleveland with a reputation as a crowd
pleaser. McCoy and Gallagher agreed to join in the Masterson-
Floto venture and to fight in the arena of the Colorado Athletic
Club, as the new organization was to be called.

Before the project had developed beyond the planning stage,
however, it was riven by internal dissension and torn by bickering
and petty jealousies. McCoy skipped out on his partners and went
to the East Coast, where he participated in some of the shadiest
fights ever perpetrated in this country. Floto secured personal

control of what was to have been the joint property and forced out
the other members. With the endorsement of Tammen and Bonfils,
his bosses on the powerful *Post*, he proceeded to run the Colorado
Club on his own hook, leaving Bat Masterson out in the cold.

A man with the capacity for intense loyalty to his friends that Bat
had evinced on many occasions is capable of profound hatred when
one whom he considers a friend turns against him. Mike Sutton and
Nick Klaine, erstwhile cronies of Bat's in Dodge City, had come to
know the boundless depths of his ire, and now Otto Floto was to
know it also.

A *Denver Times* writer pointed out in a feature article on Bat:

Although Bat Masterson's hair is beginning to turn a little gray around
the edges and he is getting along in life, he is still the same Bat Masterson
who commanded respect from the thugs who at one time posed as the
bullies of the West, and when the gray-tinged hair is rubbed the wrong
way his gray eyes flash as they used to of old and the sparks commence to
fly off in a threatening manner. Bat has by no means got to that stage of
life where he is unable to take his own part, but he has grown a little more
sedate than he was thirty years ago, when he was the best known man
between the Mississippi river and the Pacific coast. . . .[20]

Bat's hair had definitely been "rubbed the wrong way" by
Floto, and war was declared between the two men, who were
recognized as the West's foremost authorities on the ring. Although he was wooed by Floto, Reddy Gallagher remained in Bat's
corner, and other Denver sports rallied to his side. Bat wired some
of his friends in other parts of the country, and within a few days,
he was ready to strike his first blow at the *Post*–Colorado Club.

On April 18, 1899, the Olympic Athletic Club was founded, W.
B. Masterson, President. Bat leased the Haymarket Theater, for-
merly the Academy of Music, an old building on the corner of
Sixteenth and Market streets, and called in architects to begin
alterations. "I expect to get the best men in the ring in Denver," he
was quoted in the *Republican*. "The men who are associated with
me will announce their names as soon as we get organized for we
just came together today and our plans have not entirely ma-
tured. . . . I am pretty well acquainted myself with pugilists
throughout the country and I believe I can get the best men in the
country to come here. I will try to at any rate."[21]

Now Bat had a fight club of his own to rival Floto's Colorado Club. He still felt at a disadvantage, however. He was painfully aware that in the sports pages of the *Post*, Floto had a means of advertising his own club and deprecating the competitive efforts of his adversary. Once again, therefore, as in the days of the short-lived *Vox Populi* back in Dodge, Bat took up the pen as a weapon.

Bat went to see Herbert George, editor of a Denver paper called *George's Weekly*, and talked himself into the sports editor's job. Each week, he turned out a long column that almost filled the sports page of the little journal. He was, of course, lavish in his praise of attractions at the Olympic Club, and he sarcastically disparaged the Colorado Club and its scheduled entertainment. Several months after the outbreak of hostilities with Floto, he wrote:

> The game of give-and-take with the gloves has had a fairly good chance to establish itself upon a sound basis in Denver, owing principally to the efforts of the management of the Olympic Club to present well-balanced matches which were fought out on the level. Notwithstanding the dangers of adverse legislation and the attacks of rabid reformers (for a considera-tion or a prospect), the Olympic Club has gone along with the determina-tion to present only the best in the business and to see that they delivered their best goods. This honesty of purpose has not influenced the Post-Colorado Club in the slightest degree, for it has foisted some of the worst fakes and jug-handled matches on the public to the detriment of the sport. [22]

When he had occasion to refer to Otto Floto, Bat characterized him as "a former bill poster from Cripple Creek" or "the space killer of a local sheet."

By the first of July, 1899, the Olympic Club's property at Sixteenth and Market had been renovated and Bat had lined up a pair of well-known fighters named Dixon and White to headline his initial attraction. Although a Denver ordinance banned prizefighting, "sparring exhibitions" could be held after deposit, with the city treasurer, of a yearly license fee of one thousand dollars. On July 8, Bat attempted to pay the fee and was refused, perhaps on the ground that he himself had stated many times in public print that there were to be no sham battles at the Olympic, but real knock-down, drag-out fistic conflicts.

Bat was an old hand at circumventing legal obstructions; the following day, he announced in the *Rocky Mountain News*: "We shall apply to the courts for an injunction against the fire and police commissioners. That to my mind is the only safe thing to do. It will protect the fire and police board as well as ourselves."[23] On July 11, he obtained an injunction restraining members of the Fire and Police Board, Chief of Police Farley, and Mayor Johnson from interfering with the Dixon-White match, scheduled for that evening. Noted the *Times*:

> In signing the injunction, Judge Palmer failed to stipulate that the license fee of $1,000 should be deposited with the clerk of the court. Mr. Masterson left the courtroom in company with his attorney, Judge E. T. Wells, perfectly satisfied with not being compelled to deposit the $1,000 license fee.[24]

A few days later, Bat wrote to his old buffalo-hunting partner Henry Raymond on the stationery of his new concern. Although optimistic with regard to his business venture, he expressed concern with a common problem of middle age:

> The letter head will indicate my business at present it is easy and lucrative and I find I can stand a whole lot of that just now. I am 45 years old and in the best of health but fleshy. I weigh 200 pounds and I find that a moderate amount of exercise will not reduce the adipose tissues as it used to do. . . .[25]

By fall, it seemed to the *Denver Republican* that Bat had the edge in the bitter competition with Floto's Colorado Club. On November 19, the paper noted:

> To a man who can read it is very evident that Masterson practically controls the great mass of fighters who come to this city. They may raise a row and get over in other pastures occasionally, but they must come back and crook the pregnant hinges of the knee to Bat before they can secure good matches.

The Floto-Masterson rivalry raged for two years and was followed avidly by Denverites. Gene Fowler, a wide-eyed ten-year-old at the time, witnessed a meeting of the two archenemies at the corner of Sixteenth and Champa in front of Bert Davis' cigar store:

> Floto and Bat Masterson . . . were life-long enemies. Both were past

masters at appraising pugilists, being America's foremost critics of pancratia. Let a gladiator make one lacklustre feint, the slightest error in leading, the least violation of rhythm in footwork, timing of punches or coordination of brain and fist — and these Dr. Johnsons of sport would reprove the offender with galleys of bitter type.

Yet, I remember, as a lad, an encounter on the street between these two interpreters of *le boxe*. Did they indulge in fancy steps, neat left hooks, graceful fiddling? Nay. They advanced like any charcoal burners of the Black Forest, and began kicking each other in the groin! That event was richly symbolic of the critical poohbahs of any art, men who know every move, whether of pen, brush, violin bow or naked fist, and yet themselves can find no bridge from the academic to the practical.[26]

Fowler recalled that the roundhouse rights thrown by Floto and Masterson "stirred up more wind than the town had felt since the blizzard of 1883."

According to the *Denver Times* story of the fracas: Bat attempted to chastise Floto with his walking stick, and "there was a mix, Bat using a cane he carried to good advantage." Since Otto Floto had no cane, flight seemed his best recourse. He got his two-hundred-fifty-pound bulk into motion across Sixteenth Street with the two-hundred-pound Masterson in pursuit. "I used to think I was a pretty good runner," Bat was quoted in the *Times*, "but that fellow started to pull away from me on the jump, and before we had gone ten feet I saw that it was all up with me and that I could never catch him, so I just stopped and stamped my foot like you do when you scare a dog, and you might not think it possible, but that fellow let out another link and was knocking big chunks out of the time for a city block. He is the best runner I ever saw." When asked why he had taken a cane to Floto, Bat said:

> You see there are some fellows you can reason with and talk them into being decent, and there are others you have to beat to death to teach them that they have got to be decent. These fellows have got to be decent or someone is going to beat them to death. I understand that my friend Floto is carrying a derringer. The next time I see him I am going to ask him to give it to me and I will pawn it. The darn thing cost $8 and you can pawn it easy for $5.[27]

Floto may or may not have been carrying a derringer, but there is little doubt that Bat went armed in Denver with more than his walking stick. Those who have depicted Masterson as a cold-blooded killer would be hard put to explain why such a man did not use his shooting iron on this and other occasions. Even the usually reliable William MacLeod Raine, who, unlike most western chroniclers, had the advantage of meeting and talking with Bat personally, placed him in the category of the notorious western gunmen who "reserved the right to carry on private vendettas and . . . shot swiftly, on sometimes inadequate provocation."[28] It is evident, however, that Bat looked upon his gun as a weapon of last recourse, to be used only when his very life was endangered.

Although Floto and Bat limited their feud to battles of words and "groin-kickings," there were in Denver men who answered Bat's columnar attacks with more sanguinary methods. According to Alfred Henry Lewis, a man named O'Neal took offense at certain outspoken remarks of Bat's in *George's Weekly* and lay in wait on a dark street as Bat returned home late one night. In his quaintly antiquated style, Lewis describes what transpired:

> When Mr. O'Neal, with a six-shooter in each overcoat pocket, and a hand on each six-shooter, sent forward a drunken ruffian to attack Mr. Masterson, with full and fell intent on Mr. O'Neal's part of "bumping off Mr. Masterson when once entangled with the drunken one, he, Mr. Masterson, knocked the drunken one senseless with his left fist, while with his right hand he abruptly acquired the draw on the designing Mr. O'Neal. With that never-erring six-shooter upon him, Mr. O'Neal's empty hands came out of his pockets, and went into the air, like winking.
>
> "Don't kill me!" he faltered.
>
> Mr. Masterson's finger was itching upon the trigger. In an instant he shifted. Letting down the hammer, he repeated the maneuver which had worked so well in the days of Mr. Bell. Later, the wounded Mr. O'Neal, head in bandages, sent from his bed a message of peace, asking Mr. Masterson to see him, and give him an opportunity to "explain."
>
> "Well," said Mr. Masterson to the messenger, "I'll come. But tell O'Neal to be careful, and keep his hands outside the blankets while he's doing his 'explaining.' "[29]

In early 1900, Reddy Gallagher succumbed to Floto's blandishments and bolted the Masterson camp. Bat, of course, was infuriated by the defection of his chief lieutenant and ripped into Gallagher in his column. Reddy was a tough man in a ring, but he was no gunslinger. There were in and around Denver, however, many gun hands for hire, and, according to Alfred Henry Lewis,[30] Gallagher employed a professional assassin to do a job on Masterson. Jack Grace, a prominent fighter of the time, heard of the plot and warned Bat. Slipping a one-hundred-dollar bill into an envelope, Bat dispatched it to Reddy with a message stating that the money was his if he would but walk with his importation down the street "as far as Murphy's."[31] Gallagher refused the money, and the hired gunman, said Lewis, "made haste to explain that his purpose in coming to Denver was wholly innocuous."

Several months later, the *Denver Republican* published a photograph of the men who organized the Colorado Athletic Club and commented:

> The group picture of Bat Masterson, "Reddy" Gallagher, et al.
> . . . was taken a little more than a year ago. . . . Today it would be a
> most powerful influence that could draw the men into the same room.
> When the friendship that the picture commemorates was cemented as a
> thing that was to last forever, all were interested in the establishment of a
> fighting club in this city. . . . How fleeting are friendships, and how
> soon what was to last forever, and a little longer, goes to wreck on
> trifles![32]

Bat poured all of his prodigious energy into the making of the Olympic Club, acting in every capacity except that of combatant; he was matchmaker, promoter, press agent, and referee for the bouts staged there. But Otto Floto, backed by the powerful *Post*, gradually undermined the venture of his rival. Gallagher's desertion was the death blow for the Masterson enterprise.

Disenchanted with the Denver sporting scene, Bat determined in March, 1900, to leave the Colorado capital. His decision may have been influenced by his wife's concern for his safety, but it is likely that he was again suffering from an old affliction: itchiness of foot. He had maintained permanent residence in Denver for twelve years, the longest period any town had ever held him. Even during those years his inherent restlessness had been in evidence; from 1888 to 1896, he had occupied six different dwellings in the heart of the city's business and sporting district, none more than a few blocks from the others.

Bat Masterson when he was a familiar figure in every major gambling center in the West. Courtesy Kansas State Historical Society.

Turning over management of the Olympic to his partner, Gus Tuthill, he entrained for Hot Springs, Arkansas, the spa he had first visited while he was sheriff of Ford County back in 1878. Hot Springs was a free-wheeling, high-rolling gambling man's town at the turn of the century, and Bat remained for some two months. He went on to New York City, where he refereed a prizefight, and thence to Chicago. He was plainly looking for a place to light. During this time, he continued to turn out a regular column for *George's Weekly*, commenting on the sports scene as he viewed it throughout the nation.

In his absence, rumors concerning Bat circulated freely in Denver sporting circles, usually having to do with bodily harm having befallen him. In April, there was a hot item to the effect that he and Australian Jem Hall, former middleweight champion, had met in a bar and Hall had knocked Masterson stiff with one punch. The tale reached Chicago, where high-rolling gambler Parson Davies put it to rest. He told a *Chicago Tribune* writer:

I would have no hesitancy in placing any odds on the falsity of that story. Bat Masterson is one of the finest men I ever met and is by no means a quarrel seeker, but he has a reputation as a gunfighter that precludes the possibility of any such event. . . . If Jem Hall happens to be within easy distance of Masterson when he reads this newspaper concoction, he will undoubtedly communicate with his old friend for the purpose of explaining that no part of the story emanated from him. Hall, like all men who know him, is anxious to court and retain the friendship of this prince of good fellows.[33]

A few months later, it was reported that Bat had been shot in Cheyenne by a tenderfoot. A *Denver Times* reporter checked the story with the Denver police, who had heard nothing of a shooting involving Masterson. The Cheyenne police knew of no such incident. An inquiry was sent to Lou Houseman of the Orpheum Theater in Chicago, where Bat's presence had last been reported. The following wire came back:

Houseman and I just had a drink. It hasn't killed me yet. Am still making books. Four to one on Doc Holliday. Six to one on Jim Allison. Seventeen to one on Morgan, Wyatt or Bill Earp.

Although Bat must have had much more than just one drink with Houseman to refer erroneously to ''Jim'' Allison and ''Bill'' Earp, the Denver newspaperman could report that ''Bat Masterson is alive and fairly active,'' adding: ''Denver is relieved.''[34]

In September, Bat returned to sever his ties with the Denver sporting community. He sold his interest in the Olympic Club to Joe Gavin, a gambling crony; having no further need for *George's Weekly* as a propaganda organ in his war with Floto, he resigned from that sheet. The *Denver Times* commented on the Olympic Club management reshuffle:

The change of ownership is not likely to affect the prize-fight situation in the least. One of the conditions of the sale was that Gavin was not to lay down before, consolidate or play into the hands of the Colorado club in any way, and the chances are that the fight will rage just as merrily as before Masterson stepped out.[35]

Approached by a reporter for the *Times*, Bat put a verbal hex on Denver and its sporting clan. He was sending his wife to Philadelphia, he said, and would follow her shortly, after he disposed of all his interests. He hoped never to see the Rocky Mountains again, he declared. The depth of his bitterness was evident in his remarks:

> This town is the worst in the country. . . . There ain't a sport in it. The bootblacks in Chicago have more sporting blood in their veins than the whole push of Denver sports. It is actually the cheapest town I was ever in. It is filled up with a whole lot of bluffers and hoodlums and robbers and fakirs, and everyone is trying his best to skin his neighbor. Nothing is done on the square if there is a crooked way to do it, and the man who skins his neighbor oftenest during the year is a great man in the community. . . .
>
> Why, the town is known from one end of the country to the other as the greatest town for fakes in the world, and it is worth a man's reputation to stay in it over night. . . .
>
> I have been here over twenty years, but I would not have stayed here over twenty minutes if it had not been for my wife's health. Why, the big dubs do not know what it is to spend money. You go traveling around the saloons here, talking about one of the big fights, and there are stiffs there who will bet you $400,000 or $500,000 on the result, and, by gum, you cannot get a dollar bet if you would herd the whole bunch into a corner and take up a collection. Go into any other city in the country and make your talk on fights and you will see a hundred rolls flashed on you inside an hour if there is any kind of a chance for a difference of opinion. These punks here are looking for a dead-sure thing — that is, a dead-sure opportunity to get a chance to skin somebody, and then they go around all swelled up with the idea that they are sports.
>
> This place is the butt of the country. It is a great hospital in which are gathered more old, broken-down fossils, fakirs and bunks than can be gathered up with a fine comb by dragging it through the whole country. Dubs are living here and doing business who would be, and have been, driven out of almost every other community in the country. I don't want none of the place in mine, and the quicker I can get out of it, the better. I hope nobody thinks I have been living in this rotten place because I loved it or because I was making money here or because I had no other place on earth to go. I would not live with such a lot of stiffs ten minutes if I had my own way.[36]

Denverites did not hear of Bat for several months. Then, in December, he was interviewed in New York City, the story appearing in the *Denver Times* under the headline "BAT MASTERSON TALKS AGAIN." Bat took the opportunity to castigate again the Denver sporting clan in general and the Floto-Gallagher combine in particular.':

> The boxing game in Denver is in rather a bad way. There is no money for first-class talent, owing to the fact that the patrons of boxing have been educated to cheap prices, and seem to be satisfied with cheap attractions. . . . When the boxing game first opened in Denver the price of admission was fixed at $1, $2 and $3 for all good entertainments, but there soon appeared upon the pugilistic horizen a very cheap combination of fight promoters, who cut the prices of admission down to 25 and 50 cents, which, as a matter of course, made it impossible for a legitimate club to stand the outlay of bringing from such a great distance as it is from New York to Denver first-class talent without sustaining financial loss. The result is that the people are getting boxing contests that correspond with the prices of admission charged at the door. . . . Oh, yes, we have quite a bunch of sporting writers, or sporting editors, as they call themselves, and they really present an amusing spectacle to a person who has their qualifications in that line properly sized up. But then I will pass them up on the principal that the least said about them the better. Yes, from a sporting view point Denver is as wide open as it ever was, but there is no money, and the people out there want a great deal for nothing. They are not sufficiently educated in the boxing game to be able to discriminate between a good bout and a bad one.[37]

With which final embittered comment Bat removed himself from the Denver sports picture forever. But he was to return to the Colorado city once more, a move that was to bring about one of the most dramatic moments in his turbulent career.

CHAPTER TWENTY-FIVE

THE FOUR O'CLOCK BURLINGTON

Bat's travels had taken more than a year, but during that time he had maintained a legal residence at 1825 Curtis in Denver. He was, therefore, a qualified voter and never failed to make an appearance at election time to exercise his right.

A municipal school board election was scheduled for May, 1902, and a good deal of interest had been stirred up by the energetic attempt of Denver females to elect a woman to the board. Bat was one of those conservative old-timers who felt that a woman's place was in the home and not in public office. As has been shown, he took his politics seriously; the rougher the political contest, the better he liked it. He felt at a disadvantage when faced with adversaries in skirts. His inherent sense of chivalry prevented him from attacking ladies with the gusto he had displayed in election contests back in Kansas. He had another reason for prejudice against feminine politicos, also. A few years earlier, he had entertained the idea of becoming sergeant-at-arms of the Colorado Legislature. His name had been submitted, but three women members of the lower house, appalled by his reputation as gambler and gunman, worked diligently and successfully to secure his defeat.

There can be little doubt that as Bat strolled down to his polling place at the corner of Eighteenth and Larimer streets on the morning of May 5, it was his intention to cast his vote against the female candidate for the school board. He never got to cast that vote, however, and the events leading from that walk abruptly altered the direction of his life.

The precinct in which Bat lived and worked was notorious for the use of "repeaters" at election time, and a covey of women had congregated at the polling place to inspect all voters upon arrival. What happened when Masterson came on the scene was related by Bat himself to a friend years later:

I lived in the same house in Denver for nine years, and then the women got to voting. On one election morning I went down to cast my ballot in the same old precinct, when a woman who was standing around the polls exclaimed: "I challenge that vote!"

I was never so surprised in my life. I didn't know the woman, couldn't recall ever having seen her before, hadn't the faintest idea why anybody should want to prevent me for exercising the prerogative of a citizen, but I said as mildly as I could: "Madam, will you please state why you challenge my vote? I have lived in this city for fifteen years, and nine years in my present domicile."

The only answer I got was a rap across the neck with her umbrella. That was enough for me. Yes, I decided it was time to dig out for Chicago.[1]

However, according to William MacLeod Raine, Bat's decision to leave was made only after a dramatic confrontation. Having been disenfranchised by a female's umbrella, Bat is said to have gone on a monumental binge, touring the city's gin mills, six-shooter on hip and blood in his eye. Raine details the remainder of the story, taking his facts from an unpublished manuscript by Harry Lindsley, then district attorney for Denver:

Lindsley went into the office of Hamilton Armstrong, chief of police in Denver, and found him worried. . . .

"What's up?" Lindsley asked.

"It's Bat Masterson. He's on a rampage and I ought to have him arrested, but he's sore as a boil and won't stand for it without a fight. I hate to give the job to any of my boys because two or three of them are likely to get killed."

Just then the telephone rang. The call was a long-distance one from Cripple Creek.

"Jim Marshall on the line, inquiring about some guy who has skipped out from the Creek," Armstrong mentioned as an aside to Lindsley.

Marshall was a Cripple Creek officer, a man known to be resolute and fearless. He had a large experience in dealing with tough characters.

"Have Jim hold the line a minute, Chief," Lindsley said, and then suggested that Armstrong ask Marshall to come down and make the arrest of Masterson.

Marshall was reluctant to do this. In the first place, it was not his business. Also, he and Bat had been in tight places together during the old Kansas days. . . .

But Marshall was under obligations to Armstrong, and since somebody had to arrest Bat he thought he had better do the job. He promised to reach Denver early next day.

By an underworld grapevine route Bat learned what was afoot. He wired to Marshall that he would be waiting for him in front of the barber shop back of the Scholtz drugstore at ten o'clock. Bat kept his word. He had his morning shave in the shop, then planted himself in a chair on the sidewalk beside the striped pole. His fingers hovered near the butt of a revolver. From ten o'clock until eleven he sat there, his keen eyes taking in every passer. Jim Marshall was not among them. After an hour of waiting Bat left his post and crossed the street to the saloon in the Tabor Opera House block where he usually had his morning nip. To the barber he mentioned that he would be back presently, to meet the late Mr. Marshall in case he finally arrived. Bat walked up to the bar and gave his order. He lifted his glass to drink.

A familiar voice startled him. ''Sorry I was a little late, Bat.'' The glass of whiskey stayed poised in the air. Bat realized instantly that he was trapped. Jim Marshall had slipped in a side door and was standing at his right side. He was ready for business, whereas Bat's gun hand was temporarily engaged hoisting one.

Bat showed no disturbance, though he recognized defeat. He looked at the man beside him — a ruddy, hard-eyed man, not quite six feet in height, well dressed, entirely sure of himself.

Quietly Bat put the question that was engaging his attention. ''Does this mean a killing, Jim?''

''Depends on whether you are reasonable, Bat.''

''Meaning just what?''

''Meaning that it is for you to say.''

''What do you mean, reasonable?''

''Denver is too big a town for you to hurrah, Bat. Time for you to move on.''

Swiftly Masterson reviewed the situation. Most men of his reputation would have stalled as long as he could, hoping for a break. But Bat knew from long experience that the cards were stacked against him. If he reached for his pistol he was a dead man. Moreover, he had asked for this. What Marshall said was true. Denver was no longer a frontier town. He had no right to defy the law. Just now Jim Marshall was the law, and it had served notice on him. Bat was chagrined. But he had the sort of mind that had to face facts realistically. Humiliated though he was, he had to accept the terms offered. By his own conduct he had put himself in the wrong. This was not a question of supremacy between him and Jim Marshall. He had maneuvered himself into an impossible situation before the meeting.

Bob Stockton, the saloonkeeper, drew a long breath of relief after Masterson's next words.

"If I leave, how soon do I have to go?" he asked.

"Could you make the four o'clock Burlington, Bat?"

"I reckon so."

That ended the tensity. Both men knew the matter was settled. When Bat gave his word he kept it. Masterson left town that day. No newspaper gave the reason for his going. Jim Marshall visited each one in turn and saw to it that the incident did not appear in print.[2]

So it was that Bat and Emma Masterson departed Denver again, this time for good. For Bat, the Denver interlude had been like a strange echo of his Dodge City career. In each community he had achieved an enviable position of stature and respect: in Dodge as lawman and unofficial political power, in Denver as sports authority and oracle of western history written in gunsmoke. He had departed each town after a bitter defeat brought about by overconfidence in false friends; as Nick Klaine and Mike Sutton were instrumental in his downfall in Dodge, so were Otto Floto and Reddy Gallagher the leading figures of his reversal of fortune in Denver. To each city he had returned briefly, only to leave again when it became evident that social changes beyond his control had made him something of an anachronism. When he left Denver in May, 1902, it was for the last time. So far as is known, he was never seen in the Colorado capital again.

The Mastersons went to Chicago, where Bat visited many old friends, including William Pinkerton, head of the Pinkerton Detective Agency. While touring the city's sporting district, Bat ran into a number of gambling acquaintances, among them a West Coast sport named James C. Sullivan; Leopold Frank, a Chicago gambler; and a former Denver bookmaker named J. E. Sanders. Sullivan told Bat that he and Parson Davies, operator of the Store, Chicago's largest gambling house, were contemplating a trip to England for the purpose of promoting prizefights in connection with the coronation celebration for Edward VII. He and Davies would welcome Bat's participation in the undertaking if he was interested, Sullivan added. Bat was interested. Together with Sullivan and Davies, he and Emma entrained for New York City. Sanders and Frank were going to New York at the same time and since the men were mutually acquainted, all traveled together on the train.

Upon their arrival in New York the last week in May, Sanders and Frank separated from the rest of the party and went their way. Sullivan and Davies took lodgings near the Mastersons so that they could keep in touch with Bat while arrangements were made for passage to Europe. But it was not in the cards for Bat Masterson to leave this country. Within two weeks, he was placed under arrest by New York police and his name was on the front page of every newspaper in the city.

On June 6, Masterson, Sullivan, Sanders, and Frank were taken into custody by detectives and charged with conducting a crooked faro game. The four men, said the arresting officer, Detective Sergeant Gargan, had fleeced victims from Hot Springs to New York and had followed one man from Chicago to Buffalo, where they had cheated him out of $17,000. "Much surprise was expressed by the police that 'Bat' Masterson should have been discovered in company with swindling gamblers," the *New York Times* reported. "He has always been considered 'square' when he sat down to a card table." Other people beside the police were surprised, too, according to the *New York World*. The charge that Bat was involved in a braced faro game came "much to the astonishment of local sporting men," said the paper. Bat Masterson's name, it added, "never has been associated with crookedness."

The man whom Bat and the other prisoners were specifically charged with cheating was George H. Snow of Salt Lake City, son of the president of the Mormon church and himself an elder of that church. Bat denied implication in the alleged swindle immediately and emphatically. "Masterson was white with anger," reported a dispatch printed in the *Denver Times*, "and asserted that he never associated in more than a casual manner with the other prisoners. He denied that he had any part in the game in which the man from Salt Lake City lost heavily."[3]

The names of Masterson and Snow were sufficient to cause a stir around police headquarters, but after Bat was searched at the station, more excitement was touched off when "a huge revolver was found in his hip pocket."[4] An additional charge was lodged against him for carrying a concealed weapon and the gun was confiscated. Bat seemed more perturbed over the loss of the six-gun than anything else. "It's like losing all I have," he was quoted as saying. "It is like my life for it has often saved my life, and they took it away from me. Property confiscated by the police, I understand, is auctioned off, and there will be someone there to get that gun for me if it costs many stacks of blues to do it."[5] Bat refused to say whether the gun was the one with which he had killed twenty-eight men, but, under prodding from reporters, he acknowledged that he had owned it since 1877. "The weapon," noted one scribe rather disappointedly, "had no notches."[6]

The *World* described Bat as "well-built and vigorous looking," and, while allowing that "he is noted for his quiet and affable manners," reported that his record of twenty-eight alleged killings was "more or less accurate."[7] The *World* writer interviewed Bat and got the distinct impression that the loss of the gun was Masterson's primary concern. Second in importance, apparently, was the slur against his honesty, and last was his arrest by what he called a "mush-headed cop." There was plenty of the familiar Masterson acid in Bat's recital of his arrest, but touches of humor crept in as Bat emphasized the absurdity of the situation:

This fellow Gargan who arrested me is a warm baby — in his mind. He thinks all people are suckers. That's the trouble with these mush-headed coppers. Give them a political job to keep them from starving and they think they own the earth. They get a shield on their vests, a pistol and a club and then they run amuck.

I'm sore, but it makes me laugh when I think how I was arrested. I went up to see a friend in 65th Street near Columbus Avenue, yesterday afternoon. He was out and I walked back to the avenue. I saw a fruit stand and bought an orange and was walking up the street peeling the fruit when I thought I'd get a shine.

Then I walked along and met Sullivan, an old Western friend. He told me he was going to sail for Europe today, but I guess he won't, because this fresh detective locked him up too, for what I don't know.

Sullivan and I were talking, when the first thing I knew somebody tripped Sullivan and knocked him into the gutter. They slugged him hard, and then pitched him into a saloon. Then they came at me, but they were not very rough. They told me they were officers and put me in the saloon.

I didn't know what they were after, but because of the way they had slugged Sullivan I said to myself: "Gee, Sully must have committed some serious crime." When I went into the saloon I said to him: "Sullivan, what have you been doing to get arrested this way?" He said: "You mean what have you been doing."

We were both in the dark. They drove us in cabs down to Headquarters and there I saw Snow, whom I knew slightly, and I thought to myself: "Gee, the big slob has been pinched too. I wonder what he has been doing."

Then they told me why I had been arrested. I went up to Snow and asked him what he meant by having me arrested and he answered: "I don't know you at all, sir." I said to him: "Well, you ought to know me for you've caused my arrest."[8]

After this face-to-face meeting with Bat at the police station, Elder Snow began to hedge a bit on his accusation. Said one report:

Snow is not entirely certain that Masterson was one of the principals in the game which resulted so disastrously to him, but he refused to withdraw the charge and Masterson was temporarily held.[9]

Bat was not detained long. As soon as word of his arrest reached the sporting fraternity, his friends rushed to his defense. Among them were Tom O'Rourke, owner of the Lennox Athletic Club and proprietor of the Hotel Deleran, and George Considine, manager of the Hotel Metropole at Broadway and Forty-second Street. O'Rourke and Considine "came hurriedly to Headquarters and went into conference with Captain Titus."[10] Bond was set at five hundred dollars for each of the men, and Bat and Sullivan were speedily released when the New York sports came up with the money. Sanders and Frank could not furnish bond and were sent to the Tombs. A hearing was scheduled for June 9, the formal charge reading: "Aiding and abetting in gambling games and inducing men to go to their rooms to play games of chance."

At some time during the three-day interval between the arrest and the hearing, Elder Snow either discovered that he had made a grave mistake or he suddenly decided to let bygones be bygones, for he never appeared at Tombs Police Court to press charges. In the absence of a complaining witness, Magistrate Crane dismissed the case. On the secondary charge of carrying a concealed weapon, Bat was fined ten dollars. He quickly paid the fine and asked the court if he might keep the gun "as a souvenir." The request was denied.

The idea of a real, gun-toting, western "bad man" abroad on the streets of New York caught the public fancy, and for several days Gotham's newspapers published feature articles on Bat and his gun. Many of the old stories concerning his exploits — some true, some false — were dusted off and reprinted. Papers in other cities picked up the story of Bat's arrest and sent reporters to interview men who had known Bat in the old days, hoping to find more blood-and-thunder anecdotal material. Bat's friends, however, were more concerned with aspersion on his character. Interviewed in Chicago, William Pinkerton said: "I have known Bat for twenty years, and in all that time I have never heard the faintest whisper from any quarter to indicate that he was not absolutely honest."[11]

Unmollified by the dismissal of the crooked-gambling charge and never one to remain on the defensive in any sort of conflict, Bat went into civil court and brought suit for ten thousand dollars against George H. Snow for "injury to his good name." Reported the *New York Tribune*: "Vindication was not sufficient for Masterson . . . and he has now sought legal measures to solace him. He objects to the charge that he is not a 'square' gambler."[12] Elder Snow, who undoubtedly was wishing that he had never brought up the matter, beat a hasty retreat out of town. Bat never collected on his suit.

By now, Bat had given up on going to England. He decided to remain in New York for a while. Tom O'Rourke and other fight promoters enlisted his services as referee and stakes holder at important bouts, and he spent much time at the tracks during the racing season. Bat was a good judge of horseflesh and was not averse to placing a bet on a nag, but prizefighting remained his abiding interest.

In early 1903, the management of a unique New York newspaper called the *Morning Telegraph* changed hands, with Finley Peter Dunne, author of the popular Dooley stories, assuming the post of general manager and William Eugene Lewis taking over at the managing editor's desk. Twenty years earlier, Lewis, then a cub reporter, had listened to Bat Masterson spin tales of brawling frontier life. Like his brother, novelist Alfred Henry Lewis, he had followed Bat's career through the years and had been among those who welcomed the colorful westerner to the metropolis of the East. He knew

of Bat's journalistic experience in Denver and of his facile,
fearless way with a pen. He asked Masterson if he would
take a job as reporter on the *Morning Telegraph.* Bat accepted.

For Bat this step was the most auspicious of his checkered
career. At fifty years of age, he finally had found a job to
which he could fit his distinctive personality and peculiar
talents.

CHAPTER TWENTY-SIX

THE HAM REPORTER

Bat was no ordinary journalist, and the paper for which he worked was no ordinary periodical. Said the *American Newspaper Directory* in 1904:

The *Morning Telegraph* is a unique publication in every respect — the only one of its kind in this country. Its circulation is particularly among the wealthy and persons interested in theatricals, racing, automobiling and the higher branches of sport. It has a clientele distinctly its own and is read and preserved by persons who have money to spend and who spend it. . . . The paper is the brightest and the breeziest published this side of Paris.

In the early years of the new century when other Manhattan dailies were selling for two cents, the *Morning Telegraph* was proudly proclaiming on Page One: "The Only Five-Cent Paper in New York." When standard newspaper rates went to three cents, some years later, the owners of the *Telegraph* unhesitatingly boosted its price to a dime.

Recalled Heywood Broun, who worked on the *Telegraph* during those early years:

The office was on Fiftieth Street and Eighth Avenue in what had been the stable of the adjacent street-car railway, which was electrified before my time.

Each night we played poker across the copy desk. We had two copy readers and they both sat in and read copy between pots. The night editor was Shep Friedman, a good newspaperman but a terrible poker player. . . .

I doubt whether any newspaper in New York ever had quite the intimate atmosphere of the old *Telegraph*. It was like a tough Emporia Gazette. The city room was always cluttered up with people who didn't seem to have any business there. Very often you couldn't get to your desk because there would be a couple of chorus girls sitting there waiting for a friend who was finishing an editorial. Everybody wrote editorials. They were not regarded as very important because the *Telegraph* had no policy about anything except that it was against reformers.[1]

With the editorial accent on breeziness, individuality, and anti-reformism, Bat moved into the news room as if it had been his home throughout his life. William E. Lewis gave him free rein, and no one, apparently, ever used a blue pencil on any of the articles Bat composed. On at least one occasion, Bat's prejudiced presentation of a news story got the editors and himself into hot water.

In December, 1906, three years after he joined the paper, Bat went upstate to Utica to cover the Chester Gillette murder trial, a *cause célèbre* of the day. After hearing the evidence as it was presented in the courtroom, he was firmly convinced that Gillette was innocent, but the jury brought in a verdict of guilty. The story in the *Telegraph*, under Bat's byline, was highly inflammatory, with references to "lynch law," "mob rule," and a verdict rendered by "Herkimer County bushmen."[2] Three days later, Bat, W. E. Lewis, and Henry Cary, the publisher, were arrested at their offices on bench warrants charging them with contempt of court in publishing "false and grossly inaccurate" descriptions of the trial. The three were scheduled to appear in Utica a week later for trial. Lewis became ill in the interval and was excused, but Cary and Bat went to Utica, entered a plea of guilty to the charge, and were fined fifty dollars each.

The year before, Bat had taken on responsibilities other than those he held as a writer for the *Morning Telegraph*. Theodore Roosevelt had ascended to the presidency upon the assassination of William McKinley in 1901, and according to Alfred Henry Lewis, soon after being returned to office in 1904, Roosevelt wrote Bat to offer him the post of U.S. marshal for Oklahoma Territory. Although the position carried a good deal of prestige, a comfortable salary, and the prerogative of naming twenty-two deputies, Bat declined the presidential offer. He reportedly wrote Roosevelt:

It wouldn't do. The man of my peculiar reputation couldn't hold such a place without trouble. . . . I'd have some drunken boy to kill once a year. Some kid who was born after I took my guns off would get drunk and look me over; and the longer he looked the less he'd be able to see where my reputation came from. In the end he'd crawl around to a gun play and I'd have to send him over the jump. . . . My record would prove a never-failing bait to the dime-novel reading youngsters, locoed to distinguish themselves and make a fire-eating reputation, and I'd have to bump 'em off. So, Mr. President, with all thanks to you, I believe I won't take the place. I've got finally out of that zone of fire and I hope never to go back to it.[3]

That is how Alfred Henry Lewis quoted Bat as answering the President, but the phraseology sounds suspiciously more Lewisian than Mastersonian. Bat's real reason for turning down the job probably was a more prosaic one: He was content at his stage of life to remain where he was. He enjoyed working on the *Morning Telegraph*; he liked New York City, the hub of the sports and theatrical world that he knew and loved; he did not wish to tear up the first true roots he had ever put down.

Bat did accept appointment, however, as a deputy U.S. marshal for the Southern District of New York. U.S. Marshal William Henkle, in announcing the appointment on February 6, 1905, refused to verify reports that Masterson had been named at the personal request of President Roosevelt, but he acknowledged that he had appointed Bat "on the recommendation of friends who are among the best men in this country."[4]

On March 28, 1905, Bat took the oath of office and was assigned to the staff of the U.S. attorney. His salary was two thousand dollars per year. The job was a part-time one and never seemed to interfere with his work on the *Morning Telegraph*. He held the appointment until the summer of 1909, after William Howard Taft had followed Roosevelt to the White House. A new U.S. attorney, Henry A. Wise, declared Bat's services unnecessary, and in spite of Alfred Henry Lewis' appeal to Taft to retain Masterson, on August 1 his office was abolished and his services terminated.

During Theodore Roosevelt's administration, Bat visited Washington several times at the invitation of the President and was Roosevelt's guest at the White House. The last of these calls resulted in a rare display of Masterson timidity. The man who had fearlessly faced blazing six-guns fled precipitously — from a suit of evening clothes. In 1909, shortly before Roosevelt turned the nation's highest office over to his successor, he entertained Bat at a presidential luncheon. The last official reception for the Army and Navy brass was to be held soon, and Roosevelt urged Bat to attend. Bat demurred, saying that a rough-hewn old codger like himself would be out of place among such august personages.

"Nonsense," said the President. "You have got to come. Remember, it's my last reception. You'll come, won't you?"

Trapped by the famous Roosevelt enthusiasm, Bat agreed.

"Bully!" exclaimed the President.

Once back at his hotel, however, Bat's nerve deserted him, and he told a friend he could not go through with it. He would telephone the President and tender his apologies, he said.

"Forget it," said his friend. "You're just my build and you can have my evening clothes."

The valet was called, the formal attire laid out carefully in Bat's room, and the friend, after making arrangements to meet Bat for dinner at 7:30 that evening, departed. At eight o'clock, the friend was still waiting impatiently for Bat's appearance when a bellboy with a telegram entered the hotel dining room, calling his name. The wire, dated in Baltimore an hour earlier, read: "I ain't going to attend any reception. Am heading east. Bat Masterson."[5]

From time to time, Bat was visited in New York by men he had known in the West. When Bill Tilghman was in New York in 1904 as an official delegate commissioned to notify Alton B. Parker of his nomination for the presidency by the Democratic party, he called on Bat. Tilghman was in New York again in 1921, this time to take in the Dempsey-Carpentier title fight. With him was Charlie Myton, another Dodge City old-timer. Bat helped Tilghman and Myton acquire a print of motion pictures of the fight, with distribution rights in Oklahoma.

In November, 1913, Bat went down to a Brooklyn pier to see the 101 Ranch Wild West Show load onto a ship bound for Buenos Aires. He was conversing with Edward Arlington, owner of the show, when he was approached by a powerfully built young man in cowboy attire. Arlington made introductions. "This is one of the star performers of our show, Milt Hinkle. Milt, shake hands with the famous Bat Masterson."

The big cowboy looked stunned, and then a grin came over his face. "After all these years, I get to meet and shake the hand of the

By 1909, when this picture was
taken, Bat had established
himself as a newspaperman in
New York. Courtesy Kansas
State Historical Society.

man my dad defeated as sheriff of Ford County, Kansas,'' he said.

Masterson did not smile. After a moment, he snapped: ''No
doubt you are the son of George Hinkle. Which one of his women
was your mother?''

Seeing young Hinkle's face darken in anger, Bat said, ''I can see
George in you, and if you are anything like your dad, you are a
mighty man.'' He invited Milt to call on him when he got back to
New York City.

The following year, Hinkle was in town and took Bat up on his
invitation. It turned out that Milt's mother had been a close friend
of Emma Masterson before either of the girls was married. When
Bat learned this, he took Hinkle home to meet Emma and have
dinner. In 1919, Hinkle was in New York for several months
making arrangements for a wild-west rodeo, and he saw Bat often:

> We made the rounds together. He always had a pocket full of ''Annie
> Oakleys'' — passes for all the plays and movies on Broadway.
> We would go across the street from my hotel, where Diamond Jim
> Brady had his cafe and bar near Forty-Second on Broadway. I never

drank so Bat would drink enough for both of us. . . . It was not until Bat
had downed about three or four Collins, or other mixed drinks, that he
was willing and ready to talk. . . .

One night, after Bat had had a number of drinks, I said, ''Bat, have you
a picture of Dad? I would like one if you have one to spare.''

He said, ''Hell yes, I could spare it if I had one, but why in the hell
would I want a picture of him? Hinkle would let no one take his picture,
and if you don't have one, you will have trouble getting one.'' And he
was right.

Milt was aware that his father had been in some kind of difficulty
back in the days when Bat knew him and tried to persuade Bat to
supply details. Bat was noncommittal, however, except to say that
the problem was women. George Hinkle had not been a drinker,
and to Bat it was axiomatic that the man who did not drink was
certain to have woman trouble.

The bitterness Bat Masterson still felt for the West was evident
to Milt:

One night . . . I asked him if he ever longed to go back West — to
smell fresh air and see all his old friends. . . . ''Hell, no!'' he said. ''I
never want to see the West or any of them again, and I don't intend to. To
hell with everybody in the West.''[6]

On sober reflection, Bat might have admitted that his consignment
of the entire western United States to hell was a bit extreme. It is
clear, however, that mention of the city of Denver always sparked
in him a special anger.

When Gene Fowler arrived in New York to take a newspaper
job, he went to see Masterson and announced that he was from the
Colorado capital. ''Denver can go to hell,'' Bat snorted, and
Fowler said afterward he had the distinct impression that he was
included in the damnation. Fowler's stock with Bat certainly took a
dive when Masterson learned that the young newspaperman had
been assistant to Otto Floto on the *Denver Post*. Bat's enmity for
Floto never diminished. When he learned that a horse named Otto
Floto was running on the tracks, he watched the results and gloated
in his column when the horse lost. Later, the horse's owners
entered Otto Floto in some jumping races and scored a few wins.
These, Masterson ignored. Another owner named a gelding Bat

Masterson. When the horse dropped dead in the backstretch one day, Otto Floto of Denver had a picnic. In a column titled "Poetic Justice," he declared that even an elephant could not bear the weight of both a jockey and a bad name.[7]

The New York visit of one former western acquaintance of Bat's produced an incident that made the front pages of Gotham's papers. A man calling himself Colonel Dick Plunkett of Tombstone and Creede appeared in June, 1906, with a Texas editor bearing the unlikely name of Dinklesheet. Plunkett, claiming to be a real western-style peace officer and town tamer, was carrying a large revolver, according to a reporter, with "enough notches to make a good nutmeg grater." Bat Masterson, Plunkett loudly proclaimed, was a phony, a fraud, and a fake. Dinklesheet and Plunkett were in the Waldorf-Astoria when " 'Bat' Masterson, United States Marshal . . . gathered himself into the cafe with blood in his eye." Bat invited Plunkett outside and assisted him in that direction with a grip on his coat. Said the *New York Herald*:

Plunkett has a reputation for gunfighting that is said to be as brilliant as that of Masterson. But he was inclined to be submissive last night. Not so his friend E. Dinklesheet [who] got furious when he saw Masterson grab the Colonel by the coat. He rushed across the cafe and struck Masterson a terrific blow in the face. . . . The next moment Dinklesheet was sprawling on the floor from several terrific blows landed by the United States Marshal.

Bat then stuck his right hand in his pants pocket and jabbed it up against Plunkett. Somebody yelled, "Look out! Bat's going to flash his cannon!" Witnesses stampeded for the exits amid the crash of toppling bottles and highball glasses. House Detective Smith "got on the lee of Mr. Masterson and induced him to leave. He was escorted up Sixth Avenue by two policemen." Plunkett and Dinklesheet were taken out by another door.[8]

Later that night, a *New York World* reporter cornered Bat in another bistro and asked to see the gun that had caused all the excitement in the Waldorf. Reaching into his pocket, Bat produced the formidable weapon: a package of cigarettes.

The last recorded instance of a physical altercation involving

Bat occurred a year after the Plunkett-Dinklesheet affair. For several weeks, Masterson and Walter St. Denis, sports editor of the *New York Globe*, had been carrying on a running feud in their respective columns. When they met under the grandstand at the Belmont race track, fists flew, and witnesses said that Bat got in at least three good licks. The *New York Herald* reported the action on May 17, 1907, saying that "friends of Bat were inclined to treat the whole matter with levity."

The Sunset Trail, a novel based very freely on Bat's western experiences, was published by Alfred Henry Lewis in 1905. The unmitigated romanticist retold most of the old legends and sowed the seeds of others. In at least one instance, the book did Masterson's reputation an actual disservice; in Lewis' long and verbose account of Clay Allison's visit to Dodge, he added fuel to the myth that Bat was present but unseen while Clay cavorted on the streets. Although the novel was written in a humorous vein and was never intended by its author to be taken as a serious biographical study, western chroniclers for half a century have liberally quoted from it when referring to Bat's exploits.

Besides writing novels, Lewis was editing at this time a magazine called *Human Life*. In 1907, he prevailed upon Bat to write a series of articles on the gunfighters he had seen in action on the frontier. During the months that followed, Bat wrote about Ben Thompson, Wyatt Earp, Luke Short, Doc Holliday, Bill Tilghman, and Buffalo Bill Cody. Besides showing that the Masterson literary style had improved much since the days of his vitriolic outpourings in Dodge City, these pieces reveal plainly Bat's inherent modesty. In the narration of his friends' adventures, he consistently understated his own role, a practice that often required a neat bit of literary sidestepping.

In response to what he called "a tempest of inquiry touching Mr. Masterson himself," Lewis strove to rectify these omissions with an article, "The King of the Gun-Players, William Barclay Masterson," in the issue for November, 1907: "It would be among things impossible to induce Mr. Masterson to attempt the story himself. He will write biography, but not autobiography — being modest." In this piece, Lewis adhered more closely to the facts of

Bat's life than he had in his book, although he repeated once again the fiction of Allison's Dodge City raid. In closing, he said:

These and many more have been the adventures of Mr. Masterson, who, coming up through this perilous trail of smoke and blood, is now peacefully amassing ten thousand dollars a year as crack writer on a New York City paper and a contributor to *Human Life*.

Although it is doubtful that Bat was earning that kind of money as early as 1907, he was certainly doing quite well as a journalist. He had been made a staff writer on the *Morning Telegraph* and was turning out a lengthy column three times a week. The column, appearing in the Tuesday, Thursday, and Sunday editions and later headed "Masterson's Views on Timely Topics," dealt chiefly with pugilistic activities, a subject with which Bat had remained in close contact. Frequently, Bat interlarded his ring news with personal observations on the state of the world as he viewed it, and these typically outspoken asides provide our clearest picture of the crusty old frontiersman's philosophy in his later years.

As a longtime professional gambler who had had his ups and downs, Bat spoke from experience when he referred to life as a great gamble:

A good sport is a good loser and takes his medicine when . . . the "kirds" are against him. This applies as well to one line of human endeavor as to another. Pretty much everything we do is more or less of a gamble.[9]

On the decline of big-time betting:

There was a time in this country when men could be found who would bet their eyeballs out, and yours too, on what they believed to be an even thing, but that was before barbering came into vogue. Now our big operators want a flash at your hole card before loosening up.[10]

On character assassins:

In a country where a man is called to personal accountables for statements he publicly makes derogatory to another there's always a wholesome respect for character. . . . The man who will back up what he says with a fight if necessary is to be respected, while the one who assails character and then seeks refuge behind the law deserves nothing but contempt.[11]

On reformers:

Clerical humbugs and sordid politicians are certainly giving the decent, liberty-loving people of this country a lively run for their existence. How long this state of affairs will last is hard to tell. It is some consolation, however, to know that all civilized countries, where clerical humbugs and political rapscallions have dominated, succeeded in time in driving these human barnacles from power, and it's safe to predict that the time is not far distant when the free-born American citizen will rise up in his might and go for his rights. When that time comes the humbugs and political grafters will be found scurrying to cover.[12]

On sophisticated New Yorkers:

This is the biggest boob town in America. . . . All any of these hokem peddlers need do when they contemplate selling New Yorkers a bill of their phoney goods is to ask what they want and they'll be sure to get it.[13]

On American gullibility:

The American public [is] without doubt . . . the biggest aggregation of sapheads in the world.[14]

On his personal critics, as he was preparing to leave on a vacation:

My legion of anonymous correspondents are herby notified that my address for the next two or three weeks will be the Thousand Island House, Alexandria Bay, N. Y. Letters from this species of vermin are always welcome. As all mail for the Thousand Island House is thoroughly disinfected before leaving the post office at Alexandria Bay, the guests of the hotel are in no danger of being contaminated by the insidious poison these vile communications carry.[15]

On the people of China:

The Chinese, as a race, are said to be the most honest people in the world. But who in the name of common sense would want to be a Chinaman?[16]

With the passage of the national prohibition amendment, Bat cut loose with more frequent and even more embittered blasts at those he had called "clerical humbugs and political rapscallions." He could now see little hope for the nation's future:

The fanatical reformers, aided and abetted by the sordid and hypocritical politicians, have succeeded in swarming all over this country in the last few years, and, like the boll weevil in the cottonfields of the South, left nothing but sorrow and destruction in their wake.[17]

Again:

Personal liberty has become a ghastly joke in this country and the end is nowhere in sight.[18]

And again:

"The time is not far distant when red-blooded men will get guns and use them, too. They'll either have to do that or turn the country over to the modern witch-burners. . . . There is neither freedom nor bravery in this country any more. Hypocrisy, rascality and cowardice have supplanted liberty, bravery and integrity. . . . Dirty politics, treacherous politicians and profiteering reformers are in the saddle and ruthlessly riding down all that is left of Americanism.[19]

And yet again:

Matt Henkel, the Cleveland sportsman, will arrive in the city some time today and will sail for Europe Saturday. Matt feels the need of a little recreation and decided that the best way to get it was by crossing the big swim and bringing up in some country where he can order what he wanted and have it served in his room or with his meals. . . . If I had Matt Henkel's money I would be right with him and make a permanent stay of it. . . . The grafters of this country, political and otherwise, along with the hypocrites, would have to find some way to get along without me, painful as that might be. . . . What a crime it all is. When a man becomes so thoroughly disgusted with his own country that he wants to leave it and never return, conditions are certainly in a deplorable state.[20]

Most of Bat's barbs were reserved, however, for fighters, managers, promoters, or sports writers whose actions he considered detrimental to the boxing game. As Nat Fleischer has observed:

He never pulled his punches, and wrote, just as he used to shoot, with deadly accuracy. He was dogmatic in his judgments, but never unfair, and went after the boxing crooks with a persistency of a bloodhound on the trail.[21]

Bat hated sham in any form, but he hated it most when it crept into the boxing arena. "Faking . . . seems to be part and parcel of the glove game at this time," he remarked disgustedly in one of his columns. "The higher up you go, the more fakirs you find."[22]

The Carl Morris–Jim Flynn heavyweight set-to scheduled for Madison Square Garden in October, 1911, was a case in point. Morris, a behemoth of a man, arrived in the big town sporting a string of quick knockouts scored in the nation's hinterlands. His manager, a wealthy Oklahoma oil man named Frank D. Ufer, ballyhooed his giant pug as the "white hope" who would dethrone the Negro champion, Jack Johnson, and managed to get a lot of sensational nonsense concerning Morris printed in the New York papers while arrangements for the Flynn fight were under way.

Bat had never seen Morris in a ring, nor had any of the other sports writers in New York, but he watched the lumbering giant work out in the gymnasium and saw nothing remarkable in his performance. Bat thought he detected the unmistakable odor of a frame. He knew Flynn to be a seasoned, game workhorse who had faced some of the best heavyweights in the business and come off not too badly. Yet Ufer was bragging his man up and down Broadway and taking all the Flynn money he could find, while Jim Flynn, the Pueblo Fireman, remained strangely silent.

"There have been a good many cooked-up affairs pulled off in the prize-ring, as everybody knows," Bat wrote in his next column, "but hardly one quite as daring or that smells so much like a polecat as the one between Flynn and Morris."[23] Ufer retorted in an interview published in the New York Globe, castigating Masterson at length and asserting that Bat had built a phony reputation as a bad man by shooting innocent cowboys in the back.

Bat ignored the personal attack for the time being and went directly to see Jim Flynn. Without a word of greeting, he shot a question at the Pueblo pugilist: "How much are you getting to throw the Morris fight, Jim?"

It took a more experienced practitioner of duplicity than Flynn to look Bat Masterson in the eye and lie convincingly. "Seventy-five hundred," blurted the Pueblo Fireman.

"You're a fool!" snorted Bat. He went back to his desk and

hammered away at the story of the fixed fight in every column up to the day of the bout.

With the polecat out of the bag, Flynn reneged on his agreement with Ufer and promised to give the ring patrons a real show for their money. Bat duly reported the Fireman's change of heart in his column. Flynn fulfilled his promise in the ring, handing Morris a terrific beating.

Bat had prevented the fixing of an important fight and had exposed Carl Morris' artificial buildup, but he still had a matter to settle with Frank Ufer. He brought suit against the millionaire oil man and the *New York Globe*, claiming defamation. Two years later, he was awarded $3,500 in damages. Among the character witnesses who came forward to testify that the Masterson reputation in the West was not built as a back-shooting killer were Major General Frank Baldwin and Lieutenant General Nelson A. Miles, under whom Bat had served almost forty years earlier.

Once more Bat had vindicated himself, and he had gained stature in the process. Just two months after the Flynn-Morris affair, he was promoted to the vice-presidency of the Morning Telegraph Company.

Sports writers for other papers came in for a share of the Masterson brand of outspoken criticism:

A sport writer who is not willing to stand by his honest judgment . . . ought to chuck his job and try something else. . . . The fight reviewer who lacks the knack of drawing imaginary pictures and incidents that did not exist and tossing them into the story of a frame is promptly set down by the reading public as a ham reporter. I am a ham of the most pronounced type.[24]

Attests Nat Fleischer:

He was a tough hombre. Very severe critic of those who didn't tread a straight and narrow path and got into frequent disputes with sports editors of other papers whom he abused when their decisions were different from his in the no-decision days of boxing. He practically ran the *Morning Telegraph*. He . . . was given carte blanche to do as he chose.[25]

Bat made enemies in New York, as he had in Dodge and Denver, but he made a horde of friends as well. His favorite eating

Frank D. Baldwin was a
lieutenant when he commanded
the company of scouts in the
Red River Campaign of 1874.
He was a major general, much
decorated, when this picture
was taken, about the time he
testified that Bat had not built a
reputation by shooting cowboys
in the back. Courtesy Denver
Public Library.

place was Shanley's Grill, a popular steakhouse at Broadway and
Forty-third Street. There he could be found almost every evening,
hunched over a thick, sizzling steak, surrounded by a crowd of
admirers who never tired of hearing his tales of the Old West.
Later, Bat would usually adjourn to the Metropole Bar, run by the
sons of John Considine, a former gambler from Seattle. This
establishment, at Broadway and Forty-second, long was a favorite
hangout of the sports, theatrical, and gambling gentry, but it
achieved national notoriety when, in the early hours of July 16,
1912, Herman Rosenthal, New York gambling kingpin, was shot
to death on its doorstep. After a sensational trial, five men went to
the electric chair for this murder, including a close friend of Bat's,
Police Lieutenant Charles Becker, who was convicted of ordering
the assassination.

Among the habitués of the Metropole was Irvin S. Cobb, then a
rewrite man for the *Morning World*. He recalled how imperfectly

Bat's appearance fitted the stereotyped picture of a western law-man:

Mr. Masterson was sawed-off and stumpy legged, with a snub nose and a tedious sniffle; wore a flat-topped derby . . . and in doubtful weather carried an umbrella. He was addicted to seltzer lemonades and tongue sandwiches; and in general more nearly approximated the conception of a steamfitter's helper on a holiday . . . than the authentic person who'd helped to clean up Dodge City and Abilene with a Colt forty-five for his broom. Two things betokened the real man: his eyes. They were like smoothed ovals of gray schist with flecks of mica suddenly glittering in them if he were roused. But you might not notice the glint in those eyes unless you looked closely — it came and instantly was gone. And some of the men who faced him through the smoke fogs of cow-town melees hadn't lived long enough to get a good look.[26]

Among Bat's intimates were Tom O'Rourke, who had moved in the same boxing circles with Masterson since the days of John L. Sullivan; William Muldoon, another crony who traced his friend-ship with Bat back to bare-knuckles days and who was later boxing commissioner of New York; Tex Rickard, the greatest fight pro-moter of all time; Alfred Henry and William E. Lewis; Val O'Far-rell, ace sleuth of the New York police force, who in later years managed one of the nation's largest private-detective agencies; and a young reporter named Damon Runyon.

A decade later, when Runyon was achieving national fame with his humorous short stories of Broadway characters, he published a tale called "The Idyll of Miss Sarah Brown." The central charac-ter was a gun-toting, high-rolling gambler from Colorado named Sky Masterson. The story was the nucleus of a hugely successful Broadway musical and motion picture, *Guys and Dolls*, a genera-tion later. Sky Masterson had been patterned after the real-life Bat Masterson, whom Runyon had heard spin yarns of gun-toting, high-rolling Colorado gamblers in a corner of Shanley's Grill.

Bat's tales of frontier adventure also were enjoyed by the editor of the *Morning Telegraph*'s extensive motion-picture section, an ambitious and energetic young woman named Louella Parsons:

Old Bat Masterson . . . was my close friend on the *Tele-graph*. . . . When I knew Bat he was just a kind-hearted old man, a boon

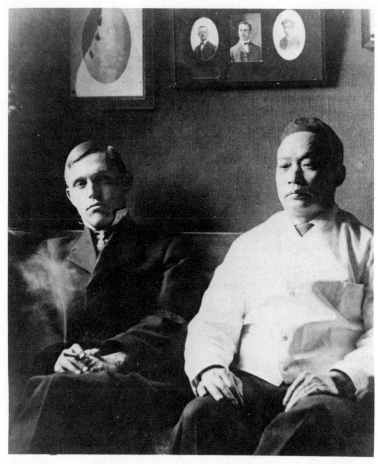

Damon Runyon with Oriental friend at the Denver Press Club in 1910. Runyon's Sky owed a lot to Bat. Courtesy Denver Public Library.

companion of Theodore Roosevelt, who used to write him to come to Washington and tell his stories of the early West, and a grand newspaper crony. But what a past the old boy had left behind him![27]

Bat's last visit to the milieu of that stormy past was made in July, 1910, when he journeyed with Alfred Henry Lewis to Reno, Nevada, to cover the Jack Johnson–Jim Jeffries heavyweight title

This photograph was taken July 13, 1910, at the Denver & Rio Grande depot in Trinidad, Colorado. Bat and Alfred Henry Lewis were returning to the East from Reno, Nevada, where they had witnessed the Johnson-Jeffries title fight. The dignitaries (from left): Tony Patrick, proprietor of Trinidad's Big 6 Saloon; John English, newspaper editor; Charley White, Chicago sports editor; Ben Springer, Trinidad barkeeper and saloon partner with Bat in Dodge; John Gysing, a local; Bat; John Conkie, former mayor of Trinidad, who appointed Bat marshal; A. H. Lewis; General E. B. Sopris, Colorado pioneer; and Charley Hungerford, who had known Bat since Dodge City days. Courtesy Old Baca House–Pioneer Museum, Colorado State Historical Society.

fight, one of Tex Rickard's first big promotions. Arriving on the scene early, Bat wired daily stories to New York, describing the preparations of the battlers and the arrival of the hordes of sports from all over the world. The event developed into a sort of grand reunion for the gambling and sporting folk, and Bat recognized men he had not seen in twenty years.

He was amazed that so many tinhorn gamblers and two-bit crooks had been able to dig up the cash to make the trip to Reno. "Men that to my absolute knowledge could not ask the captain what time the ship left if tickets around the world were a dime a smash seem to have arrived on the scene little the worse for wear," he said, marveling. There was "The Two-By-Six Kid," celebrated for his slimness and ability to obtain money "when the sun is off shift"; "Oregon Jeff," who had not won a bet, swore Bat, "since Soapy Smith dealt on the square"; and "Bull Con Jack," a second-story man who confided to Bat that he had lost a book of New York addresses that he had intended to use the following winter to further his own financial cause. "The blow is a heavy one," Bat reported, "and Jack is out with a reward for its return. He told me on the quiet he'd pay off with an IOU if he is lucky enough to have it kicked back."[28]

After reporting the action as Johnson pounded Jeffries into docile submission on the Fourth of July, Bat started back to New York. He rode over the Santa Fe line from Colorado into Kansas, the line he had traveled so often in those roaring, rollicking days that made up such a colorful period in his personal history — and in the history of the nation as well. From the window of the coach, he looked out over fields that had reverberated to the thundering hooves of thousands upon thousands of buffalo and the boom of his Sharps Big Fifty before the steel upon which he now rode had been laid. Like the buffalo, the era had passed. It lived on only in the memories of men like himself, men who had contributed to its violence, its romance, its heroism, its greatness.

Bat had his memories, but he was not a man who lived in the past. Where many another frontier veteran might have looked from that window and descried only the scenes of youthful adventures, Masterson saw what was actually there: a new Kansas. He wrote about it after his return:

In coming down the Arkansas Valley from Pueblo to Dodge . . . I could not help wondering at the marvelous change that had come over the country in the last twenty years. As I looked from the car window after reaching the Kansas line at Coolidge, I saw in all directions groves of trees, orchards and fields bearing abundant crops of corn, wheat and alfalfa. . . . The idea that the plains of Western Kansas could ever be made fertile was something I had never dreamed of.[29]

The train reached Dodge City at eight o'clock in the morning, and there was a thirty-minute layover for breakfast at the Harvey House. Bat bolted down his meal and stepped out onto Front Street to have a look at the old town. He stood on almost the exact spot where a grim-faced boy of nineteen had stood thirty-seven years before, awaiting the arrival of the train from Granada so that he could claim a long overdue debt. There, along the roadbed that he and his brother Ed graded, he had stacked stiff buffalo hides ten feet high, Old Tom Nixon, the greatest hide hunter of them all, toiling in the wagon bed at his side. How many wild-eyed law-breakers had he escorted to that old city jail across the tracks? It squatted peacefully now in the morning sun, but the bullet scars in its sturdy timbers were mute reminders of a deadly battle that had raged in the Plaza when Dodge City — and Bat Masterson — were young. Beyond the calaboose was the weatherbeaten building that had housed the Lady Gay Saloon. There, on the plank sidewalk, genial, easygoing Ed Masterson had reached the end of the trail.

As he stood at the doorway of the Harvey House, the Santa Fe snorting impatiently behind him, memories must have come flooding back to Bat Masterson: the dreams, the angers, the hurts, the triumphs. He was still touched with nostalgia for Dodge when he arrived at his New York office, and he devoted most of a column to the town and some of its lurid history. Then, with typical abruptness, he snapped back to the present:

But why dwell further on the subject — they are now but memories. . . . Dodge City is now a thriving little country village, surrounded by a thrifty farming community. There are many of the oldtimers still living there and it is doubtful if they would care to live elsewhere. They are well-to-do and happy. And may they live long and continue to prosper, is my sincere wish.[30]

From left to right: Sydney Burns; William A. Pinkerton, chief of the well-known detective agency; and Bat. The picture was taken in Hot Springs, Arkansas, and was sent as a postcard to Bat's sister, Nellie Cairnes, about 1912. Courtesy Kansas State Historical Society.

The years apparently had healed the wounds Bat received in Dodge, and he had at last forgiven his old enemies. When adversary Mike Sutton died at Dodge City in June, 1918, Bat wired Mrs. Sutton: "Your telegram great shock to myself and wife. Dear good Mike the last of my life long friends is no more. Peace to his ashes." The old-timers were dying off, and the authentic Old West had passed away also.

Even as the raucous laughter, ribald cries, and roaring gunfire echoed down the deserted streets of the last isolated boom camps, however, a new entertainment medium was sweeping the country, the motion picture, and the early west was reborn in all its epic grandeur and romance.

Surprisingly, Bat Masterson liked western films, especially those featuring the first of the great celluloid western heroes, William S. Hart. As early as 1910, when Hart appeared on Broadway in a western play called *The Barrier*, Bat referred to him as "that clever impersonator of Western characters" and applauded his performance. "Anyone familiar with the character of the cool, calculating, and daring desperado, whose presence was a part of frontier life a generation ago," wrote Bat in his column, "will recognize in Mr. Hart a true type of that reckless nomad who flourished on the border when the six-shooter was the final arbiter of all disputes between man and man."[31]

Hart treasured this plaudit above all others. An earnest student of western history, he was cognizant of Masterson's colorful career and held the old frontiersman in great esteem. "I play the hero that 'Bat' Masterson inspired," he told Louella Parsons. "More than any other man I have ever met I admire and respect him."[32]

The first meeting of the actor and his prototype took place in 1918 when Hart was in New York shooting scenes for an opus entitled *Branding Broadway*. Bat stopped in at the star's hotel to pay his respects. Hart, himself the idol of millions, was thrilled by this visit from his own personal idol:

> How glad I was to see and know him personally! We talked for two hours and it seemed like five minutes. The owner of a soft, low voice; the wielder, if the occasion required, of a virile, audacious pen; a quiet, unostentatious gentleman; a great American citizen . . . William B. (Bat) Masterson.[33]

Bat and Hart became close friends after that meeting, and the film star joined a variegated coterie of Masterson intimates that included all manner of individuals from panhandlers to presidents.

In September, 1921, Hart arrived in New York from Hollywood on a vacation and had what he called "some never-to-be-forgotten

The Ham Reporter. Courtesy
Denver Public Library.

visits with Mr. Masterson.''[34] When Hart asked to have a picture
taken, Bat went with him to the roof of the *Telegraph* building and
dutifully posed with the actor. The picture reveals that Bat, then
sixty-seven, still seemed vigorous and alert. A broad-brimmed
western-style hat, cocked low over his remarkably unlined face,
hid the thin gray hair that most prominently signaled his advanced
years. The old waterfall moustache that concealed his tight-lipped
half-smile in his earlier pictures had finally disappeared. Long
since discarded also was the flamboyant attire he had affected in
his younger days. He had always dressed to fit the occasion, and
during his years as a sports writer and newspaper executive, he was
never seen in anything but a well-tailored business suit of conservative cut and color.

   During one of his visits, Hart suggested in all seriousness that
Bat return to California and take a role in a movie with him. He
assured the surprised Masterson that he would be perfect for

One month to the day before he died, Bat sent these pictures of himself and
his wife, Emma, to his friend W. S. ("Billy") Thompson of Denver. This,
of course, was not Billy Thompson of Texas, Ben's ne'er-do-well brother.
Courtesy Amon Carter Museum.

western parts and could also act in an advisory capacity. Bat
laughed heartily but promised that he would look into Hart's offer
the next time he journeyed to the West Coast. Someone at the
Morning Telegraph offices, seeing the possibility of a good newspaper story in the movie star's open admiration for Bat, suggested
that Hart write a feature article on his hero. The actor agreed. Said
Louella Parsons:

The article, unlike many of the signed contributions from film players,
did not emanate from a press agent. Mr. Hart wrote every word himself.
He wrote it in longhand on Waldorf-Astoria stationery. It was published
verbatim October 9 — exactly as it was originally written.[35]

Hart's essay was a remarkably humble eulogy to Bat Masterson and an old sidekick of Bat's who was then living out his days in quiet obscurity on the West Coast:

Now, I am just an actor — a mere player — seeking to reproduce the lives of those great gunmen who molded a new country for us to live in and enjoy peace and prosperity. And we have today in America two of these men with us in the flesh. . . . One is Wyatt Earp, the other William B. (Bat) Masterson.

To those few who have studied the history of frontier days, these names are revered as none others. They are the last of the greatest band of gunfighters — upholders of law and order — that ever lived. Wild Bill Hickok, Luke Short, Doc Holliday, Shotgun Collins, Ben Thompson, all have crossed the Big Divide but Bat Masterson and Wyatt Earp still live — and long may they do so! . . .

Gentle-voiced and almost sad-faced, these men are today uncheered while I, the imitator, the portrayer, am accorded the affection of those millions who love the West. I appreciate from my heart of hearts all the honors bestowed upon me, and in my work I do my best to be worthy; but "lest we forget," don't let us pass up those real men — those real figures — who did so much for us in bygone days. . . .

Let us not forget these living Americans who, when they pass on, will be remembered by hundreds of generations. For no history of the West can be written without their wonderful deeds being recorded.[36]

Sixteen days later, on Tuesday, October 25, 1921, Bat Masterson sat at his desk, writing the column that would appear in the *Telegraph* the following Thursday. He had contracted a severe cold the previous week and had stayed home from his office, his column not appearing. Now he was catching up on his report of local fistic affairs. He wrote with pen and ink, rapidly, stabbing out the words as thoughts crossed his mind. As usual, his reportorial items were flavored with pointed personal opinions:

Lew Tendler received a little more than $12,000 for his scrap with Rocky Kansas at the Garden a week ago. Not so bad for a job like that. . . . No wonder these birds are flying high when they get that kind of money for an hour's work. Just think of an honest, hard-working farmer laboring from daylight to dark for forty years of his life, and lucky if he finishes with as much as one of these birds gets in an hour. Yet there are those who argue that everything breaks even in this old dump of a world of ours.

I suppose these ginks who argue that way hold that because the rich
man gets ice in the summer and the poor man gets it in the winter things
are breaking even for both. Maybe so, but I'll swear I can't see it that
way. . . .[37]

A member of the newspaper's staff, concerned about the old man's
cold, looked in at the door and asked how he was feeling. "All
right," Bat said, scratching away at the paper.[38]

Those were the last words he ever spoke, When an assistant
came into the office several minutes later, Bat Masterson was
dead. The heart of the old fighting man had simply stopped
beating.

Had Bat lived thirty-two days longer, he would have celebrated
his sixty-eighth birthday. It is unlikely that he would have expressed any regrets on his passing had he been able to do so. Things
had broken pretty well for him in "this old dump of a world of
ours," and he had departed the same way so many of his friends
had died: fast, with his boots on, and with his chosen weapon in
his hand.

He had never hoped for anything more.

EPILOGUE

Funeral services for the man who had been christened Bertholomiew, called himself William Barclay, and was popularly known as Bat Masterson were held at Campbell Funeral Home, Broadway and Sixty-sixth Street, on Thursday, October 27, 1921. The Reverend Nathan A. Seagle of St. Stephen's Protestant Episcopal Church conducted the service. Burial was in Woodlawn Cemetery. Honorary pallbearers were Tex Rickard, Tom O'Rourke, W. E. Lewis, Damon Runyon, William Muldoon, Val O'Farrell, Hype Igoe, Frank J. Price, James P. Sinnott, and Charles Thorley.

Tributes to Bat poured in to the office of the *Morning Telegraph* and were received by Bat's widow[1] from all parts of the country. Spokesmen for the world of sport in particular expressed a deep sense of loss.

Hundreds of Bat's friends and admirers gathered at the funeral home for the services, and Muldoon, New York boxing commissioner, rose and delivered a tribute that he said was "no attempt at oratory, no studied eulogium," but an honest appraisal of Bat Masterson as a friend. During forty years of intimate friendship, said Muldoon, he "had never known Bat Masterson to do a dishonorable deed, never to betray a friend, never to connive at dishonor and never to fear an enemy."[2]

Bat's passing inspired one friend to render his farewell in verse:

WILLIAM BARCLAY MASTERSON
(Affectionately known as "Bat")
by William Jerome

Good-bye, Bat,
You've gone and left us flat.
You know it wasn't like you
To do a thing like that.

But, where you've gone we know you'll find
A welcome on the mat.
You played your part — sleep on, dear heart,
Good-bye, Bat.

Good-bye, Bat,
We'll miss that mid-day chat;
The sunshine always danced around
The chair on which you sat.
With any hungry pal at all
You'd share your bit o' fat;
There's crape today along Broadway,
Good-bye, Bat.

Good-bye, Bat,
They never heard you blat
About the things you did out West —
You wasn't built like that.
That great big golden heart of yours,
It wouldn't harm a cat.
Sweet as a "gal," so long, old pal,
Good-bye, Bat.[3]

The inelegant elegy certainly must have brought a smile to the
countenance of Bat Masterson's shade, wherever it was.

NOTES

CHAPTER 1 - The Seed of Legend

1. *Ford County Globe*, November 22, 1881.
2. *Kansas City Journal*, November 15, 1881.
3. *Wichita County Herald*, February 24, 1887.
4. Cy Warman, *The Story of the Railroad.*
5. Fred E. Sutton and A. B. MacDonald, *Hands Up!*
6. Alfred Henry Lewis, *The Sunset Trail*, 1.
7. Alfred Henry Lewis, "The King of the Gun-Players, William Barclay Masterson," *Human Life* (November, 1907), 10.
8. George G. Thompson, *Bat Masterson: The Dodge City Years*, 4.
9. Stanley Vestal, *Dodge City, Queen of Cowtowns*, 273.
10. Richard O'Connor, *Bat Masterson*, 25–26.
11. *New York Morning Telegraph*, October 27, 1921.
12. This long-unknown baptismal record was unearthed by western history enthusiast Chris Penn of Norfolk, England, who published his findings in "A Note on Bartholomew Masterson," *The English Westerners' Brand Book* (April, 1967), 11–12.
13. A. T. Andreas and W. G. Cutler, *History of the State of Kansas*, 1419.
14. In his column, "Masterson's Views on Timely Topics," *New York Morning Telegraph*, October 20, 1921.

CHAPTER 2 - "A Chunk of Steel"

1. Olive K. Dixon, *The Life of "Billy" Dixon*, 81.
2. In a foreword to the Dixon biography, vi–vii.
3. Dixon, *op. cit.*, 115.
4. Henry H. Raymond to Heinie Schmidt, January 14, 1936, quoted in Joseph W. Snell (ed.), "The Diary of a Dodge City Buffalo Hunter, 1872–1873," *Kansas Historical Quarterly* (Winter, 1965), 346–47.
5. All of the Raymond diary quotations are from the edited diary as published in the *Kansas Historical Quarterly* (Winter, 1965).
6. Henry H. Raymond, "Incidents of Frontier Life," *Valley Center Index*, July 23, 1964; quoted by editor Joseph Snell in a footnote to the published Raymond diary, *loc. cit.*, 351.
7. *Ibid.*, 352.

CHAPTER 3 - The Daughter of the Hide Hunters

1. Robert M. Wright, *Dodge City, the Cowboy Capital, and the Great Southwest*, 9–10.
2. *Ibid.*, 10.

3. William MacLeod Raine, *Famous Sheriffs and Western Outlaws*, 6.
4. Henry H. Raymond, "Notes on Diary of H. H. Raymond of 1873," copy in Manuscript Division, Kansas State Historical Society, quoted in *Kansas Historical Quarterly* (Winter 1965), 360.
5. *Ibid.*, 364.
6. Quoted in Vestal, *op. cit.*, 32.
7. *Ibid.*, 32.
8. *Ibid.*, 33–35.
9. *Ibid.*, 8–9.
10. W. B. Masterson to H. H. Raymond, July 23, 1899, copy in Manuscript Division, Kansas State Historical Society.
11. *New York Morning Telegraph*, October 20, 1921.

CHAPTER 4 - Adobe Walls

1. Quoted in C. J. Phillips, "The Battle of Adobe Walls," *Hunter-Trader-Trapper* (December, 1928), 19.
2. Quoted in *The Life of "Billy" Dixon*, 164.
3. *Ibid.*, 178.
4. Zoe A. Tilghman, *Marshal of the Last Frontier*, 120.
5. Edith B. McGinnis, *The Promised Land*.
6. Dixon, *op. cit.*, 187–89.

CHAPTER 5 - Gunfire on the Sweetwater

1. The names of the scouts as recorded in the diary of Frank D. Baldwin (William Carey Brown Collection at the University of Colorado, Boulder):

    Whites

    J. D. Leach, John Kirley, C. B. Nichols, W. B. Masterson, William Dixon, A. C. Coburn, J. G. Dewalt, J. C. Frederick, J. H. Plummer, C. E. Jones, Thompson McFadden, David B. Shulz, David Campbell, W. F. Schmalsle, J. T. Marshall, J. A. McGinty, A. J. Martin

    Delawares

    Capt. Falling Leaf, Ice Wilson, Fred Falling Leaf, Charles Washington, John Kiney, Jim Coon, Elk Hair, Jacob Parker, Sam Williams, Lenowesa, John Siler, George Falling Leaf, Young Martin, John Swannock, Yellow Jacket, French Wilson, Jackson Simon, George Swannosh, Calvin Everet, George Wilson

    J. T. Marshall, a newspaperman who joined the expedition as a scout, sent letters to the *Topeka Daily Commonwealth* from August, 1874, to February, 1875, describing the campaign. The letters, edited by Lonnie J. White, were reprinted in book form by J. T. Marshall in *The Miles Expedition of 1874–1875: An Eyewitness Account of the Red River War*.
2. Nelson A. Miles, *Personal Recollections and Observations of General Nelson A. Miles*, 164.
3. Diary of Frank D. Baldwin.
4. In a letter to the *Topeka Commonwealth* dated September 4, 1874, J. T. Marshall said the bodies of twenty-five Indians were found after this engagement and as many more were carried off by the retreating warriors. "The casualties on our side were few, only three men being wounded, none killed: Michael Bartley, Co. F, 6th Cavalry, shot in left leg; Young Martin, Delaware, struck with spear in head; Geo. Everett [Calvin Everet], Delaware, bullet wound in face." Marshall, *op. cit.*, 17.

5. War Department Records, "Reports of Persons and Articles Hired, Indian Territory, 1874–1875," National Archives, Washington, D. C.

6. Robert C. Carriker, *Fort Supply, Indian Territory: Frontier Outpost on the Plains*, 102.

7. Quoted in Nyle H. Miller and Joseph W. Snell, *Why the West Was Wild*, 321. Henry Raymond married in 1874. During the winter of 1874–75, he and Ed Masterson were in and around Dodge, from which point Henry corresponded with his wife in Sedgwick. In *Early Ford County*, 172–73, Ida Ellen Rath quoted from a letter Raymond received from his wife, dated February 15, 1875: "You may tell Ed that his folks are having just the hardest kind of times. If he makes $30. per month, he ought to send $25. of it home. Mr. Masterson was here the other day. I felt sorry for him. If his people can't get feed, they can't do anything in the spring." Raymond replied on February 20: "I told Ed what you said, though if I had thought I wouldn't have told him anything about it. He seemed to take it so hard. He sends them nearly all he makes. I expect they spend it for fine clothes and extras for the policeman. He will probably give his father fits for putting up a pitiful mouth in your presence. They have such a great amount of pride, it may create a little hard feeling in some way." The policeman referred to probably was not one of the Masterson boys, but James Cairnes, who married Nellie Masterson and was serving on the police force in Wichita at this time.

8. Carriker, *op. cit.*, 103. Bat put in two stints as a teamster, working out of Camp Supply for thirty-five dollars a month; he worked from November 2, 1874, to December 26 and again from February 11, 1875, to February 25. See Dale T. Schoenberger, *The Gunfighters*, 113. On March 1, 1875, Bat was back in Dodge and was enumerated in the Kansas state census, his occupation listed as teamster. See Miller and Snell, *op. cit.*, 321.

9. Quoted in Miles, *op. cit.*, 181.

10. War Department records in the National Archives, Washington, D.C., indicate that King's real name was Anthony Cook and that at the time of his death he held the rank of corporal, although almost all later sources refer to him as Sergeant King. See Schoenberger's *The Gunfighters*, 113.

11. W. B. Masterson, "Ben Thompson," *Human Life* (January, 1907), 9.

12. *Ibid.*, 9.

13. "Gossip from Creede," *Colorado Sun*, February 25, 1892.

14. Sweetwater was renamed Mobeetie.

15. Related in Thompson, *op. cit.*, 10.

16. Stuart N. Lake, *Wyatt Earp, Frontier Marshal*, 133.

17. H. B. Hening (ed.), *George Curry, 1861–1947*, 10–11.

18. *Jacksboro Frontier Echo*, February 11, 1876.

CHAPTER 6 - "This Man Earp"

1. Lake, *op. cit.*, 143–44.

2. *Ibid.*, 139–40.

3. *Ibid.*, 142.

4. W. B. Masterson, "Wyatt Earp," *Human Life* (February, 1907), 9.

5. For a clear and nicely reasoned analysis of the story, see William B. Shillingberg, "Wyatt Earp and the 'Buntline Special' Myth," *Kansas State Historical Quarterly* (Summer, 1976), 113–54.

6. Lake, *op. cit.*, 155.

7. *Ibid.*, 146.

8. Masterson, "Wyatt Earp," *loc. cit.*, 9.

9. Sutton and MacDonald, *op. cit.*

10. Quoted by Zoe Tilghman in a letter to the author dated December 31, 1960.

11. Masterson, "Ben Thompson," *loc. cit.*, 9.

12. A fascinating story about this revolver is recounted in Robert Elman's *Fired in Anger: The Personal Handguns of American Heroes and Villains*, 306–308. In 1962, a Palatine, Illinois, gun collector named Paul Pasko purchased an old six-shooter from Paul Selley, another Palatine collector. Selley had acquired the weapon, among others, from the auctioned collection of George Walton. Before turning the gun over to Pasko, Selley had replaced the gutta-percha handles with new ones. Examining the grips some time later, he found faint scratches on the underside. Upon closer scrutiny, *BAT MASTON* was legible on one grip. The other held the cryptic letters *MH, DK, PP Wood, HCU, Dodg CY*. Selley realized that *BAT MASTON* and *Dodg CY* in all probability stood for Bat Masterson and Dodge City. The other letters were meaningless to him. He sold the grips to Pasko, who wrote Colt's Patent Fire Arms Company, describing the scratches and asking if the company had any history of the six-gun, serial number 112737. Indeed it did. This gun was one of two shipped to W. B. Masterson at Dodge City, Kansas, on July 30, 1885, six days after Bat penned his order. The history of the gun from 1885 until collector George Walton acquired it is unknown. Whether Bat carried this particular weapon very long or sold it or gave it away soon after he bought it can only be surmised. The strange scratches also remain a mystery. Did Bat put them there or did a subsequent owner? Why were they hidden on the underside of the grips, and what was their significance? In March, 1976, the revolver was sold at a Los Angeles auction to a Texas collector for thirty-six thousand dollars, as reported in the *Washington Post*, March 18, 1976.

13. Charles A. Siringo, *Riata and Spurs*, 36–37.

14. *Dodge City Times*, June 9, 1877.

15. This story appeared in the *Dodge City Times* on September 22, 1877.

16. September 29, 1877.

CHAPTER 7 - "Hurrah! For Our Officers"

1. Quoted in the *Dodge City Times*, November 24, 1877.

2. *Dodge City Times*, September 20, 1879.

3. *Ford County Globe*, February 5, 1878.

4. *Dodge City Times*, February 2, 1878.

5. *Ibid.*, February 9, 1878.

6. *Ford County Globe*, February 12, 1878.

7. *Ibid.*, February 19, 1878.

8. *Kinsley Graphic*, June 22, 1878.

CHAPTER 8 - The Trouble With Ed

1. Wright, *op. cit.*, 301.

2. *Dodge City Times*, July 21, 1877.

3. *Ibid.*

4. *Ibid.*, August 11, 1877.

5. *Ibid.*, November 10, 1877.

6. Wright, *op. cit.*, 306.

7. *Dodge City Times*, November 10, 1877.

8. *Ibid.*, November 24, 1877.

9. *Ibid.*, December 8, 1877.
10. Wright, *op. cit.*, 304–305.
11. Masterson, "Ben Thompson," *loc. cit.*, 9.
12. *Ford County Globe*, April 16, 1878.
13. Earle R. Forest, "The Killing of Ed Masterson," *The Brand Book of the Los Angeles Corral of the Westerners* (1949), 154–55.
14. Thompson, *op. cit*, 27.
15. *Dodge City Times*, April 13, 1878.
16. Wright, *op. cit.*, 307.

CHAPTER 9 - The Mistress of the Gamblers

1. Eddie Foy and Alvin F. Harlow, *Clowning Through Life*, 99.
2. *Ford County Globe*, July 30, 1878.
3. Foy and Harlow, *op. cit.*, 114.
4. June 18, 1878.
5. Foy and Harlow, *op. cit.*, 105.
6. *Dodge City Times*, July 13, 1878.
7. *Ibid.*
8. *Ford County Globe*, July 16, 1878.
9. *Ibid.*
10. *Dodge City Times*, July 13, 1878.
11. Masterson, "Wyatt Earp," *loc. cit.*, 9.
12. Foy and Harlow, *op. cit.*, 112.
13. *Dodge City Times*, July 27, 1878.
14. *Ibid.*
15. Foy and Harlow, *op. cit.*, 112.
16. Masterson, "Wyatt Earp," loc. cit., 9.
17. Henry F. Hoyt, *A Frontier Doctor*, 56.
18. *Ibid*, 56.
19. *Ford County Globe*, October 8, 1878.
20. *Dodge City Times*, October 12, 1878.
21. Lake, *op. cit.*, 218.
22. *St. Louis Daily Journal*, October 11, 1878.
23. Lake, *op. cit.*, 219.
24. Wright, *op. cit.*, 178.
25. *Ibid.*, 178.
26. Hoyt, *op. cit.*, 56.
27. Lake, *op. cit.*, 223.
28. Masterson, "Ben Thompson," *loc. cit.*, 9.
29. *Ibid.*
30. *Ibid.*
31. April 8, 1879.
32. September 9. 1879.
33. Foy and Harlow, *op. cit.*, 109.

CHAPTER 10 - "Catch 'Em and Convict 'Em"

1. February 9, 1878.
2. March 2, 1878.
3. *Dodge City Times*, April 20, 1878.

4. May 18, 1878.
5. June 25, 1878.
6. June 29, 1878.
7. August 17, 1878.
8. *Dodge City Times*, September 14, 1878.
9. September 17, 1878.
10. September 14, 1878.
11. September 17, 1878.
12. *Ibid.*
13. November 30, 1878.
14. December 10, 1878.
15. *Ibid.*
16. December 14, 1878.
17. Quoted in the *Ford County Globe*, January 7, 1879.
18. January 4, 1879.
19. Quoted in the *Ford County Globe*, January 7, 1879.
20. Quoted in the *Ford County Globe*, January 14, 1879.
21. January 11, 1879.
22. January 28, 1879.
23. January 11, 1879.
24. Wright, *op. cit.*, 308.
25. March 18, 1879.
26. August 30, 1879.
27. September 6, 1879.
28. From Governors' Correspondence, Archives Division, Kansas State Historical Society, quoted in Miller and Snell, *op. cit.*, 395.

CHAPTER 11 - Frontier Frolics

1. Wright, *op. cit.*, 299.
2. Foy and Harlow, *op. cit.*, 103.
3. Lake, *op. cit.*, 221–23.
4. *Ford County Globe*, February 17, 1880.
5. Wright, *op. cit.*, 212.
6. *Ibid.*, 213.
7. *Ibid.*, 175.
8. *Dodge City Times*, April 5, 1879.
9. Foy and Harlow, *op. cit.*, 104.
10. Quoted in Floyd B. Streeter, *Ben Thompson, Man With a Gun*, 139.
11. *Ford County Globe*, June 10, 1879.
12. *Rocky Mountain News*, June 11, 1879.
13. Quoted in Streeter *Ben Thompson*, 136.
14. Warman, *op. cit.*.
15. Foy and Harlow, *op. cit.*, 104.
16. June 14, 1879.
17. Lewis, *loc. cit.*, 10.

CHAPTER 12 - Cowboys and Indians

1. May 10, 1879.
2. Harry E. Chrisman, *Fifty Years on the Owl-Hoot Trail*, 109–10.

3. Quoted in Daisy F. Baber, *Injun Summer*, 183–84.
4. Warman, *op. cit.*
5. Frederick R. Bechdolt, *When the West Was Young*, 84.
6. Siringo, *op. cit.*, 57–59.
7. Dane Coolidge, *Fighting Men of the West*, 67.
8. Owen P. White, *Trigger Fingers*.
9. Lewis, *loc. cit.*, 10.
10. Charles W. Howe, *Timberleg of the Diamond Tail*.
11. The letter to Floyd B. Streeter is dated October 27, 1935. Quoted in Vestal, *op. cit.*, 139–40.
12. Governors' Correspondence, Archives Division, Kansas State Historical Society, quoted in Miller and Snell, *op. cit.*, 380.
13. *Ford County Globe*, February 17, 1879.
14. *Topeka Commonwealth*, February 16, 1879.
15. February 17, 1879.
16. *Topeka Commonwealth*, February 16, 1879.
17. *Dodge City Times*, February 22, 1879.
18. *Ibid.*
19. Correspondence of the Adjutants General, Archives Division, Kansas State Historical Society, quoted in Miller and Snell, *op. cit.*, 387–88.
20. October 28, 1879.

CHAPTER 13 - A New Vocation

1. *Ford County Globe*, September 9, 1879.
2. Milt Hinkle, "The Earp and Masterson I Knew," *True West* (December, 1961), 24–25.
3. *Dodge City Times*, October 25, 1879.
4. *Ibid.*
5. November 8, 1879.
6. *Speareville News*, November 8, 1879. The town is now called Spearville.
7. *Ibid.*, November 15, 1879.
8. *Dodge City Times*, November 22, 1879.
9. *Ford County Globe*, December 2, 1879.
10. *New York Morning Telegraph*, October 20, 1921.
11. Wright, *op. cit.*, 301.
12. June 5, 1880.
13. W. B. Masterson, "William F. Cody," *Human Life* (March, 1908), 9.

CHAPTER 14 - Tombstone

1. *Dodge City Times*, December 11, 1880.
2. The story of this journey appeared in George T. Buffum, *Smith of Bear City*, 119–21.
3. W. B. Masterson, "Luke Short," *Human Life* (April, 1907), 10.
4. Quoted in Walter Noble Burns, *Tombstone: An Iliad of the Southwest*, 170.

CHAPTER 15 - "Too Much Blood"

1. Burns, *op. cit.*, 57.
2. James D. Horan, *Across the Cimarron*, 58.
3. *Oskaloosa Herald*, March 17, 1881.

4. Quoted in Vestal, *op. cit.*, 221.
5. *Ford County Globe*, May 10, 1881.
6. *Ibid.*, April 17, 1881.
7. *Dodge City Times*, April 21, 1881.
8. *Ibid.*, June 16, 1881.
9. Burns, *op. cit.*, 56.
10. *Ibid.*
11. Lewis, *loc. cit.*, 10.
12. This letter is in the William Carey Brown Collection, University of Colorado, Boulder.
13. Lake, *op. cit.*, 41–42.
14. Sutton and MacDonald, *op. cit.*

CHAPTER 16 - The Deadly Dentist

1. *Trinidad Daily Times*, January 27, 1882.
2. February 23, 1882.
3. January 28, 1882.
4. March 17, 1882.
5. *Ibid.*
6. *Ibid.*
7. *Trinidad Daily News*, February 27, 1882.
8. April 8, 1882.
9. September 30, 1882.
10. *Ibid.*
11. Masterson, "Ben Thompson," *loc. cit.*, 9.
12. April 19, 1882.
13. April 25, 1882.
14. May 12, 1882.
15. W. B. Masterson, "Doc Holliday," *Human Life* (May, 1907), 5.
16. Lake, *op. cit.*, 197–98.
17. Masterson, "Doc Holliday," *loc. cit.*, 5.
18. *Denver Republican*, May 22, 1882.
19. Quoted in John Myers Myers, *Doc Holliday*, 212.
20. *Ibid.*, 217.
21. *Ibid.*, 239.
22. *Ibid.*, 230.
23. Masterson, "Doc Holliday," *loc. cit.*, 5.
24. Quoted in Myers, *Doc Holliday*, 232.
25. Masterson, "Doc Holliday," *loc. cit.*, 5.

CHAPTER 17 - The Jail of Trinidad

1. *Trinidad Daily Democrat*, July 20, 1882.
2. This notice is reproduced in James D. Horan and Paul Sann, *A Pictorial History of the Wild West*.
3. *Trinidad Daily Democrat*, September 15, 1882, quoting the *Pueblo Chieftain*.
4. *Trinidad Daily News*, August 31, 1882.
5. *Ibid.*, August 6, 1882.
6. *Trinidad Daily Democrat*, August 12, 1882.
7. *Ibid.*, August 17, 1882.
8. *Ibid.*, August 18, 1882.

9. *Trinidad Daily News*, March 3, 1882.
10. *Trinidad Daily Democrat*, August 22, 1882.
11. *Trinidad Daily News*, August 20, 1882.
12. *Trinidad Daily Democrat*, August 20, 1882.
13. *Ibid.*, September 9, 1882.
14. *Trinidad Daily News*, September 14, 1882.
15. *Trinidad Weekly News*, October 26, 1882.
16. *Trinidad Daily Democrat*, November 25, 1882.
17. *Ibid.*, November 28, 1882.
18. *Ibid.*, December 27, 1882.
19. *Trinidad Daily News*, January 16, 1883.
20. *Ibid.*, January 17, 1883.
21. *Trinidad Daily Advertiser*, February 6, 1883.
22. Quoted in the *Trinidad Daily Advertiser*, February 10, 1883.
23. *Ibid.*
24. *Ford County Globe*, February 20, 1883.
25. *Trinidad Daily News*, January 25, 1883.
26. *Ibid.*, February 20, 1883.
27. *Ibid.*, March 28, 1883.
28. *Ibid.*, March 29, 1883.
29. *Ibid.*, March 30, 1883.
30. *Ibid.*, March 29, 1883.
31. *Rocky Mountain News*, April 10, 1883.
32. *Trinidad Daily Advertiser*, April 11, 1883.
33. *Trinidad Daily News*, January 6, 1884.

CHAPTER 18 - The Luke Short Restoration

1. Miller and Snell, *op. cit.*, 521.
2. Masterson, "Luke Short," *loc. cit.*, 10.
3. *Ibid.*, 10.
4. Governors' Correspondence, Archives Division, Kansas State Historical Society, quoted in Miller and Snell, *op. cit.*, 530.
5. *Ibid.*, 531–34.
6. *Ibid.*, 534.
7. *Kansas City Journal*, May 15, 1883.
8. Miller and Snell, *op. cit.*, 538.
9. *Ibid.*, 544.
10. Masterson, "Luke Short," *loc. cit.*, 10.
11. *Dodge City Times*, May 24, 1883.
12. According to a report in the *Topeka Daily Commonwealth* of June 5, 1883, the Short adherents planned to assemble at the I. P. Olive ranch, just west of Dodge, for an assault on the town. Harry E. Chrisman, in *The Ladder of Rivers: The Story of I. P. (Print) Olive*, 319, says Olive refused to let them use the ranch. Chrisman relates a story told to him by Al Olive, Print's son, who was nine years old in 1883. Olive's rejection of the Short group angered the members of that group, Al said. When Bat Masterson made a slurring reference to Print in front of the Long Branch, Al says he saw Bill Tilghman slap Bat's face. This story is difficult to believe. First, Print Olive's sympathies always seemed to lie with Short's enemies in Dodge, and it is very doubtful that Short, Bat, Earp, *et al.* would have considered his ranch as a likely spot for a secret rallying point. Second, had Tilghman publicly slapped Bat Masterson in the face as

alleged, it is extremely unlikely that he and Bat would have remained lifelong friends, as indeed they were.

13. Masterson, "Luke Short," *loc. cit.*, 10.
14. Miller and Snell, *op. cit.*, 558.
15. Masterson, "Luke Short," *loc. cit.*, 10.
16. *Ford County Globe*, June 12, 1883.
17. Petillon sued Nick Klaine for ten thousand dollars because of this characterization. Klaine later made a partial retraction: "We shall admit the truth of the statement that Petillon is a 'Bond Extractor,' but we shall retract the statement that he is a 'pie-eater.' . . . While there is a general belief that Petillon has extracted several bonds and papers in the district court, there is an impossibility in the second allegation. We have consulted the free lunch stands in the city and find that Petillon takes in soup and beans as a duck takes in water." Quoted in William R. Cox, *Luke Short and His Era*, 143–44.
18. *Ford County Globe*, June 12, 1883.
19. *Ibid.*, June 19, 1883.

CHAPTER 19 - "The Delectable Burg"

1. *Ford County Globe*, September 4, 1883.
2. *Ibid.*, October 16, 1883.
3. *Ibid.*, November 6, 1883.
4. *Ibid.*, November 13, 1883.
5. *Trinidad Daily News*, January 6, 1884.
6. *Dodge City Democrat*, January 12, 1884.
7. *Ibid.*, February 9, 1884.
8. *Ibid.*, February 23, 1884.
9. *Ibid.*, May 3, 1884.
10. *Ford County Globe*, June 24, 1884.
11. *Topeka Commonwealth*, July 6, 1884.
12. *Kansas Cowboy*, September 27, 1884.
13. *Dodge City Times*, July 24, 1884.
14. *Globe Live Stock Journal*, October 28, 1884.
15. The only known surviving copy of Bat's paper is owned by Mrs. Merritt L. Beeson of Dodge City.
16. *Globe Live Stock Journal*, November 4, 1884.
17. Quoted in the *Globe Live Stock Journal*, November 18, 1884.
18. *Ibid.*, November 11, 1884.
19. *Dodge City Times*, December 11, 1884.
20. *Globe Live Stock Journal*, February 17, 1885.
21. *Ibid.*
22. That year, Bat's sister Minnie also died at the age of twenty-two.
23. Masterson, "Ben Thompson," *loc. cit.*, 9.
24. Wright, *op. cit.*, 218.
25. A reference to Bob and Charlie Ford and Dick Liddell, members of the James brothers' gang.
26. *Kinsley Graphic*, January 9, 1885.
27. *New York Morning Telegraph*, July 31, 1910.
28. In his letter to the *Kansas Cowboy*, August 29, 1885.
29. Quoted by Masterson in the *New York Morning Telegraph*, July 31, 1910.
30. *Topeka Capital*, July 2, 1885.

31. *Manhattan Nationalist*, July 10, 1885.
32. August 29, 1885.
33. *New York Morning Telegraph*, July 31, 1910.
34. *Kansas Cowboy*, July 4, 1885.
35. Quoted in Robert R. Dykstra, *The Cattle Towns*, 281.
36. *Ibid.*, 282.
37. *Dodge City Democrat*, March 13, 1886.
38. *Trinidad News*, March 19, 1886.
39. *Dodge City Times*, March 11, 1886.
40. Archives of the Kansas State Historical Society, quoted in Miller and Snell, *op. cit.*, 439–40.

CHAPTER 20 - From Soda to Hock

1. W. B. Masterson to Frank D. Baldwin, February 4, 1890.
2. *Denver Times*, September 7, 1900.
3. *New York Times*, October 26, 1921.
4. *Kansas City Star*, December 10, 1897.
5. February 4, 1900.
6. *Denver Times*, February 11, 1900.
7. Tom Bailey, "King of Cards," *New Magazine for Men* (May, 1958), 12.
8. Quoted in the *Ford County Globe*, August 11, 1885.
9. *Barber County Index*, December 4, 1885.
10. Masterson, "Luke Short," *loc. cit.*, 10.
11. *Ibid.*, 10.
12. Lewis, *loc. cit.*, 10.
13. *Ibid.*, 10.
14. Glenn G. Boyer (ed.), *I Married Wyatt Earp: The Recollections of Josephine Sarah Marcus Earp*, 133.
15. Reprinted in the *Wichita County Herald*, February 24, 1887.
16. Leola Howard Blanchard, *The Conquest of Southwest Kansas*, 102.
17. The register of the Delmonico Hotel is owned by Mrs. Merritt L. Beeson of Dodge City. The relevant page lists "W. B. Masterson, Lamar, Col.," as the first person to register on Sunday, October 23, 1887. He was assigned to Room B-2. The second name after Bat's is that of Ed Prather, who was killed by Bill Tilghman on July 4, 1888. Interesting also is the fact that the word "Paid" appears after the other names on the page but not after Bat's. Evidently, Charlie Heinz, the Delmonico proprietor, permitted his old friend Bat Masterson to stay for free.
18. Reprinted in the *Garfield Call*, November 18, 1887.
19. Clyde B. Davis, *The Arkansas*, 182–86.
20. William MacLeod Raine, *Guns of the Frontier*, 168.

CHAPTER 21 - A Brother of Bat Masterson

1. Hening, *op. cit.*, 47.
2. Miguel A. Otero, *My Life on the Frontier*, I, 104.
3. *Ibid.*, II, 152.
4. Hening, *op. cit.*, 50.
5. *Ibid.*, 50.
6. Bolds's account is from Horan, *Across the Cimarron*, 271–81. Newspaper sources include the *Dodge City Times*, January 17, 1889; the *Ingalls Union*, January 17, 1889; and the *Cimarron Jacksonian*, January 18, 1889.

7. Horan, *Across the Cimarron*, 280.
8. Quoted in O'Connor, *op. cit.*, 186–87. The Masterson here was Jim and not Bat as O'Connor indicated.

CHAPTER 22 - Friends, Concubines, Wives

1. *Dodge City Times*, June 8, 1878.
2. *Ford County Globe*, January 1, 1879.
3. Miller and Snell, *op. cit.*, 409.
4. *Dodge City Times*, November 24, 1877.
5. *New York Morning Telegraph*, October 26, 1921.
6. Thompson, *op. cit.*, 54.
7. Mrs. Tom Masterson to Mrs. Merritt L. Beeson, May 15, 1948.
8. Boyer, *op. cit.*, 121.
9. Hinkle, *loc. cit.*, 26.
10. *Rocky Mountain Daily News*, September 22, 1886.
11. Quoted in the *Denver Times*, September 16, 1900.
12. Quoted in George F. Willison, *Here They Dug the Gold*, 248.

CHAPTER 23 - The Last Boom

1. Arthur W. Monroe, *San Juan Silver*, 236.
2. *St. Louis Globe Democrat*, March 5, 1892.
3. "Gossip from Creede," *Colorado Sun*, February 25, 1892.
4. *St. Louis Globe Democrat*, March 9, 1892.
5. Henry Chafetz, *Play the Devil*, 156.
6. *Colorado Sun*, February 25, 1892.
7. *Ibid.*
8. William R. Collier and Edwin V. Westrate, *The Reign of Soapy Smith*, 99–100.

CHAPTER 24 - Fighting, Ringwise and Otherwise

1. Nat Fleischer, "Crusading Scribes," *Ring Magazine* (June, 1941), 14.
2. Mike Donovan, *The Roosevelt That I Knew*.
3. *New York Morning Telegraph*, January 11, 1912.
4. Quoted in Frank G. Robertson and Beth Kay Harris, *Soapy Smith, King of the Frontier Con Men*, 224.
5. *Ibid.*, 135.
6. *Denver Post*, October 25, 1921.
7. Quoted in the *New York Tribune*, February 7, 1905.
8. *Rocky Mountain News*, June 6, 1895.
9. *Denver Post*, April 7, 1897.
10. Lewis, *loc. cit.*, 10.
11. *Rocky Mountain News*, October 26, 1921.
12. *Ibid.*, April 8, 1897.
13. *Ibid.*, August 16, 1899.
14. *Guns of the Frontier*, 166.
15. *Famous Sheriffs and Western Outlaws*, 13.
16. *Guns of the Frontier*, 166.
17. Boyce House, *Cowtown Columnist*.
18. *Report of the Special Investigating Committee of the Senate of the Eleventh General*

Assembly on the Patterson-Masterson Bribery Charges and the Transcript of Testimony.

19. Gene Fowler, *Skyline: A Reporter's Reminiscences of the 1920's*, 15.
20. *Denver Times*, September 16, 1900.
21. April 19, 1899.
22. *George's Weekly*, September 23, 1899.
23. July 9, 1899.
24. July 11, 1899.
25. Copy in Manuscript Division, Kansas State Historical Society.
26. Gene Fowler, *Timber Line: A Story of Bonfils and Tammen*, 118.
27. Quoted in O'Connor, *op. cit.*, 220.
28. *Famous Sheriffs and Western Outlaws*, 183.
29. Lewis, *loc. cit.*, 10.
30. *Ibid.*, 10.
31. Murphy's Exchange, managed by Mart Watrous. This establishment was affectionately known as the Slaughterhouse by Denver sports because of the many killings that occurred there. In 1892, John P. Clow, the prizefighter Bat had managed, was killed in Murphy's by Frank Marshall.
32. June 10, 1900.
33. *Denver Times*, April 22, 1900.
34. *Ibid.*, July 15, 1900.
35. September 7, 1900.
36. *Ibid.*
37. *Ibid.*, December 2, 1900.

CHAPTER 25 - The Four O'Clock Burlington

1. *New York Morning Telegraph*, October 26, 1921. Bat always blamed women's suffrage for causing his departure from Denver. In 1912, when Theodore Roosevelt ran for the presidency as a candidate of the Progressive party, Bat told a reporter he departed Kansas when prohibition was enforced. "I couldn't stand that. I went to Colorado and stayed until the women got to running things. Then I left there and went to New York. After Teddy came out for equal suffrage the other day I began to wonder where I would go next." William F. Zornow, *Kansas: A History of the Jayhawk State*, 220 sn.
2. *Guns of the Frontier*, 167–69.
3. June 7, 1902.
4. *New York Times*, June 7, 1902.
5. *Ibid.*, June 8, 1902.
6. *Ibid.*
7. *New York World*, June 7, 1902.
8. *Ibid.*, June 8, 1902.
9. *Denver Times*, June 7, 1902.
10. *New York World*, June 7, 1902.
11. *Ibid.*, June 9, 1902.
12. July 6, 1902.

CHAPTER 26 - The Ham Reporter

1. From *The Nation*, September 5, 1936. Quoted in Heywood Hale Broun (ed.), *Collected Edition of Heywood Broun*.

2. *New York Morning Telegraph*, December 9, 1906.
3. A. H. Lewis editorial note to Bat's first article on western gunfighters in *Human Life* (January, 1907), 9.
4. *New York Tribune*, February 7, 1905.
5. Anonymous, "Bat Shows White Feather," *Santa Fe Magazine* (March, 1909), 396.
6. Hinkle, *loc. cit.*, 54.
7. Fowler, *Skyline*, 16.
8. *New York Herald*, June 23, 1906.
9. *New York Morning Telegraph*, June 18, 1911.
10. *Ibid.*, September 14, 1921.
11. *Ibid.*, February 18, 1912.
12. *Ibid.*, June 19, 1910.
13. *Ibid.*, September 29, 1921.
14. *Ibid.*, August 12, 1919.
15. *Ibid.*, August 19, 1919.
16. *Ibid.*, October 4, 1921.
17. *Ibid.*, July 29, 1919.
18. *Ibid.*, August 17, 1919.
19. *Ibid.*, July 10, 1921.
20. *Ibid.*, August 28, 1921.
21. Fleischer, *loc. cit.*, 14.
22. *New York Morning Telegraph*, August 21, 1921.
23. *Ibid.*, October 10, 1911.
24. *Ibid.*, July 5, 1921.
25. In a letter to the author dated September 27, 1955.
26. Irvin S. Cobb, *Exit Laughing*.
27. Louella A. Parsons, *The Gay Illiterate*.
28. *New York Morning Telegraph*, July 3, 1910.
29. *Ibid.*, July 31, 1910.
30. *Ibid.*
31. Quoted in William S. Hart, *My Life East and West*, 182.
32. Quoted in Miss Parsons' column, "In and Out of Focus," *New York Morning Telegraph*, October 30, 1921.
33. Hart, *op. cit.*, 272.
34. *Ibid.*, 307.
35. *New York Morning Telegraph*, October 30, 1921.
36. "Bill Hart Introduces a Real — Not Reel — Hero," *New York Morning Telegraph*, October 9, 1921.
37. In a letter to Bat's niece dated November 16, 1921, Emma Masterson wrote that he had been sick in bed for two weeks with "cold on his lungs," had got better, although he "couldn't seem to get his strength back, but no one could keep him from going out over to his office to write. "Emma said Bat had had diabetes for three years and had been on a diet: "[He] couldn't eat any vegetable that grew under the ground, had to eat a bread called gluten bread we bought at a bakery and no sweets at all and his feet were so cold every winter since he had it he wore woollen stockings in bed at nights." He had no life insurance. Bat was, said Emma, "very peculiar in some ways." Her letter is in the archives of the Kansas State Historical Society, Topeka.
38. Bat's last column was published on October 27, 1921, the day of his funeral. Coincidentally, the date was also the birthday of an old friend of Bat's, Theodore Roosevelt.

EPILOGUE

1. Bat's will left his entire estate to his wife. Emma Masterson lived on alone in New York City until July 12, 1932, when a maid discovered her body in her room at the Hotel Stratford on East Thirty-second Street.
2. *New York Morning Telegraph*, October 28, 1921.
3. *Ibid.*, October 27, 1921.

BIBLIOGRAPHY

Manuscripts

Frank D. Baldwin Diary, William Carey Brown Collection, University of Colorado, Boulder.

Letter, Jim Masterson to Tom Masterson, September 24, 1892, Manuscript Division, Kansas State Historical Society, Topeka.

Letter, Mrs. Tom Masterson to Mrs. Merritt L. Beeson, May 15, 1948, Manuscript Division, Kansas State Historical Society, Topeka.

Letter, W. B. Masterson to Frank D. Baldwin, February 4, 1890, William Carey Brown Collection, University of Colorado, Boulder.

Letter, W. B. Masterson to H. H. Raymond, July 23, 1899, Manuscript Division, Kansas State Historical Society, Topeka.

Letter, Mrs. W. B. Masterson to Nellie Cairns, November 16, 1921, Manuscript Division, Kansas State Historical Society, Topeka.

Government Publications

Report of the Special Investigating Committee of the Senate of the Eleventh General Assembly on the Patterson-Masterson Bribery Charges and the Transcript of Testimony. Printed by Authority of the Senate. Denver, Smith-Brooks Printing Co., State Printers, 1897.

Newspapers

Colorado

Colorado Sun
Denver Post
Denver Republican
Denver Times
George's Weekly (Denver)
Rocky Mountain Daily News
Trinidad Daily Advertiser
Trinidad Daily Democrat

Trinidad Daily News
Trinidad Daily Times
Trinidad Weekly News

Iowa

Oskaloosa Herald

Kansas

Atchison Champion
Barber County Index
Cimarron Jacksonian
Dodge City Cowboy
Dodge City Democrat
Dodge City Times
Ford County Globe
Garden City Irrigator
Garfield Call
Globe Live Stock Journal (Dodge City)
Ingalls Union
Kansas Cowboy (Dodge City)
Kinsley Graphic
Kinsley Valley Republican
Leavenworth Times
Manhattan Nationalist
Medicine Lodge Cresset
Spearville News
Topeka Capital
Topeka Commonwealth
Vox Populi (Dodge City)
Wichita County Herald
Wichita Eagle

Missouri

Kansas City Daily Drovers Telegram
Kansas City Journal
St. Louis Daily Journal
St. Louis Globe Democrat

New York

New York Herald
New York Morning Telegraph
New York Sun
New York Times
New York Tribune
New York World

Oklahoma

Daily Oklahoma State Capital (Guthrie)

Texas

Jacksboro Frontier Echo

Books

Adams, Ramon F. *Six-Guns and Saddle Leather*. Norman, University of Oklahoma Press, 1954.

Andreas, A. T., and W. G. Cutler. *History of the State of Kansas*. Chicago, 1883.

Asbury, Herbert. *Sucker's Progress: An Informal History of Gambling in America From the Colonies to Canfield*. New York, Dodd, Mead & Co., 1938.

Baber, Daisy F. *Injun Summer*. Caldwell, Idaho, The Caxton Printers, 1952.

Bartholomew, Ed. *The Biographical Album of Western Gunfighters*. Houston, Frontier Press of Texas, 1958.

———— .*Wyatt Earp: The Man and the Myth*. Toyahvale, Texas, Frontier Book Co., 1964.

———— .*Wyatt Earp: The Untold Story*. Toyahvale, Texas, Frontier Book Co., 1963.

Bechdolt, Frederick R. *Tales of the Oldtimers*. New York, Century Co., 1924.

———— .*When the West Was Young*. New York, Century Co., 1922.

Beshoar, Dr. Michael. *All About Trinidad*. Denver, 1882.

Blanchard, Leola Howard. *The Conquest of Southwest Kansas*. Wichita, Kan., Wichita Eagle Press, 1931.

Boyer, Glenn G., ed. *I Married Wyatt Earp: The Recollections of Josephine Sarah Marcus Earp*. Tucson, University of Arizona Press, 1976.

Breakenridge, William. *Helldorado*. Boston, Houghton Mifflin Co., 1928.

Broun, Heywood Hale, ed. *Collected Edition of Heywood Broun*. New York, Harcourt, Brace & Co., 1928.

Buffum, George T. *Smith of Bear City*. New York, Grafton Press, 1906.

Burns, Walter Noble. *Tombstone: An Iliad of the Southwest*. New York, Doubleday, Page & Co., 1927.

Carriker, Robert C. *Fort Supply, Indian Territory: Frontier Outpost on the Plains*. Norman, University of Oklahoma Press, 1970.

Chafetz, Henry. *Play the Devil*. New York, Clarkson N. Potter, 1960.

Chrisman, Harry E. *Fifty Years on the Owl-Hoot Trail*. Denver, Sage Books, 1962.

———— .*The Ladder of Rivers: The Story of I. P. (Print) Olive*. Denver, Sage Books, 1962.

———— .*Lost Trails of the Cimarron*. Denver, Sage Books, 1961.

Clark, O. S. *Clay Allison of the Washita*. Attica, Ind., G. M. Williams, 1920.

Cobb, Irvin S. *Exit Laughing*. New York, Bobbs-Merrill Co., 1941.

Collier, William R., and Edwin V. Westrate. *The Reign of Soapy Smith*. Garden City, N.Y., Doubleday, Doran & Co., 1935.

Collinson, Frank. *Life in the Saddle*. Norman, University of Oklahoma Press, 1963.

Coolidge, Dane. *Fighting Men of the West*. New York, E. P. Dutton & Co., 1932.

Corbett, James J. *The Roar of the Crowd*. New York, Gosset & Dunlap, 1925.

Cox, William R. *Luke Short and His Era*. New York, Doubleday & Co., 1961.

Crumbine, Samuel J. *Frontier Doctor*. Philadelphia, Dorrance & Co., 1948.

Cunningham, Eugene. *Triggernometry*. New York, Press of the Pioneers, 1934.

Davis, Clyde B. *The Arkansas*. New York, Farrar & Rinehart, 1940.

Dixon, Clive K. *The Life of "Billy" Dixon*. Dallas, P. L. Turner Co., 1914.

Donovan, Mike. *The Roosevelt That I Knew*. New York, B. W. Dodge & Co., 1909.

Drago, Harry Sinclair. *Wild, Woolly and Wicked*. New York, Clarkson N. Potter, 1960.

Dykstra, Robert R. *The Cattle Towns*. New York, Alfred A. Knopf, 1968.

Elman, Robert. *Fired in Anger: The Personal Handguns of American Heroes and Villains*. New York, Doubleday & Co., 1968.

Emrich, Duncan. *It's an Old Wild West Custom*. New York, Vanguard Press, 1949.

Fleischer, Nat. *The Heavyweight Championship*. New York, G. P. Putnam's Sons, 1949.

Fowler, Gene. *Skyline: A Reporter's Reminiscences of the 1920's*. New York, Viking Press, 1961.

———— .*Timber Line: A Story of Bonfils and Tammen*. New York, Blue Ribbon Books, 1933.

Foy, Eddie, and Alvin F. Harlow. *Clowning Through Life*. New York, E. P. Dutton & Co., 1928.

Gard, Wayne. *Frontier Justice*. Norman, University of Oklahoma Press, 1949.

Ghent, W. J. "William Barclay Masterson," *The Dictionary of American Biography*. New York, Charles Scribner's Sons, 1933.

Hanes, Bailey C. *Bill Doolin, Outlaw, O.T.* Norman, University of Oklahoma Press, 1968.

Hart, William S. *My Life East and West*. Boston, Houghton Mifflin Co., 1929.

Hening, H. B., ed. *George Curry, 1861–1947*. Albuquerque, University of New Mexico Press, 1958.

Holbrook, Stewart H. *Little Annie Oakley and Other Rugged People*. New York, Macmillan Co., 1948.

Horan, James D. *Across the Cimarron*. New York, Bonanza Books, 1956.

——— and Paul Sann. *A Pictorial History of the Wild West*. New York, Crown Publishers, 1954.

House, Boyce. *Cowtown Columnist*. San Antonio, Naylor Co., 1946.

Howe, Charles W. *Timberleg of the Diamond Tail*. San Antonio, Naylor Co., 1949.

Hoyt, Henry F. *A Frontier Doctor*. Boston, Houghton Mifflin Co., 1929.

Hunt, Frazier. *The Tragic Days of Billy the Kid*. New York, Hastings House, 1956.

Hunter, J. Marvin, and Noah H. Rose. *The Album of Gunfighters*. Bandera, Texas, 1951.

Jahns, Pat. *The Frontier World of Doc Holliday*. New York, Hastings House, 1957.

King, Frank M. *Mavericks*. Pasadena, Calif., Trail's End Publishing Co., 1947.

Lake, Stuart N. *Wyatt Earp, Frontier Marshal*. Boston, Houghton Mifflin Co., 1931.

Lewis, Alfred Henry. *The Sunset Trail*. New York, A. S. Barnes & Co., 1905.

Lowther, Charles G. *Dodge City, Kansas*. Philadelphia, Dorrance & Co., 1940.

McGinnis, Edith B. *The Promised Land*. Boerne, Texas, Topperwein Co., 1947.

McNeal, Thomas A. *When Kansas Was Young*. New York, Macmillan Co., 1922.

Marshall, J. T. *The Miles Expedition of 1874–1875: An Eyewitness Account of the Red River War*. Ed. by Lonnie J. White. Austin, Encino Press, 1971.

Martin, Douglas D. *Tombstone's Epitaph*. Albuquerque, University of New Mexico Press, 1951.

Mayer, Frank H., and Charles B. Roth. *The Buffalo Harvest*. Denver, Sage Books, 1958.

Miles, Nelson A. *Personal Recollections and Observations of General Nelson A. Miles*. Chicago, Werner Co., 1896.

Miller, Max. *Holliday Street*. New York, Signet Books, 1962.

Miller, Nyle H., and Joseph W. Snell. *Why the West Was Wild*. Topeka, Kansas State Historical Society, 1963.

—— and Edgar Langsdorf, and Robert W. Richmond. *Kansas in Newspapers*. Topeka, Kansas State Historical Society, 1963.

Monroe, Arthur W. *San Juan Silver*. Grand Junction, Colo., Grand Junction Sentinel, 1940.

Mumey, Nolie. *Creede*. Denver, Artcraft Press, 1949.

Myers, John Myers. *Doc Holliday*. Boston, Little, Brown & Co., 1955.

—— .*The Last Chance*. New York, E. P. Dutton Co., 1950.

O'Connor, Richard. *Bat Masterson*. New York, Doubleday & Co., 1957.

Otero, Miguel A. *My Life on the Frontier. Vol. I*. New York, Press of the Pioneers, 1935.

—— .*My Life on the Frontier. Vol. II*. Albuquerque, University of New Mexico Press, 1939.

Parkhill, Forbes. *The Wildest of the West*. New York, Henry Holt & Co., 1951.

Parsons, John E. *The Peacemaker and Its Rivals*. New York, William Morrow & Co., 1950.

Parsons, Louella A. *The Gay Illiterate*. New York, Doubleday, Doran & Co., 1944.

Quiett, Glenn Chesney. *They Built the West, an Epic of Rails and Cities*. New York, D. Appleton-Century Co., 1934.

Raine, William MacLeod. *Famous Sheriffs and Western Outlaws*. Garden City, N.Y., Doubleday, Droan & Co., 1929.

—— .*45 Caliber Law*. Evanston, Ill., Row, Peterson & Co., 1941.

—— .*Guns of the Frontier*. New York, Houghton Mifflin Co., 1940.

Rath, Ida Ellen. *Early Ford County*. North Newton, Kans., Mennonite Press, 1964.

Robertson, Frank C., and Beth Kay Harris. *Soapy Smith, King of the Frontier Con Men*. New York, Hastings House, 1961.

Rynning, Thomas H. *Gun Notches*. New York, Frederick A. Stokes Co., 1931.

Sandoz, Mari. *The Buffalo Hunters*. New York, Hastings House, 1954.

Schoenberger, Dale T. *The Gunfighters*. Caldwell, Idaho, The Caxton Printers, 1971.

Siringo, Charles A. *Riata and Spurs*. Boston, Houghton Mifflin Co., 1927.

Sonnichsen, C. L. *Billy King's Tombstone: The Private Life of an Arizona Boom Town*. Caldwell, Idaho, The Caxton Printers, 1942.

————. *Roy Bean, Law West of the Pecos*. New York, Macmillan Co., 1943.

Spring, Agnes Wright. *The Cheyenne and Black Hills Stage and Express Routes*. Glendale, Calif., Arthur H. Clark Co., 1949.

Stanley, F. *Desperadoes of New Mexico*. Denver, The World Press, 1953.

Streeter, Floyd B. *Ben Thompson, Man With a Gun*. New York, Frederick Fell, 1957.

————. *The Kaw*. New York, Farrar & Rinehart, 1941.

————. *Prairie Trails and Cow Towns*. Boston, Chapman & Grimes, 1936.

Sutton, Fred E., and A. B. MacDonald. *Hands Up!* Indianapolis, Bobbs-Merrill Co., 1926.

Thompson, George G. *Bat Masterson: The Dodge City Years*. Topeka, Kansas State Printing Plant, 1943.

Tilghman, Zoe A. *Marshal of the Last Frontier*. Glendale, Calif., Arthur H. Clark Co., 1949.

————. *Spotlight: Bat Masterson and Wyatt Earp as U.S. Deputy Marshals*. San Antonio, Naylor Co., 1960.

Vestal, Stanley. *Dodge City, Queen of Cowtowns*. New York, Harper & Brothers, 1951.

Walton, William M. *Life and Adventures of Ben Thompson*. Houston, Frontier Press of Texas, 1954.

Warman, Cy. *The Story of the Railroad*. New York, D. Appleton & Co., 1898.

Waters, Frank. *The Earp Brothers of Tombstone*. New York, Clarkson N. Potter, 1960.

Westermeier, Clifford P. *Trailing the Cowboy, His Life and Lore As Told By Frontier Journalists*. Caldwell, Idaho, The Caxton Printers, 1955.

White, Owen P. *My Texas 'Tis of Thee*. New York, G. P. Putnam's Sons, 1936.

————. *Trigger Fingers*. New York, Knickerbocker Press, 1926.

Willison, George F. *Here They Dug the Gold*. New York, Reynol & Hitchcock Co., 1946.

Wilstach, Frank J. *Wild Bill Hickok, the Prince of Pistoleers*. Garden

City, N.Y., Garden City Publishing Co., 1926.

Wolle, Muriel Sibell. *Stampede to Timberline, the Ghost Towns and Mining Camps of Colorado*. Denver, Artcraft Press, 1949.

Wright, Robert M. *Dodge City, the Cowboy Capital, and the Great Southwest*. Wichita, Wichita Eagle Press, 1913.

Zornow, William F. *Kansas: A History of the Jayhawk State*. Norman, University of Oklahoma Press, 1957.

Articles

Anonymous, "Bat Shows White Feather," *Santa Fe Magazine* (July, 1909).

————. "The Killing of Ed Masterson," *Santa Fe Magazine* (July, 1912).

Bailey, Tom. "King of Cards," *New Magazine for Men* (May, 1958).

Fleischer, Nat. "Crusading Scribes," *Ring Magazine* (June, 1941).

Forest, Earle R. "The Killing of Ed Masterson," *The Brand Book of the Los Angeles Corral of the Westerners* (1949).

Harrison, Fred. "Historic Run to Guthrie," *The West* (October, 1966).

Hinkle, Milt. "The Earp and Masterson I Knew," *True West* (December, 1961).

Lake, Stuart N. "Straight-Shooting Dodge," *Saturday Evening Post* (March 8, 1930).

Lewis, Alfred Henry. "The King of the Gun-Players, William Barclay Masterson," *Human Life* (November, 1907).

Lynch, John T. "Devil's Grin," *True West* (April, 1955).

Masterson, W. B. "Famous Gunfighters of the Western Frontier: Ben Thompson," *Human Life* (January, 1907).

———— ."Wyatt Earp," *Human Life* (February, 1907).

———— ."Luke Short," *Human Life* (April, 1907).

———— ."Doc Holliday," *Human Life* (May, 1907).

———— ."Billy Tilghman," *Human Life* (July, 1907).

———— ."William F. Cody," *Human Life* (March, 1908).

Penn, Chris. "Edward J. Masterson, Marshal of Dodge City," Part I, *The English Westerners' Brand Book* (July, 1965).

———— ."Edward J. Masterson, Marshal of Dodge City," Part II, *The English Westerners' Brand Book* (October, 1965).

———— ."A Note on Bartholomew Masterson," *The English Westerners' Brand Book* (April, 1967).

Phillips, C. J. "The Battle of Adobe Walls," *Hunter-Trader-Trapper* (December, 1928).

Proett, Patrice North. "The Parson's Pants," *Rocky Mountain Life* (June, 1949).

Shillingberg, William B. "Wyatt Earp and the 'Buntline Special' Myth," *Kansas State Historical Quarterly* (Summer, 1976).

Snell, Joseph P., ed. "The Diary of a Dodge City Buffalo Hunter, 1872–1873," *Kansas State Historical Quarterly* (Winter, 1965).

Wiltsey, Norman B. "A Man Called Bat," *True West* (December, 1956).

Zamo, Stan. "They Stole the Parson's Pants," *True West* (April, 1955).

Miscellaneous

Denver (Colorado) City Directories, 1889–1901.

INDEX

427